# THE SLOW
# BURNING
# FUSE

# THE SLOW BURNING FUSE

## The Lost History of the British Anarchists

**John Quail**

Afterword by Constance Bantman
Biographical sketches by Nick Heath

*The Slow Burning Fuse: The Lost History of the British Anarchists*
This edition © 2019 PM Press and Freedom Press
All rights reserved
Printed 2017 by Freedom Press
First published by Granada Publishing Limited in Paladin Books, 1978

ISBN: 978-1-62963-582-8
Library of Congress Control Number: 2018931532

Cover by John Yates/stealworks.com

PM Press
PO Box 23912
Oakland, CA 94623
www.pmpress.org

Freedom Press
84b Whitechapel High St, London
E1 7QX
www.freedompress.org.uk

10 9 8 7 6 5 4 3 2 1

# ACKNOWLEDGEMENTS

The work for this book has involved research at archives and reference libraries. Since I was not supported by grants or by any academic institution this could have been a rather desperate undertaking. I had, however, the sense to work part-time as a stagehand at the Fortune and Drury Lane theatres during the writing of the book, which kept my feet very much on the ground.

I would like to thank the following for the discussions and the pleasant experience of working with them: Arthur, Reg, Allen, Bob and John from the Fortune; and Alan, Kenny, Billy, Del, Brian, Tim, Tom, Jim, John, Colin, Richard and Sabba at the Theatre Royal, Drury Lane.

Perhaps as an 'unofficial' historian I have had to rely more than others on an informal network of interested, knowledgeable and helpful people. Without them this book would be rather worse than it is now. For more particular information and assistance, I must thank the following people.

First mention must go to my comrade Ken Weller. In no way, however, does this diminish the great help I have received from Nick Massey, Francis Devine, Dave Poulson, Jeffe Jeffers, Raphael Samuel, Stan Shipley, Albert Meltzer, Sheila Rowbotham, Rachel Howe, Sam Dreen, Bill Fishman, Anna Davin, Rudolf de Jong and Thea Duijker and Mieke of the International Institute of Social History at Amsterdam, the Keeper and staff of the Brotherton Collection at Leeds University, Grayson Holden, Tom Woodhouse, Jerry Ravetz, Mary Canipa and Freedom Press, Tony Bunyan, Mark Kramrisch and Nicolas Walter.

This book is dedicated to the memory of two Leeds anarchists, Billy MacQueen (d. 1908) and my friend George Cummings (d. December 1975).

# CONTENTS

# FOREWORD

John Quail's history of British anarchism was a groundbreaking document. It was one of the first books to address itself to the 'lost history' of the movement. Only Albert Meltzer had previously addressed the subject in any detail in his *The Anarchists in London 1935–1955: A Personal Memoir* which had appeared two years before in 1976. As Comrade Quail notes in his bibliography, E.P. Thompson's book on William Morris had important information on anarchist activity in the Socialist League, though, as he warned, whilst it was sourced from primary sources it has a quite pronounced bias against anarchism.

Since then we have had Ken Weller's *Don't Be A Soldier! The Radical Anti-war Movement in North London 1914–1918,* containing much information on anarchists and libertarian socialists active in this period, which appeared in 1985; Sheila Rowbotham's essay on *The Sheffield Anarchists in the 1890s* (1979), and some pieces on the history of the British movement in the magazine the *Raven* and in the Freedom Press Centenary edition book *Freedom: A Hundred Years — October 1886 to October 1986.*

In addition we have had the pamphlet *Left-wing Communism in Britain 1917–1921 ... An Infantile Disorder?* by Bob Jones (1984), Mark Shipway's book *Anti-Parliamentary Communism: The Movement for Workers Councils in Britain 1917–1945* (1988) and the anthology produced by Wildcat, *Class War on the Home Front: A History of the Anti-Parliamentary Communist Federation* (1986), all of which gave details of anti-parliamentary and anarchist activity between the wars and filled a gap in Quail's book.

Recently there has been a welter of new articles on the British movement thanks to the efforts of the Kate Sharpley Library, which reprinted important pamphlets by George Cores and Wilf McCartney, as well as providing much new information, and of the Libcom website, which has published many new biographies of British anarchist militants and histories of anarchist activities in Aberdeen, Brighton, Dundee, Manchester, Stockport, East London and the Welsh valleys.

Yet research on the history of the British movement still seems to be in its late infancy and much more work needs to be done in rediscovering individual anarchist activists and local movements hidden from history for too long. It is a sign of the renaissance of anarchism in general that the tempo of material being produced on the British anarchist movement is increasing. For too long both bourgeois historians and those allied to either the Communist Party or the various Trotskyist groups have, consciously or not, obscured or distorted the history of British anarchism and of broader movements into which anarchists had an important input. For example the anarchist origins of quite a few founding members of the British Communist Party, like Harry Pollitt, etc., are ignored by C.P. historians.

Quail's book deals in great detail with the anarchist movement up until and during World War One, and then gives brief details of the movement in the interwar period, as well as a cursory look at the re-emergence of anarchism after the Second World War. Some of his closing comments on the fate of the movement are still extremely cogent today, though I would take issue, as very much an organisational anarchist, with some of his comments on organisation in his conclusion.

John Quail's book remains an important one, a pioneering work in dragging the history of the British movement out of obscurity. Freedom Press should be congratulated on republishing it after so many years.

**Nick Heath**

# A PERSONAL INTRODUCTION

Some years ago I was talking to a friend of mine in Leeds who was doing a thesis on British labour history. He asked me if I had ever heard of a group of people who had been arrested for a bomb conspiracy in 1892, a group known as the Walsall anarchists. What? British anarchists? I had never heard anything like it. I had cut my eye teeth as an anarchist arguing with Trotskyists and communists over Spain and Russia. I had wondered why left-wing politics always had to do with foreign parts, though I had found much disputational mileage in the events in Barcelona in 1936 ('the capacity of the proletariat for spontaneous self-activity') and Kronstadt in 1921 ('the Bolsheviks were not fighting the counter-revolution, they *were* the counter-revolution'). But passionate denunciations of Leon 'Shoot them like partridges' Trotsky over many pints of beer left much to be desired. There was too much dreaming in our transference of the heady days of past revolutions in other places to the sooty backstreets and Arndale centres of Leeds. It was our own place and time we should have been talking about. Had Leeds no history of its own which made sense of the present? Its people were descendants of Luddites and Chartists, mill-burners and loom-wreckers. There had been no revolutions, we were sure of that; but perhaps there had been revolutionaries whose successes and failures it would pay us better to learn from. So when my friend asked me if I had heard of anarchists in prosaic Walsall my mind did a somersault which it had been prepared for, more or less. My intention to write a book on the British anarchists was formed that afternoon in Leeds during a cigarette break outside the university library.

A lot of things got in the way, earning a living for one thing, not to mention various agitations. Eventually the book was written. As so many authors have remarked, if I had known what was involved before I started, the book might not have been written. I suppose, however, that this makes about as much sense as someone saying that if they had known what a difficult business life was they would not have bothered to be born. Anyway, when the book reached the publishers it was greeted with cautious optimism, but I was told that I had described the British anarchist movement without explaining the general philosophy on which it was based. I thought this was a bit rough; there seemed enough passing references and inferences to make it clear. On reflection, however, I began to feel that they might have a point — anarchism has been represented too often as the philosophical creed of a bunch of bomb-carrying nutters in big black hats and cloaks, providing a general justification for causing chaos for the sake of it. But if I was to try and correct this impression how was I to do it without being balls-achingly boring? For it is an unfortunate fact that political theory, no matter how worthy or perceptive, is curiously disembodied; it gives no clues to the passions, the heroisms or the squalid conflicts that it inspired.

I could begin by saying something like 'anarchism is a political philosophy which states that it is both possible and desirable to live in a society based on cooperation, not coercion, organised without hierarchy with no element of the principle of authority'. I could add that as a human aspiration in various guises it is as old as authority itself, though as a politically self-conscious, self-defined movement it emerged in the middle of the nineteenth century. It seems to have been one response to the treatment of socialists at the hands of bourgeois revolutionaries in the 1830–1848 period of revolutions. More specifically it marks a rejection of the political structure which the bourgeoisie sought to establish — parliamentary democracy. From the earliest times when the odd socialist might take executive office, through to the development of mass ocial democratic parties, the anarchists developed their criticisms and their alternatives in parallel: from the cooperatives and staunch artisan individualism advocated by Proudhon through the decentralist revolutionary activism of Bakunin and the simultaneously intense idealism and finely detailed practicality of Kropotkin to the entwining of all these strands with insurgent trades unionism in anarcho-syndicalism. And it hardly needs to be added that an expansion of this theme would fill — and has filled — many volumes. There is much in the writings of the anarchist sages worth reading; yet they wrote for times and to concerns which only loosely approximate to our own. Should anyone wish to read theoretical works of more contemporary relevance, the works of Murray Bookchin, Paul Cardan and the situationists are recommended.

But once all this is said, perhaps the most important part remains unsaid. Political convictions involve an analysis of a situation with suggestions for change; yet they differ qualitatively from the emotionally neutral attitudes of, say, car mechanics. Political attitudes are to do with the totality of social being — which can only be seen as a series of mere technical problems at the risk of madness. Political convictions involve much more than the logical faculties; they involve a strong emotional commitment. Perhaps one reason why I have written a book about the anarchist movement is that in the lives of the people who made it I find a sense of community of emotional commitment that I cannot find in a history of theoretical development. We understand theoretical convictions more easily, it seems to me, when they are presented as a particular personal commitment.

Thus, rather than expand the themes of the previous paragraph, it might be better to explain anarchism 'from the inside', as it were, by describing how I became an anarchist. I have no way of knowing how typical I am, though, and I apologise to anyone in the movement who thinks my own case is wildly untypical.

Some time ago I was thrown out of Leeds University for failing an examination. I wanted to change subjects anyway. The result was that I spent two years working in assorted jobs and going to night school to get more relevant A-Levels. One of these jobs had been as an unqualified teacher. The school had been quite a tough one, I was too young and inexperienced and the whole business turned out to be something of a disaster. The most depressing thing was the incredible ease with which I became a parody of the authoritarian teacher. I bellowed at the kids, I hit them, I demanded an obedience I found ridiculous, I preached values that were not my own. I had started the job an unthinking socialist with a rebellious streak and ended up sounding and acting like a prison warder — if not a particularly effective one. So when I was readmitted to the University and was spending the summer beforehand working at the far more congenial job of cleaning railway carriages I had a lot of thinking to do.

In the house where I had a room there were two anarchists. Quiet and friendly themselves, though perhaps a little too un-uproarious for my taste, their conversation and their bookshelves were a revelation. For the first time

I began to see what systems of order-givers and order-takers did to people, how authoritarian roles were enforced from the outside and then more readily accepted through chronic personal insecurity. I also found examples of men and women who had not only opposed arbitrary authority but had formulated — and lived — alternatives to it. Almost immediately I began to call myself an anarchist, though it is probably true to say that it takes a lifetime to be one. It was certainly the case that some time passed before the unique combination of personal morality, political analysis, strategy and tactics fully came home to me. In the years of agitation that followed I began to put practical flesh on the simple bones of the idea that mankind can live without authority. And though the problems in the way of progress towards that happy society have proved more deep-rooted than my first enthusiasm might have allowed, I have found no reason to suppose that it is neither possible nor desirable. For every anarchist, in the present book or out of it, there has been some process similar to this. Whether through personal experience or personal observation of oppression or exploitation someone jumps from considerations of despair or piecemeal defence to the conception that the whole world can be made again. And not with 'a new boss same as the old boss' but a world without elites, hierarchy or privilege. Without some understanding of this one cannot understand what makes anarchists tick and their ways will be as strange to the unpolitical reader as the ways of Martians.

In the present book I have tried to describe the British anarchist movement from its origins in 1880 or thereabouts to its more or less total eclipse by about 1930. (Though it is worth pointing out that the movement did pick up again rapidly in the later 1930s, mainly through the influence of the anarchist contribution to the Spanish Civil War and Revolution of 1936–1939. This later period is still a matter of living reminiscence rather than history.) That the British anarchist movement was a small one compared to the mass movements of Spain or France cannot be denied. Yet though never a mass movement, when it was in tune with its times it had periods of quite extraordinary growth. These periods of growth raise some interesting queries as to how histories of the 'common people' or the 'working class' have been related. For the conventional wisdom of 'people's history' over the greater part of our period has seen the significant developments in the emergence of institutions, most particularly the trades unions and the Labour Party. (A smaller group have rather concentrated on a smaller institution, the Communist Party.) There is no point in anarchist historians trying to fabricate anarchist institutions in opposition to these — there is no evidence that any existed. Anarchism in Britain had as its high spots the two periods of great working-class unrest that occurred in our period — 1889–1894 and 1910–1919. Outside these periods, institutions formed and transformed in them represent a tidemark round the bath of history after the waters of revolt have subsided. The anarchists, on the other hand, were of the moment, a part of that revolt, sustained by it, feeding ideas into it, growing and subsiding with it. The forms of the movement were shifting and decentralised, making it rather difficult to pin down numbers, events and the particular activists involved and forcing the historian to rely on myriad snippets of information. Nevertheless it is possible to say that the anarchist movement emerges in its moments of strength as of at least equal importance to that of the Marxist groupings. More importantly, it calls into question the validity of a history which considers only the institutional superstructure of working-class activity with little or no attention given to the ebb and flow of that activity itself. Anarchism, so often called 'utopian' or 'unrealistic', would seem to emerge as a practical creed when the masses move and suddenly feel their power.

It is as a movement in relation to the ebb and flow of popular revolt that this book concerns itself with the British anarchists. Only in relation to this does it consider anarchist philosophy and its philosophers. It concerns itself with the anarchist ideas taken up by people trying to seize some control over their own lives. Recent years have seen the reissue of many of the anarchist 'classics' of our period, together with assorted attempts to assess anarchist ideas of a rather patchy quality. I have no wish to enter this field. This book is concerned with the active spreading of anarchist propaganda and the nature of day-to-day anarchist activity. Thus there is little about Kropotkin after 1890, though his major theoretical output was after this date. There is barely a mention of literati of the Oscar Wilde-type who have connected themselves or have been gratuitously connected with the movement. This was not my intention when I started the book; yet as

I fossicked through the literature and other material connected with the movement I found little to encourage their inclusion. This is significant because as Kropotkin remarks:

> Socialistic literature has never been rich in books. It is written for workers for whom one penny is money, and its main force lies in its small pamphlets and its newspapers. Moreover, he who seeks for information about socialism finds in books little of what he requires most. They contain the theories or the scientific arguments in favour of socialist aspirations, but they give no idea how the workers accept socialist ideals and how they could put them into practice. There remains nothing but to take collections of papers and read them all through — the news as well as the leading articles — the former, perhaps, even more than the latter. Quite a new world of social relations and methods of thought and action is revealed by this reading, which gives an insight into what cannot be found anywhere else — namely, the depth and the moral force of the movement, the degree to which men are imbued with the new theories, their readiness to carry them out in their daily life and to suffer for them.[1]

My experience in writing this book absolutely confirmed Kropotkin's judgement. In this "new world of social relations and methods of thought and action" I found numbers of unsung demi-heroes (and, of course, not a few unreviled villains) whose story is considerably more gripping and important than a catalogue of contributions to the more progressive reviews. Such a catalogue, however, would be easier to write. As has been said, the sources for the anarchist movement are extremely scattered no central committee minutes exist because there was never a central committee; even quite large circulation papers can only be read in sequence by following fugitive odd copies from library to library. The result of research is a large ragged jigsaw with lots of pieces missing, most convincingly lifelike in its confusion. Inevitably selections have to be made, loose ends ignored or chopped off short to present some semblance of a rounded-out story. It is true that there are dangers to an over-cut and dried history; it is probably true to say too that any history of any social movement suffers from too much structure. Yet when the raw documentary stuff of history is confronted, a welter of fragments, stories, biographies, movements, concerns and events burst over the historian. And I, like all the rest, have selected and structured and for all my attempted objectivity have doubtless constructed a piece of the past in my own image. The only way for interested readers to correct this is to fossick through the libraries, etc., in order to construct a version of their own. Of one thing, however, I am certain: there will never be a final version.

**John Quail**

# Chapter 1
# RADICALS, EXILES AND SOCIALIST BEGINNINGS

Social agitations and working-class movements in the nineteenth century were many, various and contradictory. Certain themes can, however, be picked out. Ever present was the class war in varying degrees of complexity. Certain formal political liberties were struggled for: freedom of speech and press, freedom of assembly and freedom of conscience. The fact that some people's meetings for their version of freedom were broken up by other people with a different version, or that, say, nonconformists desired freedom from Church of England interference but were in no way prepared to countenance freedom for secularists merely adds charm to the proceedings. There was wide sympathy for nationalist movements of one sort and another and for the Irish particularly; yet British imperialist adventures could count on jingoist crowds turning out in support with monotonous regularity in the latter part of the century. Even the major question of the extension of the franchise meant different things at different times.

The Chartists had tried to achieve a sudden rearrangement of political power through the 'constitutional' means of manhood suffrage. In effect, however, it was a 'transitional demand' — to use Trotsky's phrase — a demand round which people will mobilise but which would not be granted by the ruling class this side of revolution. And whether the Chartists were of a tendency towards 'moral force' or 'physical force', manhood suffrage was too revolutionary for the ruling elites. These were, for many decades after 1848, overwhelmingly representative of ancient aristocratic privilege. The slow inclusion of members of the capitalist and professional classes in no way reduced its sense of its exclusive right to rule. Reform when it came seems to have been acceptable because the political elite had decided that the artisan class that it enfranchised, though perhaps under protest, in the 1867 Reform Act did not in any serious way intend to challenge that right.

The spirit of the times seems to have been clearly enough illustrated by the cordial relations that existed between the leadership of the skilled 'New Model' trades unions and the Radical capitalists of the Liberal Party. This underlined the social stability that increasing prosperity among the working class seemed to have established. That rise in prosperity was real enough: by 1865 real wages were 20 per cent up on 1850, and 33 per cent up on 1850 by 1875. For all this, it is worth pointing out that Booth in his surveys at the end of the 1880s found that fully one-third of the population was living below a most stringent subsistence line. The misery, degradation and disease at the bottom of the social heap is more fully described in other works. Suffice it to say that Doré, who illustrated Dante's *Inferno*, found the subject a comparable challenge.

Nevertheless the sense of increasing prosperity was real in the 1860s as was the sense of stability that went with it. And while this reduced the element of insurrection founded in misery in working-class politics it heightened the sense of self-importance. Prosperity was seen as the wages of worth, and it was more readily assumed that just demands would be met, one such demand being for an extended franchise. The Chartist spirit had by no means disappeared: in London in May 1866 a demonstration calling for electoral reform turned into a riot which involved, among other things, the destruction of over a mile of railings from round Hyde Park. But the sense of demands made and met undoubtedly bound together the social groups whose place it was to ask with the groups whose place it was to give. Although a more deep-seated spirit of revolt might exist among members of the First International or groups of old Chartists, it is nevertheless true that the activity connected with the possibilities opened up by the 1867 Reform Act took little note of it.

This (self-named) Radical activity was not based on a socialist politics. In its extreme forms its enemies were the aristocracy and others who benefited by unearned income and ancient privilege like the Church of England clergy and the royal family. (There was a considerable undertow of republicanism and secularism in Radical circles.) Radicals were frequently small businessmen or artisans who could become such by employing a few men. They tended to respond most readily to an analysis which divided society into two parts: the productive classes (i.e. masters and men) and the unproductive classes in the shape of the aristocracy, Church, etc. For the most part the Radicals aimed at cutting down the influence of the unproductive classes by reform rather than by the guillotine. It was certainly in a spirit of reform rather than revolution that the Radicals began to take advantage of their new influence after 1867.

This coincided and is connected with a rapid growth in the number of independent workingmen's clubs which sprang up all over England but which were particularly important in London. It had already been noticed that "The working classes, alike physically and politically, are now a very important power in the State. Their relations both to their employers and to the country at large are full of grave responsibility for the future of the country."[1] The Club and Institute Union set up in 1862 had been designed to encourage wholesome pursuits among the working class; and on a programme of temperance, class collaboration and decorum had gained many philanthropic upper-class patrons. From this source had stemmed a number of well-appointed, highly subsidised and tightly controlled clubs.

In the late 1860s and 1870s, however, working men began to organise their own clubs, sometimes to escape into a more easy-going atmosphere without patronage and sometimes for more directly political reasons. Among clubs founded for the latter can be included the Commonwealth Club in Bethnal Green established on the initiative of John Hales and the Patriotic Club in Clerkenwell similarly served by Tom Mottershead. Both these men had been members of the General Council of the First International, and John Hales was to stand at one point as a Radical candidate. When the Metropolitan Radical Federation was established, the independent clubs were the branches.

At the height of their influence in the late 1870s and 1880s, the Radicals had a relationship with the Liberal Party amounting to an alliance of which they were the left wing. But as time went by they were absorbed and by the 1890s "became a mere appendage of the Liberal Party, putting forward or supporting Liberal candidates in elections for the School Boards, the Borough Councils and the L.C.C. Instead of capturing the Liberal Party for Radicalism it provided it with election fodder and carried out election chores."[2] Yet in the period before Radical independence faded, the clubs provided centres of political discussion and self-education which both contributed to the development of the new socialism of the 1880s and provided it with an audience. The new ideas made some headway among the Radicals: by the end of the 1880s an informant of Booth's described the typical Sunday of a member of the Borough of Hackney Radical Club — which allegedly had more influence in the Borough than any religious body — as follows: "He goes to the club in the morning about 11, sits with a pot in front of him and froths at the mouth over all kinds of socialistic rot; then he has a band which finishes up by playing the Marseillaise; in the afternoon he goes round and visits other clubs and there is more frothing of the mouth and of the pot."[3]

So socialism was to creep in and influence the Radical rank and file. But in one sense it had always been there, although as a submerged and sometimes only just discernible tradition which can be traced back through the century, from Robert Owen, various sects like the Spencean Philanthropists, sections of the Chartists and so on. Examples pop up from time to time in the present book. In the 1860s and 1870s this tradition was continued through individuals who were a part of the Radical milieu. It is clear, however, from the limited work that has been done that from the collapse of the International in the early 1870s to the development of the new socialism of the 1880s continuity was preserved, as we shall see, by small but more decisively socialist groups. Of anarchist *groups* there is no trace, though anarchist individuals can be found from time to time.

Of the socialist groups that existed in the 1870s, some were influenced by what was, at base, a more militant Radicalism, though with more emphasis on physical force. Some were influenced by theories of the mutual antagonism of capital and labour. Some socialists put this view in the context of traditional aspirations towards parliamentary representation, thus providing the earliest apostles of a party of labour (or Labour Party).

Others preserved the element of physical force, opposed parliamentary activity and argued that the working-class struggle for emancipation would, of necessity, have to be revolutionary. It was to libertarians of this shade of opinion that anarchism was later to appeal, not in a vacuum but to an already developed set of ideas and to a body of self-confident and active men. The specific and developed theories of anarchist mutualism, collectivism and communism were really only taken up by English people in the 1880s; yet foreign anarchist exiles in England before this time could and did find areas of mutual understanding with sections of the British socialist movement. How this understanding developed and where it led can perhaps be most immediately demonstrated in the lives of individuals, though we should beware of possible distortions. These men were prominent rather than pre-eminent.

Frank Kitz was born in 1848, the son of an English mother and a German father — though he seems to have been orphaned early because he was later to describe himself as "a fatherless lad."[4] From an early age he lived alone, as his mother found work 'in service' — i.e. as a domestic servant. "I supported myself," he wrote later,

> as errand boy, porter and messenger in various situations: ill-shod, badly clothed, and seldom enjoying a square meal except when my mother smuggled me into her employer's kitchen ... I decorated the walls of my lonely room with pictures of the French Revolution which I purchased out of my scanty earnings. Brought up in the neighbourhood of the West End with the evidence of wealth and luxury confronting me — wealth unearned, comfort undeserved — and with my own undeserved hardships, I needed no lectures upon surplus value or dissertations upon economics to cause me to challenge the justice of a system which confers wealth upon the parasites of society and clouds the lives of thousands as it had already clouded mine with care and poverty.

As a boy he "attended every meeting or demonstration held by the advanced movement in London. In the riot at Hyde Park," he writes, "at the time of the Reform League [i.e. 1866] my white printer's jacket made me conspicuous in the skirmishes with the police and only my nimbleness saved me from arrest. The police behaved with their usual brutality ..." He was by this time apprenticed as a dyer, which was to be his trade for the rest of his life. When his apprenticeship was finished in 1869–1870 he went on the tramp, first round south-east England where he financed himself when no work was available by taking the Queen's shilling [the traditional down payment on joining the army] and then rapidly disappearing. He then travelled through the north of England. "Here I found everywhere the same conditions — the factory with its iron discipline, the mazes of mean streets and insanitary slums for the workers, the enslavement of women and children." He returned to London and settled in Soho in late 1873 or early 1874. It was here that he was introduced by a friend to a discussion group called the Democratic and Trades Alliance which met regularly in a pub run by a shoemaker who had been blacklisted for his trades union activity. "Becoming a regular attender at these meetings," writes Kitz, "I there became acquainted with G. Odger, John Rogers, G. Milner, W. Townshend, the brothers Murray, G. Harris and G. Eccarius, all members of the lately defunct British Federation of the International. ... Most of the members were Soho tailors and shoemakers, always the most advanced among the workers. ... There I made my first attempt to open a debate, reading a paper against political action and was sat on heavily and informed that I would never be a speaker and not to try again ..."[5] It is to be noted that Kitz's first speech was to be against political — that is, electoral — activity. And Kitz is being too modest here. Whatever the reactions to his first speech it does not seem to have affected his standing among this 'steadfast old guard'. He is first mentioned as taking part in a debate on communism in August 1874. In September he took the chair at a meeting — a position of some prestige. By December of that year he had been elected secretary.

But there were disagreements within the alliance: "We had our conflicts with the purely Trades Unionist members, who, when our foreign comrades solicited our help [for a celebration of the Paris Commune] opposed cooperation. The bills announcing the celebration (and brave bills they were, with the Red Flag printed upon them) were removed from the club room notice board. The brothers Murray who represented our speaking power at the time, went unofficially to help them. Eventually we shed this fossilised element, shifted our quarters and blossomed out as the Manhood Suffrage League." This organisation was founded in 1875 and Frank Kitz was its secretary. Although the League was more to the left than its predecessor, its members were by no means all revolutionaries: "Moderate men can be found on its committee as well as extremists, and on Sunday evenings this dialectic was strongly apparent. It was always an open forum and meetings could vary considerably in their political tone.

"The most advanced politicals in London were among the members ... but the discussion was wide open and the most moderate views could sometimes prevail ..."[6]

One measure of the differences between the League and its predecessor, however, lies in the more positive attitude to the Paris Commune which caused the League to come into being. Fairly advanced Radicals like Bradlaugh, for example, baulked at the 'unconstitutional' nature of the Commune. He was reported as saying in a speech that "The Commune asked for the recognition and consolidation of the Republic. But he denied their right to do it by force of arms ..." Radicals might be sickened at the slaughter — some 30,000 people were massacred when the Commune was crushed — but for them the Commune was not a heroic beginning of a new world. The Manhood Suffrage League thought differently. Kitz writes: "Freed from obstruction and opposition, we cordially cooperated with our foreign comrades in holding an international meeting at the Cleveland Hall to celebrate the Commune. It was a most enthusiastic demonstration and marked the beginning of the revival" (i.e. of socialism). A large number of English working men attended. But whether because of the incomplete commitment to revolution of the League or the pressure of new ventures, by 1877 Kitz was no longer secretary of the Manhood Suffrage League. He mentions no particular break in his memoirs, so it is likely that he retained a connection with it that gradually atrophied over the years. Certainly by 1877 Kitz was working for the formation of a specifically socialist, revolutionary and internationalist movement in London. The international element was important. As he says, "the socialist movement in England owes its origins largely to the propagandist zeal of foreign workmen."[7]

More specifically, they were German exiles. Kitz spoke fluent German and was in close contact with them. The Social Democratic Party was growing in Germany and was an increasingly influential example internationally. It should not be assumed, however, that 'social democracy' meant then what it means now. Kitz was committed to revolutionary rather than electoral action and by *his* use of the phrase he clearly meant a revolutionary democratic socialism. The distinction was between a total social democracy and a partial *political* democracy. At that time 'social democracy' was not reducible to parliamentary reformism.

There had been German political refugees in London since the events of 1848, one of the better known of them being Karl Marx. For the most part these refugees were men mostly "past middle age and already longstanding members of some English trade union or another ..."[8] and their meetings were mainly social affairs where politics were discussed as part of a pleasant chat over a drink. There was, however, a steady influx of younger men with more activist tendencies. This influx was to turn into a flood as a result of the German Anti-Socialist Laws; yet the quickening of the German political atmosphere to which these Laws were something of a response had already affected the German exiles by 1877. One consequence was that at an informal gathering after the Cleveland Hall meeting Kitz describes how he was "urged by my comrade Johann Neve" (of whom more later) "to form an English section of the Socialist party. I succeeded in getting together a number of comrades including those of the British Federation whom I have already referred to and thus was started an English Revolutionary Society, which, working with the foreign element was to take its part in the International Socialist movement ..." This English Revolutionary Society was a part of the Social Democratic Club, which met in pubs in Soho from its foundation in August 1877 until it found permanent premises in Rose Street (now Manette Street) in 1878. There were some five sections according to nationality, with Frank Kitz as secretary of the English section. The move to club premises was important because now discussion and organisation could go ahead without the interference of landlords; and without the expense of hired rooms, says Kitz, "we were enabled to hold public meetings with greater frequency."[9]

When a wave of refugees arrived in London from Germany after the passage of the Anti-Socialist Laws in 1878, the Rose Street club became a central point for defence and aid. The general publicity given to the Laws also attracted attention to the thing they were designed to repress. "Shortly after this influx of refugees," writes Kitz, "the sections jointly issued a pamphlet by J. Sketchley, entitled *The Principles of Social Democracy* thus taking advantage of the interest awakened. ... Many thousands of this pamphlet were sold, the German section bearing the major portion of the cost, in order to aid propaganda among our own working class. The English section undertook the reissue of two pamphlets on communism by H. Glasse; they also published an address to the amnestied Communists of Paris and 50,000 copies of this leaflet were distributed …"[10] (Sketchley, incidentally, was an old Chartist.) In order to understand the reasons for and the consequences of the Anti-Socialist Laws it is necessary to explain in more detail what was happening in Germany in this period.

A German anarchist movement had existed since the mid-1870s.[11] Their propaganda was spread by wandering agitators and smuggled newspapers. It was a small movement, in isolation, yet it began to have some influence on the left wing of the Social Democratic Party. This influence grew because of the anomalous position of the party. It was rapidly increasing the number of seats it held in the Reichstag (and displaying all the tendencies towards respectability which such positions seem to entail). On the other hand, however, even a majority of seats held by the SDP in the Reichstag would have given it no real power. The Reichstag was able, under the constitution, only to advise the Kaiser and his Chancellor; and the latter were able to ignore this advice, constrained only by a wish to preserve the forms of government by consent. The extent to which the anarchists began to have influence among the party's left wing was the extent to which it began to see that even quite modest reforms might only be achievable by revolutionary means.

Yet there was no revolutionary turbulence among the German workers, as the general lack of response to revolutionary propaganda seemed to prove. At this time the anarchists were developing ideas as to how such working-class passivity could be overcome. It was suggested that a new kind of propaganda was needed, a propaganda of deeds rather than words.

Kropotkin, for example, writing at about this time, asked what separated "the argument from the deed, the thought from the will to act." He answered his own question by saying: "It is the action of minorities, action continued, renewed without ceasing, which brings about this transformation. Courage, devotion, the spirit of self sacrifice are as contagious as cowardice, submission and panic."[12]

And he goes on to say that this action will be "sometimes collective, sometimes purely individual" but that it would neglect no "means at hand … to awaken audacity and the spirit of revolt by preaching by example." This preaching by example was later to be better known as

'propaganda by deed'. The theory of propaganda by deed seemed to invite
the most spectacular actions and in Germany it led to two attempts on the
life of the Kaiser. In May 1878, Emil Hödel, and in June of the same year
Carl Nobiling, shot at the Kaiser as he was driven through the streets in
an open carriage. Both attempts failed. The failed assassins both had links
with known German anarchists and Hödel declared himself an anarchist
at his trial. He was beheaded. Nobiling died of self-inflicted wounds. No
revolutionary upsurge accompanied these attempts, any such thing being
pre-empted in any case by the frantic reaction of the German authorities.
Bismarck, the German Chancellor, irritated by the growing electoral
strength of the SDP, constitutionally circumscribed and severely legalistic
though it was, seized upon the assassination attempts as an opportunity
to smear the party. The result of his efforts was the Anti-Socialist Laws of
October 1878.

After the second assassination attempt Berlin became an armed camp. All
known socialists had their homes raided. Even before the passage of the
Laws over 500 people had been arrested and sent to jail for 'insulting the
Kaiser' or 'approving' of the attempts on his life. Some of the cases would
have been laughable had it not been for the suffering involved: A drunken
man received two and a half years in prison for murmuring "William is
dead, he lives no more." A woman talking about the Emperor's wounds was
sentenced to a year and a half for saying "The Kaiser at least is not poor, he
can afford to care for himself." A worker ... while sitting on a bench along
Unter den Linden was heard to say that "Hödel is a dumb-bell but Nobiling
planned his attempt well." This slip of his tongue cost him four years of
his freedom.[13] The results of the repression were twofold. Firstly, as far as
the left-wing socialists were concerned the mask of the democratic process
was ripped away to reveal black reaction. Secondly, socialist agitation of
any sort was made both doubly difficult and very much more dangerous.
A wave of socialist refugees left Germany and many came to London.
Frank Kitz described the situation: "Thousands were expatriated, hundreds
of families broken up, hundreds imprisoned; seizures and confiscations
were the order of the day. Of those torn from their families a number went
insane and others were irretrievably ruined; a great number sought refuge
in London and our club in Rose Street presented at times the appearance

of an arrival or departure platform at a station with luggage and cases of prohibited literature and the bewildered emigrants going to and fro."[14] The bitterness caused by the repression and the Anti-Socialist Laws probably made more anarchists than the German authorities had been able to silence by their measures. For some years London was to be the major centre for the production of German revolutionary and anarchist propaganda and the organisation of its secret distribution.

Into the embittered society of the German exiles in London came Johann Most, later to be the central figure in a case which was to prove a rallying point for the new socialist movement. When he arrived in London, Most was a dissident left-wing social democrat who had been forced out of Germany. No theoretician, as a bitterly sarcastic and humorous speaker and journalist who was popular with working-class audiences, he had earned himself some notoriety and a string of jail sentences. He had been elected to the Reichstag, which he found frustrating, until another jail sentence for a speech on the Paris Commune put an end to his political career. On his release he edited a Berlin social democrat newspaper whose circulation he boosted from 2,000 to 18,000 in a year. Further activities in this direction were abruptly halted after Hödel's attempt. Most spoke about it at a meeting and though his comments were not approving he was arrested and sentenced to six weeks' imprisonment. When this term was up he was sentenced to a further five months, which he spent in solitary confinement. In December 1878 he was released and given twenty-four hours to leave Berlin. He went to Hamburg, where the local party leaders, their nerve completely shot, advised him to emigrate to America. Most did leave Germany but went instead to London, arriving just before Christmas 1878.

Most's energy was unaffected by his prison sentences and expulsion. With the financial and practical help of members of the Rose Street club, the first issue of *Freiheit*, a paper designed for illegal distribution in Germany, was published on 4th January 1879. At first it described itself as a social democrat paper but from February 1879 onwards it steadily downgraded the importance of electoral activity; and in 1880 it began printing specifically anarchist articles. At this time, too, fairly formal links were alleged to exist between Most and "the younger generation of Bakuninists in Paris, the group that publishes the *Révolution sociale*."[15]

Once the paper was established a number of successful networks were set up for smuggling the paper into Germany. Large numbers were sewn into mattresses in a factory in Hull and exported. Sailors carried quantities of it from England to Germany via Hamburg. Each issue of the paper was given a different title so that the authorities had to first find out its name before banning it. Naturally German police spies were sent to try and infiltrate the smuggling networks and the group round the paper. Kitz relates that on several occasions "we were puzzled by the fact that the German government was aware of the new titles before the paper reached Germany, and thus forestalled us. Johann Neve and I set out to find the cause. Suspecting a member who had recently joined we supplied him with a specially printed copy of the paper bearing a title different from the one we actually intended to use. The bogus title was prohibited but the other escaped. I regret to say that this member met with a serious accident when attending a fête held in support of the *Freiheit*."[16] The spy was shot and seriously wounded on Hampstead Heath.

The mixture of political ideas in *Freiheit* at this time represented fairly accurately Most's own ideas, which took parts of left social democracy, Blanquism (i.e. putschist republicanism) and anarchism but which were marked by strident calls for revolutionary violence that grew out of a wild and bitter response to the repression in Germany. His itch for vengeance found an exemplary object in the assassination of Tsar Alexander II by Russian nihilists in 1881. *Freiheit* published an article by Most entitled 'Endlich' ('At Last') which enthusiastically supported their action. The Russian government applied pressure — pressure from the German government can be assumed to be constant — and Most was prosecuted by the British authorities. He was found guilty of incitement to murder heads of state and sentenced to eighteen months' imprisonment.

His arrest and sentence caused something of a stir in London Radical and socialist circles. A short-lived English-language paper, also entitled *Freiheit*, was issued by the English section of the Rose Street club as the organ of a defence committee. Frank Kitz was the editor. The paper printed an English translation of Most's article but avoided being enmeshed in the prosecution by presenting it as part of the speech of the prosecuting counsel at the trial! Jack Williams stood on the steps of the Old Bailey during the trial and sold many copies of this edition. Protest meetings were held, some successful as at Mile End Waste in April, some less so as at Peckham where "the Radicals combined with Tories, opposed the speakers and were only prevented by force from seizing the platform ..."[17] The prosecution of Most was opposed publicly on the grounds of the right of asylum and the right of free speech (although the first issue of the *Freiheit* did reprint some approving remarks of Disraeli's on tyrannicide). Such an approach did find quite wide sympathy — the jury at Most's trial asked that he be treated with some mercy since he might be suffering from violent wrong done to him in Germany.

The German *Freiheit* continued under caretaker editors until further publication in London was stopped as a consequence of an article applauding the assassination of Lord Frederick Cavendish by Fenians in Phoenix Park, Dublin, in May 1882. The office was raided and its plant seized. Johann Neve narrowly escaped arrest and two compositors were jailed for six and nine months. *Freitheit* was forced to move, first to Switzerland and then to the United States. In its short but eventful London career it had produced a number of important incidental effects. Through dissensions within the German exiles a split had taken place, the orthodox defence committee removing to new premises in Tottenham Street. The progressively anarchist supporters of Most remained at Rose Street until they formed a distinctively anarchist club in St Stephen's Mews, Rathbone Place, some time around 1883. The prosecution of Most had provided a focal issue around which the English socialists could organise and had more actively brought these militants into contact with foreign revolutionaries. The prosecution had also further discouraged hopes that the new Liberal government of 1880 would prove a dynamically reforming force.

Perhaps a word should be said here about the personal qualities of Kitz at this time. A contemporary related later that during the time of the Most prosecution "Kitz was having a very bad time ... and finally had the brokers in. He had £20 in his possession subscribed to the defence fund ... After much perplexity as to its safety he ... hid it in a small barrel of sand which he was using in his work. After the brokers had departed he found the barrel had been untouched."[18] He was thus able to hand over the money to the defence counsel. It was a trustworthy man indeed who could hold twenty pounds for his cause without thought of its usefulness to himself when bailiffs were stripping his house of his last sticks of furniture.

## Chapter 2

# THE LABOUR EMANCIPATION LEAGUE

Frank Kitz and his associates were not the only British revolutionary propagandists in London by the time the Rose Street club was formed. The importance of Kitz in the 1870s was that he provided an active link between the veterans of the International (and veterans, too, of earlier movements) and the new socialism of the 1880s. In the mid-1870s there might not have been much young blood about — on a visit to Oxford, Kitz was introduced as 'the last of the socialists' — but by the later 1870s there were new and interesting developments and new figures were emerging. One such was Joseph Lane. Born in 1850 in the village of Wallingford, Oxfordshire, he spent his early life "working on the land under the most enslaving poverty. Soon, by necessity, he took an interest in the infamous game and land laws and quickly developed into a thinker and a rebel." He was attending local political meetings at the age of fifteen. "In 1865 he came to London arriving at a time when vigorous fights for free speech were in progress. He participated in the struggles at Hyde Park when the authorities tried to stop meetings being held there."[1] These were the same Reform Riots that Frank Kitz had taken part in.

According to one source Lane joined the English remnant of the International in 1871. "In the early 1870s he took an active part in the republican agitation accompanying Dilke on one of his tours ... earning the nickname of 'Dilke's Boy.'" Later he became a member of the Manhood Suffrage League where he met Frank Kitz.[2] In January 1880 he was chairman at a meeting which founded branch number three of the Marylebone Radical Reform Association, with Edwin Dunn as secretary. This branch split from and veered sharply left of its parent body. The spirit and something of the politics of Joe Lane at this time can be gathered from an incident he relates in his memoirs. He, Kitz and Jack Williams were going to all the election meetings called by the two Liberal

candidates in Marylebone in 1880 and frightening them by asking them to
support abolition of the House of Lords, Home Rule for Ireland and land
nationalisation — all 'extreme Radical' demands. On one occasion, one of
the prospective members asked Lane if he really wanted the abolition of
the House of Lords. He replied, "Yes, and the House of Commons too!"
The result was a riot: "They threw all they could lay their hands on at us
on the platform and smashed up furniture and mirrors …" After a fight the
three hecklers were thrown out. Lane, it would appear, had already started
on the path of anti-statist ideas. By 1881 he was apparently calling himself
a socialist, since in that year, having moved to Hackney, he founded the
Homerton Social Democratic Club. He attended the Social Revolutionary
and Anarchist Congress in July 1881 as the delegate of the Club, the
congress taking place in the private room of a pub in Charrington Street,
Euston, London.

The international congress was basically an affair of and for continental
and Russian revolutionaries. The minutes of the proceedings reveal that
the English delegates played little part; yet many of the people involved
were more or less permanent exiles in London, and it was partly through
contact between them and the British socialists that a more sophisticated
libertarian philosophy was to develop relevant to British conditions. Thus
though the congress did not precipitate anything like an eruption of
anarchist activity in Britain it can be seen as part of a developing process.

The English delegates were Joe Lane and Price from the Homerton
Social Democratic Club; Frank Kitz, Edwin Dunn and John Lord[3] from
the Rose Street club, together with a rather suspicious unknown called
C. Hall, who could well have been the English counterpart of the French
police spy Serreaux, who also attended the conference. The forty-five
foreign delegates included John Neve, Malatesta, Louise Michel, Peukert
and Kropotkin. The latter in his memoirs puts the early socialist initiative
in England into perspective:

Aided by a few English workers whose acquaintance we had made at
the congress of 1881 or whom the prosecutions against John Most
had attracted to the socialists, we went to the Radical clubs speaking
about Russian affairs, the movement of our youth toward the people

and socialism in general. We had ridiculously small audiences, seldom consisting of more than a dozen men. Occasionally some grey bearded Chartist would rise from the audience and tell us that all we were saying had been said forty years before and was greeted then with enthusiasm by crowds of workers, but that now all was dead, and there was no hope of reviving it.[4]

Yet in France, whence Kropotkin had come, a new socialist movement was well under way. In England it was only just starting. Inevitably Kropotkin's feelings were coloured by comparison, and he was to leave England later in 1881 with the sentiment 'Better a French prison than this grave'. Joe Lane, on the other hand, was about to start work on a project of some importance in the history of English socialism, the Labour Emancipation League. This emerged out of Lane's contacts with yet another emerging socialist grouping in East London, the Stratford Dialectical and Radical Club. This had been formed as a result of a split in the Stratford branch of the National Secular Society, where the leading dissentient was a young man called Ambrose Barker. The National Secular Society was by no means devoted only to anti-Christian theology. Its members were

renowned for their 'advanced' views on all the leading questions of the day. ... They were closely associated with every species of metropolitan Radicalism and led political demonstrations, for example in Hyde Park against royal grants in 1875 and against war during the Eastern crisis [circa 1880]. ... The Secularists were definitely identified with and indeed in the late 1870s were the chief upholders of the Radical-Republican cause. They attacked monarchy, hereditary privilege and class oppression and in London secured wide general support among the working men's clubs.[5]

The undisputed leader of the N.S.S. was Bradlaugh, who was by all accounts a brilliant orator and organiser of the republicans and 'infidels'. He was not above opportunism, however, and it was this that withered the heart of the young Ambrose Barker. Ambrose Barker had been born and brought up in the village of Earls Barton near Northampton, the scenes of Bradlaugh's epic electoral battles. His father had been a Chartist and had helped to found a cooperative shop and bakery in the village. Barker remembered his father taking "a party of Radicals to Northampton to support Bradlaugh at the hustings in October 1868."[6] In 1878 he went to London at the age of nineteen to take up a job as assistant master at a school in Leyton. On his arrival he joined the N.S.S. He writes in his memoirs: "One can well imagine our joy in the election of Charles Bradlaugh for Northampton and the great satisfaction generally that a great majority had overthrown the Tory government in 1880. But that satisfaction was soon to be shattered. Reaction had ruled so long that great things were expected of the Radical-Liberal Government. But the people were soon to be disillusioned. They were looking to the Government to bring forward social reforms, instead of which a most stringent Coercion Bill for Ireland was introduced ..."

And Bradlaugh supported the Coercion Bill. Ambrose Barker attacked him in print and — a brave thing to do at the shrine of the Bradlaugh supporters — proposed a motion at the Hall of Science condemning him; but could find no seconder.[7] This 'betrayal' by Bradlaugh came on top of discussions within the Stratford Branch which had been going on for some time over the question of whether religion alone or the wider 'social question' should be their central concern. The majority favoured 'this worldism' and the more restrictedly secularist members left, taking the name of the branch with them. The remaining 'this worldists' formed themselves towards the end of 1880 into the Stratford Dialectical and Radical Club. This, writes Ambrose Barker, who became secretary to the club, "marks the inception of the Socialist movement in East London."

"We now commenced our propaganda work in dead earnest," he writes. "For myself I lectured on 'Labour', 'Social Democracy', 'The French Revolution' and many other subjects." One lecture he gave — on 'Government' — was, he claims, "the first lecture of the kind in East London or for the matter of that in London itself on the basis of Anarchism. I said, 'Governments were popularly supposed to be for the protection of the people. A knowledge of the past and the bitter experience of the present seemed to point out that it was *against* rather than by Government that protection was necessary'. 'The lecturer,' reported the *Radical* of 19th

February 1881, 'argued that people made a great mistake in looking to Government for help. It had always been the destroyer of independence.'"[8] The language here remains within the bounds of Radical thinking and at best represents only an un-anarchism. On the other hand it was to men like Ambrose Barker, with fairly well-developed socialist and anti-statist ideas, that anarchism was later to appeal.

To the club were invited speakers and writers well known to the Radicals of London. These included James and Charles Murray, Frank Kitz, Herbert Burrows, George Standring, Edwin Dunn, Dan Chatterton and Miss Le Compte, the American delegate to the international congress. Later on — in April 1882 — Kropotkin was also to speak at the Stratford Club, but on 'Russian Exiles' rather than anarchism. In fact, the first systematic propaganda defining itself as anarchist that had any effect within the socialist movement came from America in the shape of Benjamin Tucker's paper *Liberty*. Joseph Lane seems to have been the first to procure copies of the paper from the United States. He introduced Ambrose Barker to it — and probably others too — in late 1881, and Barker became a regular subscriber and commenced a regular correspondence with Tucker. Tucker was a Proudhonist and thus fundamentally committed to a society based on small proprietorship. In the American context, however, where the small landowner was often locked in battle with large capitalist interests, this did not represent the reactionary position it often did later where it could easily degenerate into an 'anarchism for small businessmen'. Tucker had a keen sense of the right of the oppressed to struggle against oppression and a good eye for revolutionary humbug. Away from his hobbyhorse of private property versus communism the paper was lively and far-ranging and even on this topic he was prepared to give space for the anarchist-communist view. The introduction of specifically anarchist ideas into the working-class movement was thus going on well before the alleged Year One of English anarchism, 1886, which saw the foundation of *Freedom*.

Yet the socialist groups were too small and, it must be admitted, too theoretically imprecise for there to be any practical outcome of theoretical differences. The immediately felt need was for a wider spread of socialist ideas of any variety. For these purposes specifically socialist clubs in pubs, etc., could have their uses. For example in 1881 James MacDonald was told by the landlord of a pub in Tottenham Street, Soho, that in another room there was a meeting of "some of the most red-hot Fenians and dynamiters in England." Intrigued, he and some of his friends investigated and found Frank Kitz, the Murray brothers and others enthusiastically denouncing the Coercion Bill. At first opposing them, he gradually became converted, and from this contact stemmed his long connection with the socialist movement.[9] But it was fairly obviously going to take quite some time for socialism to spread if all its recruits came this way. It was necessary to take the message out to the people. One way of doing that was by providing speakers for the Sunday evening meetings of the Radical clubs. As Frank Kitz remarks, they "had still a leaven amongst them of Chartists and Republicans and their platforms were at our disposal."[10] Many of the early socialists made good use of this opening. The Murray brothers, Kitz, Dunn, Barker and many others were regular speakers.

There was, however, another way of reaching the masses: public speaking in the streets. Street speaking was, by and large, the preserve of the religious or temperance sects, who not only had muscular Christian support but also friends and patrons higher up the social scale on whom they could rely. Secularist speakers had occasionally held meetings in the open air and the Radicals had their rallies and demonstrations, but there had been no "regular weekly outdoor meetings at which Socialist addresses were given, followed by questions and discussion — when nothing more untoward took place!"[11] The Stratford Dialectical and Radical Club decided to extend its work in this direction "and began to hold meetings in Mile End Road which were well attended. It was there," writes Barker, "early in 1881 that I first met Joseph Lane and formed a friendship that only ended with his death."

Joe Lane had transferred his attentions from Homerton to Mile End as a result of the forcible closure of his club. As he puts it: "The Police exerted so much pressure [on] the landlord we had to leave Homerton — the police inspector said because we printed 'Socialism' so large on our bills. Another thing: we had just had a large demonstration in Hyde Park against the Liberals' coercion in Ireland. Me and Kitz made a banner, 'Homerton Socialist Society — Labour is the source of all wealth therefore all wealth belongs to Labour' and several other mottoes. But the one that frightened the members as well as the police was 'Blessed is the hand that dares to wield the regicidal steel that shall redeem a nation's sorrow with a tyrant's blood.'[12] As Kitz tells the story, as a result of objections to the latter inscription there was a more or less pitched battle with more moderate elements taking part in the demonstration.

As a result of the success of the open-air meetings at Mile End, Joe Lane suggested follow-up discussions, and a room was booked at a pub opposite their speaking pitch. After a few of these meetings the participants formed themselves into the Labour Emancipation League. This marked the beginnings of a real penetration of socialist ideas into the East End of London's poverty-stricken, crowded, violent and miserable streets in which only those who shared or instinctively understood the lives people led could hope to communicate the new socialism. The success of the Labour Emancipation League was due largely to the energy and determination of Joe Lane and more particularly in his choice of open-air speaking as a means of getting a hearing. There was some nervousness at his approach: "James Murray told him he was young and didn't know anything about it; that the propertied classes were like a pack of wolves and would tear them apart if they went out into the streets and parks. Lane, Kitz and others went out nevertheless and blazed a trail of revolutionary action. The days of Chartism were near enough still to intimidate men who were not really courageous. Peterloo was even yet a living memory."[13]

Joe Lane proved himself to be a ferociously committed organiser. He later described his mode of operation: "Take a room, pay quarter's rent in advance then arrange list of lecturers for the three months, then get bills printed, one for each week, then paste up bills in streets all round. By the end of 3 or 6 months I had got a few members and [I would] get them to take it over and manage it as a Branch. I generally had two or three Branches on my hands in this way."[14] And this is put in its proper context when we understand that, as a contemporary put it, "He did this out of his wages as an ordinary carman [cart driver], which at that time would probably be nearer 20 shillings than 30 shillings per week."[15]

The programme of the League was: equal direct adult suffrage; direct legislation by the people; abolition of the standing army, the people to decide on peace or war; free secular and industrial education; liberty of speech, press and meeting; free administration of justice; the nationalisation of land, mines and transport; society to regulate production and wealth to be shared equitably by all; the monopoly of the capitalist class to be broken and the means of production transformed into collective or public property. The object of the League was "the establishment of a Free Social Condition of Society based on the principles of Political Equality with Equal Social Advantages for All." Thus no matter what some of its members may have claimed later, the Labour Emancipation League was not at its inception an anarchist organisation. The concerns with suffrage, free administration of justice, liberty of speech, etc., clearly have their origins in the Chartist demands and even earlier with the constitutions and bills of rights of an earlier revolutionary era. They sit a little uneasily with the demands concerning the expropriation of the capitalist class. Ambrose Barker was later to claim that "Parliamentary action was a constant topic of discussion in … the Labour Emancipation League from 1881 to 1884 … the members were fairly unanimous as to its futility." This may well have been a position that was reached by 1884, but its programme (which remained unchanged) by no means expresses an anti-parliamentary position. The fundamental importance of the Labour Emancipation League was that it provided a forum for discussion and mutual education. This has to be borne in mind when we assess its programme. The political ideas of the working class were in transition, and the Labour Emancipation League was in the best sense transitory.

The League rapidly established branches at Mile End, Canning Town, Hoxton, Bethnal Green, Millwall, Stamford Hill and Hackney. There was regular open-air propaganda at Mile End Waste, Clerkenwell Green, Stratford and Millwall, with occasional meetings in Hyde Park and Regent's Park.

## Chapter 3

# THE DEMOCRATIC FEDERATION
# AND THE SOCIALIST LEAGUE

The working-class militants were concerned with the practical problems of socialist propaganda on specific issues at the grass roots. As Frank Kitz put it, "the English Section and the comrades of the Labour Emancipation League worked with only one aim and that was to permeate the mass of the people with a spirit of revolt against their oppressors and against the squalid misery which results from their monopoly of the means of life. No thought of kudos or personal aggrandisement had entered into their efforts to spread the light, and therefore the squabbles between would-be leaders had no interest for them."[1] This assertion was certainly true of those who formed the libertarian wing of the movement in the 1880s. Whatever the accusations against them by their opponents, seeking a political career was not one of their faults. There were others, however, with more of an eye for the main chance. As we have seen, socialism developed on the left-wing fringe of the Radical movement and in this early period retained strong links with the Radical milieu. There was a wave of discontent among the Radicals when the Liberal government failed to live up to its promises of reform and this discontent made it easier for the socialists to spread their message. But this discontent also attracted more opportunist attention.

The working-class vote had been attracted to the Liberal Party by a careful wooing of the Radicals by the more 'progressive' Liberals. The Tory counter-attack took several forms. They did some wooing of their own, setting up clubs under their patronage and seeking the support of the independent clubs for 'Tory Democrat' candidates in elections. The 'Tory Democrats' represented a combination of imperialism abroad and jingoism and a gentle reformism at home. They represented something of a break with the Tories of the old school, who were straightforward representatives of the landed interest. The more far-seeing Tories made the quite correct calculation that if they could split the Radicals from the Liberal Party and set them against each other then this would split the anti-Tory vote and gain Tory majorities in otherwise unpromising seats. The most hopeful means for expediting that split seemed to be independent Labour candidates. The rise of the Labour Party and the concomitant demise of the Liberals shows how correct their thinking was, at least in the short term. It had the disadvantage, however, of being an obvious manoeuvre. Lane relates a crude approach when he was active in Marylebone before the election in 1880. He "had an offer by the Tories to pay all expenses if we would put up a candidate — wanted us to put up of course to let the Tories in."[2] The offer was refused.

It was in this rather murky political undergrowth that the Democratic Federation had its origins. H.M. Hyndman, a stockbroker and one of its prime movers, had stood as an independent Tory in Marylebone in 1880.

While canvassing the clubs in the district he met Joe Lane who recalled his impressions of Hyndman's politics at that time. He was opposed to Home Rule for Ireland and land nationalisation. On complete adult suffrage he said, "'Do you mean to tell me that a loafer in the East End was to be placed in equality with you, no the furthest I would go is that every man who can read and write is to have a vote.' He was on every point a Tory Democrat." He invited Lane to his house and asked for support for his candidacy from Lane's club. Lane was highly dubious. Hyndman wanted Lane to come on further visits to keep some kind of dialogue going, a proposal Lane found a complete waste of time. Hyndman was pressing, however, and Edwin Dunn, the secretary of the club, became a regular visitor in Lane's place. As a result of these meetings they approached Lane with the idea of "forming an Independent Labour Party" and asked Lane to call a meeting of delegates from all the workmen's clubs. Lane seems to think that Hyndman was the prime mover here while Kitz says it was Dunn's proposal. Meetings were called to discuss the matter at the Rose Street Club and elsewhere. As a result of these meetings Dunn sent out invitations as secretary of the Marylebone Radical Association to inaugurate an independent labour organisation at a meeting at the Westminster Palace Hotel in June 1881.

Professor Beesly, the positivist defender of the Paris Commune, took the chair at the meeting which included some of the more liberal politicians, delegates from the clubs, the odd Tory Democrat and some of the new socialist militants — "all sorts and conditions of men" in Kitz's phrase. Lane was one of the socialists and he says, "we drove them as far as we could and set them up with the most advanced programme we could force on them. One whom we had to fight on all the most advanced points was H.M. Hyndman ... After a hard struggle it was to be [called the] Democratic Federation with adult suffrage, Home Rule, etc ..." Lane then withdrew from the organisation. Dunn remained but Kitz says that Hyndman "soon engaged in a conflict with Dunn for the leadership, and evicted him ..." There is little doubt that it was Hyndman's intention to use this organisation as a base for further attempts at election, whether by himself or others. A faithful follower was to write later that Hyndman started the Democratic Federation out of "disgust at Gladstone and the Liberals, by genuine sympathy with real democratic movements as against party politics and by his own impulsiveness of action ... and not by any fixed idea of future definite Socialist propaganda and organisation."[3] Hyndman's Tory candidature in 1880 is similarly described as 'impulsive'. His organisation was to be impulsive again in the elections of 1885, using Tory money even if it did not stand on a Tory platform.

There is no doubt, however, that Hyndman's ideas (if not his ambitions) were in flux at the time. It is probable that his contact with the world of the working-class Radicals had encouraged new thinking. The 'official' history of the S.D.F. says that after the 1880 election his views on Ireland changed and he opposed coercion.[4] By April 1881 Hyndman and his wife were visiting Marx, who thought him 'self-satisfied' and 'garrulous'.[5] By the time of the Democratic Federation founding conference in June, Hyndman had written a little book entitled *England for All*, which he distributed there. Of this Marx wrote: "The chapters on Labour and Capital are only literal extracts from, or circumlocutions of, the *Capital*, but the fellow does neither quote the book, nor the author, but to shield himself from exposure remarks at the end of his preface: 'For the ideas ... in Chapters II and III I am indebted to the work of a great thinker and original writer, etc. etc.' Vis-à-vis myself the fellow wrote stupid letters of excuse, for instance, that 'the English don't like to be taught by foreigners', that my 'name was so much detested, etc.'" For all that, Marx thought it would make good propaganda "so far as it pilfers the *Capital*," but the incident was enough to cause a complete breach between

Hyndman on the one side and Marx and Engels on the other. Marx felt used: "All these amiable middle-class writers … have an itching to make money or name or political capital immediately out of any new thoughts they may have got at by any favourable windfall. Many evenings this fellow has pilfered from me, in order to take me out and to learn in the easiest way."[6] Whatever Hyndman had learned from Marx his jingoism and his imperialist ideas had not changed — they were to stay and plague the socialist movement for the rest of his life.

For the libertarians like Kitz and Lane the Democratic Federation held little charm, and they continued with their own work in more congenial surroundings. As far as Lane was concerned, after the founding conference "…we left them to get on with it. They went to sleep … doing practically nothing." The socialists in the Federation, as far as Kitz was concerned, "were wasting their time combating the opportunism and jingoism of their shifty leader." Yet the Federation went through a development of its own which the suspicions of Kitz and Lane did not allow them to see. Hyndman did have a real change of heart. He did change his views on Ireland, and the 'Marxism' of *England for All* did lose him support from the more respectable Radicals after the conference in 1881. He continued to develop ideas based on a mechanistic and 'British' interpretation of Marx's writings. After a series of meetings to discuss 'stepping stone' measures — immediate reforms in housing, land and railway nationalisation, education, etc., which were to pave the way for a totally reconstituted society — he produced *Socialism Made Plain* in 1883. This was adopted at the Federation's annual conference that year — "the first definitely Socialist pronouncement of the Democratic Federation." This, as it specifically denounced the capitalist class as a class, led to the loss of all those members of the Federation who were not either socialists or near-socialists.[7]

The Democratic Federation had begun to form some sort of organic whole and to pull together a number of people, particularly intellectuals, and the emphasis of the organisation had slowly shifted from an attempted independent federation of Radical clubs towards a more specific socialist grouping. Though, again, it is difficult to say how far Hyndman led this process or how far he was pushed into it. One witness says that Charles and James Murray were making the pace too fast for Hyndman's taste.[8] For all this it should be stressed that Hyndman was, without doubt, the dominant personality in the Federation, it being quite psychologically consistent that someone should have both a forceful character and imprecise ideas. And in this latter respect his understanding of Marx, one-dimensional though it might have been, was in advance of that of most of his contemporaries.

The executive elected at the conference of 1883 included Andreas Scheu and William Morris. Morris had been invited to join the Federation by Hyndman and had done so in January 1883. He had become disgusted with the Liberal politicians and their moderate trades union associates during his involvement with the Eastern Question agitation and had declared his intention of joining an avowedly socialist body. His fame as a poet, designer and manufacturer gave a considerable boost to the Federation. His developing commitment to anti-parliamentary socialism and his opposition to Hyndman's political opportunism and domineering attitudes were to help to split it. Andreas Scheu was an already committed anti-parliamentarian socialist. He was an Austrian political exile who arrived in England in 1874 and had played some part in the politics of the German exiles in London. By 1880 he was a member of the group round Most who were deeply influenced by anarchist ideas.[9] He came to know Most quite well and grew to distrust what he saw as Most's slap-happy ways with confidential documents and information and his insistence on leaving the *Freiheit* office door unlocked.[10] He began to grow irritated with his fellow Germans: "The political activity of my country-men became more and more limited to either playing billiards or cards ... in the rooms at Tottenham street," (the social democrat/'Marxist' section), "or to passing bloodthirsty resolutions at the Anarchist Club under the leadership of tried agents provocateurs; so I turned my gaze upon the purely English working-class movement which promised to move into a new phase of activity. I began to visit their meetings."[11]

Becoming involved with the Democratic Federation, Scheu seems to have quickly developed a very strained relationship with Hyndman, which compounded disputes over political tactics with Scheu's sensitivity to Hyndman's chauvinism. Morris's membership of the Democratic Federation was to bring him into contact with many socialists ranging from old Owenites and Chartists to those who held more 'modern' positions.

Among them all, according to E.P. Thompson, "Andreas Scheu ... from 1883 to 1885 was one of Morris's closest colleagues."[12]

William Morris was to play an important part in subsequent events and his particular brand of socialism was to have great influence on the movement. It is thus well worth examining the roots of his ideas. There has been something of a genteel struggle over the political remains of William Morris. Anarchists have claimed him as an anarchist, Marxists as a Marxist. In a very real sense the approach that Morris took to socialism is diminished by such a dispute; it is certainly a blinkered way to read him. Morris was a powerful and original thinker. Engels described him as "an emotional socialist"[13] which apart from the implication that only walking calculating machines are fit to be socialists, and despite the sneer that Engels intended, grasps the essential element in Morris's thought. For Morris generalised his experience of everyday life and the result was socialism expressed with great simplicity, strength and emotional conviction. He had worked to produce beautiful things in a world which mocked his efforts by its indifferent ugliness. He was steeped in the crafts and skills which had existed in a world where casual beauty had been a part of all work — no matter how hard and brutal that world had been. For the world remained hard and brutal, but it had changed work and "destroyed art, the one certain solace of labour. ... All this I felt then as now, but I did not know why it was so."[14] He wrote later:

> The hope of the past times was gone, the struggles of mankind for many ages had produced nothing but this sordid, aimless, ugly confusion; the immediate future seemed to me likely to intensify all the present evils, by sweeping away the last survivals of the days before the dull squalor of civilisation had settled down on the world. ... Think of it! Was it all to end in a counting-house on the top of a cinder heap. ... But the consciousness of revolution stirring among our hateful modern society prevented me, luckier than many others of artistic perceptions, from crystallising into a mere railer against 'progress' on the one hand, and on the other from wasting time and energy in any of the numerous schemes by which the quasi-artistic of the middle classes hope to make art grow where it has no longer any root, and thus I became a practical Socialist.

The real and general ugliness of the society around him led him to try and find real and general solutions. He had a personal need for a society within which his work would be meaningful and described it: "a condition of society in which there should be neither rich nor poor, neither master nor master's man, neither idle nor overworked, neither brain-sick brain workers, nor heartsick hand workers, in a word, in which all men would be living in equality of condition and would manage their affairs un-wastefully and with a full consciousness that harm to one would mean harm to all — the realisation at last of the meaning of the word commonwealth."

With an equal simplicity he describes the process of becoming a 'practical socialist':

> Now this view of Socialism, which I hold today, and hope to die holding, is what I began with; I had no transitional period, unless you may call such a brief period of political radicalism during which I saw my ideal clear enough, but had no hope of any realisation of it. That came to an end some months before I joined the Democratic Federation, and the meaning of my joining that body was that I had conceived a hope of the realisation of my ideal. ... Well, having joined a Socialist body ... I put some conscience into trying to learn the economical side of Socialism and even tackled Marx, though I must confess that whereas I thoroughly enjoyed the historical part of Capital, I suffered agonies of confusion of the brain over reading the pure economics of that great work. Anyway I read what I could, and will hope that some information stuck to me from my reading; but more I must think, from continuous conversation with such friends as Bax and Hyndman and Scheu, and the brisk course of propaganda meetings which were going on at the time, and in which I took my share.

He was at other times to be more dismissive of Marxist economics: "I have tried to understand Marx's theory but political economy is not in my line and much of it appears to me to be dreary rubbish. But I am, I hope, a Socialist none the less. It is enough political economy for me to know that the idle class is rich, and the working class is poor. That I know because I see it with my own eyes. I need read no books to convince me of it. And it does not matter a rap, it seems to me, whether the robbery is accomplished by what is termed surplus value or by means of serfage or open brigandage."[15] This is not quoted to score points against Marx or Marxists but rather to emphasise the basis of Morris's socialism in *experience*. This he shared with the working-class militants like Lane and Kitz who were later to become his colleagues in the Socialist League. Socialism for these latter militants grew out of the experience of poverty and exploitation. For Morris it grew out of a life work made meaningless in the face of the world. He was middle-class and comfortably off, which produced the symptoms of guilt so often found in middle-class socialists. But at core his socialism was not an acquired belief at odds with his life but a generalisation from everyday life. In Hyndman and Bax we can see the signs of expertise treated as an indication of personal worth. They were professional socialists in the sense that a lawyer or accountant is professional. In Morris this was not the case, his socialism represents a growth of self and an urgent personal need for the reintegration of man and the world and the restructuring of a disastrously fragmented society.

William Morris took a full part in the propaganda work connected with the Federation. His subject matter in this early period was always connected with the major reason for his conversion to socialism, the immense difficulty or even impossibility of reconciling art with capitalism. In various forms he spelled out his message to debating societies, to Radical clubs, to literary and philosophical societies and to little groups of socialists. He also began to speak at the open-air meetings which the Federation started in 1883, following the example of the Labour Emancipation League. No one could claim that the message he preached set England aflame in 1883 and 1884; but it is evident that Morris, though at times discouraged, used this time to work out the implications of his socialism. Meanwhile the Federation made advances. In early 1884 Morris and Hyndman went to Blackburn (where MacDonald and Williams had been sent as agitators) to address 1,500 strikers in the cotton industry. The meeting was a great success and a branch of the Federation was set up with 100 members. In April 1883 Hyndman debated on socialism with Bradlaugh at a large public meeting — Bradlaugh opposing. As we have seen, the secular societies were very open to new ideas. The publicity attendant on this debate was considerable and certainly started a number of secularists on the road to socialism.[16] *Justice*, the paper of the Federation, started publication in January 1884 and further increased the open-air propaganda effort, since its distribution "had mainly to rely on sales at meetings."[17] But as the propaganda began to move ahead, dissensions appeared within the Federation not on general principles or on the analysis of capitalist society but on the means to be used to overthrow it.

At the meeting held to announce the founding of *Justice* there was an open clash on the question of parliamentary representation. James Murray moved a resolution outlining a 'socialism via parliament' programme. To this an amendment was put urging that the "time for palaver has passed by," the working class could not rely on Parliament to better their condition and "all means were justifiable to attain the end in view." Morris seems to have taken a fairly prominent part in this discussion according to his own account — on the anti-parliamentary side. The debate "was throughout energetic and at times heated." Andreas Scheu, holding anti-parliamentarian views, clashed noisily with Charles Varenholtz, a supporter of the German Social Democrats. The whole issue did not come to a vote, and the chairman managed to paper over the cracks.[18] It certainly showed, however, that the question was already being discussed in the Federation early in its existence and clearly foreshadowed the later split.

In fact the Democratic Federation had signed a 'Manifesto to the Working Men of the World' which was issued by eleven groupings in London, both native and foreign, in 1883. Some of the signatories were anarchists, and their influence shows in such phrases as: "Governments, no matter of what party, are but the instruments of [ruling] classes and under different disguises of judges and police, priests or hangmen, use their strength and energies to support the monopolies and privileges of the exploiters ..." And again: "Experience disperses illusions of those who have believed in Governments and Laws."[19] Anti-political sentiments were clearly quite widespread in the movement.

But the dispute over strategy was made more difficult by inter-personal difficulties, which were exacerbated rather than diminished as the organisation grew. As Morris wrote later: "When I first knew of the Fed. it really almost consisted of Mr H. and a few agents of his working under his direction: but then independent men came into it who worked very heartily in the cause and who could not submit to be under his despotism."[20] Scheu, as we have already seen, together with Belfort Bax and a young disciple of Scheu's, Robert Banner, were particularly irked by Hyndman's authoritarianism.

In the late spring and summer of 1884 Scheu was urging Morris to make a bid for the leadership of the Federation against Hyndman or to attempt to split the organisation. Morris was at first reluctant and more inclined to try and patch things up, but as the August annual conference approached his attitude began to change. He wrote to Scheu in July: "…if I have any influence amongst our party … it is because I am supposed to be straight and not ambitious … and feel sure that any appearance of pushing myself forward would injure my influence, such as it is, *very much*; therefore I will not secede for any matter of mere *tactics* … but if I find myself opposed on a matter of principle … I will secede if I am driven to it." He felt incapable of leading such a split though he promised support for any such move on the grounds given and further promised "steadily to oppose all jingo business." He was worried since he had not "got hold" [sic] of the "strings that tie us to the working class members; nor have I read as I should have. Also my habits are quiet and studious and if I am too much worried by 'politics', i.e. intrigue, I shall be no use to the cause as a writer …" But he finished firmly: "If I am pushed into a position of more importance, I will not refuse it from mere laziness or softness."[21] This does not seem to have been written in the context of a general revolt against Hyndman, however, since he talks of secession in the context of joining "any men if they be only two or three, or only yourself to push the real cause." But a majority for Scheu and Morris's position was to come from a rather unexpected quarter — the Labour Emancipation League.

As we have seen, after attending the founding conference of the Federation, Lane and his comrades had gone back to the East End to carry on with their own chosen political work. Lane had no high opinion of the Federation, and there seems to have been some element of dismissiveness in the Federation's attitude to the League. Lane said: "They were very jealous of us but at the same time called us anarchist. And why? Just because we charged no entrance fee and no monthly contributions but carried out the doctrine 'from everybody according to their ability'. And the poorer they were the more we wanted them to join, not to keep them out because of their poverty."[22] There had been some contact, however, since Hyndman and one or two other members of the Federation occasionally visited the League speaking pitch on Mile End Waste.

As the August 1884 conference of the Federation drew nearer, Hyndman again approached Lane and asked him to attend. Lane said that they had their own work to do. Hyndman "said he thought we ought to because their country branches would sure to be reactionary." Lane then proposed to send a delegate, but Hyndman replied, "Oh, one is no use, you ought to send two or three from each branch." After some discussion Lane finally agreed and elections were held to send "three from each branch but no arrangements or a word said as to what they were to do when they got there." Hyndman's motives in inviting the League can be guessed at.

Confident as to his dominating position in the Federation, he was concerned to push forward those country branches that remained fundamentally Radical rather than socialist. He had seen the forceful Joe Lane in action before and he had also seen him withdraw from the fray once an organisation was saddled with "the most advanced programme [Lane] could force on them." It would also seem that as the opposition to Hyndman centred on Morris, Bax and Scheu — all middle-class men who had "not got hold of the strings" connecting the working-class members — and as Hyndman's attitude to working-class militants was patronising and rather dismissive, he had not considered the possibility of Lane and the League having a mind different from his own. More particularly, he obviously did not consider the possibility of the League cooperating with his opponents. This was a considerable miscalculation.

Three or four days before the conference Lane was invited to a meeting at Morris's house to discuss the forthcoming event. Lane took little part in the discussion. However, by the time the discussion broke up the last train had gone and Lane stayed the night. The next day Scheu arrived as a delegate from Edinburgh. Scheu asked Lane about the business arrangements for the conference and for Lane's opinions generally. Lane says:

> I told him I did not know the official business but for myself I did not believe in Gods or Devils, Kings or Emperors [and] I did not believe in permanent Presidents in Democratic organisations and that my first

business was to put an end to Hyndman's Permanent Presidency and that every member of the Council *should* preside at Council meetings in rotation. He said he agreed with it and would second my resolution but we should not carry it ... what else? I said I was going to propose our Emancipation League programme item by item and that when we started we forced them as far as we could ... it was time that [a] mere political programme should be superseded.[23] He agreed and said he would second my resolution but that their branches were so reactionary we should never carry that. I said we would. Then he asked about other things and about the future members of the Council. I gave him all the names except my own which he would insist on including. I thought I could do better work in the East End. In the afternoon Bob Banner came to Morris. He was coming to Conference as delegate from Woolwich so we had it all over again. He agreed to support. So the whole thing was hatched on the lawn at Morris's house but so far as I was concerned Morris did not know a thing about it.

The conference went much as Joe Lane had predicted. It adopted the L.E.L. programme in a simplified form — it was ironic, in Joe Lane's later view, that this left out the demand for freedom of speech and assembly. The name of the organisation was changed to the Social Democratic Federation (S.D.F.). The conference voted against fighting parliamentary elections — though for some delegates it was a pragmatic rather than a principled opposition. And it voted against the permanent presidency of Hyndman. This Hyndman did not like at all. No wonder Lane still showed rather a tendency to crow about it many years later: "when I proposed a thing up went all the hands of all those delegates that Hyndman wished sent. Talk about Bombs! The Hyndman party was so taken by surprise that they would say nothing until after the conference was over. Then at the tea party afterwards they formed little groups and talked things and looked at me so black as though I had done or said something rude ..." The council elected at the conference was composed of Eleanor Marx, Edward Aveling, Banner, Champion, J. Cooper, Amy Hicks, Mr and Mrs Hyndman, Joe Lane, Morris, Quelch, Bax, H. Burrows, W.J. Clark, R.P.B. Frost, Joynes, Sam Mainwaring, James Murray and Jack Williams. Joe Lane and Sam Mainwaring were definitely L.E.L.

members, and some of the others were too. These people, together with the Avelings (Eleanor Marx was Aveling's partner in a 'free relationship'), Morris, Bax and Banner, formed the opposition to Hyndman. Champion, Quelch, Burrows and Williams were the more prominent supporters of the former permanent president.

The next six months in the life of the Council were wretched. An escalation of feuding, backbiting and intrigue led to spasm war by Christmas 1884. Joe Lane later claimed that the political question behind it all was whether the S.D.F. should go in for parliamentary elections or not. Other accounts make it clear that this issue rather got lost in the pro- or anti-Hyndman battle.[24] In the first meeting of the council after the conference, Hyndman made it clear that he was in no mood to be demoted. He was subject to a cutting counter-attack by Joe Lane and an attempt to have him reinstated failed. It was probably the realisation that Hyndman could not and would not work in any organisation he did not control that finally braced Morris for the coming split. He wrote in August: "The time which I have foreseen from the first seems to be upon us, and I don't see how I can avoid taking my share in the internal conflict which seems likely to rend the D.F. into two or more. More than two or three of us distrust Hyndman thoroughly; I have done my best to trust him, but cannot any longer. Practically it comes to a contest between him and me."[25]

The finale was played out on 27th December 1884. At a noisy meeting packed with Hyndman supporters — the L.E.L. being excluded because, although it had affiliated to the S.D.F., it had preserved its autonomy and paid no dues — the Hyndman group was roundly defeated on a vote taken by the council members. Morris then read out a statement in which the victorious members of the council *withdrew* from the Federation. This represented a refusal to follow up their victory by expulsions and further strife and caused no little surprise. It was fundamentally Morris's idea and probably represented both a continuation of the feelings he had when his 'party' had been in the minority and a more recent desire to wash his hands of the whole business. Morris hated intrigue and personality clashes "to the point of cowardice," as E.P. Thompson remarks. And though the S.D.F. had grown in 1884 it still only had perhaps 400 members in London and perhaps 100 in the provinces. With energy and the Labour Emancipation

League (and without Hyndman) the new body that was formed — the Socialist League — could well make good its initial disadvantage.

Although the Socialist League emerged from the split in the S.D.F. in a state of some confusion, the mood was one of confidence and relief. The importance of anti-parliamentarianism for a section of the seceders meant that the new organisation both largely represented this tendency and attracted those of a like mind. But its origins in the fierce struggle against the 'despotism' of Hyndman also meant that a parliamentary faction had seceded. This was not to cause open and destructive dissension in the Socialist League immediately. The differences were apparent from the beginning, however. A draft constitution by the Avelings — as a result of the prompting of Engels in the background — was accepted by the council of the Socialist League shortly after the split.[26] It committed the League to "Striving to conquer political power by promoting the election of Socialists to Local Governments, School Boards and other administrative bodies." This draft was rejected at the first annual conference of the League in July 1885.

Two other documents issued at this time were more important, both in terms of their contents and their more accurate expression of the politics of the League. These were firstly the circular *To Socialists*, which explained the reasons for the split, and the *Manifesto of the Socialist League*. The former largely consisted of an exposition in a rather dignified sort of way of the difficulties of working with Hyndman. But it was clear in its attitude to the politics of the time and shares the same view as the *Manifesto*. A socialist body, it says, "...in the present state of things has no function but to educate the people in the principles of Socialism and to organise such as it can get hold of [sic] to take their due places when the crisis shall come that will force action on us. We believe to hold out as baits hopes of the amelioration of the condition of the workers, to be wrung out of the necessities of the rival factions of our privileged rulers, is delusive and mischievous." There had been in the S.D.F. "a tendency to political opportunism, which if developed would have involved us in alliances, however temporary, with one or other of the political factions and would have weakened our propagandist force by driving us into electioneering and possibly would have deprived us of some of our most energetic men by sending them to our sham parliament, there to become either nonentities, or perhaps our masters and it may be our betrayers."

The *Manifesto of the Socialist League* puts the anti-parliamentary position in its correct perspective. It is neither mere prejudice nor a cowardly refusal to become involved. It speaks of the economic exploitation of the producers by the possessing class and the ceaseless conflict between them: "Sometimes it takes the form of open rebellion, sometimes of strikes, sometimes of mere widespread mendicancy and crime; but it is always going on in one form or another, though it may not be obvious to the thoughtless looker on." But the competition was not only between classes but also within classes and between nations. Shoddy goods smothered the 'civilised' and 'uncivilised' world alike, the motor of working-class degradation in production and consumption, and the motor of imperialism. "This must be altered from the foundation … all means of production of wealth … must be declared and treated as the common property of all." In this way the worker would receive the full value of his labour and the essential work of the world "would be reduced to something like two or three hours daily." In this way workers would be relieved of "sordid anxieties" and their real communal tendencies could emerge. "Only by such fundamental changes in the life of man, only by the transformation of Civilisation into Socialism can these miseries of the world before mentioned be amended." It continued:

As to mere politics, Absolutism, Constitutionalism, Republicanism have all been tried in our day and under our present social system and all have alike failed in dealing with the real evils of life …

No better solution would be that of State Socialism, by whatever name it may be called, whose aim it would be to make concessions to the working class while leaving the present system of capital and wages still in operation: no number of administrative changes, until the workers are in possession of all political power, would make any approach to Socialism …

Close fellowship with each other and steady purpose for the advancement of the Cause will naturally bring about the organisation and discipline amongst ourselves absolutely necessary to success; but we shall look to it that there shall be no distinctions of rank or dignity amongst us to give opportunities for the selfish ambition of leadership which has so often injured the cause of the workers. We are working for equality and brotherhood for all the world and it is only through equality and brotherhood that we can make our work effective.

The *Manifesto* is a beautiful document. Socialism is seen as social being, not as an administrative form. The envisaged change in society is fundamental and will come about through the "crisis that shall force action on us." Socialist education will expedite that change through those socialists who "will take their due places." But though this special role for conscious socialists might imply a group apart the "selfish ambition of leadership" is particularly denounced. (What Morris, whose work the *Manifesto* is, was probably thinking of was selfless leadership.) The document, if not anarchist, is clearly libertarian in its commitment to revolution, its view of the role of socialist groups and its deprecation of state and party hierarchy. The *Manifesto* was signed by some people in addition to those who had seceded from the S.D.F. — two of them being Frank Kitz and Charles Mowbray. Working together as part of the 'English Revolutionary Society' in its various shapes and forms, they had watched the difficulties within the Federation with sardonic detachment. They had set up a print shop in Mowbray's house in the notorious Boundary Street slum, issuing anti-military and anti-rent propaganda and placarding the East End with "incendiary manifestoes." They had also been speaking round the clubs and working in conjunction with the L.E.L. When the Socialist League was formed, however, Kitz says:

> ...its purely propagandist and non-Parliamentary objects ... appealed to our members and we joined at once. We found, however, that the demands upon our scanty leisure were too great to allow us to attend to both the printing group and the League and we finally decided to merge our work into the League's, with its possibility of a wider field of propaganda.
>
> True to our anti-rent campaign, we owed some rent to the landlord of our 'printery'. At the final meeting of our group a heated debate took place as to the best method of settling this liability, some arguing in favour of cash payment and others for payment in kind. Finally it was decided to liquidate our indebtedness to the slum landlord by leaving

him our ink-slab (the previously mentioned paving stone) as being akin to his own heart.[27]

When Kitz joined the Socialist League it was the first time he and Morris had met. Morris wrote of him: "Like most of our East-Enders, he is certainly somewhat tinged with anarchism or perhaps one may say destructivism; but I like him very much: I called on the poor chap at the place where he lived and it fairly gave me the horrors to see how wretchedly off he was; so it isn't much to wonder at that he takes the line he does."[28] In February 1885 the Socialist League secretary, J.L. Mahon, was writing to Kitz as "Secretary of the Workman's Propagandist Committee," thanking him for the offer of two founts of type and other printing equipment for the use of the League.

At the same time Lane was taking steps to integrate the L.E.L. with the Socialist League. From his accounts later it appears both how much the existence of that body depended on his prodigious energies and how much his involvement in the S.D.F. Council had undermined his work in the East End. "I made one fatal mistake in allowing myself to go on their Council. That commenced the break-up of all the work we had done in the East End. If we had done as we had done before, just driven them as far as we could and then left them, then we should have had a very strong organisation in the East End of Anti-State Socialists."[29] When the Socialist League was formed, as far as the L.E.L. was concerned "if not dropped, the life was taken out of it. I handed over all my Printing plant [and] leaflets over to [the] League and gave my whole time to it. I am very sorry, I can see now if we had kept to our own L.E.L. we should have been alright."[30]

But this was written with the benefit of hindsight. In May 1885 he was circulating members of the Mile End branch in Mile End and Stratford with a view to forming branches of the Socialist League in both places. The Hoxton branch had decided to retain its autonomy as the L.E.L., though it remained affiliated to the Socialist League.[31]

Generally the Socialist League seems to have begun well. John Turner, soon to become involved with the Freedom Group, wrote later that he joined the Socialist League immediately it was formed. He was already a "convinced Socialist but having been a young freethinking Radical Republican I had the usual Radical suspicious aversion to Hyndman." This "usual Radical suspicious aversion to Hyndman" might explain part of the success of the Socialist League. It certainly went some way to encourage the accession of branches in Scotland and Yorkshire. The clarity of the League *Manifesto* in comparison with the S.D.F. material led the socialists of Norwich, whose leading light was a young man called F.C. Slaughter (later known as Fred Charles), to form themselves into a Socialist League branch. In London, apart from the accession of the L.E.L. and the English Revolutionary Society, there was increasing interest in the new anti-parliamentary body on the part of foreign exiled anarchists. Wess, later of the Freedom Group, was in regular contact with the Socialist League from March 1885 onwards, writing from a Jewish "working men's educational and mutual relief society" in Whitechapel, which formed a club in Berners Street in 1886. The Socialist League was strongly represented at its opening. Exiles were also represented in the branches. The North London branch formed in June 1885 included among its members a German anti-parliamentarian, Henry Charles; Victor Dave (a Belgian anarchist who had been involved in clandestine propaganda in Germany for Most and had been arrested there and jailed for two and a half years in 1881); and Trunk who had worked on the *Freiheit* and was a member of the St Stephen's Mews club. Other members of this branch included David Nicoll, Scheu and Mahon.

Such links with the exiled anarchist community were strengthened by the protests organized after the police raid on the German anarchist 'International Club', St Stephens Mews, Rathbone Place. At a meeting attended by delegates from the clubs — though not in the strength that had been promised — Frank Kitz described what had happened. The members had been going about their business on the night of 9th May 1885, when "without any previous notice an attack is made on the windows and doors.

"Upon opening them and seeing not only police but a large crowd they appealed to the former for protection and the answer from a sergeant was 'We will protect you D — foreigners with the Staff ' and police and crowd surged into the club ... many of the members were wounded and streaming with blood and some will carry the marks received to their graves. Police and public alike, the latter mostly contained police in plain clothes carried off beer in jars, forms, papers, books and money not even stopping at the members clothes."[32]

The area of north Soho in which the Club was situated was an area with a very large immigrant population, mainly of Germans, French and Italians. The police riot at St Stephen's Mews is largely explicable by the chauvinist hatred of foreigners to be found in immigrant areas and accentuated in authoritarian bodies such as the police. But though the members of the club were foreigners they were also foreign *socialists*; the raid was also undoubtedly connected with the general difficulties made by the police over socialist propaganda. In 1885 there was increasing harassment of open-air meetings held by socialists.

In August Kitz was arrested for obstruction at Stratford, London, but his case was dismissed. At about the same time the S.D.F. were suffering constant police harassment at their meetings at Dod Street, Limehouse. A number of people were arrested and fined for 'obstruction' at meetings held on Sundays at a place then deserted by vehicle traffic. Jack Williams made a stand and, refusing to pay a fine, was sent to prison for a month. The Socialist League offered its assistance and together with the S.D.F. and some Radical clubs formed a Vigilance Committee. This called a large meeting at Dod Street on Sunday 20th September, where Kitz and Mahon spoke for the League. As the meeting was breaking up it was suddenly attacked by the police with considerable brutality. Eight people were arrested, including Mowbray, Mahon, Kitz and Lewis Lyons, a Jewish tailoring worker and S.D.F. member. The police attack had infuriated the Radicals who really began to get to work. The subsequent court case brought wider publicity.

The magistrate, Saunders, was completely hostile to the arrested men.

After a short and farcical trial in which the police perjured themselves black, seven of the men were fined forty shillings with the option of a month, while Lewis Lyons — the only Jew — was sent to prison for two months. This caused a great uproar from the socialists in the court whom the police then proceeded to attack. In the fracas they arrested William Morris, which was a mistake. Saunders, who obviously had no idea who his famous gentleman prisoner was, let him off with a caution. Morris was greeted outside the court by a cheering crowd. This incident brought the full glare of publicity on to both the magistrate and the free-speech fight. (One illustrated magazine had a picture of Saunders tearfully blacking Morris's boots.) The result was a massive meeting on the site the following

Sunday with perhaps as many as 50,000 there. The police did not bother the meeting — or indeed any subsequent ones. The battle for free speech at Dod Street had been won.

It is necessary to stress how important such free-speech fights were for the new movement. Socialists were small in numbers, and no matter how energetic or determined their agitation in other directions they needed the streets as a forum if socialism was to spread rapidly. Such occasions as Dod Street did bring them publicity. But the primary purpose of the meetings was to spread the word, and they preferred them unharassed. At meetings they could sell literature and distribute leaflets. Discussions could take place in a freer atmosphere than that provided by the debate structure imposed by the Sunday meetings at the Radical clubs. In this way they acted as a kind of popular socialist university — though sometimes it was a violent one. Jack Williams carried a scar to his grave after being hit by a bottle hurled at him during a meeting. Opposition ('fair-traders', heavies hired by the Tory or Liberal Party, militant temperance advocates or Christians) would often disturb a meeting with more than words. Platforms were 'cleared' not infrequently — that is to say rushed and another speaker more to the taste of the attackers substituted. But in more placid moments the street meetings provided an unofficial popular education. This is a later account but accurately gives the spirit of these occasions:

> A secularist speaker received more abuse than sensible criticism but I learned from him the crushing effect of satire, where reasonable argument was futile. I also learned the art of heckling at these meetings; not the foolish obstructionist kind that merely plays into the hands of the speaker but that which turns observation to the advantage of the opposition. By an interjection at the right moment a speaker could be thrown right off the rails and much amusement caused by rhetorical catastrophes.
>
> 'If you want to know what the Conservative Party have done for the working-man look ...'
> '...inside the workhouse.' (Interjection)
> 'British working men are being thrown out of jobs by foreign dumping. If we tax these imports the workers will ...'
> '...pay.' (Interjection)

But the most enlightening moments were spent among the little groups of thinkers who carried on discussions with all the earnestness of a philosopher's council chamber. One subject merged into another, which gave an opportunity for the quidnuncs of economics to hold the torch until it was grabbed by an acolyte of the 'higher criticism' or by an apostle of the 'astral plane'. In the pallid glare of the lamps stood men and women of all stations of life, mufflered and collared, dapper and dowdy, listening with either credulous or critical mentality to the arguments, and ready to brighten their faces at the slightest joke and to appreciate the verbal contest of verbal erudition. And if there was no all-night sitting at that public parliament, it was more because of legal restrictions than want of enthusiasm for most of the members stayed till the rising of the 'House' before sauntering away in little groups, when voices and footsteps faded into the night and a happy truce was called for another seven days."[33]

But the victory at Dod Street did not mean that free speech was then automatically ensured in London or the rest of the country. Free-speech fights were a regular feature of socialist propaganda in the 1880s and 1890s. However, after Dod Street there were no particularly odious oppressions of public speaking until the 'dangerous influence' of socialism made itself apparent in the West End Riots. The winter of 1885–1886 was a period of high unemployment and great misery. But the mood of the unemployed was not one of resignation, as is too often the case. The occasion of an S.D.F. unemployed counter-demonstration to a Tory 'fair trade' meeting in Trafalgar Square in February 1886 provided the spark.

Militant — even blustering — speeches were made by Burns, Hyndman, Williams and Champion together with Sparling of the Socialist League.

According to some sources, gentlemen wearing top hats in the square had them snatched from their heads, and some of the gentlemen were thrown in the fountains. The fair traders were attacked and their platform broken up.

Engels alleged that many of the unemployed were drunk — an obvious indication to him that they were lumpenproletarians and not fit for the revolution. The mood of the crowd was pugnacious in any case. The organisers, seeing that shifting the crowd from the square would be difficult, decided to march them to Hyde Park and then disperse.

Their route, however, took them past the upper-class clubs in St James. Here the crowd raised a general hooting and jeering. The procession stopped and Burns and others spoke to the crowd outside the Carlton, the Reform, etc. There were counter-jeers and things were thrown at them from the clubs. The reply was a barrage from the crowd. It was said that one man started it: "A poorly-clad hungry-looking man, tore from his ragged breast an Egyptian war medal which he had been wearing. He forced himself in a frenzy of anger into a prominent position and addressing the members of the Carlton who were looking at him with surprised expectancy he shouted, 'We were not the scum of the country when we were fighting for bond-holders in Egypt, you dogs!'"[34] He hurled his medal at the window of the club and smashed it. The crowd then picked up loose building material which was lying around and proceeded to throw it through the windows of the clubs. They then proceeded to smash the windows of surrounding shops, which were then looted. This carried on while the main procession marched off to Hyde Park. Here the demonstration petered out after carriages had been wrecked and the livery had been stripped from servants. It had been an explosion of working-class anger rather than a socialist demonstration, illustrated by the fact that sections of the crowd marched back to the East End singing 'Rule Britannia'!

There were several results. Large unemployment demonstrations took place in a number of towns, and there was rioting in Leicester. There was a remarkable and sudden concern for the welfare of the unemployed on the part of the upper classes. Public works were set up and charitable funds for the unemployed grew by leaps and bounds. For several days the panic among respectable people was almost indescribable. As Morris pointed out in the *Commonweal*, the Socialist League paper, the strategy inspired by this panic had two sides. First there were "some palliative measures." On the other hand, they could expect selective repression of 'ringleaders'. Burns, Hyndman, Williams and Champion were arrested (to be eventually acquitted). More generally the authorities began what looked like a systematic attack on socialist meetings. The police made repeated assaults on a demonstration in Hyde Park later in February. As the weather improved and the various open-air speaking pitches were reopened there began a steady stream of prosecutions for 'obstruction'. In July 1886 we find Mowbray and Lane attending a meeting of the Metropolitan Radical Federation, trying — unsuccessfully — to drum up support for Socialist League speakers who were being harassed at the Grove, Stratford, Bell Street, Edgware Road and at the 'Bricklayers Arms', Kilburn. Nigger minstrels and Christian preachers were not interfered with, and boys were being paid by the police to obstruct the meetings, it was claimed.[35] The unhelpful attitude of the Radicals is explainable both by the West End Riot, which offended the more respectable, and the socialist candidates put up by the S.D.F. in November 1885. The latter adventure had been a farcical failure, but it had obviously irked the Radicals who looked upon the working-class vote as their own private property.

The pitch at Bell Street became the scene of sustained struggle for the right to speak in the streets. After the first case of obstruction at the site, Mainwaring of the League and Jack Williams of the S.D.F. spoke to a large meeting on 11th July. Both were summonsed and sent for trial at a higher court. Between the two hearings Morris went to the site and spoke, though he knew he risked prison. He was summonsed but in the event, being a gentleman, he was fined one shilling! Mainwaring and Williams, who were both workers, were fined twenty pounds. Williams refused to pay and went to prison for two months. And though as a result of these prosecutions the Marylebone Branch decided to leave the Bell Street pitch, another was opened immediately which remained more or less unmolested. Morris's intervention in the struggle had resulted in publicity, as at Dod Street. Morris felt his name was worth using if it helped block attempts to "clear the streets of costermongers, organs, processions and lecturers of all kinds and make them a sort of decent prison corridor, with people just trudging to and from their work."[36] But it was the determination of the rank and file to keep their speaking pitches that won through. It was now impossible for the police to close every speaking pitch without Draconian measures and massive repression and they probably became uncomfortably aware of the counter-productive results of the efforts they did make. The movement was growing and this kind of repression fanned the flames rather than doused them.

The mood at this time is given by an observer: "It is undeniable that a very deep seated spirit of discontent was very widespread … and that it was fostered by agitators who saw no other road to profit and prominence at the time — and rendered dangerous by unbridled language in the highest degree reprehensible. The English extremists advocated what they termed the Social Revolution and at street corners, in public places and elsewhere, when a crowd of working men and loafers could be mustered, they were invariably asked to give 'three cheers for the Social Revolution' and it must be admitted that they responded in greater numbers and greater enthusiasm as this dangerous movement progressed."[37] This widespread and developing discontent was conditioned by events. First there had been political discontent in the Radical milieu over the Liberal government's backsliding in the relatively prosperous period of 1881–1883. Political discontent had combined with material misery in the harsh period of high unemployment of 1884–1886. The combativeness and bitterness of this period were to develop and carry over into the more prosperous years of 1889–1890, when a burst of organising was to take advantage of the favourable 'terms of trade' for labour.[38] It was in 1885–1886, poised at the point of take-off of the working-class movement, that the first anarchist papers were published in England.

No one knows how political ideas seize the imagination of masses of people. If they did our world would look even rougher than it does. So much can be said about 'objective economic conditions,' but we still only have explanations after the event. The self-confident analysts of the past have proved to be lousy predictors of the future. Whatever the mechanism, however, that body of ideas summed up by the word 'socialism' rapidly struck root. In the ten years between 1885 and 1895 socialists changed from being a few foreigners and cranks of no consequence to a deadly danger or the wave of the future according to taste. Yet where did socialist ideas come from? A few weekly or monthly papers of small circulation; a few meetings addressed in clubs or on street corners; and when we consider the mounds of rival journals and the hordes of rival street corner speakers it seems little short of miraculous that socialist ideas were heard, let alone taken up and acted upon. So when we now consider the affairs of a few anarchist papers it is for their potential energy as much as for their immediate impact. The latter, initially, was not great.

## Chapter 4

# THE *ANARCHIST* AND *FREEDOM* ... AND DAN CHATTERTON

As we have seen, the first English-language anarchist paper to circulate in England was the American paper *Liberty*, published by Benjamin Tucker (see page 37). It is possible that the paper was introduced to the English socialists in the early days by Marie Le Compte, the American delegate to the 1881 congress in London, who evidently spoke in a number of clubs during her stay in England.[1] She was a regular correspondent from France for Tucker's paper in 1883, great interest being aroused by the trial and imprisonment of a number of anarchists (including Louise Michel, Pouget and Kropotkin) at Lyons. A number of prominent English public men and intellectuals signed a petition for Kropotkin to be released from prison on health grounds and because of his scientific work — a petition, it must be said, that Kropotkin did not solicit. But it seems evident that a wider interest in Kropotkin's political ideas was encouraged in England by the trial. *Liberty*, by giving accounts of the trial and reports on the prisoners and printing translations of anarchist-communist material played its part in introducing anarchist ideas to England.

In December 1883 two distributors of the paper in England were given. One was George Standring, a regular lecturer to workingmen's clubs. The other was 'The Science Library', Tunbridge Wells. This was run by the local secretary of the National Secular Society, Henry Seymour. He had achieved a minor notoriety by posting a 'blasphemous' bill in Tunbridge Wells and being summonsed for it at the request of local Christians. On Bradlaugh's advice he had pleaded guilty in July 1883 and was fined. The accusation of cowardice raised against him for following this advice seems to have rankled, but the fact of his prosecution had given him a certain status.[2] His interest in anarchism seems to have originated with his secularism — illustrated by his publication in 1883 of Bakunin's essay 'God and the State'. He seems to have become converted to anarchism by

1884, because there was something of an encounter between Seymour and Bradlaugh in the columns of the Secular Society's paper in September, Seymour defending anarchism and Bradlaugh attacking: "...we consider all views unfortunate which result in the cowardly and murderous use of explosives as means of agitation."[3] Bradlaugh never seems to have asked himself whether the same argument could not have been used to denounce his own political views, which, after all, had resulted in the cowardly and murderous use of almost every weapon to ensue Coercion in Ireland. It is interesting though that anarchism and bombs were seen as synonymous at this early date.

By January 1885 *Liberty* was announcing the forthcoming publication of an anarchist paper by Seymour. It appeared in March 1885, came out monthly and was called the *Anarchist*. It was a lively paper and, like Tucker's, though initially supporting a Proudhonian position of small proprietorship and staunch independence of artisans within voluntary cooperative schemes it was prepared to give space to anarchist-communist writings. Seymour also shared Tucker's admiration for the Fenian bombings. The first issue contained greetings from Élisée Reclus and the French-speaking International anarchist circle of London. It reprinted the Lyons anarchist manifesto. It also had a characteristic piece of verbal acrobatics from George Bernard Shaw and acknowledged the receipt of one pound from Pease, the later historian of the Fabian Society. All in all it represented quite a rich mixture! Further issues of the paper also make it plain that Seymour was in touch with the exiled anarchist groups in London, and one of the most interesting things about the paper was the immediacy with which foreign events (in France particularly) were portrayed. Letters from Marie Le Compte, from Kropotkin in Clairvaux prison, from Brocher, who organised the congress of 1881, gave events at first hand, allowing some insight into the emotions and personalities involved. The reader was thus able not only to grasp the facts about happenings abroad but to understand the atmosphere within which they took place. But if Seymour was in contact with the anarchist movement abroad or exile circles in London his contact with the English socialists was somewhat limited — limited, it would seem, initially to the Fabian Society.

This isolation from those groups of English socialists who were engaged in the problems of relating experience and theory, utopian aspiration and day-to-day activity, gives Seymour's theoretical contributions a certain dogmatic unrealism. When Seymour turned his hand to propaganda, however, he could turn out quite snappy stuff, like his 'Anarchist Manifesto' on the Elections in the October 1885 issue. The cross-heads on the manifesto read "Why do you vote? The people in Subjection; Labour Representation is an illusion; No need for any Government at all. Do Not Vote," and finally in huge capitals "THE SOCIAL REVOLUTION!"

A small group began to form around the paper. The third issue of the *Anarchist* in May 1885 announced that "A circle of English Anarchists is about to be formed." By July the 'English Anarchists' were meeting more or less monthly. The numbers involved were not indicated and neither were the individuals; but it is possible to make some educated guesses. Firstly, since Seymour was involved in the Fabian Society it is probable that this provided some recruits. George Bernard Shaw was later to remark that there had been "a sort of influenza of anarchism in the Society at that time."[4] E. Pease could have been one victim of the epidemic: he is described as making "public confession of his belief in Anarchist Ethics as distinct from Coarse Materialism so ably set forth — by H.M. Hyndman" at a Fabian Society meeting.[5] In December 'C.M.W.', who can be no one else but Charlotte Wilson, a member of the executive of the Society, was acknowledged as a collector of the princely sum of nine shillings for the *Manifesto* Fund, and was probably also a member of the 'English Anarchists'. She had already contributed two pieces on anarchism to *Justice* in November 1884, signing herself 'An English Anarchist'. A review of the Labour Remuneration Conference was given by someone signing similarly in the first issue of the *Anarchist*; this too could have been Charlotte Wilson. More will be said about her later as she was deeply involved with the founding of *Freedom*. Apart from Fabian Society intellectuals, however, the paper attracted a most remarkable figure in the shape of James Harrigan. Material on him shows him to have been an exceptional figure, a loner who according to his own account had espoused anarchism long before the 1880s. A shoemaker by trade, as an apprentice he had worked with one of the Cato Street conspirators, "who may have inspired [him] with revolutionary ideas."[6] Harrigan had been a member of the English Section of the First International and had once been chairman of its Annual Convention. He was to write in October 1885: "...old stagers know well enough that I have consistently and persistently advocated and defended the principles of Anarchy from the time I left the old 'International', exactly at the same time that Michael Bakounine left it and for the same reason ..."[7] "He became an open air speaker at an early age in the parks and open spaces and probably deserves the distinction of being the first open air propagandist of avowed Anarchism in England." In this early period he would attend trades union meetings and advocate the stay-in strike. He is also credited with converting Ben Tillett, later a leader of the Dockers' Union, to socialism while working with other cobblers at seasonal work opening tea chests at the Docks. "He said there was nothing he regretted more for he hated the political charlatans who used the workers' movement to make a career for themselves. Harrigan with abilities far beyond those smooth-tongued adventurers, remained a worker, a rebel in society."

In October 1885 he was pushing the *Anarchist* at meetings and had run into accusations from Charles Mowbray that he was a police spy. How this came about is almost impossible to discover — Harrigan was of the opinion that it was jealousy of someone pushing papers other than the *Commonweal* at Socialist League meetings. (There had, incidentally, been complaints from Hyndman that S.D.F. paper-sellers were being harassed at League meetings.) The incident is worth mentioning because it shows that an awareness of the activity of police spies already existed in socialist bodies. It also shows that Mowbray, who was later to declare himself an anarchist, at this stage remained like most of the Socialist League, an anti-parliamentary revolutionary socialist. His accusation of Harrigan, however, might have had something to do with the latter's style of agitation. At a large meeting to which he lectured on anarchism in South London in November 1885, Harrigan, in an aside while telling about a no-rent campaign, advised his audience "...by way of a pastime they should amuse themselves by poisoning off the landlords."[8] This could easily be taken as provocateur's talk.

These minor difficulties did not affect the paper. By the end of 1885 Seymour was writing: "On the whole, the success of the paper from a pecuniary point of view has exceeded my sanguine expectations but I am bound to say that, since enlarging its size, the increased circulation is not so large as reasons led me to anticipate." As a result he decided to bring out the paper twice as often but half the size. He printed a mocking commentary on a piece reprinted from the *Daily Telegraph* which said that anarchists were far more dangerous than socialists, that they were madmen and so on, and which went on: "Fortunately there are certainly not more than 300 Anarchists in London and their organ the *Anarchist* which appears rather irregularly sells not more than 500 copies and is not in a flourishing condition."[9] But in substance apart from saying that the *Telegraph* had got its facts wrong Seymour gave no details. It is probable that an informed guess would give a circulation of approximately 1,000 at this point. It was a recognised left-wing journal read by branches of the Socialist League and with some support in the Fabian Society and took its place as a regular if modest feature of socialist political life. It was undoubtedly a one-man effort and stood or fell with Seymour and his reputation. It had the words 'Edited by Henry Seymour' under the title on the front page in letters small enough to come within the bounds of decency but large enough to read at some distance. It was unfortunate for him that two events took place which first shook his position and then almost completely destroyed his influence in the small new movement. The first was the arrival of Kropotkin in England and the eventual formation of *Freedom*. The second was his support for Theodore Reuss, a German police spy.

Kropotkin was released, together with the other anarchists held since the Lyons trial, in mid-January 1886. He arrived in England in March. His reason for leaving France was the high probability of re-arrest and the need for a period of recuperation after his imprisonment where he had suffered from both scurvy and malaria. If he left voluntarily there would be less possibility of the authorities preventing his return. Unless he considered America as a possible home England at this time was his "last refuge from arbitrary authority."[10] But Kropotkin was also satisfied that in addition to being close enough to France to continue work on *La Révolte* there was positive work to be done in England. Seymour had been in correspondence with Kropotkin in Clairvaux prison, and Charlotte Wilson had been in touch with Kropotkin's wife during his imprisonment. On his release

Kropotkin wrote to a friend, "I am called to London to found an anarchist (English) paper; the means are existant and I will get to work busily."[11] The phrase 'to found' is interesting: it implied rather more than cooperating with Seymour on his paper. And indeed the twee picture that one is all too often given of Kropotkin as 'The Gentle Anarchist Prince' can only obscure events here — it is a picture belonging to the politenesses of drawing rooms and respectable tea parties. Kropotkin had been a soldier and had gone armed on workers' demonstrations, he had worked in underground political activity and had broken from jail. He was also something of an autocrat. Stepniak, the Russian terrorist, with whom he had both lived and worked, gives a convincing picture. While admitting all of Kropotkin's theoretical brilliance and personal talents, Stepniak says: "He is too exclusive and rigid in his theoretical convictions. He admits no departure from the ultra Anarchical programme and had always considered it impossible therefore to contribute to any of the revolutionary papers in the Russian language abroad and in St Petersburg. He has always found in them some point of divergence and in fact has never written a line in any of them."[12] The implication is, then, that any paper which Kropotkin became involved in would have to be anarchist-communist.

Seymour's attitude before (if only just before) Kropotkin's release from prison is given in a commentary on his printing of an anarchist-communist article by Henry Glasse to which Seymour was to reply on Proudhonist lines. He wrote: "There is nothing to quarrel about in the ideas of Anarchists — mutualistic or communistic. Both ... are essentially anarchistic since enforced authority is absent. ... Why then do not Communist and Mutualist sink outside speculative difference of opinion and join hands to overturn the state?"[13] This seems to have been a sincerely held view — as we have seen anarchist-communists had often featured in the columns of the *Anarchist*. It was something of a surprise, though, when after Kropotkin had arrived in England the words 'Edited by Henry Seymour' were removed from the paper and the following announcement was printed: "In accepting the economic principles of Communism as satisfactorily established I unhesitatingly and fearlessly adopt them ..." To many this seemed an over-sudden conversion. The reasons for it were clearly to be found later in this announcement: "I have succeeded in securing the editorial assistance of several scholarly and revolutionary writers, so that the paper will henceforth be conducted on lines of conjoint editorship."[14] From now on articles were to be anonymous and to stand on their own merits without personal egoism. These changes can be seen quite simply as the down payment for Kropotkin's cooperation. Only two issues of the paper under 'conjoint editorship' appeared, the second being something of a disaster — dull as ditchwater for the most part, with a peculiar stifled air to it.

The paper reappeared as Seymour's personal organ in June 1886 and, as if to celebrate the occasion, he allowed himself a war whoop over the bomb thrown at the police in the Chicago Haymarket:

> Our Chicago comrades have proclaimed a reign of terror. They have led the van in the struggle for the people's emancipation. Justice personified in bombs had stepped down and bid the Capitalist pause in his murderous career. A combination of Sulphuric and Nitric Acids and Glycerine has proved itself ten times more formidable than even a quarter of a million 'Knights of Labour.' ... Men are moving ahead.
>
> We have practically passed through those crude beginnings of the Social Revolution of the people sacking the bakeshops to appease their HUNGER and are about to enter that final phase where the people will attack the armouries and arsenals to appease their ANGER.

In this and the following issue (July) he also gave the reasons from his point of view why the short-lived 'conjoint editorship' failed. Firstly, he says that the whole conception was impractical leading to a "dull and dead level of mediocrity." He says that a particular article 'The Family as a Type of Society' which, one is forced to admit, was turgid in the extreme was ordered "by one individual member" of the editorial committee without his knowledge. It was then placed in the paper by the committee, overriding his objections. This 'one individual member' of the committee would appear to be Charlotte Wilson from other remarks he makes. He implies that she was both undemocratic and impractical, and there seems to have been quite some friction between them. Charlotte Wilson seems, for her part, to have seen Seymour and his paper as something of an inconvenience.

According to her, *Freedom* would have been started earlier if there had been no *Anarchist*.[15] She was keeping aloof from Seymour's circle by this time and had her own 'Proudhon Society,' which met in Hampstead. Seymour's group became the Central London Anarchist Group.[16] It may well have been difficult to work with Seymour, but one can understand his irritation when rumours were circulated in the London clubs saying that the *Anarchist* was finished now that Kropotkin and Charlotte Wilson had left. However, he misjudged the situation when he wrote that Kropotkin "resigned only because he saw that no useful work could be done by the committee ..." *La Revolté*, a paper with which Kropotkin retained a close connection, had written "we learn with regret that the attempt made by London friends to publish the *Anarchist* with a new programme has been abandoned. We hope that a new *Anarchist* journal will be started."[17] There is little doubt that Kropotkin was the source of both the information and the intention to publish a new paper. However, due to the illness of his wife, Kropotkin was not able to start work on the new paper for some time, and the first issue of *Freedom* did not appear until October 1886.[18]

In the meantime Seymour had the field to himself. He did not, however, use his opportunity well. He made the mistake of becoming involved in a dispute raging among the German exile anarchists in London — the *Bruderkreig* or Brothers' War. His mistake was the more serious because in the process he both became associated with a proven police spy and caused a deep split between himself and the Socialist League. The circumstances of the Bruderkreig are more fully explained elsewhere.[19] Putting it simply, however, it was a dispute involving both personalities and politics and boiled down to a conflict between Victor Dave — a trusted member of the Socialist League — and Peukert. The conflict was longstanding, having its origins in Most's rather high-handed treatment of Peukert, the opposition of Peukert to the American-based *Freiheit* (distributed in Europe by Dave) and the starting of a rival journal *Der Rebell*. This split the limited financial resources of the German anarchist movement and caused friction. Peukert was an anarchist-communist and opposed Most's more Bakuninist collectivism. Such opposition, both literary and political, incensed Most and Dave who both seem to have considered Peukert a young upstart.

There were further disagreements over the smuggling of anarchist literature into Germany, with Peukert accusing Dave of trying to take control of the whole anarchist movement. Quantities of ink were spilt in mutual backstabbings in the German anarchist press. Dave and his followers finally succeeded in expelling Peukert and his followers from their Whitfield Street club. Those expelled founded the Gruppe Autonomie, with a clubhouse at 32 Charlotte Street, in February 1886. The group grew rapidly and eventually moved its premises to 6 Windmill Street, Tottenham Court Road. The whole affair was conducted with astonishing bitterness on both sides, with every accusation from misappropriation of funds to police spy activity being thrown back and forth. Frankly, it was rather silly of Seymour to get mixed up in the business at all.

On 17th May a council meeting of the Socialist League expelled Charles Theodore Reuss as a police spy in the pay of the German police. Reuss had been quite deeply involved in the Socialist League as librarian and labour secretary in 1885. He was connected with Peukert and would thus have come under Victor Dave's suspicion, but in fact the information upon which the accusation was made came from the Belgian Social Democrats and was brought independently to the council by H. Charles.[20] Events were to prove the accusations correct. In the meantime Peukert and his followers rallied to defend Reuss. A more than somewhat biased commission cleared Reuss of the charges against him and denounced Dave as a police spy. Seymour reprinted its findings in September 1886. Almost all of the front page of the October issue of the *Anarchist* was devoted to an attack on the Socialist League for its expulsion of Reuss. This came in response to a special supplement to the *Commonweal* of 18th September marked 'Printed for Foreign Transmission Only' which emanated from Dave's club at Whitfield Street and which denounced both the biased commission of inquiry and the *Anarchist* for reprinting it. Seymour began to back-pedal a little on his denunciations as time passed, but his support for Reuss continued. It was not clever of him, for it more or less completely alienated the Socialist League, which at that time was the only grouping of English socialists which he could have allied with or even infiltrated. His misjudgement was demonstrated clearly when in February 1887, Reuss, using Peukert as an unwitting accomplice, was able to trace Johann Neve in Belgium and have him handed over to the German police. Neve was one of the most wanted men in Germany. A truly heroic figure, modest and careful, he had chosen a life of exile on the Belgian/ German border organising the secret distribution of anarchist literature, arms and explosives in Germany. His arrest was a major triumph for the German political police. Johann Neve died — or was murdered — in prison. Seymour's paper moved into a magazine format in March 1887 and steadily dwindled into insignificance.

The first number of *Freedom* in October 1886 was very different from Seymour's *Anarchist*. It was sober, respectable and theoretically coherent. All contributors were anonymous — except that everyone knew Kropotkin wrote for it. The keynote of its long life was given in its first article. After a review of the contemporary situation, man's constant struggle for freedom and the uselessness of participation in the structure of repression for achieving freedom, the piece finishes: "Such, in rough outline, is the general aspect of the Anarchist Socialism our paper is intended to set forth and by the touchstone of this belief we purpose to try the current ideas and modes of action of existing Society." Here it is made clear that the paper is not considered so much an agitational newspaper but as a general propagandist paper reviewing events as they take place *outside*. Unlike *Commonweal* or the *Anarchist* it was not designed as a newspaper of combatants. Neither did it consider itself at any time the newspaper for the anarchist movement but as the newspaper of the Freedom Group. The group was not open, its "membership was always limited and confidential."[21] The group included in addition to Kropotkin, Dr Burns Gibson, Mrs Dryhurst, Frank Hyde and his wife and Charlotte Wilson, who was effectively the editor of *Freedom*.

Charlotte Wilson remained editor of *Freedom* until 1895, and it was largely due to her efforts that the paper appeared consistently over that time. She had first become interested in anarchism during the trial of Kropotkin and other anarchists in Lyons in 1883, and by 1884 had become an anarchist. Born Charlotte Mary Martin in 1854, the daughter of a surgeon, she received "the best education then available to girls. During 1873–1874 she attended the institution at Cambridge which a few years later became Newnham College. After leaving university, she married

Arthur Wilson, a stockbroker, and settled in Hampstead, a fashionable suburb of London."[22] By 1886 they were living a somewhat expensively appointed simple life at Wildwood Farm (later renamed 'Wyldes'), on the edge of Hampstead Heath. She had joined the Fabian Society in 1884 and in December was elected to its executive. In addition to her two contributions to *Justice* on anarchism she also wrote the section on anarchism in the fourth Fabian tract 'What Socialism Is,' which was published in June 1886.

At this time the Fabian Society had not firmly espoused social democratic electioneering and was basically a discussion group for socialist intellectuals, with no fixed programme or ideology. It was its openness at this time which made the publication of anarchist material possible. But this openness was too open for some of the members and steps were taken to find out the extent of Mrs Wilson's influence and to establish a policy of parliamentary activity. At a meeting in London in September 1886 the parliamentarians proposed that the Fabian Society should organise itself into a political party. William Morris proposed and Charlotte Wilson seconded an amendment which stressed the need for the education of the people as to their position and to steadily keep the principles of socialism before them "...and whereas no Parliamentary party can exist without compromise and concession which would hinder that education and obscure those principles: it would be a false step for Socialists to attempt to take part in the Parliamentary contest." This amendment was overwhelmingly defeated. Charlotte Wilson resigned from the executive of the Society in April 1887.

The Freedom Group, however, betrayed distinctly Fabian tendencies — not so much in any penchant for electioneering as in its exclusiveness and its commitment to 'permeation' of other bodies with anarchist ideas as opposed to using the paper as the nucleus for the organisation of other autonomous groups. It can be guessed that this was Charlotte Wilson's natural preference. Kropotkin, who had taken part in more direct agitational and organisational work in the past, now also seemed to prefer a more discreet role. This was partly due to his desire not to upset the authorities with regard to his residence in England, to failing health and to his difficulties with English. French was the court language in Russia and with it he had no trouble. English was another matter: "His pronunciation was peculiar until one grew used to it. 'Own' rhymed with 'town', 'law' was 'low', and 'the sluffter fields of Europe' became a kindly joke amongst us."[23] Manuscripts in the Institute of Social History in Amsterdam show his written English to have been defective. In order to write English propaganda he needed subeditors, and the Freedom Group represents from this point of view a 'front organisation' for Kropotkin. Whatever the difficulties, though, he had great personal prestige at this time in the English socialist movement and it was his presence that rubbed some of this prestige off on to the other Freedom Group members. His discretion by no means forced him completely into the background, however. In the 1880s he is to be found lecturing to a large number of meetings, bad English or not. He also formed friendships with the Hyndmans and William Morris. The S.D.F. regularly reprinted his *Appeal to the Young* over the years. William Morris and he met at a celebration of the Commune shortly after his arrival in England. Soon they were to have long discussions and were in close contact, Kropotkin speaking occasionally at the Hammersmith branch of the Socialist League and attending some of the Sunday suppers at Morris's home. "It is doubtful that Morris made any systematic study of Kropotkin's anarchist writings, but he did have ample access to Kropotkin's ideas, and arguments during the last years of his participation in League affairs."[24] It was probably through this early contact with Morris that the *Commonweal* press facilities were used to print *Freedom*. As time went by the Freedom Group also used branches of the Socialist League to distribute *Freedom* — *Freedom* certainly reached Scotland and Norwich by being ordered through the Socialist League office.[25] It is doubtful whether this 'permeation' would have been possible without the prestige of Kropotkin.

Engels wrote in April 1886: "...the Anarchists are making rapid progress in the Socialist League. Morris and Bax — one as an emotional socialist and the other as a chaser after philosophical paradoxes — are wholly under their control for the present."[26] Yet a rather different view is given by Nettlau of this period. He points out that Kropotkin had the choice of working with the Socialist League and preferred to work with first Seymour and then the Freedom Group. Indeed Kropotkin wrote to Morris in reply to a request for articles for *Commonweal* saying he had too much work on hand with *La Révolte* and the *Anarchist* together with the scientific articles by which he earned his bread. Reasonable though this refusal might sound, it nevertheless represented a political choice, a choice Nettlau described as:

> ...regrettable, for in 1886 and 1887 the League contained the very best Socialist elements of the time, men who had deliberately rejected Parliamentarianism and reformism and who worked for the splendid free Communism of William Morris or for broadminded revolutionary Anarchism. If Kropotkin's experience and ardour had helped this movement we might say today Kropotkin and William Morris as we say Élisée Reclus and Kropotkin. Unfortunately we cannot say so. There was a latent lack of sympathy between the Anarchists of the League and those of the Freedom Group in those early years; the latter were believed by the former to display some sense of superiority, being in possession of definitely elaborated Anarchist-Communist theories ... if both efforts had been coordinated a much stronger movement would have been created.[27]

Thus it is made clear that the Freedom Group in no way wished to become organically linked with the Socialist League but were prepared to use the branch organisation of the League to distribute their paper. When members of the Socialist League were recruited — as, say, John Turner and Alfred Marsh were in 1887 — their activities in each body were kept separate. Thus it was not from the group round *Freedom* that the 'anarchists' in the League received consistent encouragement and support or received their political education — except as general readers of the paper or through attendance at anarchist meetings.

It is more than likely that Nettlau is naive in ascribing the "latent lack of sympathy" between the Freedom Group and the anarchists in the League to the alleged "sense of superiority, being in possession of definitely elaborated Anarchist-Communist theories" of the Freedom Group. This amounts to an accusation of inverted snobbery and philistinism. With the exception of Kropotkin, the militant anti-parliamentarians in the League seemed to have looked on the Freedom Group with some suspicion not as clever theorists but as "middle class faddists" to use Nicoll's phrase. He wrote "...neither Kitz, Mowbray or I were particularly friendly (to the Freedom Group). We looked upon them as a collection of middle class faddists, who took up with the movement as an amusement, and regretted that Kropotkin and other 'serious' people ever had anything to do with them. But they called themselves 'Anarchists!' and that had great influence with many of our international comrades."[28] This was a suspicion which extended to many of the middle-class members of the League. William Morris was acceptable because he was completely free of pretension and seemed prepared to take the risks and do the work. More to the point, perhaps, he seemed to understand what it meant to live the worker's life. "The whole of his poetry and prose is permeated with sympathy and love of the poor," wrote Frank Kitz, "the victims of landlord and capitalistic greed. This note of sympathy distinguishes him from many who surrounded him and who babbled of art and culture, but were mere tuft-hunters devoid of any desire to raise the status of the working class. ... Morris's preference for the society of his humbler confrères gave great offence to some superior persons."[29] Kitz is here referring to Fabians of the George Bernard Shaw-type. But one can see the reasons for suspicion of the sincerity of anarchists like Charlotte Wilson on the part of working-class militants in the face of her middle-class lifestyle. A contemporary, Margaret Cox, later Lady Oliver, wrote of a time around 1886: "She seemed to me a peaceful sort of anarchist and so did all the others who came to meetings, some of them Russian. Someone read a paper and this was followed by discussion, often very vigorous and exciting, lasting until Mrs Wilson interrupted with sandwiches and drinks, after which we all turned out on the Heath."[30] It all seemed a little too genteel.

It really seems then that the anarchism which was developing in the League received only passing encouragement from the Freedom Group. In fact, as anarchism grew within the League the Freedom Group finally disengaged from it. The anarchists in the League developed their anarchism in their own way, and in response to their own needs, which will be described more fully later on. Briefly, they were due to the need to develop the ideological counter-attack to the parliamentarians in the League and the need for a wider vision of a new libertarian society under the pressure of events.

As we have seen the working class were becoming increasingly responsive to socialist propaganda of every kind. But the socialist response — like the mass misery and bitterness which nourished it — was decentralised. This was both reflected in the self-activity within the branches of the socialist organisations and the activity of individuals too ambitious, too heterodox or too eccentric for one organisation to hold or contain. Under the first head we could put John Burns, under the second Tom Mann, neither of whom of course were anarchist. But one eccentric could be described as a one-man anarchist response to the social situation. This was the astonishing Dan Chatterton who published forty-two numbers of the wildly individual *Chatterton's Commune — the Atheist Communistic Scorcher* from 18th September 1884 until his death in 1895.

Dan Chatterton lived in one of the most miserable slums in London, off Drury Lane. In his time he was well known among London socialists, an old Chartist who had recovered the fire of his youth in the new socialist movement. David Nicoll wrote of him:

> Who does not remember ... a pale haggard old man who used to climb the platform at meetings of the unemployed, or in the closely packed Socialist lecture halls and pour forth wild denunciations of the robbery and injustice that flourishes in our rotten society, mingled with fearful prophecies of the terrible revolution that was coming. He looked as he stood in the glare of the gaslight, with his ghostly face and flashing eyes, clad in an old grey overcoat and black slouched hat, a red woollen scarf knotted around his neck, like some grim spectre evolved from the misery and crime of the London slums and middle class men who had entered the meeting from curiosity shuddered as they murmured to themselves 'Marat! Yes Marat come to life again, an English Marat.'[31]

Dan Chatterton made his living, if not a particularly lucrative one, as a bill sticker and as a seller of socialist newspapers — an indication of the mood of the time that someone could actually sell enough of them to exist on the commission.

He was well known not only in Hyde Park, but also at all meetings of the advanced sections of the social movement where he sold *Freedom* and the *Commonweal* but especially pushing the sale of his own little production. ... He usually created a sensation and considerable amusement by rapidly announcing his paper as 'An appeal to the half-starved, herring-gutted, poverty-stricken, parish-damned inhabitants of this disunited kingdom ...'

Through the *Scorcher* ran his 'Autobiography of Old Chat' which is a history of the struggles of his time, the scenes he witnessed and his frequent challenges to Bishops and priests to debate with him. These last were mostly preceded by an 'Open Letter' stating why they should meet him in debate, and he took pains to see that they received the challenge, though I think that he had no success in drawing them into battle! ...

Richard Whiting in his once famous novel *No. 5 John Street* makes Chatterton one of his main characters under the name of 'Old 48', and says of his paper: "The journal if I may be pardoned the digression, has no circulation; yet it supports '48 as he supports it. It is bought at public meetings as a curiosity and usually by persons who have in view an inexpensive donation to the British Museum. Many who purchase it make the transaction an excuse for offering the proprietor an alms. It has every note of singularity. It is printed on paper of the texture commonly used for posters and of the hue of anaemic blood. Its orthography is of the first standard; its syntax aspires to the perfect freedom of the Anarchical ideal. It is set up from a composite font suggestive of a jobbing printers dustbin, and containing so undue a proportion of Capitals they sometimes have to take service out of their turn at the end of a word. It might appear to have a large staff for no two of its articles are signed by the same person. 'Brutus' writes the leader, 'George Washington' supplies the reports of meetings, 'William Tell' gives reminiscences of the Chartist rising and 'Cromwell' acts as agent for advertisements. To the initiated, however these are but so many incarnations of the same commanding personality. When '48 has written the entire number he sets it up. When he has set it up he carries it to a hand printing press which Guttenberg would have considered crude. When the press happens to be in a good humour, he obtains a copy by the usual method. When it does not he is still at no loss: for he lays the formes on the table and prints each sheet by the pressure of the hand. Earlier difficulties of this sort were met by the cooperation of his wife, now deceased. This devoted woman sat on the formes and obtained the desired results by the impact of a mass of corpulency estimated at fourteen stone. Her death is said to have been accelerated by the sudden demand for an entire edition of a hundred and seventy copies descriptive of a riot in Hyde Park. These earlier issues are valued by collectors for the extreme sharpness of the impression."[32]

Dan Chatterton was an eccentric, a curiosity; yet he was also something of an institution. There are references to him in many papers and books of the period, and Richard Whiting's account discounts his importance as an agitator. As Nicoll remarks, his pamphlet/newspaper "reached an audience which more pretentious writers never do ... he never wrote above the heads of the people." He deserves to be rescued from oblivion.

## Chapter 5

# ANARCHISM DEVELOPS IN THE SOCIALIST LEAGUE

For all its hopeful beginnings there was a built-in time bomb in the Socialist League. The group of people that had seceded from the S.D.F. had done so for different reasons, some because of hostility to Hyndman, others because of hostility to Hyndman and his politics. There were continual attempts by the group that initially centred on the Avelings to turn the League into an electoral party. At first these attempts took no great part of the League's time or attention. The first proposals that the League should strive "to conquer political power by promoting the election of Socialists" were rejected at the annual conference in June 1885.[1] Another attempt was made the following year and was again defeated. Morris wrote: "the alterers were defeated and bore their defeat with good temper."[2] From this point on things began to deteriorate. In September 1886 Lane was putting a motion to the League Council which asserted that "some speakers of the League are in the habit of advocating Parliamentary action and palliatives of the present system as a means of bringing about socialism. The council believes that this is opposed to the principles of the League and to the wishes of a large majority of the members [and] requests those speakers to desist from advocating this means of propaganda."[3] By the summer of 1887 Morris was writing that: "I am trying to get the League to make peace with each other and hold together for another year. It is a tough job; something like the worst kind of pig-driving I should think."[4]

In two years then, the inner circles of the Socialist League had been transformed from examples of harmonious 'agreeing to differ' to a quarrelsome battleground. Without doubt the disputes were over electoral involvement, though the course of the argument is not totally clear. By 1886, however, the parliamentary faction were using the opportunity provided by the branch structure and name of the League to advocate their policy. Naturally enough, this could be expected to annoy the anti-parliamentarians in the organisation. But whereas at the base this advocacy could be seen as the occasional expression of 'personal opinion', in the council and its committee it was more clearly perceived as the deliberate policy of a faction. The conflict began to explode with monotonous regularity. On one level this took the form of a power struggle — which the parliamentarians equally monotonously won. Aveling resigned as co-editor of the *Commonweal* in early 1886, presumably for doctrinal reasons. (He was encouraged in this by Eleanor Marx and Engels — the latter after a brief honeymoon period was now calling the League and its paper a "swindle."[5]) Bax, who succeeded Aveling, also 'resigned' in early 1887 when he too began to hanker after involvement in elections. Attempts were made to dissolve the Ways and Means Committee which was, in effect, the real executive of the League.[6] This was always dominated by the anti-parliamentarians and was bitterly regarded by their opponents, particularly because it handled the information that went to branches from the council.

It is significant that the motion to dissolve it came from its one parliamentarian member who was in a position to know its activities. This power struggle emerged into full view at the 1887 and 1888 conferences, though it remained more or less restricted to the council before then.

On another level the dispute was an ideological one — or rather one from which ideology developed. *All* the seceders from the S.D.F. had been opposed to any shoddy alliances with the Radicals and related kinds of electoral jiggery-pokery. Their suspicions of Hyndman's opportunism seemed amply justified by his organisation's disastrous involvement with the 1885 general election. Yet the group round the Avelings had a general commitment from the beginning to a socialism on the German Social Democrat model, and found a natural sympathy with those who called for an independent political party of labour. The activists of the L.E.L. and the English Revolutionary Society, on the other hand, had been used to an issue-based propaganda and had an ultimate commitment to mass revolutionary action. The group round Morris was concerned to 'make socialists' by an educational propaganda without intrigue or compromise with day-to-day exigencies. For the time being the latter two groups could work well enough together and could not be expected to do other than oppose any specific proposals for electoral activity. For Morris the issue was clear; the only time that socialists should endeavour to enter Parliament was when it was time to break it up and in the meantime education was the only worthwhile activity.[7] For Kitz, Lane, Mowbray and Mainwaring and their group the situation was somewhat different. They were activists rather than educators. Their joy at every manifestation of working-class rebellion and their experience of various agitations left them hazy when it came to a formulation of a unified theory and strategy. Confronted with a body of people like the parliamentary faction who did have a coherent reformist strategy they were forced to develop or accept ideas which could provide them with a more general scenario. These ideas were progressively anarchist.

When Engels wrote in 1886 "the anarchists are making rapid progress in the Socialist League," whether he knew it or not he was not talking about any coherent anarchist faction but of a faction trying to achieve coherence through a self-developed anarchism. The only committed anarchists in the organisation were exiles like Dave. That the process of self-education was messy there was no doubt. A trades union member resigned from the council in 1886 because of its inconclusive wranglings (though it is worth pointing out that he was also a parliamentarian). He wrote: "I earnestly hope the League is not going to degenerate into a mere Quixotic debating society for the discussion of philosophic fads. I care not how angelic may be the theories of Anarchists or Anarchist-Communists. I contend that the real solid basis of the Revolutionary movement is the economic question."[8] The irritation of this correspondent seems to have been a feature of Council proceedings generally. The general wranglings were both resented and felt to be inevitable. The L.E.L. activists for example were evidently furious that so much time had to be spent on them yet felt that they had to continue to defend the original principles of the League and develop the polemic or give up the League to the parliamentarians. Lane, particularly, was irritated in the extreme that he could spend so little time on organisation in the East End.

Meanwhile the branches were carrying on in their own way and where able people were involved they were doing good work. They were being let down by the council which could have provided a forum for creative thinking but which was locked in increasingly bitter strife. It was inevitable that this would spill out into the League as a whole. As the 1887 conference approached Lane circulated a leaflet to the membership which illustrates something of what was going on. It also fired the first shots in the now public battle. He wrote:

> Comrades, Directly after our last conference which endorsed the policy carried out by the League hitherto, two separate parties were formed on the Council, caused by the fact that as early as July members on and off the Council were publicly urging the League into a parliamentary course of action; the other party wished to maintain the League as an educational party of principle.

As an attempt to make an understanding possible it was decided to draft a policy agreeable to both sides and a committee was formed with Mahon and Lane for the 'principled side', Bax and Binning for the parliamentarians. Agreement was complete except for the question of an Eight Hour Labour Bill and parliamentary action. Mahon told Bax and Binning that if this was what they wanted they should join the S.D.F. However:

> At the next meeting Mahon volunteered to draw up a policy to submit to the committee. At this meeting, of which I had no notice, Mahon presented his draft, the other two finding it a parliamentary policy and nothing more, accepted it with pleasure, threw over all previous arrangements and presented it to the Council as the report of the committee. On hearing it read to the Council I disagreed with it and claimed my right to put it in a minority report. Mahon has since regained possession of the majority report and declines to give it up or bring it before the Council except in the way of resolutions from the Croydon branch. This I was not aware of until a week after the time for sending in notices of motion for the agenda paper. I have to the best of my ability carried out the instructions of the Council in drawing up a report. The Council having declined to send the minority report to the branches, the majority report having gone

round on legs, I now further carry out the instructions of the Council in submitting it to the Branches.[9]

Lane's minority report was his *Anti-Statist Communist Manifesto* which can fairly be claimed as the first English anarchist home-grown pronouncement. Like most pioneers Lane did not write a masterpiece. He paid a disproportionate amount of attention to the religious question — though this section is interesting for its echoes of Bakunin's 'God and the State'. He shared Morris's rejection of palliative measures in Parliament or through trades unions. Yet his ideas are distinguishable from Morris's in two areas. Where Morris emphasised the necessity to make socialists, Lane emphasised the necessity to make revolution. Lane clearly called for mass violent action whereas on the occasion of the West End Riot Morris had clearly been dubious about a policy of riot. A second distinction between Lane and Morris was Lane's firm opposition to the state as an entity: "We aim," he said, "at the abolition of the State in every form and variety." Lane expected nothing but tyranny from any state machine. Morris on the other hand was less emphatic. For example, we find Morris writing in 1888: "Even the crudest form of State Socialism (which I do not agree to) would have this advantage over the individual ownership of the means of production, that whereas the State might abuse its ownership, the individual ownership must do so ..." Thus when Morris and Lane both emphasised education as the proper means for achieving their stated aims they were talking of education in different contexts.

Lane submitted his *Anti-Statist Communist Manifesto* to the 1887 conference as a restatement of League policy after the Croydon branch called for electoral activity by the League. William Morris was the proposer of a motion from Hammersmith which wanted the League to postpone any discussion of the parliamentary question for a year. Morris was obviously trying to reconcile the two extreme wings but at the 29th May conference it rapidly became apparent that reconciliation was not possible — at least not at the level of restraint that Morris was proposing. Lane, it would appear, was stressing the anti-parliamentary position to bring matters to a head. Urging that Morris's 'peacemaking motion' be withdrawn, he said, "Members from the country do not know the bitterness, jealousy, etc., shown in this matter. The matter has lasted some time in Council. Delegates ought to settle one way or another."[10] Lane would probably have been quite prepared to expel every 'politician' in the organisation. The feeling of the conference was not with him however and his *Manifesto* was not accepted as the policy of the League. On the other hand, neither was the conference prepared to suspend the issue, and Morris withdrew his motion. Finally the conference voted to accept Morris's amendment to the Croydon branch motion. This simply asserted the principles of the League as laid down in the *Manifesto of the Socialist League*. For all the fact that this reasserted the anti-parliamentarian position it did not finish the matter by any means. The 'political' faction showed no readiness to leave the League or to moderate its stance. They simultaneously left the bulk of the work of running the League to the anti-parliamentarians and made that work doubly difficult by systematically undermining the agreed policy of the League. Furthermore, the bad temper which burst forth every now and again at the conference showed that the "bitterness, jealousy, etc." had been deepened rather than dispersed by its airing. With the benefit of hindsight it is possible to say that it might have been better for the Socialist League if the matter had been pushed to a final conclusion. Uncomfortable it might have been but at least it would have been short and sharp instead of encouraging the ulcerous persistence of the dispute through the following year. Though the events of 1887 might seem to obscure the difficulties within the organisation, the 1888 conference was to show that the rival factions were growing yet more irreconcilable. For the rising social tensions of 1887 were to throw into sharp relief the choices open to the socialist movement. As both revolution and electoral gains appeared more possible their partisans became more intransigent.

For by 1887 working-class discontent was growing. In the trades unions a sharper, more militant note was being struck. At the T.U.C. conference, the young Keir Hardie clashed with the Liberal's lapdog, Broadhurst. A determined attempt to get an Eight Hour campaign under way in the Engineering Union and the T.U.C. was made. John Burns and Tom Mann were active in this latter campaign. New organisations in the provinces, the Labour Federation on Tyneside and the Knights of Labour in the Midlands, proved surprisingly effective and grew rapidly. New organisational attempts also met with some success among the seamen. This new militancy was both spread by socialists and proved responsive to them.

It was a period of high unemployment, and the mood of the unemployed was restive. The lesson of the West End Riot were clear enough — trouble meant attention and attention meant aid. But the authorities had been alarmed and were taking steps to make sure nothing like it happened again. Sir Charles Warren was appointed to reorganise the police in London and was being encouraged to keep the streets clear of 'loafers' and other members of the dangerous classes by the Tory government and press. As if to underline the fears of the authorities and the respectable classes, on Friday 14th January the unemployed rioted at Norwich. The riot broke out after the unemployed had marched from a meeting addressed by Mowbray and Henderson of the local Socialist League branch to the Guildhall to demand help. Here "the insulting tone of the Mayor, the unconcealed contempt for their fellows on the part of the councillors and aldermen ... angered the crowd and they broke away."[11] The mansions of the wealthy had their windows smashed and shops in the centre of Norwich were looted. Mowbray and Henderson were arrested and sentenced to nine and four months respectively for their part in the affair. The riot, if anything, made the League more popular and there were large demonstrations to welcome the men on their release. The situation improved somewhat over the summer, but as winter approached unemployment rose again. A placard posted in Norwich in October 'by unknown hands' was threatening: "Notice to all concerned: The unemployed do not intend to starve any longer. If employment is not found for them, they will soon make some."[12] As a result 200 special constables were sworn in. More sensibly the local authorities tempered their show of force by providing public works. *Commonweal* later quoted two councillors:

How much extra did it cost ...?
£150!
Well ... none of us will grudge that. *It's a damned cheap price to have kept them quiet for.*

The correspondent commented: "it seems after all that fear of a repetition of rioting was their motive. Let the unemployed learn the lesson this teaches."[13]

In London, however, the authorities seemed determined to solve the 'problem' of the unemployed by force alone. In the earlier part of 1887 the S.D.F. had organised many parades by the unemployed — to Westminster Abbey during services among other places. While individual members of the League had participated in them the League as a whole rather saw them as intended to be advertisements for the S.D.F. There were sporadic outbreaks of looting — for example, after a meeting in February on Clerkenwell Green. Due, apparently, to some internal difficulties in the S.D.F. that organisation discontinued its parades some time in the summer. As unemployment increased during the autumn mounting numbers of the unemployed began to meet daily in Trafalgar Square and between 400 and 600 homeless people were sleeping there at night. Socialists began to hold meetings in the square on a freelance basis and increasingly violent threats were being uttered by them. While it would seem that one of them at least was a police paid agent provocateur, the violence being urged was a violence the unemployed felt. Prominent in the agitation in the square was an anarchist-inclined Socialist Leaguer called James Allman, who had already served a month's imprisonment earlier in the year for 'obstruction' while addressing a meeting.

Processions were organised. One to the Bow Street magistrate on 12th October was met with a blank refusal of aid and a suggestion that the unemployed enter the workhouse. "Asked if he would give them food and shelter in prison if they sacked bakers shops he replied that they were 'exceedingly impertinent' and 'deserved no compassion.'" *Freedom* noted that "unfortunately this did no more than cause a march through the City."[14] The police had already begun to attack processions of the unemployed, though these attacks met with stiff resistance. On 15th October the police attacked a meeting of the unemployed in Trafalgar Square itself with both foot and horse "hustling, charging, striking and trampling the people." Attacks on meetings in the square continued daily with ever-increasing numbers of police involved until the unemployed were finally driven out on 19th October. The centre of the agitation then moved to Hyde Park. "For days the conflict was carried on in and around the Park. On one occasion the gates were closed on the people and the mounted police charged the crowd thus hemmed in and helpless." Many stragglers were arrested, beaten and sentenced to vicious sentences on often perjured evidence. "But in spite of police court terrorism and sentences of hard labour by the dozen, the people defended themselves with sticks and stones and their fists and held their meetings just the same. And on Sunday, 23rd October they returned to the square in a solid mass, filling the huge square to overflowing and afterwards marching to Westminster Abbey."

The escalating conflict had brought protests against police violence from the liberal press and screeches from shopkeepers in the area of Trafalgar Square, who claimed their takings were being hit by the demonstrations. It was quite clear whose views Warren took to heart. The police continued to attack the daily meetings until, on 8th November, Warren banned all further meetings in the square on the grounds that it was the private property of the Crown. This brought a storm of protest from the Radicals, who had taken no part in the unemployed agitation but were very strong on the right of free speech. As a reply to the ban the Radicals announced that they would hold a mass demonstration in the square on 13th November to protest at Coercion in Ireland. The demonstration was to converge in a number of processions from different parts of London. It could be readily assumed that the police would have no intention of allowing the processions to reach the square and that violence was to be expected; yet the morale of the various large contingents was good. Lane said that Morris "quite thought the revolution had come."[15] The marchers were to be brutally disabused of any such opinion.

Knowing the time of the demonstration, the direction from which the contingents were to come and their approximate size allowed Warren every advantage, a fact that he used to the full:

> The 'Square', i.e. the sunken space, was guarded by foot-policemen four deep, whose business was simply to guard it and who had orders not to stir from their posts, outside these were strong bodies of horse police who took careful note of any incipient gathering and at once scattered it.
>
> This defence was ample against anything except an organised attack from determined persons acting in concert, and able to depend on one another. In order that no such body should be formed and no such attack be possible, the careful general had posted strong bodies of

police, with due supports to fall back on if necessary, about a radius of about a quarter of a mile of the square, so that nothing could escape falling into the meshes of this net.

Into this net we then marched.[16]

The contingent which included most of the League marchers was attacked at Seven Dials and taken on the flank. Though they fought back as best they could they were confused and taken by surprise. Morris wrote: "I was astounded at the rapidity of the thing and the ease with which military organisation got its victory." The police behaved with utter savagery. One witness said, "As I was being led out of the crowd a poor woman asked a police inspector ... if he had seen a child she had lost. His answer was to tell her she was a damned whore and knock her down."[17] The story was the same with the other contingents and only unorganised and confused stragglers reached the square itself where they were quickly dispersed. Three people died as a result of injuries received from the police on 13th November, and another man was killed the following week when police horses were again clearing the square. Many arrests were made and jail sentences were liberally handed out. The day is properly remembered as Bloody Sunday.

Reactions from the participants were quite naturally angry. But there were a variety of responses beyond that. E.P. Thompson suggests that from the time of Bloody Sunday onwards Morris drastically extended his timescale for the achievement of socialism. The ease with which the large bodies of people had been dispersed profoundly depressed him and persuaded him of the vast power at the disposal of the authorities. This neither changed his general political strategy or his ideas but did reduce his intense political activity. For others, too, Bloody Sunday represented a crisis in any belief they might have had in the likelihood of an incipient revolution, but, unlike Morris, it pushed them steadily towards a more reformist position.

For the majority of the League activists, however, it seems to have been treated as a lesson in not fighting against impossible odds. Bloody Sunday did indeed mark a defeat, but this did not in itself represent a defeat for a policy of riot. There was little doubt that they shared *Freedom*'s opinion of events: "...the inclination of the people increases to rush on the smallest pretext to demonstrate in the streets. There have been more or less tumultuous street gatherings during the past year [i.e. 1887] in London, Glasgow, Norwich, Northampton, in Wales and in Ireland. ... The increase in such stormy gatherings marks the arrival of the period of action. Before the next new year it may well happen that we shall find ourselves amid the first crisis of a Social Revolution."[18]

Anarchist ideas began to appeal more specifically to the activists of the League in 1887. The context was the increasing class confrontation represented by the unemployed demonstrations culminating in Bloody Sunday. The example that fascinated them was the trial and judicial murder of the Chicago anarchists. Four men were hanged after a series of events in Chicago in 1886 which had culminated in a bomb being thrown at police who were attacking a peaceful meeting. Chicago was a militant centre of anarchism and had seen a series of strikes in pursuit of demands for the eight-hour day. Pickets had been shot and beaten by Pinkerton thugs and police. (The meeting attacked by the police had been called in the Haymarket to protest against police violence.) After the bomb explosion, which killed one policeman, the police arrested eight men who were all either anarchist editors or active propagandists in the eight-hour struggle. The anarchist press in Chicago had been stridently calling for preparation on the part of the working class for armed revolution. For all that, none of the men could be proved to have had anything to do with the bomb. They were all charged with complicity in the murder of the policeman. After a series of farcically unfair trials they were condemned to death, though three of them, Fielden, Neebe and Schwab, had their sentences commuted. The dignity and conviction of the condemned men in the face of a frenzied hate campaign compelled attention. One can go far towards understanding the motives of an anarchist assassin when one is confronted by the truly bestial relish with which the newspapers described the details of the preparation for the hanging, and the execution itself. Albert Parsons, one of the men who were hanged, had every chance to go into hiding but returned to face trial since his status as a native English-speaking American might just tip the balance for his foreign comrades. Louis Lingg appealed for revenge for their imminent deaths and as his parting words to the court said: "I despise you. I despise your order, your laws, your force propped authority. Hang me for it!" Lingg chose to take his own life by exploding a smuggled dynamite cartridge in his mouth. On the scaffold Engel said, "Long live Anarchism!"; Fischer said, "This is the happiest moment of my life!"; Spies said, "There will come a time when our silence will be more powerful than the voices you strangle today." The men were executed on 11th November 1887.

The hate campaign in America was matched by the Tory press in Britain. To counter their propaganda a series of protest meetings were organised by the Freedom Group, the Socialist League and branches of the S.D.F., both jointly and separately. Propaganda tours were made through the radical clubs. Accounts of the trials of the Chicago men were sent to the *Commonweal* from America by Henry Charles and the Socialist League devoted much space in the paper and considerable organisational effort to the campaign in defence of the condemned men. The Freedom Group and the Socialist League not only cooperated with each other in the organisation of meetings, they jointly issued and distributed a thick pamphlet, *The Chicago Martyrs*, which gave the lives and speeches of the condemned men and described the events leading up to their execution.

In late 1887 and early 1888 the biographies of the eight Chicago men were serialised in the *Commonweal*. The courage and fortitude of the Chicago martyrs, the cooperation with the Freedom Group, the increasing penetration of anarchist ideas within the League both from longstanding foreign anarchist members and from *Freedom* itself, the ideologies developing out of the struggle with the parliamentarians — all these were intertwined in the *Commonweal* and the minds of the activists. The Chicago men were hanged on 11th November. Bloody Sunday was on 13th November. Close connections were drawn between them — they were both commemorated at the same meetings the following year. Naked force, it appeared, was the final answer of the state when the dispossessed insisted on pressing their claims — and claims for what? For work or bread, for an eight-hour working day. Why then did the people not claim *all* and have done? These were the feelings of the militants.

In the months after Bloody Sunday there was a deceptive calm in the Socialist League. Cooperation was a simple matter when it came to decrying the violence of the police. Receptions for those people jailed after the fighting were occasions when comradely feeling was easy. Yet the annual conference of the League on 20th May brought to a head the infighting that had simmered since the conference of the previous year. The obvious desire of William Morris to reconcile the politicians, now concentrated in the Bloomsbury branch of the League and the more peremptory anti-parliamentarians had in no way changed the situation. Joe Lane had been proved right in his objection to the proposal "that the matter be adjourned for twelve months, the result of which would be that the battle would still be carried on, weakening our propaganda forces."[19] Reasserting the principles of the League had been equivalent to an adjournment.

The run-up to the conference started in earnest when the Bloomsbury branch sent in their resolutions. There were four, three of them proposals on organisation which could only increase the control of the large, rich Bloomsbury branch. The other resolution, number two, proposed that the "Constitution be amended ... adding 'That its objects shall be sought to be obtained by all available means; and that Branches of the League be empowered ... to run or support candidates for all the representative bodies of the country." In the internal circular of 7th May the seriousness of the threat was underlined, the Ways and Means Committee asserting that "the carrying of this resolution in the opinion of the committee would involve the immediate dissolution of the Socialist League."[20] It was an indication that this time there would be no attempt at compromise. A better example of the mood of the anti-parliamentarians came in other documents. The 14th May internal letter revealed that Sam Mainwaring had called for the immediate dissolution of the Bloomsbury branch at a council meeting though he was prevailed upon to leave the matter until the conference. The reasons for his angry gesture can be found in two internal documents, one circulated by Lane and Charles, the other by the Hackney branch.

The first document listed all the anti-parliamentary policy statements of the League and then proceeded to its real business. Lane and Charles reprinted what appear to be the purloined minutes of a meeting of the parliamentary faction which took place on the day after their defeat at the 1887 conference. Aveling was in the chair and present among others were Eleanor Marx-Aveling, A.K. Donald, Bax and Tom Binning. The most interesting section reads:

> *Shirley* — proposed to make Bloomsbury a Head Centre of Socialism.
> *Utley* — To become active working members of the L.E.L. without withdrawing from the S.L. Stay in League till we can work it for our own party.
> *E. M. Aveling* — Sorry we left the S.D.F. Reverse our blunder made there and get the League into our own hands. Get a Conf. in about three months and reverse the decision of this last one. Make W. Morris give up the paper. Work the L.E.L. and suggest that every parliamentary supporter joins the L.E.L. Force the hands of the Council by joining the L.E.L. and if resistance is offered, resign and leave the League, but hold on to League for time being.
> *E. M. Aveling* — Branches in harmony with party subscribe funds for working provincial branches.[21] That Branches pay subscriptions to L.E.L. and pay as affiliated bodies to League.
> *Tom Binning* — L.E.L. could arrange early meeting.

Lane and Charles then go on to say that "the attempt to use the L.E.L. for their party purposes was an ignominious failure and they have therefore adopted the course of proposing these resolutions from the Bloomsbury branch."[22] No one can deny that the anti-parliamentary faction had also been lobbying for support[23] but the shoddy self-advancing and opportunist tone of these minutes would by no means calm tempers.

Neither could the second internal document circulated by the Hackney branch. This concerned the proposals designed to increase the control of large, rich branches like Bloomsbury. Now the Hackney branch had an interest here; it was a small branch. But it was also emphatically anti-parliamentarian. The secretary was George Cores and its members included two anarchist members of the Berner Street club, one of whom, W. Wess, was a member of the Freedom Group. In addition its delegate to the conference was Joe Lane. The real point of this circular issued by the branch was the sentence "Those who know how the large numbers of the Bloomsbury Branch have been obtained namely by inducing very many members of the S.D.F. to join while still members of the S.D.F. merely for the purpose of swamping the votes of others."[24] It was this allegation that had made Sam Mainwaring want to dissolve the Bloomsbury branch at the council meeting before the conference.

The Bloomsbury branch made no attempt to circulate serious material of their own before the conference. In addition they put some effort into being provocative at the conference itself. Their report in what appears to be a late entry boasts of joint activity with the S.D.F. in promoting candidates for the St Pancras Board of Guardians.[25] Furthermore their mandates for delegates were written on the back of a leaflet made up of the text of a simultaneously perceptive and rather silly letter which had been refused by the *Commonweal*. This read in part:

> The S.L. has followed so closely in the steps of that society which Socialists desire to overthrow, that in it has arisen a curious phase of Jingoism. The jingo patriot exalts devotion to the State into a virtue far higher than devotion to the cause of humanity, and similarly there are many of our comrades who have put devotion to the S.L. before devotion to the cause of Socialism. ... While our present Executive exists any branch or any member exercising the right of thought or free discussion runs the risk of expulsion.[26]

This explicitly referred to Mainwaring's attempt to expel the Bloomsbury branch. It might have been less irritating to use this to write mandates on if the people checking branch credentials had not been Lane and Mainwaring.

The conference was structured in such a way that it allowed everyone plenty of time to lose their temper before the Bloomsbury motions were debated. There were wrangles over whether branches existed or not and Bax's branch (Croydon) was declared collapsed. There were wrangles over the control of the *Commonweal*. It was not until 6pm after a day of it that the Bloomsbury motions were discussed. This immediately started with a spat between Donald and Lane. 'Bloomsbury number two' was taken first, immediately amended by Morris and Mowbray to convert it into a reassertion of anti-parliamentarianism. The debate was noisy and disorderly. Eventually the amendment was carried by nineteen votes to six. The other Bloomsbury motions were defeated as heavily. But this time it was not intended to leave it at that. A further motion was put by Davis and Morris recommending the League to "take steps to reconciliate, or if necessary, exclude the Bloomsbury Branch from the Socialist League." This was carried by eighteen to seven. The Bloomsbury branch then replied with a motion to divide the assets of the League. They were again defeated.

Thus the conference ended any hopes the Bloomsburyites might have had of capturing the Socialist League. It seems clear, though, that it was less of an attempt to persuade and more of a wrecking expedition. The resolution calling for the division of the League assets sounds like an attempt to have themselves bought out, since most of the assets of the League were bought by Morris, and as he had written, "the parls. cannot do without us moneyly as we have found most of the money; if you think it mean to say this I must say in turn that they have rather speculated on my known horror of a split in their machinations."[27] Their tactics remained disruptive after their clear defeat at the conference. They issued and distributed an "illustrated squib" derisive of the conference, and at the next council meeting the branch was suspended. They then insisted on attending the next council meeting and refused to leave. A final attempt at reconciliation was made by Morris but failed. The branch claimed its "complete autonomy." Finally at the 25th June meeting of the council it was resolved to dissolve the Bloomsbury branch. And here the battle ended.

But there were still birds limping home to roost. The Labour Emancipation League at Hoxton decided to withdraw its affiliation to the League in June and the Walsall branch similarly seceded in August. These resignations were received with regret and it was hoped that cooperation could take place on points where they were in agreement. But an important stage had been reached in the life of the League. No matter how firmly Morris and the other committed anti-parliamentarians had stated their case since the inception of the League, it had become, particularly in the provinces, a gathering point for socialists of every description. The reasons were twofold. Firstly, many people found Morris both as a man and as a socialist more attractive than Hyndman. The political differences between them seem to have figured little initially. This, at least, is the impression one gains reading memoirs by early members of the League.

Secondly, the looser branch structure of the League suited some provincial socialists, and the provincial branches of the League represented more or less a federation of local socialist societies. The struggle between the parliamentary and anti-parliamentary factions was primarily a struggle involving those members whose socialism was more theoretically specific. Thus Walsall and Hoxton were branches where the parliamentarians had a base of a kind — Walsall probably because Donald of the Bloomsbury branch had been working nearby. Meanwhile the only branches who specifically endorsed an article entitled 'The Policy of the League', which underlined the anti-parliamentary stand of the League were Norwich, Hackney and Hammersmith, influenced by Charles, Lane and Morris respectively. It has already been said that the struggle had started in the council of the League and had been kept there until it boiled over at the 1887 and 1888 conferences. It is not at all surprising that those branches to whom the generally humanitarian socialism of Morris was the most attractive feature of the League would shrink back somewhat from this 'irrelevant' and passionate conflict. Some of them, Leeds for example, had quietly lapsed as branches in any real sense between the 1887 and 1888 conferences. For them systematic electoral activity was as yet unconsidered on practical rather than ideological grounds. They shared Tarleton's opinion at the 1887 conference and "objected to parliamentary action by a body of 800. Party action [had been] damaging so far because [it had been] used by Conservatives to damage Radicals." Yet when there seemed to be real prospects of success in elections the bitter disputes of the 1888 conference would be repeated up and down the country.

The conference of 1888 left the Socialist League now completely committed to an anti-parliamentary policy. The sordid tail end of the dispute with the Bloomsbury branch lingered on for a few weeks, but the tension of that dispute had left the organisation. Morris had plainly felt disgusted with the whole thing even before battle was joined. Before the conference he had written: "Plainly speaking, the shadow of corruption which we should certainly tumble into if we became Parl. is already on us, and there has been a great deal too much intriguing going on."[28] After the conference he withdrew to a certain extent and his letters take on a gloomy tone. He began increasingly to see himself out of the mainstream of activity and to immerse himself in literary and other creative activity. But if the 1888 conference left Morris feeling rather flat it was not a feeling shared by the majority of the new Council. This was now dominated more or less by the progressively anarchist group of activists including Kitz, Lane, Mainwaring and Tochatti. The secretary of the League was now Charles, who had been in Switzerland looking for evidence against Peukert as a police spy. Lane had persuaded him to stand on his return. It should be stressed that this group did not have a policy of taking over the League — "there were no definite plans to alter the League or make it more Anarchist but agitating always to keep it to its manifesto," Charles was reported as saying many years later.[29]

This would seem to be flatly contradicted by Morris writing in December 1888: "there seems to be a curse of quarrelling upon us. The Anarchist element in us seem determined to drive things to extremity and break us up if we do not declare for Anarchy — which I for one will not do." Yet the real cause of the curse of quarrelling is revealed later in the same letter. The Hammersmith branch, he says, is "getting into bad odour with some of our fiercer friends, I think principally because it tacitly and instinctively tries to keep up the first idea of the League, the making of genuine convinced Socialists without reference to passing exigencies of tactics, whether they take the form of attacking (or running away from) the police in the streets, or running a candidate for the school board ..."[30] Morris apparently did not see that by this time one man's refusal to take account of "passing exigencies of tactics" could be another anti-parliamentarian's withdrawal from the fray. The events of the years 1888 to 1890 were summed up from the latter point of view by Frank Kitz:

> There existed in the League itself opposing elements which eventually led to its disruption. The merely negative policy of Anti-Parliamentarianism could be endured by the West End branches, of which Hammersmith was the strongest, and in which Morris's personality was dominant: but the East End comrades, confronted by a fierce struggle for existence and in the midst of gigantic Labour conflicts, drifted towards a definitely Anarchist attitude. A quantity of ink has been shed over the question of the split between the West and

East End branches which caused the dissolution of the League; but the temperamental differences have always been ignored. Many of the West End members would have found a more suitable environment and method of exposition of their ideal within the ranks of the I.L.P. or the Fabian Society; and … it was only Morris's personality which caused them to give lip service to opinions from which many of them have now seceded. They seemed to be afflicted with the timidity of anaemic respectability.[31]

The position of the Socialist League in the first years of its existence has often been called 'purist'. But its purism can be seen in two ways: one, as an educational propaganda speaking to working-class movements, with which it is not involved, from the outside; the other, as the simple recognition that possible avenues of reform from electoral activity to trades unionism do not imply the fundamental changes that their socialism demanded. The question here is one of emphasis. Educational propaganda alone implies a deliberately withdrawn position which often expresses itself as a superior defeatism. Suspicion of reform dressed up as revolution on the other hand, means a different kind of involvement or propaganda. Every member of the League on the anti-parliamentary side can be accused of 'educational defeatism' in the early years. Yet the class war hotted up as the 1880s drew to a close, and it became impossible for some people in the League to insist that there could be no socialist action without socialist theory. The unemployment battles of 1887 and the industrial struggles from 1889 onwards seemed to have something of the stuff of revolution about them. It became impossible for the activists to stand aside. For them socialism became something that the working class learned in action out of the practical experience of solidarity and confrontation. The new conflict in the League was over the question of whether action or theory came first.

In the early part of 1888, just before and after the conference, Lane and Charles were preparing for a massive effort to propagandise the East End of London. Their intentions were described as follows:

The East End branches of the Socialist League and our foreign comrades at the Berner Street and Princess Square Clubs have just formed themselves into the East End Socialist Propaganda Committee and are commencing a systematic distribution from house to house in all the streets, lanes, etc. of leaflets, pamphlets (which are left in the houses of one street one week, then called for and taken to another street the following week) and other literature as well as pasting up leaflets, bills, etc. on the walls, hoardings, lamp-posts, church noticeboards and other similarly available places. They have besides commenced holding regular open-air meetings at about 20 places in the district. ... In view of the threatened anti-foreigner agitation they specifically appeal for the assistance of the foreign comrades in London to show that they are not the enemies of the English worker but comrades working with them for the emancipation of labour the world over.[32]

This campaign represents something of the energies released at the end of the unprofitable dispute with the Bloomsburyites. In early June they had surpassed their projected twenty speaking pitches and had managed to man twenty-seven in a week. They had drastically overextended themselves, however, and by August and September the East End pitches had shrunk to ten per week. Morris was describing the agitation as a failure by this time, which was both true and a little unfair: Lane, who was undoubtedly the architect of the East End Propaganda Committee, was in ill-health and was to be prevented thereby from taking any active part in the League from that point on. (He was eventually to leave the League in 1889 after a silly squabble with Sparling.) Charles left London and a number of other people who were active left the East End districts. And as Morris had already said in July, "the whole of the work in London is now on the shoulders of the section of principle."[33]

The propaganda effort of the League was greatly enhanced before the end of 1888 by the visit of Lucy Parsons — the widow of Albert Parsons, hanged in Chicago. She had been an active propagandist both before and after the judicial murder of her husband and had been involved in the restarting of Parsons's paper, the *Alarm*. This was being distributed in England by the League and an internal circular from the Council in July was urging branches to order it at once. By September the East End Propaganda

Committee was calling on the Council to bring Mrs Parsons to England for the commemoration meetings planned for the Chicago men and the victims of Bloody Sunday in November. She came and made a strong impression both at her London meetings and on her provincial tour, which was also arranged by the League. She was no pathetic, sorrow-struck victim. She came as a propagandist to whom tragedy had given a stronger voice. Her visit, more than any other factor, accelerated the drift towards a "definitely Anarchist attitude" in the Socialist League. But even without her aid this process was well under way in 1888. The Freedom Group were holding regular public discussion meetings in the Socialist League Hall, Farringdon Street, which certainly attracted a number of Socialist League members. Apart from cooperation with the Berner Street club (whose members were mainly Jewish anarchists) in the East End Propaganda Committee, the Berner Street club was also the meeting-place of the Hackney branch of the League. Similarly the North London branch met at the Autonomie Club, an anarchist centre with mainly German and French members.

The increasing anarchist influence did not, as Glasier slanderously asserts, lead the League into the paths of sloppy incompetence.[34] Charles, it was true, proved a failure as a secretary, yet Kitz took over this position later in 1888 and proved vastly more effective. He had proved his organisational stamina in the latter part of 1887 and in the early part of 1888 when he had been stumping round London attempting to boost the sale of *Commonweal* through retail shops. The Ways and Means Committee had taken over the printing of the paper and were able to significantly cut production costs. The circulation of the paper had fallen after the conference (its circulation just before had risen to 2,600, largely as a result of Kitz's efforts) and continuous effort was needed to try and boost circulation. Five thousand copies were ordered for the Chicago Martyrs/Bloody Sunday meetings, but generally the sale remained static at somewhere just over 2,000. The problem was partly the paper itself, which was rather dull, reflecting its editor's rather withdrawn and gloomy mood. A noticeable brightening of the paper took place when David Nicoll became co-editor (with Sparling and Morris) after the 1889 conference. This conference reflected the fact that the League was now almost completely an anarchist organisation — except for the delegates from the Hammersmith branch all the 1889 council members were at some point to be identified with the anarchist position.

Throughout the earlier part of 1889 a discussion on anarchism between committed anarchists was printed in the *Commonweal*. The bone of contention was individual liberty and the voluntary principle. The contributions of the anarchists were over-abstract and wilful in comparison with Morris's determined attempts at clarity. The anarchists insisted too much on philosophical principle and not enough on social practice. Morris wrote: "I am not pleading for any form of arbitrary or unreasonable authority, but for a *public conscience* as a rule of action: and by all means let us have the least possible exercise of authority. I suspect that many of our Communist-Anarchist friends do really mean that, when they pronounce against all authority."[35] The anarchists H. Davis and James Blackwell were too ready to take issue with Morris's phrase 'the least possible exercise of authority', failing to see that the 'public conscience' he proposed as the basis of communism was the culmination of the voluntary principle in a society where it had become custom and habit. If Morris chose to call that a situation where authority was exercised then the dispute was semantic.

The events of the summer and autumn of 1889 were to cure many of them from over-abstract philosophising. Many of the League anarchists were experienced in political propaganda and confrontation with 'law and order' on the streets, yet their experience until the early part of 1889 had been of difficult work, inching itself forward. To be sure the unemployed in 1887 had shown themselves in a pugnacious mood and their clashes with the police had been spectacular. But their struggle, starting with demands for maintenance, had been reduced to a defensive battle to keep the right of assembly, particularly in Trafalgar Square. And they had lost that battle. Thus when the Socialist League militants and anarchists from other English groupings (James Blackwell was recruited from the S.D.F. by the Freedom Group) talked of revolution and the future society they were talking of something which had no basis in action around them. Inevitably their talk was abstract, though it need not have been as abstract as it was. The industrial battles from the summer onwards, however, provided an environment and example of aggressive organising by the working class. Here at last was the spontaneous upsurge with its solidarity and mutual aid which they had predicted and hoped for. If the upsurge turned out to be more containable and co-optable than they had hoped it was a revelation and lesson which would have to be confronted later.

The impact of the strikes of 1889 was clearly powerful. In June–July the London gasworkers organised in a union which had only been started in March of the same year and managed to force a reduction of hours from twelve to eight on their employers without a strike. It was an example which proved infectious. A strike in the South-West India Dock by a small number of men over a wage demand on 13th August sparked off a strike in the whole of London's dockland. Its beginnings were quite spontaneous, though the strikers very quickly came to rely on Ben Tillett, the secretary of a small dock union, and other organisers he brought in, notably Tom Mann and John Burns. The example of the dock strike inspired other workers, first those with some connection with the docks and then others, to similarly strike for increased wages or shorter hours. "Coal porters and car-men, printers labourers, iron workers, tin-plate workers, rope making and jam factory girls, tobacco workers, orange porters, candlemakers, tailors, bricklayers and their labourers, basket makers, chemical works employees, screw makers and other workers ceased work."[36] The atmosphere in the East End was electric. The area was in a state of near general strike and to some of the Leaguers it seemed that London was on the verge of revolution. David Nicoll wrote: "The cry is still they come! The workers are pouring by thousands from their workshops — printers, labourers and brass finishers. The coal heavers leave their yard in response to the shouts of their comrades. Bands of them are marching round the Northern suburbs turning out the men at every yard. The police are powerless."[37]

He described the almost carnival atmosphere in the East End. "I saw a ring of factory girls at the gates of a rope factory performing a Carmagnole dance, occasionally bumping against the gates as if with the intention of forcing them in. Further down they were bringing out men, boys and girls from a biscuit factory, a good humoured crowd standing at the door laughing and chaffing the strikers in a most fraternal manner. ... I entered a quiet street where there was already some appearance of fermentation. Gathered round a sweaters shop was a large crowd; the shop was guarded by a strong force of police, who were evidently apprehensive of having their windows broken."

In the streets the children were parading and playing at strikers. (They were later to strike themselves at several East End schools.) Processions of dockers were taking place through the City and daily meetings were being held at Tower Hill or Hyde Park. Other workers, too, were parading in the East End and nightly vast meetings were held on Mile End Waste. Streets normally gloomily gaslit and empty at eleven o'clock at night were now ablaze from light from open front doors and excited groups in the street were discussing the latest news — and the latest rumours: "'The tram men have revolted, cars have been left on the road out Bow and Bromley way'; 'Rioting has broken out, the docks are to be fired'; 'The strikers are marching to attack the railway depots and turn the carmen out'; 'Deptford meat market is in the hands of the insurgents who won't allow London to be fed.' ... The East End is like Paris in the first revolution."[38]

The organisation of picketing was effective after a number of blacklegs were imported because of the opportunity provided by too many parades. The dock strike was effective too on the level of its supply lines, "showing the powers of the working men for organising the supply and distribution of food for a large population of strikers" as Kropotkin later noted.[39] As happens in most strikes, the paying of rent became less than a priority for the strikers — and the cry of 'No Rent' was raised and met with some response. The strike at one point threatened to escalate from a virtual general strike in the East End to a general strike in the whole of London — but the call for this was withdrawn almost as soon as it was issued by the Strike Committee. It was this that explains Kropotkin's later (private) accusations of cowardice against Burns in the face of a potential revolution. Kropotkin had misjudged neither the mood of the time nor had he misjudged the dependence of the strikers on their leaders for the next step to be taken. The crisis point passed. The edge of desperation in the strike was taken away by a massive influx of funds from Australia in support of the strikers. The edge of class conflict was blunted by the good offices of Cardinal Manning and the Lord Mayor of London. Finally the demand for the 'docker's tanner' — sixpence an hour — was met by the employers and the men returned to work. Once they were back the employers began steadily to chip away at every condition they had agreed to. The many small strikes which had accompanied the big dock strike were to suffer a similar fate. Burns, meanwhile, had already got himself elected to the new London County Council and was beginning a political career which was to eventually gain him a Cabinet place in a Liberal government.

While the dock strike was at its height, socialists had been very active. *Freedom* remarked: "One of the most satisfactory features of the agitation was the apparent disappearance of the various Socialist bodies as such. The names of organisations seldom transpired but Socialism and Socialists were everywhere. ... Political humbug disappeared from the Socialist programme as soon as our comrades in the various societies found themselves face to face with a live workers movement."[40] Pearson, Blackwell and Turner from the Freedom Group were active speakers — the first named being another recruit from the S.D.F. From the League, Kitz, Mowbray, Nicoll, Brookes and W.B. Parker "addressed large meetings and tons of literature and leaflets have been distributed. More work could be done but funds are lacking."[41] In one sense these people were tourists, advocating policies from outside the struggle. It is to be expected that the necessity for revolution as opposed to 'mere palliatives' would be stressed, as too would the necessity for the preparative general strike. This 'outsideness' is stressed by a note which appeared in the *Commonweal* in reply to inquiries and which said that of course members of the Socialist League could take part in strikes, but they should not become so involved in such struggles as to forget their revolutionary propaganda.

It is worth examining a little more closely the message that was being preached. John Turner, in a debate with Herbert Burrows of the S.D.F. on 'Anarchist Communism versus Social Democracy', outlined something of the anarchist approach. Criticising the social democrats for advocating palliatives and at the same time "continuously writing and speaking to the effect that these palliatives, if put into operation tomorrow would be of little use ...," he goes on to say:

> We Anarchists have a line to work upon, to teach the people self-reliance, to urge them to take part in non-political movements directly started by themselves for themselves. ... Look at the strike now in progress. When the Anarchists have said that as soon as the people learn to rely upon themselves they will act for themselves without waiting

for parliament, it has been disregarded. But their words have come true. We have an example of this truth in London now. The strike has gone upon the old Trade Union lines but had it started on the lines of expropriation, who knows how rapidly it might have spread. We teach the people to place their faith in themselves, we go on the lines of self-help. We teach them to form their own committees of management, to repudiate their masters, to despise the laws of the country — these are the lines which we Anarchists intend to work along. Let them, if they will, commence by claiming the right to elect their own foremen. This very day I have suggested to the men on strike that the trade unions should take over the work rather than the contractors. They might follow this up until they gradually get control of the whole concern, and they would find the capitalists as unnecessary as monarchs have been found to be.[42]

But if the anarchist speakers were tourists as far as the dock strike itself was concerned, they were increasingly speaking as participants in other industrial struggles. The passing of the crisis in the dock strike by no means stopped the grumbling labour war. Though the ending of the dock strike took away a central focus of activity, disputes, both small and large, continued to flare up throughout 1889 and 1890. The successes of the Gasworkers Union and the Dockers Union inspired imitation. The organisation nearest to the dock workers was that of the carmen (cart drivers). Many of them had struck during the dock strike in sympathy — without assistance from the strike fund, be it noted. As a result many of them were sacked. This provided the impetus to form a Carman's Union and *Commonweal* reported that "now they have their own organisation and are winning all along the line."[43] Active in this union was Ted Leggatt, an anarchist member of the St George's in the East branch of the League who had been battered, arrested and jailed on Bloody Sunday. He was later to become the union's full-time organiser. Mowbray was active in the tailors' strikes both in the East and West End. He was a lay official of the West End Society himself and helped the sweated Jewish workers in the East End through his friends in the Berner Street club. Kitz and Reynolds of the Merton branch, were active in organising carmen, labourers and laundry women into a small Surrey Labourers Union. A handbill issued in October 1889 advertised its intentions "to obtain shorter hours and advance the wages of the working men of Surrey" and to form a branch in Croydon in addition to those already formed at Mitcham, Streatham and Merton.[44] In West London, Tochatti and Lyne of the Fulham branch, together with Jack Williams of the S.D.F., were active organisers and 'outside agitators' during a strike at Thornycroft's factory. Also active in West London was a Shop Assistants Union formed by Turner and others.

Nobly active in this union was Edith Lupton who would take a job, sign up the assistants working there, resign and take a job somewhere else. (She remained active in the union until late in 1890 when she was organising a laundry women's co-op.) Samuels was in Leeds organising tailoring and slipper workers. These are the more prominent examples, it is to be expected that every trades union member of the League would take part in disputes in his trade.

So the League anarchists and the Freedom Group activists were by no means outside the labour organisation of the time and took an active part in every phase of its development. There was no doubt that their unwillingness to commit themselves totally to trades union work made them less prominent than the social democrats — without going further into the area of invidious personal comparisons. Their reservations about trades union activities were expressed in phrases which indicated that the anarchists did not think them revolutionary enough, even though they might be "palliatives in the right direction," as *Freedom* put it. This lack of revolutionary fire was often blamed on the personal cowardice of the leaders. As it rapidly became apparent that these leaders saw the next step in terms of electoral activity, the accusations changed to those of personal ambition. Yet behind the personal accusations lay hardly grasped worries of a more general kind. There seemed to be a connection between over-prominent leaders, electoral proclivities, the denial of revolutionary aims and increasingly exclusive attitudes within the new trades unions themselves. Some of these factors could be fitted into a general anti-election critique, but there were obviously loose ends which did not fit so well.

Where the question of elections was concerned the pronunciations were clear and forthright. The anti-parliamentary socialists of the League had always said socialism and elections did not mix. With other matters objections were made piecemeal. When John Burns started denouncing the "dead-beats and riff-raff" who hung round the docks waiting for odd hours of casual work, the *Commonweal* could only put its objections in negative form: "Emphatically, Revolutionary Socialism does not mean the carving out of a new close order of labour, which will kick those already down."[45] Gradually there began to creep into the anarchist press through 1890 the beginnings of criticisms of the new union leaderships as a social phenomenon rather than as a collection of cowardly or ambitious men. The notes of the *Commonweal* in December 1890 are interesting here. Tom Mann and the other dockers' officials are described as 'bureaucrats' who are keeping an exclusive grip on decision-making in the union, "it seems that these superior persons have a 'plan' which they will not allow more impetuous — not to say energetic — warriors to interfere with." And simultaneously these officials were blaming some branches for their apathy. There was discontent in the rank and file and Mann had attended a stormy meeting at which strong complaints were made that union officials were aloof and difficult to contact. These are strangely modern complaints. It is no way claimed however that such criticisms were the core of the anarchist misgivings about the new unions.

In any case the main concern of the anarchists was to find answers to the more pressing social situation, and their criticisms tended to be a spin-off from consideration of the practical problems facing the working-class movement. By the summer of 1890 all the high promise of the previous year seemed to have become dissipated. The new unions were now much more on the defensive. Over the winter of 1889–1890 the Gasworkers Union had fought and lost two strikes, one at the South Metropolitan Gas Company and another at a large rubber factory in West Ham. Similarly the Dockers Union had lost a five-months' strike at Hays Wharf which ended in May 1890. Attempts to organise the postmen failed after a disastrous stoppage. Outside the capital, dockers were defeated at Southampton. Other organisational attempts were bitterly fought and often defeated. To shrink back in the face of this onslaught seemed to the anarchists to be a grave mistake. Their concern was given greater point in July 1890, for they were already noting the early-warning signs of a new depression on the way.

Whatever had to be done had to be done quickly before the masses were again starved into submission. The May Day demonstrations had shown them the less adventurous direction the new unions were taking. Out of two chaotic international socialist conferences in Paris in late 1889, one clear proposal had emerged. This was that in pursuit of the eight-hour day and in memory of the Chicago Martyrs an international one-day general strike would be declared on 1st May. In England the Socialist League and Jack Williams's 'Federation of Trades and Industries' (composed of a number of small new unions) were the only organisations to declare for a strike on 1st May 1890. The rest of the socialist bodies and the larger new unions held a march on the following Sunday, 4th May. The difference in the way these two demonstrations were treated was striking. The Sunday demonstration received every assistance from the police. The smaller 1st May marches (10,000 as opposed to 100,000) were considerably harassed. An East End contingent was attacked in Aldgate by the police, a French contingent from Soho was ambushed in St Martin's Lane and women strikers from an envelope factory assembling at Clerkenwell Green for the march were similarly attacked. It seemed to the anarchists that the movement was being split into respectable and dangerous socialists, and respectable socialists would never make a revolution.

To the anarchists it seemed imperative that a new initiative should be taken to bring the workers back to the pitch of excitement and the sense of possibility of the summer of 1889. To this end two small conferences, one of anti-parliamentary socialists in March and another of "London revolutionists" in June, pledged themselves to propagandise for an international general strike and a universal rent strike. There were further discussions on the action to be taken "in the event of a crisis." At first the discussions represented something of a post-mortem on the 1889 dock strike, which was now seen as something of a lost chance. The English anarchists were later described as a small group of "fanatical enthusiasts ... who spend their time mainly in deploring the lost opportunity of the Dock Strike ..."[46] The hopes that such a crisis might present itself again were greatly raised by the course taken by the stormy and successful Leeds gas strike, which culminated with a massive riot on 2nd July. The events were described as follows by a participant:

...the City Gas Committee demanded that their employees should engage themselves for four months at a time, having no power to strike within that period and that the stokers eight-hour day should be increased. The men refused the terms and were locked out.

Blacklegs were imported and fierce fighting took place between the townspeople and the military who guarded the newcomers. The gas gave out and for five nights Leeds was in complete darkness.

Hundreds more police and a regiment of cavalry were sent for.

The cavalry tried to convey fresh blacklegs through the town, but was trapped under a railway bridge which was crawling with furious men and women. One mob faced the soldiers ahead, another poured down on their behind; and meantime the townsmen on the bridge literally pulled it to bits with their bare hands and hurled down tons of brickwork, stones and rubble on the helmeted soldiers and their struggling horses.

Slowly the defenders were forced off the ruined bridge; bitterly the struggle went on in the streets below till nightfall and fog blotted it out. Women flung themselves against the flattened sabres, children stood on the outskirts of the whirling crowd and flung stones into it at every gleam of a red jacket.[47]

It was thus with new hope in the hearts of the participants that a large Revolutionary Conference was held at the Autonomie Club on 3rd August. This was called, as the others had been, to consider "United International Action" by revolutionaries "in the event of a European crisis" and to determine "the best means of propaganda." Present were many of the foreign clubs and groups, some English anarchist-communists and eleven branch delegates of the Socialist League. The account of the conference reveals it to have been unable to come to any organisational conclusions; yet there was a consistency in the contributions that made it clear that a generalising of particular struggles should be encouraged to "light a fire that would end the whole damn thing" as Charles put it. Mowbray felt that "In the event of a crisis at home the first thing to do was to fire the slums and move the people into the West End mansions." Kent said that a coal strike was near: "Leaders would be required to prevent people acting all together in mobs and to utilise them individually. We wanted to know where the Gatling guns and other instruments of destruction were kept so that we might find them when wanted. So we wanted to know where the storehouses of food and clothing were that we might take them." The organisational problem was most clearly faced (if left unresolved) by Malatesta:

...the problem of the best means of assuring combined international action had been often discussed. The authoritarian solution was to have committees everywhere. The committees were always too late or ill-informed, and consequently the movement was paralysed. Another system was to renounce all system. The results of this course were no better. By all means trust to individual initiative, but let every individual have a clear idea of what he should do, without necessity for any kind of word of command. To establish an initiative of this kind the individual must know the strength behind him. As a rule men were not heroes and they wanted to be assured that if they did some great thing they would have the sympathy of their comrades. For practical purposes, too, we should distinguish future plans from present action. ... Let us urge the people to seize the property and go and dwell in the mansions of the rich; do not let us paralyse our efforts by discussion as to the future. Some organisation was desirable. There was an authoritarian system which encouraged spies and accustomed the people to the system of delegation; but there was also a system of organisation which was spontaneous and Anarchist. A party which did not believe in organisation would do nothing; a party which believed in organisation only would soon join the Social Democrats or the politicians. In all things we went from one exaggeration to another before finding the mean. It was so in discussing the problem of how to make the Revolution. At one time Anarchists had abandoned trade-unions and strikes and thought of nothing but making the Revolution by force. Then we found the bourgeois too strong for us on this ground, and after the great Dock Strike we began to fancy that the General Strike would do everything. A strike however was not the Revolution but only an occasion to make it. The General Strike would be good if we were ready to make use of it at once by immediate military action whether by barricades or otherwise.[48]

Malatesta was a 'professional' from a country with a revolutionary tradition. He had his own ideas about action in a revolution. But making a revolution happen was still a problem neither he nor anyone else had solved. It was not surprising that the English delegates could make but a small contribution to an answer. As far as the discussion on the best methods of propaganda was concerned a number of suggestions were made. From the Socialist League came their suggestions for an advocacy of the general strike and the total rent strike. There was also a fair amount of reference to 'individual initiative'. Not to put too fine a point on it, this was a barely veiled reference to propaganda by deed, particularly through dynamite. This was still an underground matter at this point, but it was steadily coming to the forefront and was to contribute to the deepening crisis in the Socialist League.

For while the anarchists were looking for a means to make a speedy revolution, the 'educators' who were their fellow members were looking on with deepening unease. On the surface the Socialist League had survived moderately well into 1890. It had twenty-two branches (nine in London) and manned nineteen speaking pitches a week in London. The *Commonweal* sales were going up a little. Yet in real terms the organisation was static at a time when the S.D.F., for example, had doubled its membership between 1889 and 1890. Every new trade agitation took people away from the organisation, and the League could not cash in on the new unionism like the S.D.F. because of their position of (necessarily) critical support. The anarchists in the League wanted a revolution but were unclear about how to achieve it on the level of immediate action. The S.D.F., on the other hand, were quite prepared to use revolutionary rhetoric about eventual aims but had an immediate 'practical' means to offer their members, namely elections. The anarchists might be correct in their call for a general strike as a solution for the difficulties the labour movement found itself in, but they did not have the means at that point to convince the mass of workers that it was a real possibility. Meanwhile their cult of immediate revolution was causing opposition within the League itself. Morris was writing in

April 1890: "Outside the Hammersmith Branch the active(?) members in London mostly consider themselves Anarchists but don't know anything about Socialism and go ranting revolution in the streets, which is about as likely to happen as the conversion of Englishmen from stupidity to quick-wittedness. ... Now I must do notes for *C'weal.* I don't like the job as I have a new book which amuses me vastly."[49]

The anarchist influence was undoubtedly growing fast in the League.

Out of the Freedom Group discussions at the Socialist League Hall a number of activists had been recruited to it. The paper had remained more or less Charlotte Wilson's preserve, however, until she fell ill in early 1889. As a consequence it was announced in March that some of the new recruits had formed "a committee of workmen ... to manage the publication and sale of the paper." (One of them, James Blackwell, had been manager of the S.D.F. paper *Justice.*) The new group proved a distinct improvement and by August a column devoted to accounts of the 'Propaganda' had been started to cover the increasing activity. At first the reports were mainly of debates and discussions, particularly with S.D.F. members. (One report from Manchester, however, gave accounts of meetings where "Anarchy pure and simple" was being preached.) But by the end of 1889 it was becoming clear that anarchism was a matter for assertion rather than debate. Kropotkin began what was to be a heavy schedule of talks throughout the country in 1890. In addition to the centrifugal force of trade disputes, the making of specifically anarchist propaganda began to attract away members of the Socialist League. Samuels, Mainwaring, Cores, Mowbray, Davis and others are all to be found as anarchist propagandists in late 1889 and 1890. In April 1890 it was reported from Manchester that the Socialist Leaguers there "like those of Norwich have largely adopted Anarchism as their political ideal." By July there were two groups of anarchist-communists in London. One, in St Pancras, was mainly composed of Freedom Group activists. The other, the East London Group, was basically some members of the Clerkenwell branch of the Socialist League wearing different hats. The group had taken over the branch propaganda sheet, the *Labour Leaf,* which now appeared as the *Anarchist Labour Leaf* and was used for free distribution at public meetings. And the tone of the anarchist propaganda was getting sharper.

By July Morris was writing to Nicoll to protest over a piece which had appeared in the *Commonweal*, sent from Samuels in Leeds describing the gas strike riots. After describing the hail of missiles "on to the horse and foot soldiers, police, scabs, mayor and magistrates" Samuels continued: "The consternation and confusion baffles description; and if the people had only the knowledge (they had the pluck) the whole cursed lot would have been wiped out. As the horses and men picked themselves up, it was seen that many were bruised and bleeding but, alas! no corpses to be seen.

The party on the bridge got off without trouble or hurt."[50] Morris wrote to Nicoll: "I think you are going too far — at any rate further than I can follow you. You really must put a curb on Samuels's blatant folly or you will force me to withdraw all support. ... Please understand that this is meant to be quite private; and do your best not to drive me off. For I assure you it would be the greatest grief to me if I had to dissociate myself from men who have been my friends so long."[51] (Morris had by this time given up the editorship of the *Commonweal* to Nicoll.) The tone of the Revolutionary Conference in August cannot have helped things much and an open breach was threatened in October. The dispute concerned the first part of an article on 'Revolutionary Warfare' by Nicoll.

This did little more than repeat Nicoll's earlier support for a general strike and a No Rent campaign, though the language and title used were stronger. Kitz says, "The publication of a second instalment of it was made a test case by the Hammersmith Branch, and as he refused to withdraw it, they severed their connection with the League."[52] The dispute over Nicoll's article more or less coincided with the meetings to commemorate Chicago and Bloody Sunday in early November. At a meeting at the Kay Street Radical club on 11th November it was evident that little sympathy existed between Morris and the other Socialist League speakers. Samuels said: "We socialists ought to feel very sad that night and try if we could not find some means to avenge our friends' deaths. He did not advocate force but sooner or later force might have to be resorted to if we were attacked ..." Burnie talked of paying back the debt of Trafalgar Square "with compound interest." Kitz said that the worker's life was shortened by what he suffered. "Why then should he fear bloodshed, if bloodshed were to come?"

Morris in his speech spoke directly to these remarks: "The essence of the Revolution was the intense desire and settled intention of the people to be free ... by the realisation of equality of condition. If that feeling once grew in people's hearts it could not be put down. Something had been said about revenge, but the only real revenge we could possibly have was by our own efforts bringing ourselves to happiness. Only unhappy people thought of revenge: when we were happy we should forget it."[53] During his speech Samuels said that, with others, he had intended to "polish off" the judge in the trial of John Bingham of Sheffield if Bingham was found guilty. (Bingham had been charged with incitement to kill blacklegs in a speech in 1889.) Nicoll later asserted that these remarks were responsible for Morris's final decision to leave the League. Morris was only to refer in his letters to "Nicoll's folly," but the question remains open. What is certain is that when Morris walked out of the hall that night he was walking out of the Socialist League.

He went back to Hammersmith and wrote the article he described as his farewell — it is said on the same night. This was entitled 'Where are we now?' and appeared in the issue of the *Commonweal* following the meeting. It was written without bitterness, and in it Morris emerges as the more remarkable a man in his objective treatment of what he obviously felt to be a defeat. It does not diminish his humanity to add that he was better able to bear this defeat since he no longer believed in imminent social revolution. In his article he reviewed the obvious advance of socialist ideas and underlined his belief that socialism was ultimately inevitable. The major questions, he felt, were now questions of method. Morris's own preference was to "put forward the simple principles of Socialism regardless of the policy of the passing hour." The danger he saw was that socialists would seize on "the methods of impatience":

There are two tendencies in this matter of methods: on the one hand is our old acquaintance palliation, elevated now into vastly greater importance than it used to have, because of the growing discontent, and the obvious advance of Socialism; on the other is the method of partial, necessarily futile, inconsequent revolt, or riot rather, against the authorities, who are our absolute masters and can easy put it down.

   With both these methods I disagree; and that the more because the
palliatives have to be clamoured for and the riots carried out by men
who do not know what Socialism is, and have no idea what their next
step is to be, if contrary to all calculation they should happen to be
successful. Therefore our masters would be our masters still because
there would be nothing to take their place. *We are not ready for such
a change as that!* The authorities might be a little shaken perhaps, a
little more inclined to yield something to the clamours of their slaves,
but there would be slaves still, *as all men must be who are not prepared
to manage their own business themselves.* Nay, as to the partial violent
means, I believe that the occurrence of those would not shake the
authorities at all, but would strengthen them rather, because they
would draw to them the timid of all classes, i.e. all men but a very few.[54]

While he had made out a strong case against the policy of riot he could
not (and did not) expect the anarchists to accept it. The reasons are clear
enough. For them, Morris's position implied doing nothing and doing
nothing implied defeat. At the back of the anarchist rejection of Morris's
'defeatism' was a feeling, never fully articulated, that people learned their
power — and what to do with it — through riotous action. The expected
progression of events was seen by Nicoll as follows: "Individual assaults
on the system will lead to riots, riots to revolts, revolts to insurrection,
insurrection to revolution."[55] This was putting it at its most hopeful and
implied a change of consciousness as the scale of events grew greater. But
at the very least the anarchists were asserting the immediate material
advantage to the working class of 'palliatives by riot' and urging the use
of new weapons to resist the most immediate forms of repression. There
were two replies to Morris's last article, from John Creaghe and Charles
Mowbray. Creaghe said, "Every man should take what he requires of the
wealth around him, using violence wherever necessary and when dragged
before his enemies he should tell them plainly that he has done what
he knows to be right and what he is proud of having done. His example
will soon find imitators ..." Mowbray wrote the first piece ever to openly
advocate dynamite in the *Commonweal*: "I feel confident that a few
determined men ... who are prepared to do or die in the attempt could

paralyse the forces of our masters providing they were acquainted with the power which nineteenth century science has placed within their reach."[56] The tone of these replies shows that Morris was quite right when he wrote after his article had been published: "It was and it was meant to be, directly opposed to anything the anarchist side would want to say or do. If I had remained in the League after that I must have attacked them persistently. And why should I? I shouldn't have converted them."[57]

Morris's presence in the League had, however, kept the more violent incitements out of the *Commonweal* — his letter to Nicoll over Samuels had a real effect. In addition his money had enabled the paper and organisation to function relatively smoothly. (He had been spending in the region of £500 per year on the League.) When Morris left the League his moderating influence and his money went with him. But perhaps more importantly the organisation lost its enormous prestige as Morris's own. These losses threw everything into turmoil. The morale of even the firmly anarchist members was severely shaken, and many of them seem to have assumed that the end of the League was nigh. From December 1890 onwards the *Commonweal* was temporary issued monthly instead of weekly. The League moved into much less salubrious quarters at 273 Hackney Road. A circular from the Hammersmith branch (now renamed the Hammersmith Socialist Society) explaining the reasons for their secession seems to have isolated the *Commonweal* from the provincial branches that had no strong anarchist influence. By December 1890 the branches of the League had shrunk from nine to two (North Kensington and North London) if we except the group round the *Commonweal*. Matters were not helped by rumours that the League and the *Commonweal* were finished, rumours put about by "ink-slingers" who had left the League earlier when it passed "the drawing-room and aesthetic stage of the Socialist movement," in Kitz's words. All this inevitably put strains on the small numbers left to carry on the work. Kitz and Mowbray fell out after some dispute, and Kitz left in March 1890 just as things seemed to be getting better. It is more than likely that the dispute had something to do with Mowbray's inclinations towards the power of nineteenth-century science. In April 1890 Kitz had written: "Some of the younger and hotter amongst us, disheartened at what appears to be a hopeless task … either give up in despair or dream of more forceful methods of agitation. … As well prepared and willing as any to make reprisals should there be a determined effort on the part of the 'haves' to suppress the murmurings of the 'have nots' ... I still contend that in agitation and education ... and in preaching the gospel of discontent lays our chief chance of success."[58] The loss of Kitz was serious, as Nicoll was forced to admit in the *Commonweal*: "The defection of the late General Secretary caused much confusion and loss, but every effort has been made."[59]

The anarchist section of the League in London (now renamed the London Socialist League) only just survived these ructions. That it survived at all was due to the efforts of Nicoll and Mowbray to keep the *Commonweal* going. Nicoll wrote later: "The paper had been carried on after Morris had left us by the scanty pence of workmen who often lacked food. It was edited by a man who in the few hours he had left from the *Commonweal*, for there was no money for salary for the editor, barely enough for the compositors, had to pick up a living from stray journalism."[60] (Nicoll had exhausted a small legacy.) In April 1891 the London Socialist League was in a bad shape, with an estimated membership of no more than 120. Only six speaking pitches were being kept open. From this point, however, having overcome its most immediate internal and material difficulties, the organisation had more time for agitation and began to expand. From 2nd May the *Commonweal* again came out weekly, though only in an edition of four pages. Nicoll came under some pressure to formally declare the paper anarchist, pressure he resisted for some time. From his point of view, giving anti-parliamentary revolutionary socialism a specifically anarchist brand name seemed to unnecessarily restrict the paper's readership. Nevertheless from the first new weekly edition of the *Commonweal* in May 1891, the subtitle described it as 'A Revolutionary Journal of Anarchist Communism'.

In one sense the anarchists had been ahead of their time in 1890 when they urged more dynamic action on the working class and made carping criticisms of the 'new' unionism. By 1891 it was clear that the boom was over. In the winter of 1890 to 1891 there had been a financial crisis in the City and Barings Bank nearly failed. Trade was slack, unemployment was rising, the incidence of blacklegging (organised or otherwise) was increasing and the new unions were very much on the defensive. Audiences could now be found who responded to more revolutionary sentiments. A Christian socialist paper was clearly worried at the new trend: "Violence has been openly advocated by the more extreme journals, and at meetings of angry workmen revolutionary speeches have been hailed with delight, while more moderate and more reasonable speakers have been listened to with but scant patience. Such sentiments as 'putting a little more devil into the strike'; 'don't let all the corpses be on one side'; and vague threats of 'fanning the class war into a blaze which shall fire the world' are heartily echoed by thousands of excited workers in different parts of London and throughout the provinces."[61] By no means, however, had this new bitterness become focused by the anarchists. The 1st May demonstration in 1891 was called by the anarchists alone and only mustered some 700–800 people in Hyde Park in the daytime. An evening meeting fared somewhat better. When the speakers arrived at Mile End Waste they found a very large body of police, both foot and mounted, waiting to "prevent any disturbance." The police did not attempt to break up the meeting but their presence attracted large crowds to hear speeches by Cantwell, Nicoll, Arnold, Mainwaring, Yanovsky and Mowbray. As if to underline the point made by the Christian socialist paper, the *Commonweal* reported that the audience, mainly composed of dock and riverside workers, responded most enthusiastically to "the most revolutionary sentiments." Judging by the *Commonweal* the action urged on the people was the strike conducted in the Leeds style and riotous looting as a method of feeding the unemployed.

As 1891 progressed a number of agitations were conducted by the League anarchists which showed some real life. A fund was set up to finance propaganda in the army. This seems to have initially involved Charles Mowbray's son, who was sentenced to a prison term and discharge from the army for these activities. Mowbray and Charles then took up the work, visiting Colchester, Rochester and Chatham. At Colchester 500 special (?) numbers of the *Commonweal* and 2,000 leaflets were distributed in the barracks. At Chatham 1,000 copies of the *Commonweal* containing an 'Address to the Army' were handed out. The 'Address ...' urged the soldiers to remember their working-class origins and to refuse to fire on the people if they were ordered to do so. The agitation seems to have been met with some success. At the very least it was in tune with the dissatisfaction that existed in the army at that time — semi-mutinies were being reported in some Guards regiments. A further agitation was conducted around the question of rent. A 'No Rent League' was founded, and their meetings in the Boundary Street slum were excitedly attended by the residents. The choice of Boundary Street was shrewd. The new London County Council had paid the owners of this notorious rookery a generous compensation after acquiring it. The gist of the anarchist propaganda was that it was the residents who needed compensating. This, it seemed, could be most easily achieved by their refusal to pay rent. This campaign, too, met with some success. As a result of people withholding rent, bailiffs were called in and this led in turn to the formation of an Anti-Broker Brigade to protect people from their depredations.

The No Rent agitation was enthusiastically taken up in Sheffield by Dr John Creaghe and others. Creaghe, an incredible man who had spent much of his life in Argentina, practised what he preached. When bailiffs attempted to distrain goods he drove them out with a poker. This appears to have led to the penning of a little ditty which was put on No Rent propaganda from that point on. It ran:

> Hurrah! for the kettle, the club and the poker
> Good medicine always for landlord and broker;
> Surely 'tis better to find yourself clobber
> Before paying rent to a rascally robber[62]

The Sheffield anarchists were noticeably active at this point. They were unusual for their time in that instead of remaining a faction within a Socialist Society or Socialist League branch where one existed, they struck out on their own and formed an anarchist group early in 1891. They unfurled their banner at the Monolith, the regular speaking pitch, on May Day with the motto 'No God, No Master' written on it. They regularly held meetings there and in other parts of the town and established a club. They were popular in the working-class districts, Creaghe's activity with the poker being particularly well received. Among the middle class, however, there was great hostility and in September *Commonweal* reported that "well dressed rowdys" had attacked the club and broken windows by throwing pennies. Taking the money as payment the anarchists had replied by running out and scattering revolutionary literature among the attackers. The Sheffield group also produced several issues of a local paper, the *Sheffield Anarchist*, which had a short and outrageous career in 1891. And Sheffield was not the only provincial town where anarchists were beginning to establish themselves: the Leeds anarchists were, it was alleged, responsible for riots in Bradford during a big strike at Listers Mill through their insistence on holding strike meetings which had been banned by the police.

But these beginnings of an activist anarchism adapted to English conditions were to be thrown into greater prominence by events early in 1892. In February 1891 a casual note had appeared in the *Commonweal*: "Our comrade Mendelsohn has been warning the British public that the Russian police have been good enough to transfer a portion of their attention from Paris to London, and that we may therefore expect to hear of sham dynamite plots here ..." The warning, it turned out, was not regarded seriously enough.

## Chapter 6
# THE WALSALL ANARCHISTS

The arrest, trial and sentencing of the Walsall anarchists in 1892 deserve more attention than they have received from the historians of the left in Britain. From the point of view of the more liberal, there was a disconcertingly straightforward use of agents provocateur by the police.

From the point of view of historians of the growth of institutions connected with the working-class movement, the existence of options for propaganda by deed and the reasons for the rejection of these options should have given more cause for thought. In any case, the circumstances were unusual enough for notice. As ex-Detective Sergeant McIntyre was to say, "Quite a sensation was caused at the time by the appearance of this new class of revolutionist. It is safe to say that no conspiracy of quite the same nature had been known in England during this century."[1]

On 6th January 1892 Joe Deakin, an anarchist living in his native town of Walsall, was arrested in Tottenham Court Road on his way to the Autonomie Club. He was remanded in custody at Marlborough Street Court the following day on a charge of manufacturing bombs. Immediately after the court appearance Inspector Melville went to Walsall by train and on the evening of the same day Victor Cailes, a Frenchman, and Fred Charles were arrested at the Socialist Club in Goodall Street, Walsall. Later William Ditchfield and John Westley were arrested in Walsall and Jean Battola, an Italian, was arrested in London. Deakin and Battola were transported up to Walsall to stand trial. They were all jointly charged with what amounted to manufacturing bombs. At their first appearance at the Walsall police court, Mr Young, prosecuting, asked for a week's remand on the grounds that "The authorities both in Walsall and London had received very important information with reference to what he might call a widespread conspiracy throughout the country."[2]

The evidence brought against the accused men was as follows: In Charles's possession was found a sketch of a bomb with instructions in

French on how to make it, a model of a bolt allegedly to fit the top of the bomb and a manifesto in French in Cailes's handwriting entitled *The Means of Emancipation,* which said in part, "Let us occupy ourselves with chemistry, and let us manufacture promptly bombs, dynamite and other explosive matters much more efficacious than guns and barricades to bring about the destruction of the actual state of things, and above all, to spare the precious blood of our comrades. Courage, companions! Long Live Anarchy! Walsall, 1 September 1891." In Cailes's possession was found a length of fuse and a large number of anarchist publications in French, including issue number 7 of *L'Internationale,* which gave instructions on making bombs and how to use them for the destruction of public buildings. At Ditchfield's workshop "a plaster cast of a bomb similar to the sketch produced" was found and at his home a bolt "for the head of one of the missiles." In the basement of the Socialist Club there was "a quantity of clay mixed with hair, evidently for moulding purposes." On the "sworn information of the Chief Constable that all the persons had in their possession or under their control explosives under such circumstances as to lead to the conclusion that such substances were not in their possession or under their control for a lawful purpose" the magistrate — in this case the Mayor of Walsall — remanded *all* the men in custody. This was done even though no evidence at all had been brought against Battola, Westley or Deakin; and in the case of the other men, whatever suspicions might have been aroused by what was found in their possession no explosives had been produced at all, and it was unlawful possession of explosives 'with intent' that lay at the centre of the charge.

As it stood, this evidence could not have faced an energetic defence in court. It was fortunate for the police, therefore, that at the next hearing, on 21st January, a most incriminating set of confessions by Deakin were produced. As the *Times* put it:

> On the 15th inst. Deakin told witness [Chief Constable Taylor] that he should like to tell all, as he had come to the conclusion that Charles was a police spy. The following day he handed in a statement, in which he wrote that the parcel of chloroform found in his possession when he was arrested in London was given to him by Cailes to be given to an

acquaintance of Cailes. This was the man charged at the Court under the name of Battola. As for the castings and models, Ditchfield and Charles arranged to get them for Cailes.

Deakin added that he understood the things were for use abroad. A second statement made by Deakin ... was of a great length and of a sensational character. It showed that in the summer of last year [i.e. 1891] Charles went to the Walsall Socialist Club, of which Deakin was the secretary. As he was known to the members of the club through the socialist papers and also slightly known to Deakin who had met him in July 1889, in Paris,[3] he was permitted to have the run of the club. He mentioned to Deakin and to other members that a London comrade named Coulon had written to him. It was decided to have the man over. This was during the months of June and July.

A few weeks later Charles met two Frenchmen at the station and Deakin was introduced to them. One of these men was Cailes, who stayed in Walsall, the other man returning to London. Cailes spoke very little English.

One night in October or early in November 1891, Cailes and Charles spoke to him about a letter written in French, which Cailes had received and which enclosed the sketch of a bomb produced in the police court. The letter was sent in the name of 'De Farney'[4] and Cailes not knowing the name wrote to Coulon, 19, Fitzroy Square, London, asking whether it was all right. He afterwards got an affirmative reply. Deakin understood that the bombs were wanted for use in Russia. They came to the conclusion they should want a pattern for the bomb to be cast from. One Sunday Cailes, Westley, Charles and Deakin met to make one. Then came the question of having it cast. Charles said he would pay the cost and it was agreed that they should call the bomb an electric cell. A letter was sent to Messrs. Bullows by Charles in the name of La Place. Subsequently a letter was received from London by Cailes saying that someone would fetch the things. The stranger who went down was the man Battola.

The reading of the statement caused some excitement in court.[5]

This was something of an understatement. Deakin was denounced as an informer and liar in the *Commonweal*. There was little else to do for what Deakin's statement did was to link up the accused and lay them open to charges of conspiracy. All the bits and pieces in their possession which separately meant very little now had a great collective significance and were admitted to have been for a common and violent purpose. Things now looked very bad indeed for the men. They were again remanded.

It is a little difficult to get at the truth of how this confession was obtained. Nicoll gives the story as Deakin told it later but it rings oddly. Ditchfield had been threatened and bullied by Melville and Taylor but without much information being obtained from him. He did not have much to tell. Deakin was then taken from his cell to the private room where Inspector Melville and Chief Constable Taylor started a conversation with him on socialism. Deakin was a simple enthusiast and he was soon worked up to a high pitch of excitement. In the dead of the night he was taken back to his cell and while there he heard what he thought was the sound of the voices of two of his companions, Charles and Ditchfield, confessing all about the plot to the officers. Under the impression that he was betrayed he made a full confession, which was just what the police wanted.[6] When Deakin found that Charles and Ditchfield had not made this confession "he declared to a friend that a trick must have been played upon him and that someone must have imitated the voices of his comrades." How much reliance one can put upon this story it is difficult to say. For myself, I think it more likely that Melville and Taylor told Deakin that Charles and Ditchfield had made full confessions, and even told him that Charles was employed by them. And as we shall see, they would be able to give all sorts of 'private' details of what had been going on which would seem to substantiate their story. It might only have been necessary to hint that Charles was a police spy, since this had already been rumoured in the movement — Nicoll alleged later that the rumour originated with members of the Freedom Group "who so persuaded Kropotkin of its truth that he said to Charles 'If you are not in the pay of the police you are doing their work.'"[7] Faced with this apparent betrayal Deakin then confessed since he does not seem to have been the stuff that martyrs are made of. Finding that he was alone in his confessions, 'hearing voices' would appear to be a way of saving face or a convenient resolution of the situation by his unconscious.

Deakin's confession, however, mentioned the name of one co-conspirator who had not been arrested — Coulon. Coulon's career linked the defendants together. Events were to show why a man so obviously compromised remained free and unpursued. Who was Auguste Coulon?

He had taken some part in the Dublin branch of the Socialist League and had some official correspondence with the League in 1886.[8] He "left that body and went to France where he formed some connection with the Possibilist Party. Thence he came into the movement in England, in January 1890. At this time ... he was living at Notting Hill and joined the North Kensington branch of the Socialist League. Here he posed as a very violent Anarchist. He occasionally visited the Hammersmith Branch of the Socialist League where he chiefly occupied himself by endeavouring to sell a little French book *L'Indicateur Anarchiste* containing instruction concerning the manufacture of bombs and dynamite."[9]

Coulon described himself as a professor of languages but had been "chronically out of work ever since he had been in England. He had largely been supported by the generosity of comrades in Hammersmith and North Kensington," says Nicoll, and as a consequence of these sources drying up he appeared at the Autonomie Club saying that he'd been expelled from the Hammersmith Socialist Society. In this he was appealing to and deepening the split in the Socialist League — there were, for example, raiding parties from the West End which disrupted meetings at Hammersmith. At the Autonomie his ability to speak several languages recommended him for the job of assistant to Louise Michel who could speak only French, in a school which was started for her by the foreign anarchists for the education of the children of the foreign socialists of north Soho, in the autumn of 1890. There was little money available but Coulon declared himself willing to sacrifice himself, his wife and children for the good of the cause. He made himself busy and soon had the entire business management of the school in his hands — he received all money and his name appeared as prominently in advertisements and circulars as that of Louise Michel herself. His connection with Louise Michel, naturally enough, made him appear a man to be trusted. A further indication of his apparent trustworthiness was the work he engaged in for the refugees from France after the stormy events around May Day in 1891. There had been riots and fights with the police.

"Nine people were killed by the police at Fourmies. At a riot at Clichy Levallois three men were wounded and arrested after a gun fight with the so-called 'forces of order'. The wounded men, all anarchists, were taken to Clichy police station and there brutally assaulted by the police and not even given facilities for bathing their wounds."[10] Two were eventually sentenced to long terms. (It was in revenge for their treatment that Ravachol was to set his bombs.) One of the refugees was the Walsall defendant Victor Cailes, who was wanted by the French police for incitement to "incendiarism, murder and pillage" after a riot in his native town of Nantes on May Day. Cailes was sent to Walsall through the contact Coulon had with Fred Charles, who by this time was living there.

Charles, "out of employment and in a desperate mood" in London, had gone first to Sheffield to find work.[11] In Sheffield he had helped Dr Creaghe start the *Sheffield Anarchist*. Creaghe wrote of that time:

> I cannot forget the time that Charles who was then out of work started with me the first number of the *Sheffield Anarchist*. He would do nothing for himself. If his chances of getting a £1000 depended on his keeping an appointment, I am certain he would not be there and I was astonished how actively and steadily he worked for the cause he loved. I cannot say how often I regretted it when he had to leave me, for we spent some happy hours in that anything but sweet smelling den which served us for a club and office at 47 West Bar Green, Sheffield. How we laughed as we scribbled and enjoyed in anticipation the horror and rage of the enemy.[12]

Whether because of this activity or for other reasons he did not manage to find a job. He then went to Walsall about July 1891, and was fixed up with work by local comrades. Charles was known to Deakin in a business capacity from 1888 when Deakin, then secretary of the Walsall Socialist League, had regularly written to Charles for copies of the *Commonweal*, pamphlets, etc.[13]

As far as the socialist movement in England was concerned the men arrested at Walsall were almost unknown except for Charles. Apart from being a known activist he had an incredible reputation for open-handed generosity. Practically all his earnings and possessions were given away to tramps or the unemployed. He had been known to take off his coat and pawn it in order to be able to give something to a fellow worker who was without money. Ted Leggatt told how he had seen Charles "take his best boots off his feet and the last half crown out of his pocket and give them to a man he had never seen before, who pleaded poverty to him at a meeting at the Berner Street club where William Morris was lecturing. Others can verify my statement."[14] Nicoll said of him, "I, who knew him well, have often thought that Charles, Atheist and Anarchist as he was had more of the spirit of Christ about him than those who talk so loudly of their Christianity."[15] Coulon had helped Charles when he had been hard up — Charles had "like many other fine natures, suffered much from the ingratitude of those he had befriended and was therefore charmed with Coulon's 'generosity'. This is a man after my own heart he thought, and after he left London for the North, he still kept up a correspondence with Coulon."[16] Through this correspondence Cailes arrived in Walsall.

Charles and Cailes were accepted as members of the Socialist Club on 10th August 1891. The conspiracy might well have been started as a result of a conversation which took place on Saturday, 29th August, at the Autonomie Club. Deakin, returning from an international congress at Brussels, was in the bar "chatting to a group of Anarchists to whom he was known. Someone asked after Charles: 'Oh he's all right,' said Deakin, 'he's at work in an iron foundry.' 'Oh, he will do to make bombs for us,' cried Coulon, who was present." Two months later the letter signed 'Degnai' containing the sketch of the bomb was sent to Cailes at Walsall. Not knowing the name, Cailes, as we have seen, wrote to Coulon who replied that the letter was "all right." This was the letter which the police were to say was in Battola's handwriting. Cailes and Charles were connected through Coulon — and on closer inspection it was found that Coulon had not only underwritten Battola's reputation for the men in Walsall but was directly responsible for bringing him into the conspiracy. Battola lived next door to Coulon in Fitzroy Street and they were in constant communication. He did not speak English but did speak fluent French, as prison letters testify.[17] Battola did not know Cailes or Charles: the only connection conceivable between them is through Coulon. As Nicoll says:

Supposing Battola wrote the letter did he not do it at Coulon's suggestion. Battola an exile burning with hatred against the tyranny that had driven him from his native land, might be easily worked upon to assist Coulon in his nice little plot of manufacturing 'bombs for Russia' ... according to Deakin's confession, Coulon was writing to *hurry them up,* from 19 Fitzroy Street. In truth he kept up a vigorous correspondence with the Walsall people 'pressing' them to hurry on with the bombs. ... At last a letter arrived from Coulon informing the Walsall men that a man would call on Saturday, December 5th for some of the bombs which it was expected Bullows would have completed by this time. On December 2nd, the man arrived in the shape of Battola.

Coulon had been busy in other areas too. His command of several languages seemed to recommend him for the 'International Notes' section of the *Commonweal*. His style was chatty — and his basic subject was dynamite — e.g. "Our Austrian Comrades beat the record this time! Dynamite seems to grow as thick there as rotten potatoes in Ireland. Only last week, I mentioned two bomb explosions in Ruchenberg, and here again, we record another infernal and diabolical machine that has thrown terror and dismay into the mind of the capitalist class";[18] and "No voice speaks so loud as Dynamite and we are glad to see it getting into use all over the place."[19] Nicoll, as editor of the paper, says he was unwilling to interfere on what might appear to be ideological grounds but finally lost his patience with Coulon's notes when "he sent me in a paragraph celebrating the blowing up of a cow in Belgium as a great and good revolutionary act and as I would not publish it Coulon has never forgiven me."

In October 1891, Coulon was organising chemistry classes. "The class consisted of mere boys and one of them M — [20] was sent to Mowbray and Nicoll asking if they would join. They declined with thanks ... and the class was dropped." However M — was provided with a bottle of nitric acid and a bottle of glycerine and encouraged to start the production of home-made nitroglycerine. Luckily this exceedingly dangerous proceeding was prevented by the lad's father finding the materials and pouring them out onto a patch of ground. Another "enthusiast C — , medical student,[21] under the direction of the arch conspirator, translated Most's *Revolutionary*

*Warfare* this was to be privately printed and distributed to all the anarchist groups in the country ... this book contains simple directions concerning the manufacture of dynamite and bombs." So, all in all, Coulon had been a very active fellow. But among sections of the foreign anarchists Coulon had become the object of some suspicion. "He had become a petty tyrant, and there were even graver charges against him. The result had been his dismissal from the International School at the end of October. ... He moved into Fitzroy Square, taking a highly respectable dwelling for a man 'with no visible means of subsistence.'" At the Sunday meeting at the Autonomie Club on 10th January 1892 — the Sunday following the arrest of Deakin on the 6th and Cailes and Charles on the 7th — "Coulon was openly charged with betraying the Walsall men. 'You do no work; how do you get your living if you are not a police spy?' he was asked. He replied, 'I am a true Anarchist; I live by plunder.' The explanation was not considered satisfactory and he was expelled from the club." By this time, however, it was a little late.

The arrests of the Walsall men and the sudden accusations of Coulon burst upon the English anarchist scene as a complete surprise. Even in Walsall, the business of getting the bomb cases cast does not seem to have been known about outside those immediately involved. It seems unlikely that the members of the Walsall Club should have been so blithe about their treatment of the detectives who began to dog the footsteps of the 'prominent members' in early December. "They took the detectives for long walks into the country by the banks of the canal, where discussions were held as to the advisability of giving them a ducking. In fact they made the detectives' lives unbearable by dint of chaff, insult and ridicule. So the game went merrily on." Among the English movement bomb plots seemed not to be a major concern at the time of the Walsall arrests. Activity was concentrated in more traditional areas. One of the major concerns of the socialist world was the fight led by the S.D.F. at the World's End, Chelsea, for the right of free speech which had been going on since November 1891, resulting in many arrests. It was being taken up by assorted Liberal/Radical bandwagon jumpers. Among the London anarchists there was something of a skirmish going on connected with John Turner's United Shop Assistants Union. A shopkeeper in the Harrow Road, named Haile, who would not accede to the Union's demand that he close at the earlier time of 5pm on Thursdays, was picketed by members of the union together with some 'outside agitators'. In Turner's words, "the local excitement had grown week by week with the result that riots occurred, the shop was raided and the mounted police were called out."[22] Earlier on in the struggle, pickets had been charged with minor offences — Tochatti, for example, was arrested for causing a disturbance and fined in October.[23]

The union had paid the fines involved. As the struggle escalated, however, "a more serious view" was taken of the situation and three pickets, one of whom was David Nicoll, were arrested and prosecuted on a more serious conspiracy charge. Convicted, they were sent to prison for a month with the option of a fine. The hard-pressed union, almost bankrupted by the struggle, took three days to raise the money to get the men out of jail. Nicoll was in jail when Coulon was accused of being a police agent.

If anybody was thinking of examples of 'individual action' immediately before the Walsall case broke, they would probably be mostly concerned with the rather farcical action of John Evelyn Barlas (a poet whose collection of poems, *Phantasmagoria*, was published under the pen name of Evelyn Douglas). On 31st December 1891, a policeman first heard and then saw him discharging several shots from a revolver at the Houses of Parliament at about 9 o'clock in the morning. The policeman ran towards him. "Seeing witness [i.e. policeman] he [i.e. Barlas] handed him the revolver saying, 'I am an Anarchist and I intended shooting you but then I thought it is a pity to shoot an honest man. What I have done is to show my contempt for the House of Commons.' Magistrate, 'Was the prisoner sober?' Witness, 'Perfectly.'"[24]

The accusation against Coulon and his expulsion from the Autonomie Club was the subject of great debate. Nicoll was probably typical of the English movement:

> I was totally ignorant of the existence of the conspiracy (like everyone else connected with the *Commonweal*), I thought it extremely improbable that Coulon could know anything about it; therefore I reserved my opinion. Coulon remained in London, till the Thursday that Battola was arrested, professing all the time to be very much afraid of arrest. He disappeared directly after Battola was taken.

I still remained incredulous as to Coulon's part in the conspiracy till Deakin's confession was published. Then I saw at once who was the instigator and the betrayer of the plot.

Deakin's confession made it clear how deeply Coulon was involved in the conspiracy. Evidence that Coulon was a police agent was at first circumstantial — his various instigating activities combined with a surprising freedom from interference by the police. More solid evidence was to emerge. Nicoll, on his release from prison, started a defence fund and then became secretary of the defence committee for the prisoners. He says, "The friend of a wealthy French Anarchist had an interview on a matter of business with Coulon's brother, who has a shop in the neighbourhood of Old Street. They mentioned Coulon, and the brother, who was unaware that the gentleman knew anyone in the Anarchist movement, said, 'Yes, my brother is in the pay of the police. He tells me he has been in the employment of Melville for two years. But I did not think till now Melville was at Scotland Yard, I thought he was a private inquiry officer.'" This information came into Nicoll's hands and though the man was in no way willing to be publicly mixed up in the affair he was prepared to repeat his conversation with Coulon's brother to W.M. Thompson, the barrister hired by the defence committee.[25]

With this information and some letters written by Coulon to various people before his disappearance, Thompson cross-examined Inspector Melville at Walsall police court:

Inspector Melville said he had some experience of these cases. ... He had not been engaged in any cases abroad, but he had made inquiries abroad as to foreigners. ... Among the foreigners he had inquired about there was not one named Coulon. He knew a man of that name who was a well known Anarchist. He had often been in Coulon's company but not at Scotland Yard. To his knowledge, Coulon had never been there. He could not swear that he had never given Coulon anything to do for him but he did not remember having done so. He would not swear that he had not paid Coulon money, for he had paid lots of Anarchists money. Mr Thompson: 'Have you paid him any money?' Witness asked the Bench if he were to answer such a question and Mr Young, the prosecuting counsel, said that if these questions were designed merely to get the name of the informer they could not be put. Mr Thompson: 'My theory is this, that any suspicious element in the case is the work of this man Coulon who is an agent of the Police.' (Loud applause) The Mayor (who was on the Bench): 'If there is any more of this, we shall clear the court. We decide that on the ground of public duty, the question should not be put.'[26]

Inspector Melville's replies are more than a little shifty here and much the same could be said of his replies on the following Monday, 15th February, when Thompson offered him Coulon's address from one of his letters. It looked very bad indeed that the police should decline to accept information leading them to a man directly cited in the confession by Deakin as being a central figure in the conspiracy. But it is possible that W.M. Thompson made a great mistake in bringing up the question of police provocation in the police court. By the time the case came up at the Stafford Assizes the Inspector was warned, the prosecution was warned, and steps could (and were) taken to evade the question where it might actually have helped the defendants — in front of a jury. In a small and reactionary town the forces of law and order have a tendency to try and impress prestigious visitors from London. If that meant remanding prisoners in custody on no evidence except the belief of the chief constable that they were guilty, keeping them almost completely without bedding in the middle of winter and feeding them sufficient food 'only to keep body and soul together' as the chief constable put it — if this was what seemed required they were glad to do it. W.M. Thompson should have understood that the Mayor of Walsall would not know how to listen to allegations of malpractice against the celebrated Inspector Melville of Scotland Yard. And since he did not know how to listen he would not bother to try. The prisoners were committed for trial at Stafford Assizes and remanded in custody at Stafford Gaol. There, however, the conditions were somewhat better.

There was some measure of press hysteria over the case which particularly made hay with *The Means of Emancipation* and another text entitled *The Anarchist Feast at the Opera* that were found in Charles's and

Cailes's possession. The hysteria communicated itself to the police, who arrested a Swiss named Cavargna in nearby Handsworth on the grounds that he was a dangerous anarchist. He was nothing of the sort — he had invented some small explosive shells for exterminating rabbits in Australia and could produce correspondence with the patent office to explain why he had explosives in his possession. He spent forty-eight hours in jail, however, before the police rather reluctantly released him.

The scene was also enlivened by the activities of a most unattractive person named McCormack. A complete parasite, he thieved from comrades who helped him and, in fact, had followed the ever-generous Charles to Walsall.[27] There he had managed to disgrace himself completely as far as the Socialist Club was concerned. When the Walsall case broke he offered his services as informer to Chief Constable Taylor of Walsall, was accepted, installed in lodgings in the police station and paid two shillings a day. However, after some research into his background it was thought expedient to release him from this employment. McCormack then went to Birmingham and sold a story to the *Birmingham Daily Argus* entitled 'The Adventures of a Police Spy' which eventually appeared on 16th February. In the meantime McCormack got drunk on the proceeds and stood up and addressed a crowd in the streets of Birmingham on anarchy — whether for or against is not recorded. Arrested for being drunk and disorderly, he appeared in court the next day and much to the embarrassment of everybody said that he had been employed by Scotland Yard in "getting up evidence" against the Walsall prisoners and "had worked hard for the police as Inspector Melville of Scotland Yard could testify." He was given seven days. (He was not completely cast off by the police, however: some measure of protection was afforded him at various later appearances at Tower Hill, etc.)[28]

Meanwhile, the anarchists did what they could to defend their comrades and to point out the politics of the situation. George Cores, an ex-Socialist League anarchist, came to Walsall from Leicester to coordinate the local propaganda campaign. After the six men were committed for trial the first number of what was presented as a regular local weekly paper was published from the club at 18 Goodall Street on 27th February. It was in fact the issue of *Commonweal* of that date with its heading changed to read the *Walsall Anarchist*. It covered the use of police agents in the case and attempted to counter the frenzied anti-anarchist propaganda in the local press. It reprinted a letter sent by Cores to the *Birmingham Daily Argus* which gave a vigorous exposition of anarchist communism and also attempted to mend the damage done by *The Anarchist Feast at the Opera*, which had already received quite a lot of publicity in the local press. This latter piece of Grand Guignol was a detailed account of how to cause the maximum amount of carnage in an opera house by the simplest methods.

Comrades were to buy seats in the cheapest, highest gallery in the building and as opportunity presented itself — in an interval for example — the comrades were to cut the gas pipes which serviced the house lights sufficiently to allow large quantities of gas to float up to the ceiling as the performance proceeded. The comrades were then to push incendiary devices through slits in the seat covers into the stuffing. These would spontaneously combust after a period of time sufficient to allow the comrades to slip away. Then the gas would explode and great would be the destruction, the moaning and the gnashing of teeth.

This may seem horror-comic stuff to us now, but at the time it was used to great effect against the anarchists. (Furthermore, Most had given detailed instructions for delayed-action incendiary devices in his *Revolutionary War Science*.) *The Feast* "purported to be a translation from a French Anarchist Paper," wrote Cores.

It advocated the burning of theatres and went on to express the joy of the writer could he hear the frizzling of human bodies and taste the broiled flesh of the rich. This has been freely used to show what an awful class of people we Anarchists are. Well, I know with what horror and disgust I read the article referred to, and I have been gratified to find every Anarchist I have met of the same mind. More, from my knowledge of Anarchists, they would be among the very first to save life not to destroy it. And in a burning theatre it is the workers, their wives and children who suffer most from any panic. The rich have the best chance of escape. Human suffering brings no joy to the heart of an Anarchist. It is the existence of human suffering that makes him such a determined foe of all forms of oppression and misery. The paper I have alluded to (so French Anarchists tell us)[29] is published by an agent of the French Secret Police to discredit the Anarchist movement. It is not like any ordinary Anarchist organ — published by a known Anarchist society and distributed or broadcast, but secretly and sent only to prominent revolutionists.

But George Cores was swimming against the tide. The local socialist movement was dismayed and cowed by the arrests and the trial with all the attendant publicity. The club was closed and local reactionary forces were mobilised against them, though local meetings held for some weeks wore out this opposition by sheer bloody-minded nervous energy.

Matters were not helped by behind-the-scenes bickering over the finance and policy of the defence of the Walsall men. At the same time that Nicoll was asked by members of the Autonomie Club to set up a defence fund for Charles and Battola, Robert Bingham in Sheffield had approached Edward Carpenter to ask him to set up a fund for Charles. (Charles had spent some time in Sheffield, as we have seen, and Carpenter certainly met him, for he writes most affectionately about him in his memoirs.) Nicoll's fund was publicised through the columns of the *Commonweal*; Carpenter's through *Freedom*. Carpenter asked Nicoll to put his fund in with his. Nicoll and the Autonomie Club people flatly refused — Nicoll does not say why but we have already noticed the attitude of Nicoll to the Freedom Group. As 'middle-class faddists' they might not be relied upon to provide a hard enough defence. Carpenter, apparently was very angry at this refusal — or so Nicoll said. In fact, we have to rely rather heavily on Nicoll's account here.[30] He says that the solicitor friend of Carpenter's, H. Gore, whom Carpenter employed in the case, was indignant with W.M. Thompson for raising the question of police provocation in the police court. And it does not seem that it was for reasons of a better tactical use of the relevant evidence — the barrister (Willis) hired by Gore never referred to police provocation in his presentation of the defence case at Stafford Assizes.

Nicoll also says that Gore stopped some contributions reaching Nicoll's fund, so much did they disapprove of the "police provocation" line: "These respectable people seem as indignant as an old Tory reactionary at any attacks on Scotland Yard." The difficulties this conflict brought about — an unfocused and messy defence for the accused among other things —

did not compare, however, with the news from France, which created an atmosphere which would have severely tested the toughest defence.

The news from France was of bomb explosions. On 11th March a bomb exploded at the house of M. Benoit in the Boulevard Saint-Germain, Paris. No one was seriously hurt but there was considerable damage done. Benoit had been the presiding judge at the trial of the two anarchists condemned to jail sentences after the fighting at Clichy Levallois on 1st May 1891. On 18th March a bomb exploded at the Lobau barracks. On 27th March there was an explosion in the Rue de Clichy, Paris, at the apartment of M. Bulot, in which five people were injured and much damage was done to the building. Bulot had been the prosecutor at the Clichy Levallois trial. The bombs at the judge and prosecutor's residences had been set by Ravachol. (No one was accused of the Lobau barracks bombing until some time later when Meunier was extradited from England and sentenced to life imprisonment for this and another explosion at the Café Very.) Due to incredible indiscretions on his part Ravachol was arrested in Paris, on 30th March 1892. The details of his bombings, robberies, and of his arrest and trials can be found elsewhere.[31] What concerns us here is the considerable effect these events were to have on the trial of the Walsall men. The Paris correspondent of the *Times*, for example, was sending really quite frenzied reports:

> No possible political end can be adduced to justify or explain the detestable acts which have startled us all. It is clearly the war of disorder and chaos against order and law. It is crime for crime's sake. It is murder and havoc acting in the service of covetousness, hatred and all evil. Undoubtedly all Anarchists are not assassins but all assassins are ready to increase the army of Anarchists and it really is with an army of murderers that society has now to deal.[32]

Since it had already been made quite clear that the bombs had been aimed at members of the judiciary in revenge for the sentences at Clichy Levallois and, furthermore, since no one had been killed in these attacks, the language of the Paris correspondent seems a little over-inflated. The centre of the matter, however, is made clear a few lines later. "In the stress of so wide a danger there should certainly be an international league preventing every murderer of this sort from finding a place to linger even for a night in any country under the sun." And, neatly switching the emphasis but preserving the odium, he continues: "Anarchists should not be regarded as members of a political party, and it should not be possible for an Anarchist to hurry away from Paris to find an asylum in Brussels, in Geneva or in London."

This was to become a familiar theme. Governments whose dissidents had escaped abroad resented strongly their ability to continue to cause them difficulty from their exile by publishing propaganda and distributing it from a safe base. The very existence of a safe place to run to tended to make the as yet un-exiled dissidents bolder in their actions. The result was that many continental governments were to exert considerable diplomatic pressure and to indulge in considerable public relations work in order to close the more liberal havens to political refugees. The relative security (or lack of it) given to political refugees was often a bargaining counter in diplomatic manoeuvrings and ententes. As far as native British chauvinism went, the cry for anti-anarchist legislation was mixed in with 'fair trade' demands, demands for the throwing out of 'pauper aliens' and so on. The smokescreen thrown up by professionally excitable fellows like the Paris correspondent of the *Times* allowed the authorities a certain latitude in their handling of immigrants. It certainly made the lives of political exiles in London harder and saddled the English anarchist with a reputation that was both dangerous and difficult to live up to.

The trial at Stafford Assizes of the six Walsall men began on 30th March — the same day that Ravachol was arrested. On 4th April the newspapers reported Ravachol's confessions, which not only quite breezily admitted the bombings but also showed him to be genially unrepentant: "...if I had not been taken I would not have been satisfied with these explosions. None of those who had helped prosecute our mates would have escaped."[33] He would, he said, also have paid some attention to the deputies responsible for putting forward the alterations in the dynamite laws which made threatening the use of explosives as heinous a crime as attempt to murder.

The newspapers of 5th April carried news of a narrowly averted attempt by anarchists to bomb the Spanish Chamber of Deputies.[34] They also reported the end of the Walsall anarchists' trial.

The prosecution at Stafford Assizes was conducted by the attorney general, which gives some idea of the importance given the trial by the government. The judge was Justice Hawkins (already nicknamed 'Hangman' Hawkins). The trial itself apparently proceeded with dignified irrelevance — reading the *Times* reports of the trial one gets no sense of a battle either to prove guilt or to assert innocence. The evidence brought forward by the Crown was that given to the police court together with evidence from explosives and handwriting experts and some additional evidence that the prisoners had been seen together. The true nature of the trial is better expressed by the repressive atmosphere in the court. *Freedom* reported "... the system of spying has been dreadful throughout. Every remark made by the prisoners to their solicitor, or vice versa, in the court was eagerly picked up if possible by a band of attendant detectives. Almost everyone interested in the case was 'shadowed' at Stafford."[35] Some people were refused entrance because they had the wrong face. The Crown — the whole court — assumed guilt and the defence, as far as one can see, put up a miserable display of shadow boxing. The attempts by Deakin's counsel to have his confession set aside, on the grounds of its having been obtained through inducements, were pathetic. W.M. Thompson's attempts to get Inspector Melville to again make injudicious references to "paying lots of Anarchists money" were ineffectual.

Neither of these two lawyers seemed prepared to hammer away at the only two points which could have saved the men — the confession from Deakin, obtained by threat or inducement, together with the activities of Coulon in setting up the plot and his relations with the police. Nor did they make any real attempt to throw doubt on the impression given by the Crown that the psychotic fantasy of *The Anarchist Feast at the Opera* — which was read in full — represented the views of the men on trial. The counsel for Charles — Willis, paid for through Carpenter's fund — proposed as the core of his defence that since no explosive substances had been found they could not be found guilty under the Explosives Act. And if a paragraph of the Explosives Act referred to the illegality of "any apparatus, etc., used ... or adapted for causing, or aiding in causing any explosion ... also any part of any such apparatus," nobody was in any mood to accept his subtle distinction between patterns for bomb cases and bomb cases themselves. Having made little difference to the course of the trial, in his final speech he took it upon himself to explain in effect that desperate situations sometimes breed desperate acts — which was not really a clever thing to say in what was supposed to be a conciliatory defence. On 4th April the jury retired and after an hour and three-quarters returned to pronounce Charles, Cailes and Battola guilty; Deakin guilty but with a recommendation for mercy; and Westley and Ditchfield not guilty.

The convicted prisoners were then asked if they had anything to say. And it was only here that something like daylight fell upon the whole vicious buffoonery of the legal process. Charles stated openly that the affair was a police plot and referred to the memoirs of the police chief Andrieux, of Paris, who had arranged for explosions to take place in order to incriminate anarchists. He stated that the bombs had been represented as being intended for Russia — finding they were not, "he at once abandoned any connection with them." Battola — who put on the bravest front among them — made a long speech through an interpreter. Completely unawed by his surroundings — though prudent enough to deny any connection with bomb-making — he accused his accusers "who had kept him from his wife and children ... of all the crimes of the age, of all the murders prompted by want and all the suicides."[36] He also denounced Coulon as the instigator of the plot. Cailes, too, spoke defiantly. But it was too late, far too late. Justice Hawkins declared that "no part of the sentence he passed was because they were Anarchist or because of the possession of those documents." Charles, Battola and Cailes were given ten years each, and Deakin five. the *Times*, however, was a little more honest:

The offence with which the prisoners were charged is one of the most dastardly and wicked which it is possible to conceive. Like treason it is aimed at the very heart of the State, but it is not designed to destroy the existing Government alone. It strikes at all Governments, and behind all Governments it strikes at those elementary social rights for the defence of which all forms and methods of civil rules exist. The crime of which the Walsall prisoners have been found guilty was no isolated act. ... Hate, envy, the lust of plunder and the lust of bloodshed are stamped on every line of the Anarchist literature read at Walsall and on every word of the confessions made by RAVACHOL.

The sentences, the *Times* recognised, were severe. But, it said, "our columns this morning contain abundant evidence that this is no time to deal lightly with such crimes ..." It was referring to the attempt on the Spanish Chamber of Deputies, news of other attempted outrages and a list of fairly recent, mainly Fenian, bomb explosions in England prepared by H.M. Inspectors of Explosives.[37] The prisoners of Walsall were suffering not only for breaking the law but for the dastardly crime of making the ruling class nervous.

As the case proceeded the anarchists did what they could to publicise the case and to provide back-up support for the imprisoned men. At the centre of this activity was David Nicoll, the editor of the *Commonweal*. In addition to raising money for the defence he spoke at meetings, researched the background of the case and lobbied the radical press and anybody else who might have been useful. His efforts were even recognised by *Justice*, the S.D.F. paper, in a backhanded sort of way: "Though we entirely differ from Nicholl [sic] we must give him the fullest credit for the work he did in securing a defence for his Walsall comrades. He spared no pains in this direction and sacrificed himself in every way. Such noble and courageous conduct renders us the more sorry that so much enthusiasm and zeal should be thrown away on the hopeless cause of Anarchism,"[38] etc., etc. The importance of David Nicoll's activity in the defence of the Walsall anarchists was also recognised in a rather different way by Auguste Coulon. The latter, who had disappeared after Battola had been arrested, was holed up in Brixton where he was traced by one of the ex-pupils of his bomb-making school who was acting for Nicoll. From here he issued two really quite scandalous leaflets denouncing Nicoll as a police spy. One gave a highly coloured account of Nicoll's younger days when he had affected 'aesthetic' modes of dress and had got into trouble when he threatened a printer who had refused to print one of his poems. His behaviour had been weird enough to result in his being held at the workhouse as a lunatic. He had been rescued by his family. Coulon's conclusion from all this was that Nicoll had been rescued from a lunatic asylum by Inspector Melville to spread mayhem in the anarchist movement.[39] The second leaflet was better — in psychological warfare terms — because it was more plausible. Nicoll and Cyril Bell, who had probably aroused Coulon's animosity by taking over his position at Louise Michel's school after Coulon's dismissal, were accused jointly of collecting money to print the *Emancipator* (which I take to be Most's *Revolutionary Warfare*) and pocketing the proceeds. Nicoll, a "quaker shaped spy without any human feelings, leaves his wife and child at the mercy of charitable institutions. It is this jesuit who never dares look at you straight in the face in private conversation who is now giving his private address where money should be sent for the propaganda. Seeing himself ousted at our last congress he hit on a bold stroke. He went to Peter Edlin to get 24 hours of prison ... to save his reputation ..." (Peter Edlin was the judge in the Harrow Road/Shop Assistants Union case.)

Cyril Bell, who as we said earlier had acted on Coulon's suggestion in this, is accused of being an agent provocateur "in sending letters to form a secret conspiracy of which he would be No. 1, for the fabrication of explosives. ... His shortsightedness and deafness added to the repulsiveness of his manners make him an object of disgust."[40] The major point about this leaflet is that it asks comrades not to send money to Nicoll "but to some trustworthy comrade of which there are plenty in London."(Presumably he meant himself.) Apart from revenge for being exposed as a police agent by Nicoll, the intention of the leaflet was probably to stop money going to the defence fund for the Walsall anarchists. Inspector Melville also played his part in these accusations according to Nicoll: "Melville had told several people that Coulon was 'All right' but it was Nicoll that had given information."[41] Melville had reason to feel spiteful towards Nicoll. The work Nicoll had put in had made the role of Coulon more apparent and had led to Melville's embarrassment by W.M. Thompson in the Walsall police court. Further, Nicoll had publicised his embarrassment in the *Commonweal*. Nicoll tells how he met a friend who had been at the trial at Stafford. "He told me that he had seen Melville who had stated to him that he was very indignant at the way he had been libelled in the *Commonweal*. He was not responsible for Coulon acting as an agent provocateur. 'If a man comes to me with information what can I do?' Then with a sudden burst of temper, 'If that fellow Nicoll goes on telling lies about me, *I'll have him*'." And Melville was to get his chance.

When the sentences were passed on the convicted Walsall men there was considerable shock in the socialist movement generally. "Alas! Alas!

*Ten* years for Charles," wrote Edward Carpenter, "it is too bad. An evil conscience makes them cowards."[42] But in addition to such handwringing there seems to have been a sudden shudder of fear through the movement. While the trial had been going on, several protest meetings over the prosecution had taken place with quite considerable numbers of people attending. The first open-air meeting after the convictions, on Sunday, 10th April in Hyde Park, was very sparsely attended. It is true it had been hastily organised but so had the others — fear seems to have played its part in keeping people at home. Nicoll says, "Detectives positively swarmed in the crowd. There were enough there to take the whole crowd into custody. In fact these gentlemen were so numerous that several comrades would not come to the meeting."[43] The speeches were made by David Nicoll and John Turner and amounted to a rehash of the facts of the case with particular attention to the role of Coulon, together with a general appeal to the workers to rally to the cause of anarchy, at least to the extent of demanding the release of the prisoners. Subsequent attempts to prove that Nicoll had made a speech inciting to violence failed. However Nicoll had already more or less committed himself in an article written for the *Commonweal*. Nicoll had been rather unrealistically optimistic about the chances of the accused men at Stafford Assizes. It seems likely that deep and sympathetic acquaintance with the evidence for the defence had allowed him to assume that the judge and jury had an acquaintance equally deep and sympathetic.

> I believed ... that the men at Walsall were trapped by an agent of the police into making castings for the purpose of manufacturing bombs for 'Russia'. I thought also that the admissions which Mr Thompson had obtained from Inspector Melville had made this pretty plain to judge and jury. What was therefore my surprise and indignation at hearing of the brutal sentence passed on three of the men of ten years penal servitude ...
>
> The day on which I heard of the result of the trial was Tuesday. Our paper goes to press on Wednesday. I went down to the office full of rage and indignation against those who had so cruelly and shamefully treated a dear friend of mine. It was there I wrote the article.[44]

This hastily written piece published in the issue of 9th April 1892 bears all the marks of angry indignation — one of them being a measure of incoherence. What is clear from the article, though, is that Nicoll advises workmen contemplating violent revenge on their oppressors to avoid conspiracies and act alone. Further, the responsibility for the savage sentences rested firmly with a police plot constructed by Mathews (the Home Secretary) and Inspector Melville, carried out by Coulon and connived at by justice Hawkins. Finally he asks if the men named "are fit to live." It was a cry of anguish, of hate and, it has to be said, an expression of impotence. Nevertheless, reactionary papers had already started demanding that the government prosecute over the article on the evening of the day it was issued.[45] There was a steadily rising chorus of such demands and questions were asked in Parliament. Yet Nicoll's cry of anger had probably broken the silence that settled when the sentences were announced. He was lobbying a number of newspapers and was hopeful that the details of Coulon's activities would soon become known to a wider audience — in more ways than one he was keeping the issue alive. The week after the sparse meeting in Hyde Park, on 17th April, in Manchester's Stevenson Square, Nicoll, Barton, Stockton and John Bingham addressed a meeting of protest and had an audience of several thousand people who listened "with great attention and evident sympathy."[46]

The *Commonweal* of the previous day had naturally enough taken up the subject again, though in more temperate language. This was not the only difference. He said, "The reader must not suppose that there was 'a widespread conspiracy' save on the part of the police and their accomplices. It was Coulon who had twenty plots in hand at the same time; all distinct from each other. Coulon knew everything, the rest of the 'conspirators' only knew what they were doing. *The true story of the Walsall Police Plot has yet to be told, and we shall begin to tell it in our next number.*" Nicoll believed that it was this announcement that caused or at least precipitated his arrest, and circumstances would seem to justify this belief. When the 'Are these men fit to live?' article came out a close watch was kept on premises connected with the *Commonweal*. "Our offices in the City Road and Socialist Cooperative Federation, where our comrades sometimes met" (John Turner was the manager of the Federation)[47] "were closely watched by spies and a few nights before my arrest my wife came to me and said 'She could not understand, but she was sure there was a man watching for someone in our street.' She did not know that I was threatened with prosecution. I told her I thought it must be her fancy."[48]

Nicoll returned from Manchester to find encouraging news from the newspapers he had tried to interest with the case. The *Commonweal* had the first instalment of the promised revelations concerning the Walsall case set up in type — what became 'The Sketch of the Bomb', the first chapter of the pamphlet *The Walsall Anarchists Trapped by the Police*. A few days previously Coulon had, with the most incredible brass face, sent a letter to the *Star*. That letter was published, with his address in full — 29 Fitzroy Square — above a resolution passed by a workman's organisation calling upon the government to prosecute him, as the condemned men at Walsall had accused him in open court of being the chief instigator of the plot. "I wrote to the paper," said Nicoll, "and pointed out that though Coulon gave an address a few yards from the police station where Deakin was arrested, yet he was untouched by the police. That afternoon, on which the letter appeared in the *Star*, the police arrested, not Coulon, but me."[49] As he returned home from the *Commonweal* office on Tuesday 19th April, he was taken, almost on his doorstep.

> At that moment, the article 'The Sketch of the Bomb' was on its way to Scotland Yard under a strong escort of police. Melville and Littlechild with a posse of Scotland Yard detectives had stormed the offices of the *Commonweal*, and had carried off anything that might compromise them. They had seized the new *Commonweal* that had been set up, type, manuscript and all …[50] They were assiduous in their inquiries as to a certain book on explosives which Coulon had been getting out, but which had never been printed. If they could only have found a few copies what valuable evidence it would have been. Tom Cantwell told them in jest, 'We have been expecting you for some time, and do you think we should be fools as to keep anything here likely to get men into trouble?'[51]

W.C. Hart tells a rather different story. In his book *Confessions of an Anarchist* he says that the *Emancipator* — for this was the book referred to — was set up in type when the police raided the offices of the *Commonweal*.

In the act of removing the formes of type from an upper shelf for the police to inspect, someone — presumably Tom Cantwell — 'accidentally' dropped them and the type was pied.[52]

Charles Mowbray was also arrested. He was the publisher of the paper, while Nicoll was its editor but was not involved with the paper when the 'Fit to Live?' article was published, because he was nursing his wife who was desperately ill. While Nicoll was being arrested and the *Commonweal* office was being raided, another group of detectives under Detective Sergeant McIntyre were searching for Mowbray. The last address they had for him was at a house used as a Socialist Club in Bethnal Green. It was closed and empty. McIntyre and his men had to rush up and down the streets of Hoxton and East London looking for him — finally locating him through his signboard in a window ('Working-man's tailor. Articles made up cheap for the working classes.') There was no other way to find him, says McIntyre. "It was useless to seek information from any of the Anarchist Fraternity, for no matter what disguise was adopted they would be sure to spot a 'Yard' man and give the tip to Mowbray."[53]

When the police finally located Mowbray they found a desolate scene. A matter of an hour or two before their arrival, Mowbray's wife had died and her body was lying upstairs:

> he was sitting down to a scanty meal with his little children when the detectives entered and seized him. 'This is a job,' said Mowbray, 'my wife is just dead and what are these children to do?' and he burst into tears. It was vain for him to declare he did not agree with the article. That he had never seen it till the *Commonweal* was published and that he had then severed all connection with the paper. All these statements were quite true but it made no difference. The law must be obeyed. He was dragged away.[54]

The cruelty of this arrest, leaving as it did, Mowbray's children alone in the house with their dead mother, certainly affected Sergeant McIntyre, and his 'softness' towards Mowbray at the police court hearing probably contributed to the later harsh disciplinary proceedings brought against him which led to his leaving the police force. The magistrate, however, suffered from no such inconvenient sentimentality and remanded Mowbray in custody and with reluctance said he would allow Mowbray to attend his wife's funeral, and then only under police guard. However, the circumstances of Mowbray's arrest underlined by this final example of judicial indifference led to something of an outburst in the press calling for Mowbray to be released on bail. Mrs Besant rather noisily took temporary care of his children, and William Morris offered to stand surety. On this bail of £500 Mowbray was released. His wife's funeral, as a result of these events, became a public occasion:

> The various London groups of Anarchists decided that the funeral should be a public one and the cortège was announced to start from the Workpeople's International Club, Berners Street, Commercial Road, East, at 3.30. Long before that time several thousand persons assembled, a brass band and some twenty anarchist banners being in attendance. ... A number of prominent Anarchist and Trades Unionists had assembled including representatives of various provincial groups, Louise Michel, Hunter Watts (representing the Social Democratic Federation), W. Votier (Boot and Shoe Makers Union), M. Brochean (Brocher? — French Anarchist Section), M. Malatesta (Spanish Anarchist section [sic]), Mr Ramsey (Freethinkers) and others.

Mowbray was so upset as hardly to be able to speak; finally, however, he thanked the people for their sympathy and asked them to avoid confrontation as his bail would be put in danger.

> Before the cortège started, the crowd which had assembled in the street were addressed from one of the windows of the club, and the conduct of the police authorities was strongly denounced. It was not until nearly half-past four that the funeral procession, headed by a banner bearing the following inscription: 'Remember Chicago; there will be a time when our silence will be more powerful than the voices you strangle today' and with the band playing the 'Dead March' in Saul began to wend its way towards the cemetery. ... On each side of the coach men carried large red flags, to one of which was attached a copy

of the suppressed edition of the *Commonweal* while another bore a placard stating 'The *Commonweal* still alive. Our office plundered. Bogus charges. Our editor in gaol. Published every Saturday.' While the cortege was passing across Commercial Road a tram car driver attempted to make a way through. His horses were at once seized by a number of the processionists, who despite the efforts of three police officers, held the animals' heads and forcibly prevented the car from proceeding until the whole procession had passed.

At the graveside Touzeau Parris "said that the sister they had buried had gone to a place where there was no labour, no sorrow, no sweating. ... Mr Hunter Watts who followed said that their comrade, Mary Mowbray, was lying at their feet slain by the accursed capitalist system."[55] And here lies the relevance of the quotation at the head of the procession. Albert Parsons; the Chicago anarchist martyr, was hanged. Mary Mowbray's death (from consumption) was in great measure due to bad conditions, malnutrition and overwork. For the anarchists, both were victims of capitalism, the differences being a matter of degree rather than kind.

Revolutionary speeches at funerals were, in any case, no new thing in the anarchist movement. In 1886, at the funeral of Gustav Knauerhause, a procession with brass band set off for Manor Park cemetery and "about 800 comrades followed the Hearse and revolutionary speeches were delivered over the grave in English, German and French." He too had died of consumption.[56]

The demonstration at Mary Mowbray's funeral, despite its melancholy origins, represented a further breaking of the spell that the Walsall convictions had over the anarchist movement. As we have seen, the *Times* reported an attendance of some several thousand people, and Nicoll's perhaps rather foolish outburst in the *Commonweal* had opened out the questions surrounding the Walsall convictions. Furthermore, the raid on the *Commonweal* and the carrying away of documents and type caused an uneasy stir in Radical ranks. They might not sympathise with anarchists but they were jealous of 'English Liberties'.

On the following Sunday, 24th April, there were protest meetings all over the country at the raids on the *Commonweal* and the arrests of Nicoll and Mowbray. In London there was a meeting in the morning in Regent's Park and in the afternoon at Hyde Park. Here "a tremendous crowd" heard Harding, Cantwell ("much amusement was caused by his mimicry of Littlechild and Melville who told him they were Anarchists ..."), Morton, Miss Lupton, Tochatti, Fox, Parker, Atterbury "and others giving outspoken addresses." All their literature was sold out. *Commonweal* gradually went up in price. "Starting at 2d then 3d, 4d, 6d, to 1/- while in some instances as much as 2/- was given for a copy."[57] A second edition was printed on the Monday. Large meetings were held, and the paper completely sold out at Manchester, Leeds, Leicester, Walsall, Norwich, Newcastle-on-Tyne, Glasgow, Birmingham, Sheffield, Aberdeen, Burnley and other places. The anarchists were also able to make a fairly impressive showing on 1st May — May Day — which fell upon a Sunday. At the demonstration in Hyde Park after a procession numbering some 18,000 people calling for an eight-hour day, which had been organised under the auspices of various trades unions and socialist bodies, the anarchists held a separate meeting at the Reformers Tree, where they mustered over a thousand people. Since anarchists were also speaking from other platforms in the main body of the demonstration who presumably had their support in the crowd this was an indication of growing anarchist strength. The Walsall convictions and the prosecution of Nicoll and Mowbray had given the anarchists the stamp of seriousness. For all the distortions to which such spectacular happenings progressively subjected the anarchist message in the public mind, they seem to have led initially to a great increase of activity and interest. This not only seems the case from anarchist evidence but is confirmed by contemporaries: Detective Sweeny says as much in his memoirs.[58]

The anarchist meeting on May Day also in no way took up a defensive stance, except for Ted Leggatt who was thinking, perhaps, more of the chances of securing the acquittal of Nicoll or of an earlier release for the Walsall men. Behind the platform were two large banners, one reading 'Anarchist Communism' and 'Revolution and Anarchy', and the other 'If the people when oppressed are silent such is stupidity, the forerunner of the downfall of public liberty.' Tochatti denounced police spies. H.B. Samuels followed Leggatt's assertions that anarchism did not imply violence with counter-assertions as to the necessity for it and praised the example of Ravachol to cheers from the audience who had listened with some impatience to Leggatt's disavowals. Louise Michel then spoke, in French, saying that as fast as anarchists were jailed new anarchists sprang up to take their place. John Oldham "rejoiced that all his life he had been a notorious poacher. He was one of those who refused to starve," and Parker spoke on the anti-rent campaign: "In the East End they had started an 'anti-broker brigade' and in several instances the broker's man had been forcibly ejected from the house he was distraining on and the furniture had been carried away by some 20 or 30 of their comrades." The meeting broke up after three hours with three cheers for anarchy.[59] It is worth noticing that the 'violent means' versus 'peaceful means' (or more particularly, the pro- or anti-dynamite) debate and the vigorous grass roots direct action and propaganda (of which Parker gave an example) are fundamental to the anarchist movement of this period. They are themes which recur again and again.

Nicoll and Mowbray were tried on Friday, 6th May, at the Old Bailey before the Lord Chief Justice, and the prosecution was conducted by one of his successors to that office. Mowbray was represented and Nicoll defended himself. The prosecution used as evidence the 'Fit to Live' article in the *Commonweal* and some new evidence from two policemen who had been present at the sparsely attended meeting on Sunday, 10th April, in Hyde Park to protest at the Walsall convictions. These policemen alleged that Nicoll had said, "Four men are responsible for the conviction of the Walsall comrades, Butcher Hawkins, Melville, Mathews, and Coulon. Within a fortnight two of them must die …" Nicoll brought a number of witnesses to show that he had said nothing of the sort. Then one of the policemen, Detective Sweeny, returned to the witness box. He attempted to adjust his account so that it was compatible with Nicoll's witnesses but preserved the murderous sentiments by saying that Nicoll spoke the words in a second speech. It was a little too transparently obvious an attempt to strengthen the case against Nicoll. The judge became irritated, Nicoll accused Sweeny of perjury — in fact, Sweeny was quite regularly referred to as 'Sweeny Todd the Perjurer' in later anarchist papers — and the prosecution discreetly indicated that they would proceed only on the basis of the 'Fit to Live' article.

Mowbray's prosecution rested on the fact that on paper he was the publisher of the *Commonweal*. However Nicoll had made a statement to the police the day after his arrest taking full responsibility for the article and specifically saying that Mowbray was not responsible for it. Further, evidence was brought by Mowbray's counsel at the trial to show that Mowbray disassociated himself from the article in question: the printer of the *Commonweal* said that "Mowbray had denounced the article that appeared on the 9th (to him) and said that if such things were printed in future he should withdraw his name from the paper. He said such language was foolish at the best and damnable at worst. He gave witness (i.e. the printer) notice as the registered proprietor, not to print off the copies if he found such expressions had been put into type, but to detain the type and send for him."[60] This, incidentally, would seem to be a clear indication that Mowbray's relationship with the Commonweal Group had become strained before Nicoll's arrest or imprisonment. (If the 'Fit to Live' article aroused his anger, it had many predecessors which were equally irritating.) This evidence, together with Nicoll's further statement in court that he took full responsibility and the circumstances surrounding Mowbray's arrest and initial imprisonment, were sufficient to guarantee his acquittal.

Nicoll's defence rested on the grounds that he had been angry and upset at the blatant injustice of the sentences on the Walsall men and that his words were not to be taken literally but as an expression of that anger. This must not be taken as an indication of cowardice on Nicoll's part. He spelled out the role of Coulon in the Walsall conspiracy and placed him firmly in the tradition of the English agents provocateurs and spies at the close of the Napoleonic wars. His role was, as theirs had been, to provide the Tory government of the day with suitable bogey men to scare the "rich and the timid among the respectable classes" and persuade them of the need for strong and bloody-minded government, which the Tories could provide. But, Nicoll said, there was more to it than that. Hyndman had said, in 1885 on the Embankment, that if the government remained deaf to the cries of the starving then "by God, some of them should die" — and the bombs had been exploding in London then, not Paris. John Burns said something in 1887 in Battersea Park about the desirability of "sending Joseph Chamberlain to heaven by chemical parcels post." Why were they not prosecuted for incitement to murder? Nicoll says that in his case the police were not at all concerned about such incitement but were concerned to suppress the revelations he was about to make about the Walsall anarchists, so concerned to suppress them, in fact, that they carried away the set-up type at the *Commonweal* and were prepared to perjure themselves to secure his conviction.

But there was, he said, one final reason why he was prosecuted where others had been let go free. He was an anarchist. This was the hidden charge against him. An anarchist was not necessarily an incendiarist or assassin, though "anyone who has seen as much of the poverty and misery of the East End as we have and not use strong language would be absolutely heartless." And as if to prove his point he went on to discuss the dynamitards:

Ravachol! Why, your civilisation — that drives the poor into misery and degradation, that drives women into prostitution, and men to crime, by enslaving and sweating them to pile up wealth for the rich — is breeding Ravachols by thousands! Breeding them into its fever dens, breeding them in its slums, where good dies and where only vice and crime can flourish. Ravachol! Your civilisation is only fit for Ravachol. And to Ravachol we leave it. Let the monsters you have created devour you.

But why had Ravachol actually happened in Paris and not in London? The difference lay in the fact that the French repression far outdid that in England. Or at least that had been the case so far; but now the state was locking people up for their opinions.

Well go on with your policy, but you know what it will lead to. You will not suppress us or our ideas. Do you think that this prosecution has prevented the spread of our principles? Have you suppressed them?

Why, you have not even suppressed the *Commonweal* which has now six times the circulation which it had three weeks ago.

For my part, I am willing to suffer for my ideas, knowing full well that our friends increase with persecution and I am quite willing to suffer in a good cause. I only tell you that you will not crush the movement by repression. You will only make it more revolutionary and dangerous.[61]

This was a brave speech. In defending himself and by this final speech for the defence, Nicoll takes his place among those immoderate heroes and martyrs in the cause of a free press; a modest place it is true but a place nevertheless. The main weakness of his defence was not in the words used but in the distribution to a wide audience. It is natural that the newspapers should print nothing of his allegations concerning the activities of Coulon. It is surprising however that he should not have made arrangements to have his defence speech properly circulated; so much of the importance of this type of trial lies in the realm of theatre and the spectacle. Unless, of course, Nicoll was expecting to be acquitted. He had nourished sanguine hopes in the Walsall case. However, it seems that the activity of detectives in the court who were stopping people taking notes was sufficient to prevent the text of the defence appearing until after Nicoll's release. At the very least, it seems to me, a copy of the defence speech could have been taken out of the court by Mowbray or his counsel. This elementary precaution against the possibility of suppression does not seem to have occurred to Nicoll. (Another possibility is that fear or some other kind of pressure was being brought to bear.) Further, no proper arrangements seem to have been made for anyone to take up the work connected with the Walsall anarchists. The defence committee seems only to have been composed of Nicoll himself. The extent to which he played close to his chest is indicated by the fact that even his wife didn't know that he was threatened with arrest. So when he was found guilty and sentenced to eighteen months' hard labour for a rather foolish article the movement gained a martyr but lost a lot of information[62] and also lost the opportunity to quickly develop a campaign in response to the convictions of the Walsall men. And the publicity surrounding the trial was not all Nicoll had intended in the way of advertising the cause.

For their part, the authorities were careful to give Nicoll and Mowbray a 'fair' trial. After all, the raid and the 'unfortunate' publicity surrounding the arrest of Mowbray had aroused quite noisy protests. It was as well to be careful. The Lord Chief Justice was the soul of courtesy throughout and even allowed himself a few words of praise for Nicoll: "...you conducted yourself today perfectly well and you have shown marks of considerable education and force of character."[63] But praise from such quarters is rather like being given the privilege of being eaten by a crocodile with especially clean teeth. It is true that Nicoll could have been sentenced to five or ten years' imprisonment; but the sentence of eighteen months represented nothing more than a careful calculation. As the *Times* put it: "Many, no doubt, would have acquiesced in a much more severe sentence than the Lord Chief justice has passed. The danger is that severity may arouse sympathy and that a prisoner who has really got no more than his deserts may become an object of public commiseration, not only among his confederates or personal friends."

So Nicoll started his sentence. Unless activity within prisons links up with the wider movement, I have restricted the accounts of anarchists' prison experiences. In Nicoll's case, however, his experiences were to explain much of his later attitudes and activities in the movement. It is for these reasons that I present it in this history, although it deserves to take its place among prison literature as yet another example of the viciously pointless nature of those institutions — pointless, of course, unless their purpose is revenge. In the latter case, the state was well revenged on David Nicoll for his presumption in inquiring about the fitness to live of its representatives. The first part of his sentence was passed at Pentonville prison. For the first month he walked the treadmill and for the rest of his time there was set to picking oakum — oakum being "sections of ship's cable, thickly encrusted with tar and sometimes with paint. Often the tar has hardened with age and then the work is much harder." The point of the exercise is to shred the oakum by hand which if it is done without using all the little tricks that experience teaches, leaves the prisoner with broken nails and bleeding hands, and a sense of running a crazy race against time to produce the amount demanded. Dr Creaghe was to write to the *Commonweal*, "I fear that hard labour will be terribly trying to a man like comrade Nicoll." He was right.

Nicoll was moved on 13th June to the gaol of the small country town of Chelmsford. As at Pentonville he worked in his cell in solitary confinement at oakum picking. In the 13th August issue of the *Commonweal* it was made clear that he was finding the work no easier. When two comrades arrived to visit him "a consultation took place as to whether we should be allowed to see him at all since he had not picked enough oakum the day before and had been put on bread and water in consequence ..." The comrades found him in a cheerful enough mood at this point. He had thought on going into prison that his "sentence seemed so unjust that I could not believe I should serve the whole of it." But it was at Chelmsford that it finally came home to him that there would be no premature release from prison. Taken with this, the limited food, the solitary confinement and then finally the news that the *Commonweal* had suspended publication plunged him into a deep mood of despair.

Then he started hearing voices. They took the form of supposed readings from the popular press by the warders concerning the doings of anarchists. Then it appeared that the police were raiding the houses of anarchists all over London. But public indignation was rising. Then John Burns himself decided to speak at an anarchist protest meeting at South Place. The reports of this meeting were that it had been a great success and that there was to be a huge demonstration in Trafalgar Square on Sunday 13th November, calling for an amnesty for all the arrested anarchists, including Nicoll. John Burns had provided the money for the *Commonweal* to be restarted under the editorship of Mowbray. On the Saturday before the meeting Nicoll heard murmuring crowds outside the jail. The meeting "was a glorious success and my release seemed certain." Then the crowds outside the prison started singing to Nicoll, versions of the 'Carmagnole' — "Hurrah for the *Commonweal*/Socialist League/Socialist League ..." — and after this happened several times, the whole thing reached a climax after

> a manly voice ... made solemn proclamation that 'John Burns will be down tomorrow at eight o'clock with a free pardon from the Home Secretary ...' Bedtime came, and I retired to bed, but not to sleep. The female voice returned with a chorus of others, chanting wildly the 'Carmagnole'. They made the night hideous with this melody, which rang wildly through the darkness. Swifter and swifter ran the magic tune. Wilder and wilder grew the dance and louder the chant, till it sounded as if a host of witches were keeping Sabbath around the prison. Hell was let loose. At last, at a late hour I fell asleep amid the wild discords of the ghostly revel.

Naturally enough, no pardon arrived, the events described by the voices having no relation to events outside Nicoll's imagination. From this point on, Nicoll complained of voices from the next cell asking prying questions about anarchists in London. On complaining about this to a visitor — an objection which was passed on to the Home Secretary via John Burns — he spent some time in the infirmary being pronounced to be suffering from delusions induced by solitary confinement. This Nicoll indignantly denied, and in the pamphlet *The Ghosts of Chelmsford Gaol*[64] gives accounts of other people hearing whispers in prisons and blames the voices and singing on a conspiracy of prison warders and bought-over prisoners. Apart from the fact that the masterminding of such a conspiracy required a creativity beyond the reach of most prison warders, whose interferences with prisoners tend to be more physically immediate and brutal, there are quite obvious inconsistencies of a bizarre nature in Nicoll's account, which would seem to indicate that he underwent some kind of paranoid breakdown. When the immediate pressure of solitary confinement was released and he was put to work in the prison garden "my life was almost uneventful" (as he says) and the useless and pointless days passed by until the sentence passed on him was completed.

While the immediate excitement of Mowbray's and Nicoll's arrest, May Day and the trial was going on, the *Commonweal* was edited by George Cores, the man who had done his best to secure a continuation of anarchist propaganda in Walsall. And as Nicoll pointed out at his trial, the circulation of the *Commonweal* multiplied six times in three weeks. Certainly Cores was an able editor who produced a lively paper; and certainly the publicity given to the anarchists by the raid on the *Commonweal* office and the arrests, following after the Walsall trial, attracted serious inquiry as well as idle curiosity. Yet the fundamental reason that Nicoll could claim a huge increase in circulation at the time of his trial was that the protest demonstrations and then the May Day demonstrations had given the anarchists a readymade market for their papers. Temporarily the mountain had come to Mahomet. As the 7th May *Commonweal* said of the May Day demonstration: "All over the Park our women folk [sic] were selling *Freedom* and the *Commonweal* and the sale was the largest ever known." In Manchester, at the 1st May demonstration there, twenty quire of *Commonweals* had been sold. This level of sales was not sustained. The problems of distribution which bedevil oppositional newspapers had only been temporarily transcended by opportunity and enthusiasm. For the paper to have sustained these sales either mass left-wing demonstrations where the anarchists could have sold it would have to have happened continually, or they would have to have had a sales force able to reach a much more greatly dispersed body of sympathisers or sensation-seekers. When their audience was not readymade the sales of the paper would be a more true indication of their organisational strength and their ability to reach potential supporters and comrades. A start was made on the formation of a number of autonomous anarchist groups in London. The *Commonweal* for 14th May announced that H.B.

Samuels was now the publisher of the paper and also announced a list of groups and secretaries "and it only remains for comrades and sympathisers to attach themselves to the groups they can best work with." It was either lack of forethought or a noble lack of opportunism which caused this organisational attempt to miss the mass audiences of 24th April and May Day. This move, however well or badly planned, did represent something of a departure. Up to this point the English anarchists had grown within other bodies, as in the case of the Socialist League, or around a periodical, as in the case of *Freedom* and the *Anarchist*, or through individual contact and general association with anarchists in the political clubs. The activity of the new anarchist groups was to remain propagandist, but now they were prepared — even eager — to sharply differentiate themselves within the socialist movement not only ideologically but organisationally as well. Eight groups were given in the *Commonweal*. They were the Commonweal Group (secretary, T. Cantwell); Hammersmith (Tochatti); Holborn (H. Bird); Paddington (W.B. Parker); North London (J. Presburg); Stratford (F. Goulding); Tottenham (H.B. Morgan); Whitechapel (E. Leggatt). In the next issue two more groups were added: South London (F.A. Fox) and *Freedom* (Mrs Hyde). (The fact that the latter was included as something of an afterthought is some indication of its status among the *Commonweal* anarchists.) A programme of outdoor speaking was started, with three pitches, rising to five by 4th June.

Nevertheless, the paper went into a steady decline once the excitement of Nicoll's trial was over. Nicoll himself was to blame this exclusively on

Samuels's editorship: "the paper," he said, "was edited in such a bungling manner that its subscribers rapidly dropped away and it finally went under."[65] On one level this was unfair. The paper was subject to a degree of harassment from the police which made publishing the paper rather more difficult. Firstly, the type seized by the police when they raided the *Commonweal* at the time of Nicoll's arrest was not returned until mid-June. It took a great deal of trouble, with applications through the courts and through direct application to Scotland Yard, with a large number of obstacles placed in the way. Even when the type was returned, the made-up type — including the first part of Nicoll's revelations concerning the Walsall men — was 'pied', that is, broken up, on Home Office orders. The *Commonweal* was also evicted in late June from its office in City Road. This followed some mysterious measuring activity indulged in by the police — presumably to see if the office transgressed some siting regulation. This proved not to be the case. The *Commonweal* alleged that the police then went to the landlord and whispered in his ear to such effect that he gave the paper notice to quit. After enjoying some weeks' tenure rent-free and after fighting the possession order in the courts — unsuccessfully — the paper removed itself before the bailiffs arrived to the premises of the Berner Street club.

However, on another level Nicoll was quite right to blame the editorship of the paper for its decline. Firstly, Samuels edited a boring paper. Secondly, he seems to have provoked internal dissension in the Commonweal Group in such a way as to ensure that even if the paper did get produced there was no enthusiasm to ensure its proper circulation. The paper was boring because it lacked journalistic sense: the accounts of Nicoll's trial were perfunctory, and although the text of his speech was promised "as soon as we can get it from the clerk of the court …" it never appeared. Creaghe sent letters reporting on his faction fights in Burnley with the S.D.F. which made excellent reading. Similarly he sent a plea that "I hope you will let us know in the *Weal* as often as possible how the comrades are getting on in Stafford as well as Nicoll." Yet accounts of the Walsall men never appeared, and certainly no agitation was started concerning the role of the agent provocateur Coulon. Nicoll was mentioned and his letters were reprinted from time to time but no demands for his release were made. None of the comrades left in the movement, it seemed, had Nicoll's obsessive organisational and agitational ability, as shown in his campaign around the Walsall affair — except perhaps for Cores. The reason for the latter's sudden disappearance from the scene after editing the paper so successfully was not made at all clear in the *Commonweal*. If the published estimations of Samuels's character are anything to go by it is probable that Cores left after a quarrel between the two men. The reports of the movement, like Creaghe's contributions, were squeezed out by material made up of serialisations of theoretical matter. This is not to say that it was of a low standard: Kropotkin's 'Representative Government' appeared through May and June and was followed by 'Revolutionary Government'. Other serialised matter, too, was worth producing — in pamphlet or book form. But in an agitational newspaper it was a great mistake to fill the greater part of it with overlapping wads of theoretical saga. In fact, it can be no accident that an article entitled 'Too Abstract' appeared in the 25th June edition. This article — reprinted from *La Révolte* — starts with the words:

> 'You are too abstract', 'You are not accessible to the masses', 'You are too monotonous'. Such are the reproaches which we find too often in the correspondence which we have with comrades interested in the propaganda, and who think that it is due to a wish to appear very scientific. We have often admitted that as regards the workers our paper is, for those who begin to study the social question, sometimes undoubtedly very dry.

The article goes on to argue that in order to change the world we have to understand it, we have to be clear about the direction we are attempting to take, the workers' revolts of the past have failed because they were too confused to make their revolts into revolutions, etc., etc.

Now the article argues the point clearly and it is a point worth making. The suppressed premise, the unarticulated context of the argument, is the assumption that the understanding of this world and our aspirations for a better one can only be understood through a particular style of discourse. But the songs, the utopias, the cartoons, the humour of the movement were more than the dross surrounding the pure metal of 'theory', all of these things could be more or less coherent, more or less creative. All of them were more or less effective ways of understanding the world in order to change it. A revolutionary journalism has many styles to choose from. There was thus no particular excuse for converting the *Commonweal* almost exclusively into a series of overlapping political analyses. Neither could it be said to represent the efforts of the Commonweal Group to understand the world from their own specific viewpoint — most of the material was reprinted. It seems to me that they aspired to the philosophical glitter of *Freedom*, the editorial group of which were themselves actively engaged in developing the theory of anarchist-communism. The Commonweal Group, to put it simply, did really want to appear very scientific and philosophical. In producing a copy of *Freedom* they inevitably produced an inferior version of the original.

But there were also internal difficulties in the group producing the paper. The main difficulty centred round attitudes to Ravachol. The dispute only surfaced in occasional flashes in the paper and to a certain extent one has to read between the lines. As we have seen, H.B. Samuels praised Ravachol to cheers at the anarchist demonstration on May Day. The developing saga of his trial, first for the bombings of the homes of the judicial worthies and then for the murder and robbery of the hermit of Chambles, occupied the press from April until his execution in July 1892. In the circumstances anarchists found it necessary to define their position in relation to Ravachol's acts. The trouble was that for some the subtlety of claiming Ravachol the bomber but disavowing Ravachol the robber and murderer smacked of lack of determination. In the *Commonweal* of 2nd July we find H.B. Samuels writing "...we are anxiously awaiting the advent of some English Ravachols" and describing him as "a man who has shaken capitalism to its foundations." The fundamental confusion of identifying the fear and panic that Ravachol caused among the French bourgeoisie with a comparable degree of damage to the bourgeois system itself seemed to be shared by most of the correspondents. Alf Barton wrote in to oppose H.B. Samuels, finding it impossible to accept the murder and robbery of the hermit as a great revolutionary act. Similarly he could not stomach Ravachol's attempted grave robbery. "No doubt deeds speak louder than words," he wrote, "but the deeds should have some humanity and heroism about them." Burnie wrote to associate himself with Barton's letter; Cantwell wrote to say that if one did not like the killing one had to admit that Ravachol was to be praised for refusing to lie down and starve to death like so many workers; while a W. Jackson wrote in a letter of strong approval for all Ravachol's acts. Meanwhile, at a meeting at the Berner Street club on Saturday, 16th July, "speeches in French, German, English and Yiddish were delivered to a crowded and most enthusiastic audience who cheered every allusion to Ravachol's struggles against society …" On Tuesday, 19th July, at the Athenaeum Hall, Tottenham Court Road, "another crowded audience listened to speeches from several comrades who urged the necessity of individual activity against society." It would seem therefore that there was a certain popular groundswell of opinion in the anarchist movement which was enthusiastically in favour of Ravachol-style propaganda by deed. This was not enthusiasm from afar either, particularly among the foreign anarchists in exile in Britain. Two of these exiles — François and Meunier — were being assiduously hunted by Melville and the political police for their alleged bombing of the Café Very in revenge for the arrest of Ravachol after a tip-off from one of the staff. Thirty police under Melville raided the house of Delbaque, a French anarchist, at 30 Charlotte Street, on 27th June, enthusiastically smashing open locked doors but finding no one. The police raided 39 Compton Street, Tavistock Square, on 27th July, causing more damage but coming away equally empty-handed. Meetings certainly took place at the Autonomie Club, where pro-and anti-Ravachol factions argued out the matter. One not altogether reliable source implies that François particularly had been basking in admiration at the Autonomie, being greeted as he walked in through the door with shouts of 'François! François!' Since, apparently, he was in the habit of boasting to all and sundry about his exploits it is not surprising that Melville knew he was in London. Given the circumstances he took a remarkably long time to catch the two men.[66] Both Cantwell and H.B. Samuels seem to have shared the pro-Ravachol enthusiasm, and occasional bursts of verbal terrorism in the *Commonweal* express the fact. Others, like Mowbray, if we remember his remarks about Nicoll's article being "foolish at best, damnable at worst," and Leggatt, who disavowed Ravachol at the anarchist demonstration on May Day, could be assumed to be in opposition to the line taken by Samuels and Cantwell. One has to remember that Nicoll had been arrested for verbal terrorism. It can be quite readily understood that some members of the group, particularly Mowbray, would be firmly opposed to 'provocative' material for the sake of it. Mowbray and Leggatt were by no means opposed to violence when it was a matter of mass mobilisation of the working class or as part of the organising process or defence, but presumably just did not see the point of putting the paper at jeopardy for the sake of rhetoric. As far as the *Commonweal* was concerned the group which included Mowbray and Leggatt seems to have been strong enough to stop any further articles in praise of Ravachol appearing after July. The side effect was, however, that reprinted theoretical material formed the bulk of the paper, which was now unleavened by even wilful extremism.

By August it was apparent that things were not well in London, though it was announced in the *Commonweal* that anarchist groups had been formed in Manchester and Leeds. A peculiar paragraph appeared in the paper after an announcement that a meeting to discuss the propaganda campaign for the autumn and winter would be held at the Berner Street club. It said, "Inspector Melville the premier liar of Scotland Yard has been boasting openly that he has succeeded even beyond his hopes in splitting up the anarchists into factions and has set them fighting each other instead of carrying on their work of propaganda. Those who are not of Melville's opinion will attend above meeting so that these hounds may have a little more work on hand. No plots but a discussion of steady serious propaganda ..." By 20th August, the outdoor speaking pitches in London were down to three. In the issue of 28th August there was a Notice to Readers which said: "It is with regret that we have to announce that unless more funds are forthcoming we shall not be able to publish next week. Donations to the Printing Fund should be forwarded to the *Commonweal* Office ..." In the following issue the number of groups had fallen to six (from ten in May) with the disappearance of Paddington, Holborn, North London and Whitechapel. This issue, 4th September, was the last in 1892. It was 'explained' why in a 'Parting Word to Our Readers':

The fluctuations of industry, have for a time without the aid of the police, scattered several of our groups, our comrades having to travel about in search of a livelihood, thus being prevented from doing a steady propaganda. This fact and the persecution which the name of Anarchist entails, have somewhat hindered the steady propaganda by means of which the *Commonweal* has hitherto existed. … In order that the Revolutionary movement should not be without a mouthpiece for too long a time, we ask comrades to consider the advisability of forming a fund to start a paper, outspoken and fearless on the first of May next, with funds behind it sufficient to avoid the necessity of these appeals.

The appeal to trade fluctuations as an excuse will not do in itself. Unemployment was greater, and yet anarchists were more numerous and active in 1893 and 1894 than in 1892.[67] The social disruption caused by the undoubted rise in unemployment in 1892 could not help but affect the anarchists too. The erosion of the working-class gains of 1889 to 1890 was proceeding steadily and in some areas at a disastrous rate. But for all this I feel sure that the fundamental reason why the paper stopped publication was that the particular combination of people running it could see no point in going on the way they were. The crisis was a crisis of morale. Nicoll was later to allege that "It was proposed to dismantle the office and sell the plant to the *Freedom* people."[68] He wrote an indignant letter from prison which, he says, the group did not publish. The implication is that it was only as a result of his protests that it was proposed to restart the paper the following May. Be this as it may, it is worth pointing out that any suspension of publication gave the group that restarted it an overwhelming claim of ownership. The winter of 1892–1893 gave time for shifting allegiances, reshuffles and arguments to do their work. When the paper restarted the editor was the same, but the character of the group and the nature of the paper had changed somewhat. H.B. Samuels had used the time well.

## Chapter 7
# H. B. SAMUELS AND
# THE *COMMONWEAL*

The *Commonweal* restarted on 1st May 1893, under the editorship of H.B. Samuels. Other members of the Commonweal Group included John Turner, Carl Quinn, Ernest Young, Tom Cantwell and Joseph Presburg. Financed by Max Nettlau and Dr Fauset Macdonald, it came out in an edition of eight pages and was issued, except in times of crisis, fortnightly. The early political career of H.B. Samuels is impossible to give in detail but he first appears on the scene in 1886. A tailor by trade, he was then in touch with the *Commonweal* and according to his own account took part in the West End Riots.[1] According to Nicoll's extremely prejudiced account, he first saw Samuels at a meeting to celebrate the acquittal of Hyndman, Burns, Williams and Champion on 'incitement to riot' charges after the West End affair. Samuels, "supported by a mysterious German in spectacles," asked Hyndman why he did not advocate, among other things, the blowing up of the London reservoirs. Hyndman, apparently, found it an easy enough question to answer.[2] By 1888 Samuels was playing an active part in the Socialist League, speaking at various open-air pitches with (again according to Nicoll) rather a penchant for violent rhetoric. He went with Mowbray and others to observe one of the trials at a free-speech fight in Yarmouth and was responsible for sending reports to the secretary (Charles). He became a member of the Socialist League Council in 1889, attended the International Socialist Congresses in Paris and went to Leeds to organise Jewish workers in the clothing and slipper trades in the same year. We have already seen the effect of his dispatches on the relationship of William Morris with the League. Yet in no way was Samuels the pariah of the movement which the later writings of David Nicoll would have us believe. He had served his time and played his part sufficiently well to be trusted by sections of the movement.

Nevertheless, Samuels, to use Max Nomad's phrase, was a terrorist of the word and, as later events were to show, a terrorist of the deed too, as long as the deeds were done by others. His rhetoric was by no means modified by his responsibilities as editor and played an important part in the stormy period that was about to begin. It must be made clear, however, that while he was the most influential of the advocates of more or less indiscriminate terror he was by no means alone in his advocacy. In the editorial of this first *Commonweal* of the new series he writes that the poverty of the workers leads them to the struggle for the emancipation of labour. So far this is nothing new. We are then given, however, the keynote of almost all his pronouncements: "In a struggle like this we hold that all means, however desperate, are justifiable. Individual and collective action are alike necessary and urgent." Desperate means and individual actions, be it noted, that tended in Samuels's writings to be separated from their purpose as prescribed by the theoreticians of propaganda by deed, namely the rousing of the masses to revolt. In a November 1893 issue of the *Commonweal* he wrote, "Smashing windows, robbing misers, coining counterfeit or smuggling are not means ... to the end; but ends in themselves and though we do not claim them as means ... still we welcome such acts of daring and lawlessness as they do not strengthen but weaken the present machinery of Government and exploitation." Nowhere, however, does Samuels ever attempt to *prove* that "ordinary" crime weakens "the present machinery of Government and exploitation." Crimes against property are in general an escape from a life of drudgery, boredom or want for the criminal but remain for the most part quite consistent with the principles of individual enrichment upon which our society is based. Where crime becomes an exemplary communalisation of property then it does represent an attack on the property relations of our society. This is a distinction that escapes H.B. Samuels. Let us take some examples.

In the *Commonweal* of 30th September 1893, he writes that taken with the good news of bomb explosions and illegal printing presses outside England "comrades here were cheered with the news that someone had smashed a jeweller's window and expropriated a tray of diamond rings valued at £420..." But the villain of the piece had been caught and appeared at the police court. This was "our Comrade Harry Conway [who] was charged with burglary. He bore himself well and with a disdainful mien refused to question the witnesses. He boldly acknowledged the act and declared himself an anarchist." In an article in the *Commonweal* (14th October 1893) Conway expanded on the reasons for his act. As far as the problem of unemployment is concerned, he says, every unemployed person "could soon solve this problem altogether, every individual for himself, by simply doing something that would mean either comfort out of prison or in it." He was sentenced at the end of October to eighteen months. His statement only shows a little more than a pessimistic realism. He did urge people to copy his act and kept his dignity in refusing to try and wriggle out of a conviction. But the dignity and the proceeds from the smash-and-grab were not designed to be shared.

On the other hand, there was the case of C.C. Davis of Birmingham. At the time that these events took place Davis, a brickmaker and gasworker, was, like Conway, unemployed and starving. He had been deeply involved in the unemployed agitation in Birmingham for several months. Thrown out of home by a vicious and drunken father at the age of eleven, he had drifted from labouring job to labouring job with every promise of turning out like his dad. But on coming into contact with the anarchist movement he started to read and think and had developed into a person of "wide culture" as *Freedom* put it.[3] The *Times* report describes his desperate act as concisely as a telegram:

Yesterday before the Birmingham stipendiary magistrate, a young man named Christopher Charles Davis was charged with damaging the plate glass window of a jeweller's shop to the extent of £25 and stealing 12 rings to the value of £100. He had been arrested while throwing the contents of the window into the street and the 12 rings were found in his hands. On hearing the charge the prisoner said, 'I ought not to be charged with stealing at all but with taking them. I had no intention of taking them at all; I merely wished to throw them into the road to give other people the chance of taking them.' The bricks with which the windows were smashed were wrapped in copies of the 'Walsall Anarchist' and a circular entitled 'Anarchism; work for all; overwork for none' was found in his possession. The prisoner was committed for trial. He shouted 'Hurrah for Anarchy' and the shout was echoed by two young men in the rear of the court who were promptly arrested and charged with disturbing the proceedings but dismissed with a caution.[4]

This almost crazy act of defiance, this one-man West End Riot, was designed literally and metaphorically for public consumption. The disinterested attack on property, the reference to the Walsall prisoners and the message of the circular all go to make up a remarkable minor example of the propaganda by deed.

And the message was clearly understood. As *Freedom* put it: "An epidemic of window smashing followed Davis's act. But although about 15 shop windows have been smashed and goods stolen, only a couple of arrests have been made. A peculiar instance occurred 4th February. A number of young men drew lots as to which of them should smash a shop window in Aston Street, Birmingham. When the bobby rushed up to arrest the one who did smash the window he (the window smasher) cried out, 'Three cheers for Anarchy.' So say we all." Davis himself underscored the point at his trial: "If the whole army of unemployed workmen who had assembled outside the Council House during the month of January to demand work had gone and done in a body what I have done alone, it would have had more effect on society than all the agitation in the world." He appealed to the jury not to bring in any verdict at all and to walk out of the court. He finished "Long live Ravachol, long live the Walsall anarchists!" Yet what did H.B. Samuels have to say about this? "Our comrade C.C. Davis … has been sentenced to 15 months hard labour. … His action proves to us the necessity of similar acts and also the desirability on such occasions, not merely of throwing valuables in the street, but of keeping as much as possible for the sustenance of persons and principles." This is more than a little crass. As Nicoll puts it: "It must be clear to all that Mr Samuels would degrade a bold act of revolt on the part of a starving man to the level of an ordinary theft."[5]

No matter what criticisms are put forward, however, the paper generally gave expression to the real desperation of sections of the working class at this time. While Samuels reduced everything to its lowest common denominator of illegality and the spectacular there is no doubt that his rhetoric evoked some deep responses. Furthermore the anarchist movement definitely grew during his editorship, though how much of that is due to Samuels is, of course, open to question. There were seven open-air speaking pitches advertised in the first issue of the new series of *Commonweal*. By June there were eighteen, and this was being kept up in September. These certainly do not represent the total number of anarchist speaking pitches in London at this time. These were regular speaking sites — *Freedom* gives a greater number of temporary ones. The blank statistics give no indication of the increasing difficulties the movement was labouring under. Police spies and agents provocateurs were now often in attendance, particularly in the foreign quarters of London.[6] The police were more ready than ever to disperse meetings, and Christians of various persuasions continued to try and break them up. Faction fighting, particularly with the S.D.F., was on the increase, exacerbated by mutual provocation and some successful membership-poaching by the anarchists.[7] The police were prepared to scrape the barrel to bring charges against anarchists. For example, *Commonweal* advertised a series of "indignation meetings to protest at the waste of wealth" on a royal wedding. On 29th June 1893 Cantwell and Young were arrested for fly-posting bills advertising the meetings which did not bear a printer's or publisher's name and address. The bills read:

### Royal Marriage
The London Anarchists will hold an indignation meeting on Sunday July 2 at Hyde Park, at 3.30 to protest at the waste of wealth upon these royal vermin while workers are dying of hunger and overwork. Fellow workers prepare for the revolution and that he who would be free must strike the blow.
DOWN WITH FLUNKEYISM![8]

The two men were remanded in custody for two days. Meanwhile the police had searched them, taken the *Commonweal* office keys and riffled the premises at Sidmouth Mews. The next issue of the *Commonweal* finds Samuels saying that as a result of this a cheque is missing from a letter and so is a revolver kept "to protect ourselves from burglars (legal or otherwise)."[9] The two men were eventually fined.

All things considered, however, the *Commonweal* office remained remarkably unscathed during H.B. Samuels's editorship and no further raids or searches were made until 1894 — after his forced resignation. This was despite a continual stream of inflammatory propaganda and despite promptings to the authorities from various respectable quarters. The *Morning Post* of 5th August, for example, quoted some remarks made by Samuels and added, "If this is not a provocation to breach of the peace and lawlessness, we would like to know what is. Mr Asquith should keep an eye on this inflammatory organ." And in the following issue of the *Commonweal*, H.B. Samuels proudly quoted the *Morning Post*. As in the case of C.C. Davis, industrial affairs were to be transmuted somewhat in Samuels's hands. A good example is the miners' strike of 1893. Samuels seemed incapable of separating *effective* direct action from spectacular direct action. In the 1st and 16th September issues of the *Commonweal* appeared two bitter pieces from George Tallis, an anarchist and a small shopkeeper in Pendlebury in the Lancashire coalfield. The first is a polemic against the various social democrats who urge voting and political education on a worker who "starves and watches his family and class being slowly murdered. He knows that the present system is wrong and requires to know how to alter it … he knows that the idle vicious class called masters bleed him to death, that he has no freedom, no liberty only to starve and he requires to be told how to prevent it: but that is not the education thought of by labour leaders, Fabian orators etc. Oh no! they want him to learn how to vote; that's all, my dears." The second piece carefully computes the surplus value extracted from the miner's toil and condemns the desultory Lancashire miners' leaders. And both articles make the suggestion that since the coal stocks held in reserve by the masters were their bargaining power then the coal stocks should be fired. This point and the suggestion made by John Turner that the local shops should be looted to feed the starving men were repeated in an *Anarchist Manifesto to the Miners* "issued and circulated by the comrades in the mining districts." The anarchists in Leicester and other places held meetings to protest against the dispatching of armed police and soldiers to the coalfields. (One result of this movement of troops was the Featherstone massacre of 7th September 1893, when two miners were killed and six wounded when troops fired on a crowd.)

But George Tallis's bitterness and his advocacy of direct action sprang from his first-hand experience of the miners' suffering. A collection at a meeting in Trafalgar Square on Sunday 17th September was sent to Tallis. He used it to buy food wholesale to distribute free from his shop. His description of this occasion is pitiable:

"…400 people turned up. The time arranged was 4.30 but children and women were at my shop at 12.30 and waited. The crush was something extraordinary, little children were crushed down and women fainted in their frantic endeavour to get a few potatoes, onions, carrots and turnips. I never saw people scramble so for anything … we had not half enough for the poor souls who begged for two potatoes or carrot and turnip at the finish. … Such a crowd would have made a graven image cry."

One understands immediately why Tallis should wish the miners to make real attacks on the forces that oppressed them. But compared to Tallis Samuels merely comes across as a man obsessed with violence. When he advocated the policy of the *Anarchist Manifesto to the Miners* he added that the miners should vary the monotony of looting food shops with marches to the pit head "to play games with trucks and trollies." After the 17th September meeting in Trafalgar Square the *Commonweal* reported that "Mr Butcher drew the attention of the House to some incendiary remarks … by a Mr H. Samuels, who speaking on the present crisis in the coal trade advised the miners to imitate the young Polish Jew Berkman who shot Frick … and if they could not fight the masters together they should fight individually 'with the torch, the knife and the bomb.'" The Home Secretary replied that the regulations governing the use of the square did not allow him to ban the anarchists as such and was of the opinion that prosecution would only give "undue importance to the remarks."[10]

H.B. Samuels's consistent reprinting of these remarks and grumblings from the authorities fills out the impression of him as a determined self-publicist — he seems more pleased that his spectacular remarks should be publicised in a hostile press than annoyed that their theoretical underpinning and their basis in mass suffering should be ignored. As time went by his spectacular remarks became more spectacular and his notoriety consequently became greater. It is difficult to believe that he did not cultivate this notoriety, and it is difficult to forgive him the fact that the consequences of it fell on others. A straw in the wind was the next anarchist meeting in Trafalgar Square on 14th October. This had been called to 'explain' to the unemployed where the S.D.F. was wrong in its tactics — another skirmish in the continuing anarchist/social democrat battles. On this occasion the police abruptly stopped the meeting, claiming that the allowed time was up. Carl Quinn continued his speech and was pushed off the plinth. He climbed back up and tried to carry on but was again hurled off by the police.[11]

A struggle for free speech had already begun in Manchester by the anarchist group there. It seems from the first to have been a specifically anti-anarchist affair and really marks the beginning of a sustained repression of anarchist propaganda. The Manchester anarchists had been holding meetings at Ardwick Green for some time. (Readers should not be fooled by the rural sounding name, Ardwick Green was a sooty park in an inner suburb of Manchester about a mile from the city centre.) These meetings had been increasingly harassed by militant Christians. On 4th October four anarchists were told to move on by the police while speaking.

They refused, were arrested and fined. The following week another anarchist, Kelly, was arrested under similar circumstances. He too was fined and warned that he or any other anarchist "would be severely dealt with" in future. By this time audiences were growing and the anarchists were attracting support from other socialists. At meetings of two and three thousand the arrests continued through October. Wider sympathy was evident: in the *Commonweal* for 11th November the Manchester anarchists reported: "we have the sympathy of the workers; and a pious sneak who makes it his business to create disorder at our meetings was ignominiously hustled out of [Stevenson] Square by the indignant people while a temperance orator who attacked us at New Cross and abused us had to run for his life." However from 12th November onwards the 'ringleaders' were being jailed or, more insidiously, being given the option of either finding large sureties or going to prison. The pressure was very great on the slender finances of the Manchester group. Their ability to resist was further undermined by the defection of the more timid socialists after the continental bomb explosions culminating in Vaillant's bomb in the French Chamber of Deputies on 9th December. They were forced to give up Ardwick Green on 7th January, though a militant note was attempted by the fact that a somewhat stormy meeting of protest took place on that date in Albert Square. By 11th January the anarchists were only speaking at their old stations at Stevenson Square and New Cross.[12] (It is interesting to note that a policeman, one Caminada, who made his name by his repression of these meetings at Ardwick Green was prosecuted later in the 1890s for taking bribes and kickbacks from brothels.) In London another demonstration of police hostility had taken place on Nicoll's release from prison. His welcome party emerged from Liverpool Street Station on 1st November singing the 'Marseillaise'. A crowd gathered and Nicoll's call for three cheers for the miners was "enthusiastically responded to." At this point a body of police charged out of the entrance to the Underground and began "punching and kicking everyone they could reach." The crowd was dispersed and his comrades got Nicoll away by bundling him on to a bus.

The chorus calling for repression of the anarchists grew louder in November. On the evening of 7th November a bomb allegedly thrown from the balcony of the Liceo Theatre in Barcelona exploded in the stalls. Thirty people died and many were wounded. The *Times* correspondent commented: "The barbarous atrocity of this deed calls for just reprisals on the part of the governing powers not only in Spain but of the combined civilised world. The outrage which has been committed against Barcelona society may tomorrow be repeated in some other large city."[13] This was the context in which the Chicago Martyrs meetings at South Place Institute, the Grafton Street club and Trafalgar Square caused "a howl of terror from our masters," as H.B. Samuels put it. At South Place at an "earnest and defiant meeting" Samuels made, according to David Nicoll, "his famous speech which soon rendered him notorious in London."

I claim the man who threw the bomb at the theatre as a comrade. We must have our own some day, they murdered our comrades and we must murder them. Twenty-three killed, how sad? ... An eye for an eye. Aye, twenty eyes for one eye. I claim that unknown comrade has done better work than any philosopher. That unknown comrade ... has caused such a terror that the rich dare not walk the streets of Barcelona for fear of the bombs. I don't believe in organising bodies of men to meet the Gatling guns. We will fight the bloodsuckers by any means. I don't blame these men because they are bloodsuckers. I don't blame a dog but I will kick him damned hard if he bites me. We expect no mercy from these men and we must show them none.[14]

A packed meeting took place at Grafton Hall on 11th November and "a few words from a couple of comrades were the means of starting a regular crusade against us in the daily press." This, thought H.B. Samuels, made a good advertisement for the movement. On 12th November, the meeting in Trafalgar Square ("the best meeting we have yet held there") was the cause of more "howls of terror." An MP asked for the adjournment of a debate to discuss a speech by John Murdoch. This admitted that "the affair of Barcelona was a horrible thing ... not the act of an anarchist, but that of men rendered desperate by existing conditions," but went on to say that "There would be something of the same kind here before very long, for men would not always be content to die in the gutter."[15] The *Daily Telegraph* devoted three consecutive leaders to anti-anarchist vituperation. At this point, towards the end of November, Herbert Burrows of the S.D.F. wrote to the *Commonweal* commenting on the blaze of publicity over the question of terror. He asked whether the capitalists of France and Spain had "disgorged" anything as a result of the bombings and commented: "Platform talk of making tyrants tremble is futile. They may tremble but they also laugh and hold on."[16] He had a point. The bombings carried out by Ravachol had been in revenge for the physical and judicial brutality shown by the French authorities over the May Day demonstrations of 1891. The Café Very bombing had been in revenge for the arrest of Ravachol through information given by a waiter. The Liceo Theatre bombing had been in revenge for the massacre of peasants in revolt in Xeres. Revenge may have been sweet but Ravachol had been executed as had others after him and savage repressions had been unleashed. And no capitalists disgorged. Yet Herbert Burrows misunderstood the point of the bombs. In France and Spain the workers' movement had its back to the wall.

In England demonstrations were often attacked by police with batons. On the Continent they were often fired on. The bombs represented, in Stuart Christie's phrase, "the rearguard of the proletariat": they were an expression of violent resentments which could find no other outlet. In France and Spain these 'last ditch' activities of the anarchist bombers are inextricably entwined with the early history of working-class movements with more room for manoeuvre — the revolutionary general unions, the C.G.T. and the C.N.T. What Samuels had done was to take the 'image' of such bombings out of their context. The meaning of the bombs was immediately perceived by sections of the working class on the Continent; but this was not true of England. Appeals from the English anarchists to the unemployed or starving strikers to loot shops or use sabotage and violent means *could* be perceived as relevant, but the 'ultras' like Samuels were undermining the clarity of such propaganda. They had narrowed the propaganda by deed until it became propaganda *for* the deed.

As a result the wider propaganda rather went by the board as discussion of the bombings engaged an excited press and Parliament. Time and energy had to be put into putting the bombs into context — largely by those sections of the English movement who were opposed to bombing as a useful tactic. The Freedom Group issued their first pamphlet on this question — *Anarchism and Outrage*, written by Charlotte Wilson. Distaste for bombing rhetoric was the basic reason why James Tochatti started his magazine *Liberty*, the first issue of which appeared in January 1894. The manifesto in the first number went to special pains to insist that anarchists were not dynamiters and said, "we believe that bombastic talk and glorifying the acts of men driven to desperation by circumstances can only serve to retard the progress of anarchist ideas by alienating the sympathies of the mass of the people." Tochatti had remained in close contact with the Hammersmith Socialist Society after it had split from the Socialist League. His magazine was in fact to use contributions from many ex-members of the League, and those not necessarily anarchists. The most prominent of the ex-League anarchists to cooperate with him was Sam Mainwaring.

Meanwhile the authorities were taking steps to restrict anarchist propaganda under the cover of the 'howls of terror.' The committee at South Place issued a statement after the 11th November meeting saying that they would no longer let their hall to anarchists. The speeches at Trafalgar Square on 12th November put the future use of the square by anarchists in doubt. An article entitled 'Bombs!' by H.B. Samuels definitely closed the square to them, rules or no rules.[17] Samuels said:

> A bomb has burst in a theatre in Barcelona, and the English people are trembling about it even now. Very strange that an explosion a thousand miles away should arouse such mixed feelings here. Or is it because somebody said it was a good job. Well I am one of them who welcome this affair as a great and good act — not on the part of those concerned, but because of the death of thirty rich people and the injury of eighty others. Yes, I am really pleased; and in spite of the fact that comrades and friends have been talking at me over it, I cannot feel sorry there.

Nevertheless Samuels wrote asking for the square on 3rd December so that speakers "could explain to the people the aims and principles of Anarchist Communism" and was refused. The meeting — or an attempt at one — took place anyway. The Commonweal Group went to the square, distributed leaflets and gathered a crowd of about 1,500. Quinn, after persistent attempts to speak, was kicked, thumped and arrested. Lawrence then managed to hurl himself over the double cordon of police round the column and began to address the crowd. He was pulled off and arrested. Another couple of arrests were made and the crowd began to get restive and push the police around. Banham then got on a bus and began to speak to the crowd from the top deck. At this point mounted police were called in and the police began to try to clear the square. This took some time; there were a few brisk fights and bricks were thrown. The *Commonweal* asserted that "the battle of Trafalgar Square has recommenced" but made little attempt to carry on the battle themselves. The following Sunday (10th December) it was Nicoll who attempted to hold a meeting. Despite wet weather there were 4,000 people in the square. Unlike the meeting held by the Commonweal Group this received very little publicity in the anarchist press. *Freedom* gave it a bare mention, adding "Nicoll was set on by a gang of roughs, set on, some say by the police."[18] *Commonweal*, for reasons which will become apparent, did not mention it at all. It is a measure of the mood of the time that on the Sunday following (17th December) what seems to have been a quite spontaneous meeting took place. By 3.30pm 1,500 to 2,000 people had gathered and were milling about. Eventually a man named Inchua who had been active in the unemployed demonstrations of the previous winter gave a short speech and led a march down the Strand which was broken up by the police.[19] It is not clear what happened after this point, though by 21st December Nicoll was writing to Nettlau that the matter was "satisfactorily settled" and claiming that the anarchists by causing trouble had forced the authorities to rescind their ban. If it was a victory it was a temporary one.

It was noticeable that there had been no fulminations in the *Commonweal* calling for a campaign of terror to force the opening of the square. Was this not an occasion when Samuels's own statement applied: "I do not blame a dog but I will kick him damned hard if he bites me." In fact from this point on there is a distinct quietening in the tone of H.B. Samuels's writing. On the bomb thrown by Vaillant (9th December) he can only say that his act was the natural, desperate result of "long years of unrequited labour and misery."[20] On Émile Henry's bomb in the Café Terminus (12th February 1894) he says that execution is no deterrent to men who are too desperate to care if they die. By the issue of 10th March 1894, with its black-bordered front-page memorial to Martial Bourdin killed in the Greenwich Park explosion, he is writing: "Now that the governments of Europe are considering the advisability of taking combined action against the anarchists, we, of necessity, are driven to consider ways of preserving ourselves against them ... it is imperative that we consider the new position. The workers, generally, are against us because they do not understand; therefore our work is to make them understand us, to understand us is to know their friends from their enemies, and to know one's enemy," he ends with a slight rally, "is the one thing essential towards action — offensive and defensive." At the Commune commemoration meetings of that March he is back-pedalling distinctly. Why do anarchists not throw bombs in England? he asks. Is it because the English anarchists think that the capitalists should get off scot-free or because they do not care about suffering humanity?

No, it is because we see the impression our ideas are making upon all sorts and conditions of men; it is because we feel the strength of our moral and intellectual position that is made possible by the freedom of speech, pen and platform that we enjoy in England. As long as I have that freedom I will decline to advocate or employ forcible and destructive methods though I will not answer for or condemn others. ... The bomb is the direct result of the throttling of the right to free speech.[21]

At the Commune meeting at the C.I.U. Hall he went so far as to assert the most dubious proposition that if there was free speech in France the bomb would disappear.

Thus from December 1893 onwards a really quite sudden moderation came over H.B. Samuels. It is possible to suggest several reasons. The sudden closing of Trafalgar Square and South Place to the anarchists might have brought him up rather short. It might well also have been the "fact that comrades and friends have been talking at me over it." The comrades and friends could easily have been foreign anarchists. Vaillant's bomb in December had unleashed a fierce repression in France, with anarchist newspapers being forcibly closed and 2,000 arrest warrants being issued. Some anarchists were arrested, but many went into hiding or fled, and many French anarchists arrived in London at this time. The events in France were a tangible lesson in the repressive powers of the state which it was impossible to ignore. And it looked as though something similar was being prepared in England. A French newspaper correspondent quoted in the *Times* says: "The approval expressed by all the Tory and most of the ministerial papers of the measures taken by the French Government makes the Anarchist refugees fear that rigorous measures will be taken against them in England also."[22] This correspondent then goes on to detail the day-to-day harassment of the refugees in London:

> At the bars frequented by them detectives are mixing with the customers and regularly 'standing treat' and try to catch up the conversation. Search warrants not being as easy in England as in France, the police stop in the streets any Anarchist bearing a suspicious bundle. On being taken to the station he is questioned, the bundle is inspected and while he is awaiting the officers' decision he is photographed if this has not already been done and he is then released. This device

which is particularly exasperating to the Anarchists has of late been daily repeated. What still more disquiets them is that Scotland Yard has carefully drawn up a list of refugees in London and that English employers are more and more disinclined to engage them. Many of them, in spite of the help of their comrades are reduced to extreme poverty and look forward to the time when unless they are to starve they will be forced to quit England. The subscriptions of the leaders are steadily falling off and the expenses of the propaganda have swallowed up the reserves. The rich men of the party, moreover, afraid of being considered accomplices in outrages are reducing their contributions.

It was at about this time that Detective Sweeny burgled a printing shop used by a group of French exiles. He did not have to repeat this manner of making inquiries, since he came to an arrangement with the landlady to inspect the contents at will after hours.[23]

But if caution in the face of a possible repression explains Samuels's new moderation there are also explanations for the timing of his most spectacular pronouncements at South Place and in his 'Bombs!' article. In the eyes of many anarchists he held the editorship of the *Commonweal* in trust until the release of David Nicoll. A conference of London anarchists had taken place at Grafton Hall on 24th September 1893, and "so much had to be discussed that after six hours it was decided to hold a national conference about two weeks after Nicoll's release."[24] No agenda was published for the Grafton Hall conference, but it is not unlikely that it was similar to the one published for the later one which centred on *Commonweal* matters and included as a separate item the question of editorship of the paper.[25] The question of who was to be editor was still, therefore, open when Nicoll was released from prison. And the welcome given to him on his release showed Nicoll's tremendous popularity in the movement. At the public meeting of welcome on 3rd November, Nicoll was given a tumultuous reception. *Commonweal* quoted a "capitalist paper" on the subject: "The reception accorded to Nicoll when he appeared on the platform was enough to un-nerve the strongest man and as Nicoll is not the strongest the wonder is that he did not entirely break down." In the same article, Anarchist Jack writes: "As soon as his health permits and he has completed his provincial engagements he will resume his old place on the *'Weal*, when, we have no doubt, its size and circulation will soon increase ..." Yet in the same issue Samuels was writing: "Some comrades may be surprised at our not making the editorship of the paper at once over to Nicoll." He explains that things have taken a new course and that the paper has "a different crew of capable determined men." When Nicoll examines the facts, he says, he can form an opinion, but in the meantime he "must be allowed to have what rest he desires and needs and to write what and when he feels able to." H.B. Samuels sounds decidedly unwilling to give up his position.

Behind the scenes there seems to have been some amount of pressure put on Nicoll. There had been changes in the group. Nicoll wrote: "When I came out of prison the character of the old *Commonweal* group had completely changed. Except Turner, Presburg, Samuels, Cantwell and Mowbray hardly any of its former members belonged to it, and Mowbray attended very little." Nicoll also alleged that members of the old group had been driven out by "calumny and slander" emanating from Turner and Samuels. But it was one of the remaining "old members," Presburg (later Perry), who gave Nicoll a file "of Mr Samuels *Commonweal* and suggested that I should read it, and that, if I could see my way clear to adopt a similar policy, the Group would 'kindly let me edit the paper.'" Nicoll says he declined this offer since he did not wish to advocate bombs, "coining counterfeit and robbing misers." There was disagreement in other areas too. Shortly after his release Nicoll wrote to Nettlau, "The Commonweal Group has decided that I am not to edit the paper till the Christmas Conference has decided whether my principles are sufficiently advanced. It appears I am not strong enough upon the great question of advancing the revolution by picking your comrades' pockets i.e. Expropriation ..." Nicoll was not prepared to take this quietly. "I kicked up a row at the Group," he says, "and demanded my former post." And he went further than that: "I expressed my opinion pretty freely regarding Mr Samuels. I said if he was not a spy he was being used by one." This was a clear reference to Samuels's friendly relations with the "French group" of ultras at the Autonomie Club. This group continued to support Coulon: "Saint Coulon ranks next to Saint Ravachol among the

French group." Nicoll told Nettlau that he believed Samuels to be a puppet of Coulon's though he was too stupid to be a spy himself. The French group was of the opinion, apparently, that Nicoll was a "damned Social Democrat like Merlino, Malatesta, Kropotkin and everybody but Samuels. Samuels is the true and only Anarchist."[26] Nicoll might have been justified in his anger over being excluded from the editorship but the accusations of spying against Samuels could not be countenanced by the group at this time, and the result was an open breach.

So Samuels's speech at South Place and his 'Bombs!' article can therefore be seen as attempts to assert his position of influence in the face of the 'threat' from Nicoll. Both occurred shortly after Nicoll's release. It seems quite consistent with Samuels's personality that he should equate Nicoll's evident popularity in the movement with his notoriety in the press. So Samuels took steps to become notorious. And the threatening response to his pronouncements might explain their quite rapid fall in temperature once that purpose had been achieved. Samuels was confirmed as editor of the *Commonweal* at the conference held at the Autonomie Club on 26th December 1893. Nicoll alleged, however, that the conference was rigged. It seems clear that Nicoll hoped to appeal over the heads of the Commonweal Group to the movement at large since, as he says, "I was on good terms with most Anarchists in London" and had as the result of his imprisonment some status as martyr. He was writing to Nettlau in late November, "I don't think Samuels will retain the editorship after Christmas." But according to Nicoll the conference was "very well managed":

Tom Cantwell acted as porter and excluded all 'possible disturbers'. The usual pretext was they were 'not members' of the 'Commonweal Group'. Most London Anarchists were not, the Commonweal Group consisting of about a dozen members. ... If however a man's principles were alright, i.e. if he were a friend of Mr Samuels, they let him in. Besides the benefits of 'scientific packing', Mr Samuels had the advantage of the official support of the *Freedom* people. There were two delegates present — Agnes Henry and Dr Macdonald. Miss Henry was neutral, Dr Macdonald supported Samuels with enthusiasm. ... Seeing how everything had been 'arranged' I threw up the editorship.'[27]

"I have got the sack," he wrote to Nettlau, "because I am not advanced enough."

There is one further reason for Samuels's relative restraint after December 1893. It is more than likely that he had started considering possibilities open to him in what was to become the I.L.P.! While attending a conference of Scottish anarchists around Christmas 1893 he took the opportunity to visit the annual conference of the Scottish Labour Party, which was to form a constituent part of the I.L.P. after January 1895. His account of this visit in the *Commonweal* is long and, considering the treatment handed out to the S.D.F. and social democrats generally, is surprisingly warm and friendly. He was invited to make a short speech and writes admiringly of Keir Hardie. And indeed after the events we are to describe in the next two chapters Samuels did indeed gravitate towards the I.L.P. By May 1894 he had already displayed noticeable political ambitions.[28] In 1895 he joined the Kilburn branch of the I.L.P. and was almost immediately adopted as their delegate to the Newcastle conference.[29] The I.L.P., which hesitated to openly call itself a socialist body at that time, could hardly be expected, even by H.B. Samuels, to accept into its ranks an advocate of the random slaughter of members of the upper class in the name of the class war.

## Chapter 8

# THE GREENWICH PARK EXPLOSION[1]

If H.B. Samuels had only been a self-publicising terrorist of the word perhaps the worst one could say of him would be the assessment made by a contemporary anarchist who knew him quite well, Louise Sarah Bevington: "about the most rubbishy character possible. ... The keynotes of his character are vanity and vindictiveness."[2] But the circumstances surrounding the explosion of a bomb in Greenwich Park which killed the man who was carrying it led some anarchists, the most prominent of whom was David Nicoll, to assert that Samuels was an agent provocateur employed by the police. This further led to accusations that Samuels was responsible for this man's death. Anarchist bombs in England were now more than a matter of talk.

At 4.40pm on Thursday, 15th February, there was a loud explosion near the Royal Observatory, Greenwich Park. When a park keeper and some schoolboys rushed to the spot they found a man very badly wounded but still alive. His left arm had been blown off and he had a large hole in his stomach through which his guts protruded. He died soon after being found. The police were called and they rapidly came to the conclusion that the man had been carrying a bomb which had exploded. Documents found on his body, including a membership card for the Autonomie Club, showed him to be Martial Bourdin, who was "well known among the Anarchists of London."[3] Presumably, therefore, both he and his associates were known to the police. Yet the police were a little lackadaisical. Had they wished they could have had the details of the case collated with other information on Bourdin and could have made raids the same night. Shortly before the day of the Greenwich Park explosion Coulon had written to the *Pall Mall Gazette* saying that "There are few [anarchists] whose dossiers are not filed at Scotland Yard," though anything Coulon might say has to be taken with a pinch of salt. In any case the documents the police had were enough to give

suggestive addresses. It can hardly have been a question of legal niceties —
after the arrest of Deakin in London they had not waited for a warrant to
raid the Walsall Socialist Club. Neither was it the case that the police had
been lulled into a sense of false security by general anarchist inactivity.
Émile Henry's bomb had exploded at the Café Terminus in Paris on 12th
February 1894, i.e. three days before the accident at Greenwich, and the
sensation was still at its height. Indeed the English press, already full of
the deeds of the continental anarchists, took the Greenwich explosion as a
confirmation of its direst predictions of similar outrages in England. It was
the main item of news for over a week and hysteria knew no bounds.

It is a little surprising, then, that the police did not move until the night
of the following day. This allowed the dead man's fellow conspirators
(of whose existence the Central News was quite certain) to be warned
by accounts of the explosion in the following morning's papers.[4] Indeed
Nicoll said later that Bourdin's landlord had told him that after Bourdin's
death and before the police raids, one of Bourdin's friends had warned
him of the likelihood of police activity, and the landlord had destroyed
Bourdin's personal papers. When the raids came they were restricted to
Bourdin's lodgings and the Autonomie Club — both of them unlikely
places to find conspirators under the circumstances. The Autonomie
Club, in any case, was in bad odour in the movement because of the large
numbers of police spies who hung around the place. Without the fact of
Bourdin's involvement with the club it would thus have been avoided by
anyone who felt it necessary to be careful.

The police raid took place at 10pm on Friday, 16th February. Inspector
Melville gained admission to the Autonomie Club through knowing the
'secret knock' necessary — or so the papers alleged. Once inside he replaced
the hall porter with Sergeant Walsh[5] and other policemen who were ordered
to allow people in but not out. As people came in they were hustled down
into the main hall of the club in the basement. Only one person seriously
resisted, but he was overpowered ("a diversion, which it must be confessed,
was greatly enjoyed by the officers").[6] From 10.30pm until midnight the
members of the club were interrogated. The club was searched and nothing
in the way of explosives was found, although there were many leaflets and a
poster that had been printed in London and read 'Mort à Carnot!'[7]

Simultaneously raids took place on 18 Titchfield Street and 30 Fitzroy Street nearby. At Titchfield Street they were more lucky: hidden at the bottom of a wardrobe under a pile of newspapers was a small flagon of sulphuric acid, identical in detail to the one reconstructed from fragments at the site of the explosion in Greenwich.[8]

So in fact nothing new really emerged from these raids. No accomplices had been arrested. 'Explosive' material had been found at the house of the man who had blown himself up — interesting but not surprising. Yet further details were to emerge in the press over the following week which clearly implicated the now notorious H.B. Samuels. On the afternoon of the day of his death Bourdin "was observed in company with another man, in the neighbourhood of Hanover Square and later on the two parted company in Whitehall, Bourdin then walking over Westminster Bridge and taking the tram to Greenwich."[9] This 'other man' was Samuels. In a statement to the Central News Samuels "admitted that he had been in Bourdin's company on the day of the explosion at two o'clock and had remained in his company a considerable time." He also displayed some knowledge which might have encouraged the police to interview him. He said, "had this unfortunate accident not occurred, the consequences I feel certain would have been terrible. I don't mean that Bourdin intended to commit any outrage on Thursday, but I do think that it was the commencement of an extensive plot. I have an idea, but I have no proof of its being correct, that the manufacture of bombs for Continental purposes has been going on here for some time."[10] In later statements, Samuels said that he had been followed to Whitehall by detectives when he had been with Bourdin. It seems possible that Bourdin was under fairly systematic observation: the wretched Coulon alleged (in the *Morning Leader*) that he had been following Bourdin for some days though not on the day he died.[11] It is rather remarkable that in the face of all this Samuels was not even questioned by the police, particularly since Samuels was Bourdin's brother-in-law.

Samuels was to display further knowledge of the details surrounding the death of Bourdin; but this was not until a much delayed issue of the *Commonweal* came out after Bourdin's funeral. The funeral itself was a sombre lesson to the anarchists in the extent to which the ultras had misjudged the power of bomb explosions to encourage the workers to revolt. Even before the funeral the *Times* wrote "everywhere, even in the streets near the Autonomie Club, the unpopularity of the anarchists is striking. To issue from the door is to encounter a storm of abuse which albeit coarse is distinctly animated by a proper spirit."[12] Yet despite this, the anarchists seemed intent on trying to make Bourdin into a martyr. Their model in this was probably Vaillant, who had been executed on 6th February 1894. His grave at Ivry cemetery had become a kind of shrine, with huge queues of people filing past throwing on flowers and wreaths. The anarchists were not alone in the light they gave to Bourdin's death: Jack Williams of the S.D.F. did not find it forced to praise in the same breath the courageous examples of Vaillant and Bourdin at his unemployed meetings at Tower Hill.[13] At this point the possibility of a public anarchist demonstration at Bourdin's funeral was being openly discussed in the press. Martial Bourdin's brother was reported unwilling to "permit the Anarchists at large to make a great parade." But the question rather depended on whether or not the police returned to his family the £13 in gold found on Bourdin's body and was settled by the police declining to hand it over on the incredible grounds that it was "part of Bourdin's equipment for an unlawful exercise." Since the family could not afford a private funeral without this money, the anarchists took over the expense and management of the funeral.

The funeral procession was scheduled to start at 1pm on 23rd February. But by noon the crowds were already gathered outside the undertakers in Marylebone and in Fitzroy Square where the procession was due to call.

According to the *Times* there were 10,000 to 15,000 people in Fitzroy Square and although there were many anarchists and sympathisers present the general mood in both places was hostile and violent. In Fitzroy Square there was sporadic fighting and six medical students were arrested. A group of men went to the Autonomie Club stoned it, breaking several windows. Outside the undertakers was quieter until the coffin appeared. A large cordon of police held back the crowd and an attempt by a group of anarchists carrying red and black flags to burst through it was a failure. When the coffin was carried out to the hearse there was a great deal of booing and confused shouting and the crowd surged forward. Anarchists who attempted to link arms and form up behind the hearse were swallowed up in the crowd. The police held the people back as best they could and directed the hearse north — away from Fitzroy Square to the east — and blocked the road in a series of holding operations to prevent the crowd from following it. But people kept on running round these roadblocks through side streets and it was not until the hearse, moving at a fast trot, reached St John's Wood, about a mile away, that the pursuers had been left behind. The *Times* said, "few can doubt that, but for the police, Bourdin's funeral car would have been wrecked and Bourdin's body would have been torn to pieces." There was another largely hostile crowd at the cemetery. The police were stopping people at the gates, but despite this several hundred people were crowded round the grave and were pushed back into a circle. The coffin was quickly lowered without ceremony into the grave. "Hardly had the coffin reached the bottom of the grave before a tall, fair-haired man whose name is believed to be Quinn leaped forward. He had been admitted within the ring of police as one of the mourners and he was evidently ready to utter a funeral address. He succeeded so far as to shout 'Fellow anarchists ...'" He was seized immediately by the police and hustled away towards the gates. "A mob of a hundred or more followed and soon a cry of 'Hang him' was raised and re-echoed all around."[14] The grave was rapidly filled and the crowd dispersed.

There was an element of sightseeing in the whole affair. The *Times* reported that sensation-seekers had been visiting the undertaker's to gawp at Bourdin's body. The presence of medical students at Fitzroy Square indicated that a reactionary mobilisation of some sort had taken place. The nature of the coarse remarks hurled at people emerging from the Autonomie Club was most probably racialist. The bulk of the newspaper comment on the Greenwich affair was to the effect that it marked the beginning of an importation of nasty foreign practices to England's green and pleasant land. Socialism of any kind had been labelled 'foreign' from the beginning. But whether sensation, reactionary mobilisation or chauvinism had drawn sections of the crowd, the fact remained that more or less spontaneously a crowd of mainly working people had gathered to attack the funeral of a man that the anarchists were trying to present as a martyr in the worker's cause. It was a melancholy moment for the movement. The anarchists had faced harassment from the police and opposition, violent or otherwise, from identifiable groups with an axe to grind; but they had never had to face anything like a mass gut reaction hostility before. The extent of this hostility seems to have come as something of a surprise to the authorities, and they were to absorb and act on its implications. But it was a severe shock to the anarchists. There had been a tendency to think that, as George Tallis had put it, "the worker knows that the idle vicious class called masters bleed him to death, that he has no freedom, no liberty only to starve and he requires to be told how to prevent it." The workers, it was assumed, were passive anarchists, and all that was required was exemplary action for them to become active. But if this analysis was correct there was something deeply wrong with bomb explosions as exemplary action as far as England was concerned. It must be understood how grave an admission it was for H.B. Samuels to write in the first issue of the *Commonweal* after Bourdin's funeral "The workers are generally against us ..."

On the black-bordered front page of the issue of 10th March there is a long memorial to Martial Bourdin which sets this admission in the specific context of the events at the funeral: "Our noble comrade lies now beneath the sod. At an early age he risked his future chances of comfort, pleasure and life itself for the benefit of suffering humanity — ignorant, brutish suffering humanity — that greeted his funeral cortège with derision, contempt and hatred ..." But this memorial also gives further background to the reasons for Bourdin's presence in Greenwich Park in the first place. Samuels wrote after enumerating Bourdin's qualities: "Such a comrade ... undertook the conveyance of dangerous explosive compounds to a secluded spot, where none could have been injured, in order to put to the test a new weapon of destruction that would have furnished the revolutionary army with another means of terrorising those who consciously or unconsciously consign so many innocent lives to destitution and despair." At the same time Samuels was boasting in private of a closer involvement:

> Samuels having as it is said on good authority supplied him [Bourdin] with the 'new compound', suggested to him to take it somewhere for the purpose of 'experiment'. Well Bourdin in all good faith thought

'experiment' *meant experiment* and hit on Epping Forest as a place where he would have a good chance of exploding his compound against a big tree without great danger of its being heard, or him seen before he could get away. ... Well as the fates had it, Samuels met him just as he was starting with his ingredients. 'I'm going,' says Bourdin, touching his pockets significantly. 'Where to?' 'Epping Forest.' 'Oh don't go there, go to Greenwich Park.' 'Alright.' And they went together as far as Westminster where they were seen; and one of them accordingly was made the butt of the police. How do I know Samuels told him where to go? Because Mr Samuels, whom I used to see very often at that time, *told me*. Why do I repeat the conversation above? Because Samuels himself, before he was suspected by the Group and while he was desirous of seeming an important character in the eyes of sundry gaping comrades, boastingly related it.

The writer is Louise Sarah Bevington in a letter to Nicoll, reprinted in his pamphlet *Letters from the Dead*. She does not write as one who opposes the use of explosives, her attitude being summed up in the final lines of one of her articles for the *Commonweal*: "Dynamite is a last and very valuable resource and as such is not to be wasted on side issues."[15] She had also published poems in praise of Lingg, Ravachol and Pallas, and her suspicions of Samuels — she was clearly convinced that he was a police agent — are not tinged with questions of interest as Nicoll's are. Though Samuels had somewhat moderated his printed statements he seems in private to have continued to urge bomb attempts on all and sundry. His first 'success' was Bourdin, though there seems to have been something of a lull in these activities after this which is easily explainable by the funeral and its aftermath.

In order to understand subsequent events it is necessary to widen the focus somewhat to show the pressures the anarchist movement was acting under. We have seen that there was some measure of popular hostility. This was to combine with police harassment and the activity of agents provocateurs and made the anarchists jumpy and more prepared to take a jaundiced look at the super-militant among them. In one sense this represented a loss of nerve. It certainly tended towards a fragmentation of the movement. And one result of these combined circumstances was the end of the *Commonweal* as a paper that had any organic connection with the development of anarchism within the Socialist League.

## Chapter 9
# THE COLLAPSE OF THE *COMMONWEAL*

The anarchists had become the apostles of total destruction in the more gullible sections of the popular imagination. The mad professor in *The Secret Agent*, the anarchists in G.K. Chesterton's *The Man Who Was Thursday* and the figure in cloak and wide-brimmed hat carrying a bomb marked 'BOMB' in *Pip Squeak and Wilfred* cartoons were all variations on a stereotype developed in the early 1890s. This was obviously related to some of the activities and statements of recognised anarchist militants. But it was also to do with the activities of agents provocateurs like Coulon, whose *Anarchist Feast at the Opera* had been read to such effect at the Walsall trial, and the quite blatant use of anti-anarchist 'black' propaganda in the press. We have seen the worst that Samuels and Coulon could do. Yet how does it compare with an article which appeared in *Tit-Bits* on 10th Match 1894. The writer of the piece says that through a "Gentleman holding a high position in the detective force" he is able to get an introduction to a "swarthy, beetle-browed ruffian" who is a souteneur (i.e. pimp) and an anarchist. The gentleman in the detective force really seems to know his stuff, because this anarchist would appear to be a very dangerous man indeed — so dangerous, in fact, that one wonders what a detective is doing introducing him to reporters when he should obviously be thrown into the deepest dungeon available. The 'anarchist' talks at length about poison and bombs and "war to the death against Society." Air is to be introduced into the gas mains so as to cause terrible explosions. Two comrades are in Berlin busily studying the culture of dangerous germs "so as to be able to infect some of the poorest and most squalid districts in the End of London." Others are engaged in collecting the clothes worn by cholera victims on the Continent so they can be brought to Britain to start epidemics. Our reporter asks the detective whether the 'anarchist' is serious about all this. The detective, in that tight-lipped way detectives have, answers that the projected libertarian cholera epidemic is 'interesting' in the light of a previous incident. A notorious foreign anarchist had a parcel addressed to him from Havana, but he did not claim it. The parcel was then opened:

> It proved to contain a lot of old clothing which was almost immediately burned, but three days later the two Custom House Officials who overhauled the stuff sickened and died; 'I thought then,' said the detective, 'that the deaths were due to accident. Now I think it was probably a case of murder.'
> 'And the weapon used by the murderer was ...?'
> 'Yellow fever!' replied the detective grimly.

This kind of 'black' propaganda opened several useful possibilities for the authorities. It could be used to tar the left generally. This tended to scare other groupings and to isolate the anarchists — the S.D.F., for example, refused to cooperate with the anarchists in organising a demonstration on 1st May, 1894 because "bomb-throwing was prejudicial to the case of socialism."[1] It tended to neutralise opposition to repressive measures used first against anarchists, which then became sanctified by precedent and could be used against other groups. In certain cases it could inspire a popular reactionary backlash — even if this had to be helped along a bit. As a result of the "capitalist press inciting all and sundry to attack and lynch Anarchists" a mob of 'constitutional Peckhamites' attacked an anarchist meeting in Peckham on 15th March. They were assisted by Detective Sergeant Walsh of the C.I.D. "who exhibited his manliness by getting behind little boys and pushing them on us. ... They surged up to the platform and tried to seize the red flag. A fight for possession ensued which ended with the flag being ripped to shreds."[2] The speaker, Forrester, was arrested and charged with assault and causing a disorderly crowd to assemble. He was found guilty and bound over in £25 for six months with the option of a month in prison. Agnes Henry was refused permission to stand surety because she was a woman, and H.B. Samuels was refused because he would not swear on the Bible. After Forrester had been in jail for a week, W.B. Parker was eventually accepted to stand surety. The following week the Peckham group again held a meeting and:

an enormous crowd assembled. ... Comrades Quinn, Banham, Carter and Alsford addressed the meeting which was perfectly orderly for some time until an organised gang of blackleg gas-stoker and detectives started hooting and pushing, finally breaking up the meeting by force. The police were present in large numbers watching eagerly for the least opportunity for a 'charge'. These meetings have now had to drop owing to the fact that local comrades will not turn up and support but the propaganda will be kept up in other ways by the distribution and sale of literature.[3]

The police, it appeared, had won.

The 1st May demonstration was the occasion of a further 'popular attack' on the anarchists managed and instigated by the police. The anarchists had two platforms at Hyde Park. One of them was left alone (speakers: Samuels, Louise Michel, Mowbray), but at the other one (Quinn, Turner and Leggatt) there were "constant interruptions, interjections and abusive epithets from a portion of the audience at the rear." Both *Freedom* and Samuels state that those responsible were detectives "and those too who are tolerably well known to us." They had been manoeuvring about "now closing ranks in a circle to hold a conference; now scattering and looking around as if expecting more to come. After an hour and a half, groups of roughs, mostly youths of between 14 and 17, appear on the scene, forming the bodyguard of Melville's gang. A hoot, a yell from these youths, jogged on this side and that by the Scotland Yarders, and the orderly assembly is rudely interrupted."[4] There seems to have been some measure of hostility to the anarchists, for Samuels says that the audience were content with these interruptions though the detectives were not.

So when they saw a chance to urge on some fools to upset the speakers' rostrum they did so, pushing themselves through the people until, when within reach, they deliberately struck at, and with both fists, any comrade they knew (and they know us now pretty well) following them up and chasing them with the ready assistance of contented slaves out for a bit of fun. I saw Banham punched and kicked, Tochatti brutally struck in the head and face. ... One of our flags and a platform were

destroyed by a rush of detectives, who justified the criticism Leggatt
had bestowed on them by knocking him down and kicking him. ...
All this was done directly by the detectives (whose names I know) and
others at their instigation.

The police were clearly using — or organising — elements hostile to
anarchism which had revealed themselves at the funeral of Bourdin. The
1st May incident was, of course, represented by the press as a popular
attack on the anarchists by outraged citizens. According to *Freedom* an
attempt at a similar incident by the police on the 'first Sunday in May'
and 'official' demonstration was rapidly discouraged by the crowds of
socialists present. There was a lesson there if the anarchists would but
have seen it.

The *Commonweal* was obviously under closer scrutiny by the police.
From the issue of 28th April 1894 until its demise, the *Commonweal*
printed alongside its business address the following advice: "if a receipt
is not forwarded within three days, notice should be sent to M. Galbraith,
82 Beresford Street, S.E. The authorities have great difficulty in delivering
our letters to time or indeed at all in a number of cases where money has
been enclosed." It need hardly be said that this was only a roundabout
way of saying that mail was being held and opened by the police. This
surveillance was extended to individuals. In L.S. Bevington's letter to
Nicoll (August 1894) which we have already quoted, the first sentence
reads, "Kindly send a postcard at once to let me know if this letter reaches
you safely, the post gets increasingly uncertain." The increased surveillance
seems to have followed the Greenwich Park explosion. Bourdin may have
been French, but it had been made apparent — not least by H.B. Samuels
— that contacts between the foreign exiles and the native movement were
close. Well-publicised arrests among the exiles kept the pot boiling. In
early April a French anarchist called Meunier was arrested and extradition
proceedings were begun. He was wanted for the Café Very explosion —
despite the fact that the same accusation had been made by the French
police about François, who after extradition from England was acquitted.
Between twenty and twenty-five people in all had been posted at one time
or another as wanted for this crime. Inspector Melville was alone when he

arrested Meunier on Victoria Station; which was perhaps a brave thing to do, except that it made him eligible for all the reward offered for Meunier's arrest. This was a considerable sum of money, amounting to some £2,000. A defence committee was organised by the Liberty group, but despite their efforts Meunier was extradited in June and sentenced to penal servitude for life in July in France.[5]

On 14th April, Giuseppe Farnara and Francis Polti, two Italians, a blacksmith and a traveller respectively, were arrested for being in possession of materials intended for bomb-making. They had aroused the suspicions of the owner of a small engineering shop where they had gone to buy an iron pipe and had made inquiries about the possibility of having two screw caps made to fit it. This case caused quite a splash in the press since it became apparent that the bomb had been intended for use in England. When Farnara was arrested he apparently raved on about throwing a bomb into the stock exchange and threatening to kill every political policeman in England with a dagger. At his trial (before the repulsive Justice Hawkins) he pleaded guilty. Though his statements on arrest had been leaked to the press, they were not used at his trial; but he did not help matters by announcing to the court, "I wanted to kill the capitalists." He was sentenced to twenty years of penal servitude and on 4th May Polti was sentenced to ten years. A third man, called variously Carnot, Piermonti or 'the banker', seems to have instigated the plot and to have provided Farnara with chlorate of potash. (This ignites when in contact with sulphuric acid, which was to be used as detonator.) This third man was never caught, and there was great suspicion in the anarchist movement that he was an agent provocateur.[6]

On 1st June, a German anarchist named Fritz Brall, a member of the Autonomie Club, was arrested in Chelsea. At his home the police found apparatus for forging coins, a quantity of chemicals and electric batteries. They also found a portrait of Vaillant, "written recipes for the manufacture of the most violent explosives, letters from prominent Anarchists in various languages and a copy of a pamphlet by the Anarchist Johann Most entitled 'The Scientific Revolutionary Warfare and Dynamite Guide.'"[7] At the committal proceedings it was revealed that Brall had been connected with Meunier and François, the two anarchists extradited in connection with a bomb explosion in Paris. It was also said that the Autonomie Club was defunct. Already viewed with disfavour at the time of Bourdin's death as a haunt of police spies, the club seems to have been closed as a result of police raids, publicity and arrests. Brall had been given the counterfeiting apparatus by a fellow member who was never arrested. It seems, in view of contemporary events, worth asking whether this was another police agent. However, the defence at Brall's trial was efficient, and since the major charge concerned an eighth of an ounce of an explosive substance — the scrapings from an 'empty' jar — and convincing witnesses were produced to explain circumstantial evidence, he was found not guilty. Possession of the forging equipment was technically not an offence since it was for non-English currency.

The use of agents provocateurs had spilled out from the foreign movement into the English groups. W.C. Hart, secretary first to the Peckham and then the Deptford anarchist group, relates the following incident. A friend of Hart's sheltered a Frenchman who had claimed acquaintance with the Walsall anarchists — at one point the friend even pawned his carpenter's tools to buy food for the stranger. Pressure was put on the Englishman to 'commit an outrage', but he knew nothing about explosives. So a letter was written by the stranger on his behalf to be sent to Jean Grave in Paris asking for a copy of the *L'Indicateur Anarchiste* (which contained bomb recipes) "as he intends making an act of propaganda for the cause in London." However, Hart read the letter before it was sent, and smelling a rat he put it in the fire. The Frenchman had gone out that morning and never returned. For some weeks afterwards Hart's friend was followed by detectives. Hart was later told (interestingly enough "by a representative of Scotland Yard") that the Frenchman, confident that the letter would be sent, had informed the French police of its likely arrival, and they in turn had informed Scotland Yard. Had the bomb recipes arrived, Hart's friend could have been charged with conspiracy and in the atmosphere of the time could easily have gone to prison.[8] There were other similar incidents: "A man who had made himself prominent as the exponent of extremist views in politics — he was, in fact, an avowed Communist-Anarchist — received by post an ingenious working drawing showing how a soda-water bottle might be converted into a very destructive bomb." He also received another drawing showing how such a bomb might be launched by springs.

The day after the arrival of these drawings the man's house was raided but nothing was found, because the man was suspicious and "on its receipt he packed it up and sent it off to Scotland Yard."[9]

The harassment and surveillance of the English movement took place in an increasingly feverish atmosphere. Arrests led to suspicion and paranoia. The news of bombings and assassinations abroad mixed strangely with the sense of helplessness and rage in the face of the power of the authorities to smash up meetings, as at Peckham, Manchester and Hyde Park. The mass mobilisation of the workers to offset this was not within the anarchists' power. The organisations which had blossomed since the apparently pre-revolutionary days of 1889 and 1890 were increasingly committed to constitutionalism and electioneering. For some sections of the anarchists the result was a retreat into a fantasy world. The fantasy resided not so much in the feasibility of the assorted schemes put forward, though sometimes this was questionable, but rather in the small likelihood of their being carried out and the gap between the means and their stated aims. It represented a desire for revenge which was largely satisfied by bellicose words and schemes never designed to become flesh. It is a familiar psychological manoeuvre. Hart tells us that schemes were put forward to drop lice on the rich in the stalls from the galleries of theatres; to fill the carriages of the bourgeoisie with hydrogen sulphide, which has a rotten-eggs stench; to catapult small incendiary bombs from the top deck of a bus into the upper storeys of the rich mansions of the West End. None of these schemes were put into effect, and even if they had been their precise relationship to the social revolution is not clear. Such proposals were not given the sophisticated gloss of a French anarchist leaflet issued in 1894 entitled 'Long Live Theft!' ('Vive le Vol!')[10], which for all its 'logic' remains firmly in the realms of fantasy:

First and foremost has it not long been admitted that production much exceeds consumption? Is this not so? And why this difference between the two which should not exist among humanity? With the purest logic we can reply that the fault is firstly in the capitalist system and secondly in the idiots who believe they are duty bound to produce for 10, 12 or 14 hours a day for a meagre wage without consuming the things they need! Therefore to re-establish equilibrium between these two elements, the most simple solution is to suspend production and to consume as much as possible so that equilibrium is restored and the Revolution achieved. This is the best of all general strikes to talk about. ... The more theft multiplies, the more property is divided and the sooner the Social Revolution is brought about. ... In consequence, comrades, let us preach in our propaganda the necessity for theft in existing society as a right of war and as the strongest weapon against the capitalist bourgeoisie. Here is our most logical means of combat. So: long live theft! For it will surely lead us to the remaking of society. Vive l'anarchie!

The document is signed 'les Impurs Universels'. While undoubtedly some anarchists had made out a case for theft which was based in the desperate want of the working class in the face of the indifference of the rich, this piece is fundamentally designed only to shock. Feeding off publicity, it seeks to generate more. However, the 'revolutionary theory of theft' had day-to-day consequences which were destructive of the sense of fraternity in the movement. Following on from the leaflet 'Vive le Vol!' further leaflets were issued justifying thieving between comrades.[11] Sympathy among the English anarchists for the sometimes desperate plight of the exiles in London seems to have laid them open to exploitation. Any resulting sense of outrage was initially numbed by a barrage of theoretical justification and abuse concerning the residual bourgeois attitudes of the exploitee. Hart, for example, is very bitter on the subject. He says that 'comrades' of this persuasion would *rather* steal from other anarchists "relying on the victim's detestation of the law not to hand them over into its clutches" and adds that he himself had been "a victim of these rogues time and time again." In fact the only reason he gives for leaving the anarchist movement in his bad, if sporadically informative, book is his complete disillusionment with the 'companions'. He says, "I left them ultimately in utter disgust, they themselves having convinced me of the utter folly (not to say criminality) of the whole Anarchist scheme."[12] His objections to anarchist theory are fundamentally little more than post-hoc rationalisations of this bitterness. Such off-putting tendencies were not only to be found in the French movement. Max Nomad describes, in his memoirs, how:

a German anarchist old-timer pointed out to me, at a distance, a middle aged German worker by the name of Konrad, whom he described as the last relic of a particularly unsavoury phase of the movement in England, a phase characterised by certain German-language periodicals, published during the 1890s — as a rule short-lived ventures of which only a few issues ever appeared. The editors of these publications constituted a class by themselves. They were either, as most of the London anarchists suspected, police agents hired to discredit the movement by their propaganda, urging burglary (one of their organs actually bore the title *Der Einbrecher*, which means *The Burglar*), counterfeiting, murder and robbery, as revolutionary 'techniques'; or else they were psychopaths. Konrad was one of the latter. He suffered from coprolalia and was unable to write a single paragraph without using unprintable expressions ... he had never violated the law in his life, except by the printing of his obscenities; and was actually the most timid of men. His ultraradicalism was obviously a sort of compensation for his sense of inferiority.

In one case his mania resulted in tragedy for a German philosophical anarchist. On a visit to London, he had come across a pamphlet written by that maniac and had thoughtlessly put it in his suitcase with the intention of showing it to his friends in Berlin as evidence of how crazy some of these London ultras were. That pamphlet recommended arson as the best means for overthrowing the capitalist system. Konrad's argument culminated in the sentence: 'Even a beggar can afford to own a few matches and paper can be found in any shit-house.' Found by the customs inspectors on the visitor's return to Germany, that brochure resulted in the luckless man's being sentenced to four years' hard labour. His protests that these were not his ideas were of no avail. He was a broken man when he left prison.[13]

To try and work anywhere near the ultra sections of the anarchist movement meant living with black anti-anarchist propaganda and overblown rhetoric on the part of anarchists themselves. Strangers could be the next martyr, an agent provocateur or a con man pure and simple. There was constant harassment, surveillance and arrests by the police and identifying police spies was a constant problem. And who the spies were depended on the group or clique who were making the accusations or were being accused. A French 'counter-espionage' anarchist group who signed themselves 'Anonymat' distributed mysterious little leaflets making accusations. One of their leaflets accused Coulon (who undoubtedly was a spy) together with Tochatti (who equally undoubtedly *wasn't*) and regretted not paying attention to one man but excused themselves on the grounds that they were "occupied with the Croydon nark on a bicycle." Furious accusations and equally furious denials flew back and forth.[14] It was in this context that the accusations against H.B. Samuels were made. As we have seen, Samuels was openly boasting of his involvement with Bourdin. Towards the end of May 1894, says L.S. Bevington: "Samuels came to my house ... and without more ado, sat down and proceeded to give the most minute instructions for making and charging bombs. He described all the ingredients and the quantities, where to get them, what pretext to give on buying them, everything about the *latest* (and simplest) materials used — and after an elaborate lesson he said, 'I am telling this to everybody; there are soon going to be English acts too; it is high time there should be.'"

At about the same time, Nicoll tells us, Samuels was working with another tailor "whom we will call R—." The man was a sympathiser and not believing Samuels's constant boasts of knowing about and being able to provide explosives asked him to provide him with some. To his surprise Samuels turned up one day with a large bottle of sulphuric acid from which he poured out a phial-full and presented it to his fellow worker. Samuels informed him that he was going to distribute the rest of it to various other people. R— was scared stiff and threw his acid away.

But that night in the street he met an acquaintance who was evidently in a high state of excitement. 'Have you heard the news,' he exclaimed, 'Samuels has been giving explosives to J— and *two days later J—'s house was raided by the police*. They evidently expected to find something, for they *tore up the boards of the floor*.' J— was a French Anarchist one of the leading spirits of the ultra-revolutionary school. He was extremely excitable and hot-headed but not likely to commit an act of violence. He was a fair speaker and most of his influence was due to this circumstance. For some time his house and shop had been raided again and again by Melville and Co. and they seemed bent on 'having him'. It was thoughtful, to say the least of it, of Mr Samuels to supply him with 'a small bottle of sulphuric acid'.[16]

Samuels had also provided other anarchists with acid and according to William Banham had been distributing "some other stuff" which combined with the acid would, Samuels said, produce a "beautiful and interesting experiment." Nicoll says that this was potassium picrate, which had been the charge in the bomb carried by Bourdin. Samuels's distribution of explosives and the raid on J—'s house made people acutely suspicious of Samuels. The result as Nicoll tells it was that "…one evening a young man who once believed in Samuels arose solemnly at the weekly meeting of the Commonweal Group and denounced him. Samuels was dumbfounded, he could only ejaculate, 'They asked me for it.'" The question was left hanging for two weeks until a full hearing could be given to accused and accuser. At this meeting Samuels "admitted that he had given away sulphuric acid, but said he had done it at the request of his accusers. As to the Bourdin affair, he declared he had stolen the explosives out of the house of a comrade D— (Dr Fauset MacDonald) who had them for use in his business, and given them to Bourdin and that since that affair he supplied sulphuric acid, etc., to J— and R— from the same place." He admitted that it was he who had accompanied Bourdin to Westminster Bridge and that they had been followed by detectives. Nicoll goes on "after the death of poor Bourdin, this calm philosopher, Mr Samuels wrote that interview with the Central News and received three guineas for his trouble. Mr Samuels ought to have a career in journalism."[17]

Someone remonstrated with Samuels when they heard this. 'You ought not to have done it,' they cried. 'You go and — yourself,' said Samuels, 'I shall make money how I like.' But the questions grew pressing and inconvenient and some more facts might have come out for R — and others were about to ask some questions when he suddenly recollected something, 'My wife is downstairs,' he said, 'I'll bring her up.' He brought her up and she immediately began to assail the group with violent abuse and threw the whole meeting into turmoil. 'I suppose I must go,' said Samuels and he went taking his wife with him. This saved him a troublesome cross-examination which might have been awkward.[18]

After Samuels's farcical exit the Commonweal Group decided to depose him as editor and expel him from the group. No public statement was made about the accusations against him, the only indication on the surface being a note by Samuels in the *Commonweal* of 9th June, which, to say the least, was low-key.[19] It read, "In consequence of lack of funds the next issue of the *Weal* will be held over until sufficient money is received to make a fresh start. There is a feeling here among comrades that it would be advisable to alter the policy hitherto adopted by the paper so I have tendered my resignation as editor which has been accepted by the group pending the settlement of the attitude the group will adopt in the reissue ..." The Commonweal Group seemed anxious not to wash its dirty linen in public. However understandable this was it allowed rumour and suspicion to bubble under the surface in a way which could only be disruptive. If a precise body of charges had been brought against Samuels and examined by an impartial 'court of honour' much of this disruption could have been prevented. David Nicoll was to press for such a course, but meeting with no response he felt forced to air his suspicions openly and unilaterally. While the turmoil after Samuels's departure and disruption caused by police action are one explanation of the group's lack of energy in the question, with every week that passed inactivity began to provide its own justification.

The group was not able to publish another issue of the paper before it was hit by the arrest of Cantwell and Quinn and the occupation of the *Commonweal* office by the police. Of necessity this took attention away from the question of Samuels; and the arrest and trial of the two men forms something of an interlude. The whole thing started ordinarily enough. Cantwell and Quinn had gone to the new Tower Bridge, which was to be opened the next day (30th June) by assorted royalty and politicians. They intended to address the workers who had built it and their message was clearly written on a placard Cantwell had printed for the occasion: Fellow workers, you have expended life, energy and skill in building this bridge. Now comes the royal vermin and rascally officials in pomp and splendour to claim the credit. You are taken to the workhouse and a pauper's grave to glorify these lazy swine who live upon our labour. The placard finished with the following lines from William Morris's poem 'The Voice of Toil':

I heard men saying, Leave tears and praying
The sharp knife heedeth not the sheep;
Are we not stronger than the rich and the wronger
When day breaks over dreams and sleep?

Cantwell spoke first and made the points expressed by the placard. But this area in the vicinity of Tower Hill was a prominent speaking-pitch and thus tended to attract 'professional' anti-socialists. Further, they had chosen a rather sensitive time to preach anarchism, as the anarchist Santo Caserio had five days previously assassinated President Carnot of France with a dagger. The matter was still an extremely live issue. Cantwell was asked about Carnot's death, the prosecution alleging more and more bloodthirsty replies as court hearing succeeded hearing. The defence was to claim that the question was 'turned aside,' and this would seem to be confirmed by the fact that press reports of the meeting mentioned no incitement to follow Caserio's example. The explanation for this omission given by a reporter, who had been present, at the trial that "the evening papers do not care for sensational reports" can be safely disregarded.

When Cantwell had finished speaking Quinn took over. Cantwell, however, was soon in trouble in the crowd. According to one of the chief prosecution witnesses at the trial, one Braden, he said to Cantwell, "You are a dirty dog. Are you a specimen of an Anarchist?" to which Cantwell replied "Yes." Braden then called him a dirty dog again and pushed him.

Several other people seem to have joined in, for Cantwell found it necessary to run for it. He was finally arrested in Gracechurch Street, where the policemen who did so said Cantwell "was waving a red handkerchief and shouting, 'I'm an Anarchist.' There was a mob of 400–500 persons around him. Some of them shouted, 'Lynch him'; others attempted to strike him with large pieces of wood ..." Being pursued by people who were trying to hit him with large pieces of wood obviously amounted to disorderly conduct and Cantwell was arrested and so charged. At the police station, however, anarchist literature was found on him and it was revealed that he was a "dangerous Anarchist well known to the C.I.D." and on these grounds he was remanded in custody at the police court since "on the next occasion more serious charges would be preferred against him."

Quinn meanwhile had slipped into a church to get away. He had then gone home. With more courage than sense he went to the police station the next day "to see fair play for Cantwell" as *Freedom* put it and was himself arrested. The meeting at Tower Bridge had been a bit hectic but unexceptional. The language of the placard was no different from those which announced in indignation meetings on the royal marriage in 1893.

The consequences on this occasion were to be rather different. In the index to the *Times*, the name of the person charged is given, followed by the nature of their offence. In Cantwell and Quinn's case the offence is simply given as 'Anarchism'. Their trial was something of a travesty easily explained as the consequence of political hostility.

Through various court appearances the two men were kept in prison for a month. Almost immediately after their arrest (on 1st July) the *Commonweal* office was raided and occupied by the police. They stayed in possession of it until 30th July, drinking vast amounts of beer, opening all letters that arrived and breaking up formes of type. The grounds for occupation were that Cantwell lived in the office, and that they were guarding Cantwell's property until the legal owners of the office claimed it. (It was ironic that these should turn out to be David Nicoll and Frank Kitz.) The feeling in the movement at this time is given by John Turner in a letter to Nicoll: "This affair has put us in a fair mess, I can assure you — the police still in possession of the office and doing all they can to ensure a conviction of Cantwell and Quinn. Should they secure a conviction we believe it means the suppression of all open propaganda."[20] It would appear from the eventual charges against the two men that the police were doing all they could to secure a conviction. Cantwell and Quinn were eventually committed for trial on four charges: (1) Incitement to murder members of the Royal Family and assorted politicians; (2) seditious libel on the Royal Family; (3) the publication of the leaflet *Why Vaillant Threw the Bomb*, and (4) a charge under the Explosives Act on the grounds of a manuscript found at the Sidmouth Mews office. Taking the charges in order, the incitement to murder largely depended on witnesses at Tower Bridge. The evidence given was contradictory and one of the witnesses for the prosecution admitted in court that he had "done things for the police which I do not wish mentioned." Detectives "were overheard by the clerk of the solicitor for the defence zealously coaching up the witnesses outside on what they were to say." As far as printed material was concerned the incitement to murder was alleged to reside in the William Morris line about "The sharp knife" which "heedeth not the sheep," where the Royal Family, etc., were interpreted as the lambs for the slaughter. This is a complete inversion of the sense of the lines, which clearly call the workers the sheep and capitalism the knife. William Morris was called to explain this point but was cut short by the judge, who said, "It does not matter what the writer implies, the question is what the prisoners imply." The charge of seditious libel boiled down to the fact that they called the Royal Family rude things and they were certainly guilty of this — as guilty as the editor of every socialist paper in England.

The leaflet *Why Vaillant Threw the Bomb* consisted of Vaillant's declaration at his trial and a biographical piece which said that the workers should recognise his act as heroic. No evidence except the belief of Sergeant Walsh was offered to prove that Cantwell had printed the leaflet, which was, in any case, a rather mild affair. As to the manuscript found at Sidmouth Mews, *Freedom* described it as "some old lectures long ago publicly delivered" but not by Cantwell or any member of the Commonweal Group. This manuscript had been sent to the "*Weal* office to see if they would print it. They had no intention of doing so and did not even know it was still there, but unluckily when the office was raided the police found it amongst some old papers." Another source alleges, however, that the manuscript was found behind a loose brick in the wall.[21] Wherever it was found it is worth speculating whether this was Cyril Bell's translation of Most's *Revolutionary Warfare* or the text of Coulon's chemistry lessons to the Young Anarchists. But whatever its origin and despite the plea that the responsibility for the manuscript lay with the editor of the *Commonweal* (i.e. Samuels!) there is no doubt that it told heavily against the two men.

Five defence witnesses said that the prisoners had said nothing about bombs, assassinations or Carnot; these subjects were introduced by people in the crowd and 'turned aside' by the speakers. As to these people in the crowd, a policeman turned cab-driver "suggested that the disturbance was caused by a small clique and the crowd in general was not hostile to the speakers." The defence was given short shrift by the judge, who repeatedly interrupted, to the cheers of prosecution witnesses who remained in court.

Defence witnesses on the other hand were only allowed one at a time into the court and some were threatened by the police, who packed the corridors outside. Spectators were kept out of the court if the police considered them friends of the prisoners and 'dangerous characters'. One such (unknown) dangerous character who was shut out wrote to the *Westminster Gazette* saying that the undersheriff told him "he wondered a member of the well-to-do classes should take an interest and adding 'Our object is to get such men out of the way as quickly as possible.'" Cantwell and Quinn were found guilty and given six months apiece.[22]

While the trial was occupying the Commonweal Group, in another quarter the question of Samuels's alleged police spying was not being allowed to rest. Nicoll, by now in Sheffield and the editor of his own paper, the *Anarchist*, determinedly made the matter public. On his release from prison he had commenced work on his pamphlet *The Walsall Anarchists*, which he published at the end of January 1894. He had addressed many meetings, speaking at Regent's Park with Cantwell through December 1893. As we have seen, he tried to hold a meeting in Trafalgar Square when anarchist meetings were banned there. As we have also seen, very little of his activity was noted by *Freedom* and even less by the *Commonweal*. The cause of this was obviously the dispute over the editorship of the latter.

Samuels would be unlikely to publicise a rival in his paper, and as far as *Freedom* was concerned the general London report was written by Presburg, a close associate and admirer of Samuels who had shown Nicoll copies of Samuels's *Commonweal* as the sort of thing required of him. Nicoll also tells us that on his release he offered the text of his speech at his trial (later published as *Anarchy at the Bar*) to C.M. Wilson, the editor of

*Freedom*: "Mrs Wilson sent it to Carpenter, Carpenter sent it to Gore [the Freedom Group's solicitor in the Walsall case]. Gore said it was 'libellous' and Mrs Wilson declined to print it."[23] This was not very brave of Mrs Wilson, and Nicoll can be excused for feeling that he was being subjected to something of a boycott. No doubt this feeling was considerably deepened by the circumstances, surrounding the conference in December 1893, which confirmed Samuels as editor of the *Commonweal*. Nevertheless Nicoll offered the *Commonweal* the text of his Walsall pamphlet. This offer too was refused. Nicoll was not sure whether it was because Samuels was "scared of a criminal prosecution for libel" or because of its accusations against Coulon, with whom Samuels had preserved relations.[24] Nicoll was being forced to plough a lonely furrow.

Nicoll left London in early February 1894, shortly before the Greenwich Park explosion, to fulfil some speaking engagements. He had also decided to try and start an anarchist paper in the provinces. He went first to Leicester, but the anarchists there were not keen on the idea. He then went to Sheffield where his paper was designed to be a revival of the *Sheffield Anarchist*.[25] Thus Nicoll was not in London when Samuels was accused at the Commonweal Group meeting, though letters of his to London could have been an instigating factor. It has to be said, though, that Samuels was under suspicion from more than one quarter and for more than one reason. William Wright, an anarchist cab-driver active in the cabmen's strike in 1894 wrote: "I had my suspicions aroused some four months ago because I noticed that Samuels did not like Quinn because Quinn did not let him boss the show. It seems so strange for them to prosecute Cantwell and Quinn while Samuels has wrote *three times more than that* in the *Weal* and nothing was said about it. I tell you that from the time of the Bourdin affair, Quinn has been followed about and persecuted wherever he went."[26] After Samuels was expelled from the Commonweal Group Nicoll wrote a rather gloating piece in the *Anarchist*. He reviews Samuels's "distribution of explosives" and the subsequent police raid on J— , he then goes on to discuss his relations with Bourdin and his charmed life throughout. He ends, "When people are arrested for quoting some lines of a poem by a great writer and another man is tried at the Old Bailey for having a bottle in his possession with a few grains ... of what a Government 'expert' is pleased to call 'fulminate of mercury' it is time to ask — Why people who incite to murder and supply others with explosives are allowed to escape?"

There was a mixed response to this article in the movement. (It has to be remembered that this was the first time that the nature of the accusations against Samuels had appeared in print.) Nicoll received the first of what proved to be a series from Samuels: "You are a cowardly envious liar and I shall make you eat your paper the next time I see you. No comrade in London places any reliance on what you say or do as it is well known that you are an imbecile and not responsible. H.B Samuels." John Turner wrote to Nicoll, "Your facts re Samuels are a bit out but otherwise it is *all right.*"[27] Nicoll interpreted this to mean that Samuels had not distributed explosives but sulphuric acid, which, however, Nicoll says is an explosive under the meaning of the Explosives Act. Another result of Nicoll's article was that Dr Fauset MacDonald and Herbert Stockton of the Manchester group travelled to Sheffield to try and persuade Nicoll "to make no disclosures in the *Anarchist.*" MacDonald "said he was firmly convinced 'Samuels was not a police agent.'"[28] The interview was a somewhat heated one, for Dr MacDonald's surgery had provided the chemicals that Samuels had distributed, and Nicoll was of the opinion that MacDonald himself was not above suspicion.

Nevertheless, Nicoll did agree to print nothing more on the matter on condition that a committee of inquiry was set up to look into his allegations. Herbert Stockton wrote to Mrs Wilson and to Dr MacDonald asking for the opinion of the London comrades on the matter. Stockton continues in a letter to Nicoll:

I told Mrs Wilson what happened at Sheffield and stated you asked her to take an initiative in the matter — requesting the favour of an immediate reply. This was last week directly I arrived home but Mrs Wilson has not replied yet. MacDonald wrote at once stating that the affair had died a natural death and almost forgotten and that the comrades had too much real work on hand to bother about personalities, expressing the opinion that if a conference was called nobody would attend. So it is out of my hands and your liberty of action remains unfettered.[29]

As a result Nicoll returned to the subject in the following issue of the *Anarchist*. He added one or two points of interest. Firstly, he alleges that Samuels had been in regular correspondence with the 'Secret Police Agent' (which is how Coulon was described in a newspaper article) for four months. Of course, he says, this could be quite innocent: "Some people if caught in the act of taking money from detectives would no doubt plead that they did it 'for the good of the cause' and perhaps some people might believe them."[30] He then goes on to ask why an innocent man would, however, do his best "to dodge and evade all enquiry?"

This article drew a sharp response from John Turner. In a letter dated 29th August he wrote:

> I never read anything more stupid in my life. ... Is it your own fevered imagination, fanned by a feeling of spite for the unfair way H. Samuels treated you re editing the paper? If so you are losing the confidence of the London comrades — not in your integrity but in your common sense. ... If it were not for the annoyance it causes, by the S.D.F. using it at outdoor meetings to prove what they are always saying: That the Anarchists are either fools or police spies, you would, be merely laughed at by those that know. ... The Commonweal Group has made all the enquiry it deems fit. ... The conclusion the group came to was that there were suspicious elements in the case; circumstances connected, with some actions of Samuels which prevented *absolute* confidence in his conduct. The question of getting up *dynamite plots* has not been raised here. ... You are acting against your own interests, as your 'spy mania' as it is called here, being reflected in your paper prevents comrades pushing your paper as they would. He — Samuels — is not thought to be a police spy, but it is thought he is not above making a bit by journalism.[31]

This is quite a contrast to his earlier mild statement that Nicoll's facts on Samuels were "a bit out." It is probable that MacDonald had been doing some lobbying — he and Turner were co-members of the Freedom Group. The question of Nicoll's 'spy mania' might well have been raised by MacDonald, since at a later stormy chance meeting between Nicoll and

Samuels in 1896, Samuels said, "I could put you away if I liked. MacDonald says you are insane!"[32] Certainly Nicoll's reasonable request for an impartial committee of inquiry was being evaded by references to personal spite, public difficulties with the S.D.F. and veiled hints that the London distribution of the *Anarchist* would lack efficiency if embarrassing articles continued. If there were "suspicious elements in the case" they amounted to rather more than "making a bit by journalism." The very vagueness of Turner's phrases encourages speculation. Samuels quickly disappeared from the movement without much effort to clear himself. Though the Leeds group offered to pay his fare, Samuels did not attend the northern groups' annual anarchist picnic in the Peak District in August 1894, where he and Nicoll could have thrashed the matter out in front of an impartial anarchist audience. An appearance at an open-air meeting by Samuels for the Canning Town group on 5th August is the last mention of any activity connected with the anarchists. Nevertheless Turner's letter did have the immediate effect of stopping Nicoll raising the matter in print for three years. The disputes surrounding these later writings are considered in a later chapter.

It is worth considering, however, just what evidence there was that Samuels was a police spy. Despite the interesting analogies Nicoll was to later point out, the evidence was circumstantial and boiled down to two points. One was Samuels's charmed life through his noisy editorship of the *Commonweal* and his known relationship with Bourdin. The second was the distribution of 'stuff' to several people and a police raid on one of them shortly afterwards. There is no doubt that Samuels knew how to make bombs; in all probability was involved in the making of Bourdin's bomb; and that he urged others to make and use bombs. But the fact that he was not arrested by no means proves that he had police protection. Samuels's 'incitements to murder' were general bloodthirsty fulminations which might have landed him in the same situation as, say, Quinn, if he had not preserved a rather low profile in open-air appearances. Unlike Nicoll, Samuels had not 'incited to murder' specific people and was not trumpeting his intention to publish material damaging to the police. The distribution of sulphuric acid and a police raid shortly afterwards are not necessarily connected. Nicoll himself says that there had already been a number of raids at the same premises, and this could have been merely the latest in the series. Samuels's relationship with Coulon remains unexplained and suspicious. All this could amount to little more than the fact that Samuels was a reckless aficionado of propaganda by deed who combined a certain self-preservative caution with a useful portion of luck. Yet it should be pointed out that it was largely fortuitous that Coulon's role in the Walsall affair became anything more than a matter of speculation. Only the opening of the police files can finally decide the matter.

It was 25th August before the next issue of the *Commonweal* appeared. It was four pages only and appealed more strongly than usual for funds. In their search of the *Commonweal* office the police had found documents which showed the finances of the paper to be in a parlous state and had announced as much at the trial of Cantwell and Quinn. It was rather an unconvincing piece of rhetoric on the part of Ernest Young (who co-edited the paper with John Turner) which asserted in the face of the evidence in this issue that "the 'last legs' are of a rather tough description and before very long both the *Weal* and the *Torch* will appear weekly ..." Only two more issues were to appear — one in September and one in October 1894. By the September issue morale had dropped perceptibly: "We hope all comrades will help us in our present condition. New comrades are coming to our side and helping all they can; but old comrades must not get disheartened because we are impoverished by the persecutions. Our poverty keeps us honest ..." It is possible that money was no longer forthcoming from MacDonald after Samuels's departure and no other source of patronage had been found. The October issue demanded, "Is the *Commonweal* to continue? If so we must have money at once." In this last issue there was a story about F. Goulding of Stratford East, who had refused to send his child to board school on the grounds that "he knows what education he wants his children to have." The child was sent to truant school for three months. There was bitter infighting in Burnley between the anarchists and the S.D.F. — Billy MacQueen was proving a little too successful in his oratory in that market square for the social democrats' taste.

Ted Leggatt, who had been blacklisted by the wharfingers of East London for his Carmen's Union activities and his anarchist opinions, had been able to find no work for ten weeks and was in great distress. Ten open-air speaking pitches were advertised for Sunday meetings in London. The movement continued, but the *Commonweal* was dead.

## Chapter 10
# THE MOVEMENT IN 1894

In the years 1889–1891 there had been a positive orgy of trades union organising. There has been no satisfactory attempt to describe and analyse this phenomenon as a whole, much needed though it is. It is clear though that the 'terms of trade' had swung in favour of labour, which made such organisation very much more simple. The combativeness had obviously been stimulated by the unemployed agitation and socialists in the previous years. The gains of 1889–1890 began to be eroded by unemployment and the counter-attack of the employers. Unemployment rose seriously between 1891 and 1893. Yet the earlier gains were not given up without a struggle. Defensive strikes occurred in many places. Some were of a massive and riotous nature and mobilised many more people than were involved in the strikes themselves. In December 1892 a fund raising procession in Bristol in support of a strike was banned. It took place anyway, and the authorities were unable to enforce their ban until dragoons had made repeated charges involving the free use of lances and sabres on a crowd estimated to number some hundreds of thousands. In the Hull dock strike in May 1893, gunboats were moored in the Humber, there was arson in the docks and many confrontations took place between strikers and police. It was not only in connection with industrial disputes that the people demonstrated their readiness to take direct action. The August 1892 issue of *Commonweal* reported that 3,000 people had first pulled down the railings protecting a railway that had been run across common land at Leyton, near London. They then proceeded to wreck the railway itself. The spirit of the times also made itself manifest in more local eruptions: when broker's men seized the goods of a widow in Clerkenwell, a quickly gathering crowd attacked the men, smashed the seized goods and used the bits, together with lumps of coal, potatoes and garbage, to attack police when these subsequently arrived.[1]

In fact this period after the 'boom' of organising, when the working class was in an embattled and bitter mood, proved a more responsive one for the anarchists. The period 1889–1890 had led to something of a scattering of the libertarian wing of the socialist movement. Insofar as there had been any anarchist organisation at all it had been based in London on the London Socialist League. Outside London, branches of the Socialist League in their various states of disintegration or transformation had provided temporary haven, particularly where socialist clubs had been formed. It was not until mid-1892 that a federation of anarchist groups was formed in London and not until a little later that specifically anarchist groups were formed in the provinces. The one exception was a group formed in Sheffield in early 1891. This group however was formed round the exceptional personality of Dr John Creaghe, and when he left Sheffield towards the end of that year it went into something of a decline. The anarchists at this point were not really able to sustain an organisation separately. The Walsall anarchists, for example, were based on the Socialist Club in Goodall Street, which had evolved from the local Socialist League branch. While they seem to have dominated the club ideologically by late 1891, they do not appear to have tried to make it exclusively anarchist. Leeds, to take another example, had seen a dispute within the ranks of the socialists in 1890 between anarchists and electoral socialists, including Tom Maguire. The basis of the argument was "which of the two courses is the correct one to take bearing in mind the events of the gasworkers' struggle" which had culminated in a massive riot and the strikers' victory. Maguire and his friends "in response to the men's wishes and in accordance with our ideas of policy considered a Labour Electoral League should be formed and accordingly this was done." The anarchists attacked the Electoral League and its sponsors and "finally told the people that no policy should be entertained but physical force."[2]

Though the dispute was bitter and relations remained cool the Socialist Club did not break up. A separate anarchist group was not formed until August 1892, probably in response to more successful attempts to organise electoral activity which culminated in the formation of an Independent Labour Party in Leeds in November of that year.

In Glasgow a split in the Socialist League ranks did not take place until late 1892 or early 1893. "A few-of the members had become Parliamentarians and the remainder (the majority by far) who were really Anarchists for some time, in order to make their position clearly understood, resolved to abandon the name of Socialist," which the parliamentarians had besmirched "and declared themselves Anarchists." The group evidently had a shaky start, because it was not until October 1893 when the group reorganised itself that they really set to work. In March 1894 they were announcing that they had "five times the members we started with. ... The Labour Party from whom we have been draining a number of recruits have become so alarmed" that no anarchist speakers were being allowed on their platforms or being allowed to speak in discussions. All anarchist literature was banned from their halls. The anarchists were working closely with the S.D.F., "many of whom are Anarchists in all but name."[3]

In their success and their recruiting ground the Glasgow group were typical, though the London situation was somewhat different since the I.L.P. (of which the Scottish Labour Party was becoming a constituent part) did not make ground in the capital in the early 1890s. There the anarchists were most successful in recruiting from the S.D.F. — the cause of some bitter faction fighting. We can understand bitterness in the S.D.F. when we consider the London report in *Freedom* in June 1894: "The whole Canning Town branch of the S.D.F. have embraced Communist Anarchist principles and have formed a most energetic group and we hear that a Communist Anarchist group is in formation at Horton and Woolwich. The Wimbledon S.D.F. branch have been so disgusted by the reactionary policy of the Central Council in sending a circular to all their branches calling upon all Anarchists in the S.D.F. to resign that all the branch but two (who are still Social Democrats) sent back a resolution condemning them ..." A report the following month somewhat modified its statement concerning the whole Canning town branch of the S.D.F. becoming anarchist and now called it a split — but also added Mile End to the list of anarchist influenced S.D.F. branches. At Canning Town the anarchists and the S.D.F. held open-air meetings in close proximity. In August the *Times* reported: "Lately the attendance at the gatherings has largely increased, and between the Socialists ... and the Anarchists considerable friction has been caused, the various speakers accusing each other of treachery and backsliding. These scenes have nearly led to a serious breach of the peace."[4]

A more or less independent paper, the *Weekly Times and Echo*, assessing the progress of anarchist propaganda, had already said in December 1893 that

the social democrats were being considerably influenced by the anarchists
— "we are by no means so sure that the anarchist is not covering two miles
to the Social Democrat's one." It suggested that the workers were beginning
to think that the anarchist was "the practical man, the only social reformer
who goes to the root of the matter."[5] As far as estimating the number of
anarchists at this time we can only make an informed guess. One of a series
of articles (which it has to be said were not taken very seriously by the
anarchist press) which were published in December 1894 gave the following
figures for London.[6] There were at that time, it says, some 7,000 to 8,000
anarchists, of whom 2,000 were Russian Jews in the East End, 1,000 were
Germans living mainly round Soho Square and the Middlesex Hospital plus
a small and violent colony of 400 French anarchists living in the Charlotte
Street area. Of the English anarchists it said:

> they number between 3,000 and 4,000 … the latest adherents being in
> Canning Town and Deptford with groups of over 100 each. … Their
> ranks are recruited largely from the extreme socialists especially those
> of an 'Individualistic' tendency and among the classes such as tailors,
> shoemakers, cabinet makers whose work allows greater freedom of
> ideas. The dockers and the hard toilers and moilers remain for the
> most part stolid soldiers in the ranks of Socialism where their thinking
> is done for them and their will power delegated.
>
> Yet it is significant that recently a band of comrades headed by a
> young and highly intellectual lady have been pursuing their work at the
> docks with absolutely fanatical earnestness and have swept into their
> associations considerable numbers, notably of the younger men.

The "young and highly intellectual lady" was Olivia Rossetti and the
"comrades" were the *Torch* group with which Ted Leggatt, a carman in the
East End (and later a union official), was connected.

Yet the figures given here seem far too high. We have some confirmation
for the suggested numbers in the Canning Town group and perhaps in
the Deptford group at around the one hundred mark. Yet these were
exceptional groups. For there to be 3,000 to 4,000 anarchists in London
there would have to be 25 to 35 groups of a similar size, allowing for the

isolated, the unorganised and hardy independents. This was certainly not the case. The English anarchists could mobilise 600 people in London on a working day and upwards of 1,000 on a Sunday, when there were rival attractions. Larger numbers on special occasions can be accounted for by foreign anarchists and other socialist sympathisers. This would seem to indicate a *maximum* of 2,000 English anarchists in London at that time — a generous estimate. Equally generously we could double that number for a national total. As far as the circulation of English-language anarchist newspapers goes, there seems to be little reason to dispute George Woodcock's figure of a total of 10,000 for all of them. Thus, though these suggested figures indicate that the anarchists had not broken out from the status of sect into that of movement, there had been something of an explosion in numbers since the time William Morris had calculated the membership of the London Socialist League to be 120 in 1891.

For two years, in 1894 and 1895, the anarchists seemed poised for take-off into a self-nourishing movement. The collapse of the *Commonweal* and the closure of the Autonomie Club had been a blow to the ultra section of the movement. The events surrounding these occasions had had a disruptive effect on the movement in the West End, tending to split the exiles and the English anarchists. In political terms this largely meant the end of the influence of the advocates of bombing and more random acts of terror. By no means did such propaganda cease, however; it merely became less prominent. And in point of fact there were several anarchist bomb explosions in London after this time. In August 1894 the first of a series of post offices in South London was blown up at New Cross. A member of the Deptford anarchist group, Rolla Richards, was eventually arrested for causing these explosions. He was brought to trial in April 1897 and sentenced to seven years in prison. On 4th November 1894, at 11pm, a bomb exploded on the doorstep of the Tilney Street, Mayfair, house of Reginald Brett, M.P. The door was blown in and many windows in the surrounding houses were smashed. The bomb seemed to have been of the French anarchist style of manufacture, and the whole business was rather bungled insofar as it was generally assumed that the bomb was really intended for Justice Hawkins who lived at another house in Tilney Street. There was no particular reason why anyone should bomb Brett, but Justice Hawkins was detested in anarchist circles for his savage sentences on the Walsall anarchists and Farnara and Polti. Another explosion took place in April 1897 in an underground train, killing one person and injuring several others. While the anarchist press ignored this bomb or denied any part in it — David Nicoll went so far as to accuse the police of planting it — it was generally attributed to an anarchist. There were certainly lunatics in the movement capable of such an act; but the question has to be put as to what point, if any, could be made by such an explosion in such a place. Since no one was arrested for the bomb in Mayfair or the train the question remains open in both cases.

With the decline of the influence of the 'bombing' faction the movement became dominated by what might be termed (as in Nicoll) the 'revolutionist' faction. A simple expression of their position can be found in the *Manifesto* in the first number of the *Anarchist* which Nicoll published from Sheffield in March 1894:

> We are Revolutionary Anarchists and declare for the complete destruction of the existing society. We seek to put in its place free cooperative associations of workmen who shall own land, capital and all the means of production. We would sweep away all forms of Government and we desire neither to rule others or to be ruled ourselves.
>
>   We seek to realise that freedom which is only possible by every man being ready to defend his own liberty without seeking to trample on the liberty of others.
>
>   We are Communists. We do not seek to establish an improved wages system like the Fabian Social Democrats. We do not see that it is possible to reward a man according to his deeds; nor do we think that lack of skill or ability shall be any reason why any man should lack the necessaries of life. There is enough for all; then all who are willing to work should have enough …
>
> ### DYNAMITE IS NOT ANARCHY
>
>   It is the weapon of men driven to desperation by intolerable suffering and oppression. Our ideal can be realised without it, if the rich will let us. Our work for the present lies in spreading our ideas among the workers in their clubs and organisations as well as in the open street. So long as we can express our ideas freely we shall be content with advocating

PASSIVE RESISTANCE

All we need can be obtained by the general refusal of the workers to pay rent to a landlord or to work for a capitalist.

NO RENT AND THE UNIVERSAL STRIKE ...

This represented more or less the line of the anarchist papers in existence after the collapse of the *Commonweal*. In 1894 these were *Freedom*, the *Anarchist*, *Liberty* and the *Torch*. (The *Torch* was founded by the Rossetti sisters, Helen and Olivia, and seems to have been designed to continue the work of the *Commonweal*. Both sisters had contributed articles on Italian affairs to the *Commonweal* and one, at least, had been present at the meeting which had expelled Samuels. The group producing the paper included some Italian exiles, Ernest Young and Cantwell when he was released from prison.)

Yet the situation was, in fact, wildly unstable for the anarchists. They still spoke to the real desperation of sections of the working class. Their commitment to revolution was a severe embarrassment to those erstwhile revolutionaries who were now busily trying to get themselves elected to various bodies. As a result the socialism of these people had become transformed into 'practical proposals' which would be stepping stones to socialism via a series of reforms. Electoral activity tended to force this kind of presentation on socialists thus involved. Beckoning careers tended to confirm this approach. 'Class war' rhetoric was rather pushed into the background, because mass passivity — or at least partial demobilisation — was implied by electoral representation. The resulting fragmentation of electoral socialism meant in effect that the anarchists with their 'impossibilist' position had greater theoretical clarity than their rivals. But when the militancy of the working class had shrunk back from its flood tide their 'impossibilism' left them with no activity but propaganda. Individually they were involved in every aspect of working-class life except those areas which could be described as 'political' — that is, as an administrative part of the status quo. Thus there were anarchists who were active trades unionists, anarchists who were cooperators, anarchists who organised clubs. Yet it was only within the anarchist movement, for better or worse, that the anarchist word became flesh. Group meetings were held on the Quaker pattern: "Anarchists do not have a Chairman, but when enough people had assembled, a man stood up and began to speak,"[7] "anyone could speak when and how he pleased, so long as he received the approbation of the meeting. Generally speaking the meetings were very orderly!"[8] Groups within which this democracy operated were autonomous, freely federated without hierarchy. The movement could contain men with a considerable will to power, though the terms in which this was expressed were somewhat mutated. As Nettlau remarks of one conflict: "The aim is always a periodical without an editor, i.e. without X, which is produced spontaneously, i.e. by Y."[9] Yet if the anarchists had made a movement which demonstrated something of its principles within itself, it had no new methods to offer the workers once open class conflict diminished.

While the anarchists presented a critique of existing forms of struggle it was a critique which assessed these forms against one yardstick: the bringing of the revolution. And since trades unionism or cooperation were not revolutionary in any sense that implied violent, immediate and massive class conflict or the construction of the new society they were dismissed as *anarchist* forms of struggle though it was readily admitted that such activities were inevitable and necessary under capitalism. Thus, as individuals they were involved in them and were always ready to urge direct action in trades union struggle; yet collectively there was a distinct carelessness in their analysis of such struggle, a carelessness which applied in other similar areas too. Yet despite this, anarchists through dogged courage or a more finely attuned sensitivity to spontaneous developments were able to make contributions which will be given in more detail in a later chapter. Yet on any criteria of success the anarchists were to be hopelessly outpaced by the reformist politicians in the later 1890s. Despite the inauspicious beginnings of the electoral strategy in the Tory gold scandal in 1885, by 1895 the situation was more encouraging for the reformists. It was true that the parliamentary road was not altogether encouraging: in the 1895 election the I.L.P. put up twenty-eight candidates and the S.D.F. four and they were all defeated. Yet these were no joke candidates; the I.L.P. was becoming a mass organisation and despite its defeats had a high morale. The S.D.F. remained relatively small, with an estimated membership of between 2,000 and 4,000. Yet both organisations achieved significant electoral success in local bodies. As far as vestries, boards of guardians, school boards and councils were concerned, in the nation as a whole in 1895 the I.L.P. held 800 such positions and the S.D.F. 250.[10] It was from this developing base in local affairs that successful Labour candidates were to be launched on some scale in 1906.

The anarchists could stand on the sidelines of this activity and snipe — and they did, sometimes to great effect. Yet in the face of their inability to provide practical proposals to go with their critique of electoral reformism the latter made steady progress. The dilemma had been summed up in a hostile way in *Justice*. In a reply to a letter from an anarchist criticising election activity it said, "If our correspondent means that he objects to political and municipal action as expressed by running candidates and voting in parliamentary and municipal elections, then we fear that no organised body can be kept together or fed on mere abstractions."[11] To say the least this puts the cart before the horse and their choice of a tactic designed to preserve the organisation rather than achieve the revolution marks a considerable change from their earlier brave remarks that all methods must be tried to achieve socialism, whether bomb, bullet or ballot box. They were perceptive enough, though, to ask what the anarchists were going to do if they eschewed elections. The anarchists had found a nourishing environment in the bitter aftermath of the 1889–1890 boom and had no desire to preserve anarchist organisation for the sake of it. They found themselves scattered, stranded and impractical when the wave subsided. As the 1890s progressed the circumstances which encouraged free-speech fights, the window smashing of C.C. Davis, the anti-broker brigade of W.B. Parker, the No Rent campaign, not to mention expansive and confrontation-oriented trades union organising, seemed to have passed. The anarchists were left with propaganda activity only.

And even when that propaganda was directed against attempts to achieve socialism through elections it was no less reduced to 'mere abstractions'. Whereas electoral socialists could argue that they were at least "doing something practical" the anarchist contention that this would give practically nothing to the working class was as yet only a prediction and not a demonstrable fact. Taken together with the rising tide of imperialist-inspired popular patriotism, which was to reach its peak in the Boer War period, this caused a catastrophic drop in anarchist numbers and morale in the later 1890s. Sporadic local revivals would take place where exceptional agitators were active. But the continual complaint was to be working-class apathy and lack of activity and response. By the end of the nineteenth century history seemed to have passed the English anarchists by. David Nicoll wrote in 1898:

'There is desperit fightin in the streets of Milan; the roar of the cannon resounds; barricades rise on all sides. Bread or Death is the cry of the masses. Comrades prepare for the Westry elections and all will be well.' This is the cry of the Sosherlists of the Parliamentary School. ... The Sosherl Revolution by means of vestry elections is advancing by rapid strides.

And it's having a great influence on the party. Ten years ago they were rough blokes like you and me and they used to fight the police like winking. They wore courduroys and 'obnailed boots. Now they are nice-looking, Sunday School young men; they part their 'air in the middle, wear clean collars and cuffs and a top 'at and frock coat on Sunday, and when you attend a branch meeting you think you are in the Young Men's Christian Association ...

But there ain't the go about the propegander the way there used to be. The 'obnailed boots and courduroys 'as gone for ever but something else 'as gone and that's the spirit of revolt. If you talk about the Sosherl Revolution the young men snigger. They don't believe in it, they don't want it. They are too damned respectable. But the 'obnailed boots and courduroys was 'ungry sometimes and they got wild; they broke winders and sacked shops and made things lively.

They did believe in the Sosherl Revolution, they *did*.[12]

As the 1890s proceeded all the symptoms of a decline were to appear. Papers closed down. Propaganda activity became sporadic. Bitter disputes based more on personalities than politics had a lasting and damaging effect. Yet despite it all, anarchism, though badly bruised, was not fatally injured by the experience and made something of a comeback in the years before World War One. That is worth remembering while we relate the events of the lean years of the anarchist movement.

## Chapter 11
# THE MOVEMENT IN DECLINE

It may seem peculiar to open this section with an account of the active campaign for the release of the Walsall anarchists. Yet it is right that it should come under the heading of the decline of the movement. It was a campaign which was sparked off by information printed in a reformist newspaper and carried on by means of lobbying and 'influencing public opinion'. Despite the fact that its major organiser, David Nicoll, was an anarchist, the campaign was not — and under the conditions of the time could not be — carried out by the anarchist methods of direct action. Strikes, riots or even kidnapping and organised jail-breaks, which have all been used to force the release of political prisoners, were not seriously considered. For by April 1895 when *Reynold's News* printed the memoirs of ex-Detective Sergeant McIntyre concerning the arrest and trial of the Walsall anarchists a head of steam seemed to be missing in the movement. The 'revelations' of McIntyre, who had been forced out of the police for being more or less "soft on anarchists,"[1] were quite important. They made it clear that Coulon had been a paid police agent — something that could only previously be inferred from hearsay and circumstantial evidence. This clearly gave great credibility to the anarchist contention that Coulon had a financial interest in instigating and then denouncing the conspiracy. McIntyre wrote:

> Some time previous to what was known at the Walsall bomb conspiracy, Coulon wrote a letter to Scotland Yard offering his services to the police. Now, the police generally take advantage of any offer of this kind, in view of the necessity of keeping secret political agitators under surveillance.
>
> I have myself employed informers, and paid them reasonable sums for their information. But, in doing so, I took particular trouble to satisfy myself that they never acted the part of *agents-provocateurs*.

There is in my possession a letter from a member of the Autonomie Club stating that he could commence making dynamite with some others, that he could then give me information, and that thus I should be able to make an important capture. I had employed this man to go to the club in question, but after this letter I got rid of the unscrupulous scoundrel as quickly as possible.

Coulon's offer was accepted, and he forthwith got to work. ... Without the slightest doubt, there was an attempt at Walsall to obtain the manufacture of a bomb. According to my information, Coulon represented to the men that one was wanted for use in Russia, and, like all Anarchists, they were in sympathy with the victims of despotic government in that country. Thus they probably thought that they were acting in the interests of humanity in lending their aid to the instigator of this formidable plot.

McIntyre also made it clear that Coulon was Inspector Melville's 'property', and no evidence is offered that Melville authorised Coulon to instigate the Walsall plot. Yet the implication is that Melville did not take particular care to satisfy himself that Coulon never acted the part of agent provocateur. McIntyre points out that Coulon certainly had a financial interest in the affair:

The last time I heard of him [Coulon] he was living in the neighbourhood of Brixton in a style that favourably contrasted with his humble circumstances when I first knew him. Anyhow, the Walsall business appears to have enabled him to migrate to a semi-fashionable district.[2]

Clearly, such allegations received greater attention when they came from ex-policemen rather than from friends of the accused. Shortly after they were published Nicoll announced in the *Anarchist*: "An Amnesty Committee of men of all shades of opinion is forming in Sheffield. Our first work will be to issue a leaflet containing extracts from McIntyre's revelation with a short history of the case. We shall scatter these broadcast among the people and this will be followed by vigorous action and agitation. Our friends in

Norwich, Aberdeen, Leicester and Canning Town are working actively."[3] And the agitation did go ahead. Committees were formed in various towns. The anarchists held meetings and collections. Resolutions were passed at the S.D.F., I.L.P. and union branches. *Justice* threw open its columns for letters on the case. The *Labour Leader* printed an article by Carpenter. A deputation of anarchists in Aberdeen met with the local M.P. and held a joint demonstration with the S.D.F. Keir Hardie was sympathetic and persuaded Asquith to receive a statement of facts and a petition on the case, though the 1895 election run-up interrupted any action that he might have taken. The statement of facts was printed and circulated among Members of Parliament "and other people of influence."[4]

By April 1896 the new Home Secretary (Sir William White Ridley) had rejected appeals for amnesty for the Walsall prisoners. Nicoll had addressed seven 'large meetings' in February and March in Lancashire, Yorkshire and Derby. In fact the energy that Nicoll put into this agitation was phenomenal when we consider that he was singlehandedly bringing out a monthly paper and having to make a precarious living by penny-a-line journalism. Difficult enough for a man of his revolutionary reputation in London, this was to prove well nigh impossible in the provinces. His activity was not limited to places within fairly easy reach of Sheffield. Three large meetings were held in London with anarchist, trades union and socialist speakers. A resolution was moved by Ben Tillett, G.N. Barnes and W. Parnell at the T.U.C. and passed by an overwhelming majority calling for the release of the Walsall men. All this was largely due to Nicoll's activity. Despite the fact that funds had run out by early 1897 Nicoll was again preparing for a further provincial tour of protest meetings.[5]

But it was all in vain. Resolutions passed at socialist or union meetings — no matter how large — were unlikely to move the Home Secretary of a victorious and reactionary Conservative government. Moreover the government was most unlikely to release prisoners when it would mean such a retrospective slap in the eye for the police. Despite a number of scandals to do with blatant police perjury and corruption in this period the Conservatives were distinctly unwilling to undermine confidence in the forces of law and order by admitting that the police could make mistakes — whether by accident or design.[6] Coercion of the government by more direct means was not in the power of the anarchists or any other of the socialist groupings. The amnesty agitation faded away.

The movement as a whole was clearly in difficulties by 1896. Indications of numbers are extremely difficult to come by. There seems to have been no particular drop in the number of people who called themselves anarchists — there were perhaps even increases in their ranks. Yet most, of these people did not seem to be particularly active nor did they appear to enthusiastically support their papers to the extent even of distributing them or funding them sufficiently to keep them afloat. There is no particular contradiction here. It took consistent effort and organisational enthusiasm to keep outdoor speaking pitches open. These tended to be given up or become sporadic when morale slumped. Most of the papers were sold at open-air meetings, not through subscriptions, so that it was quite possible for anarchists to retreat into friendship networks which were not necessarily efficient channels for distributing literature but which would keep the movement together — although in a fragmented and apathetic form. C.T. Quinn described the anarchist movement as "very dull and sluggish" in January 1896.[7] He clearly saw symptoms of fragmentation around him, attributing it to "the ordinary anarchist policy of always separating whenever a difficulty occurs." He could only mean by this, disagreements which had led to the existence of several different groups and their papers out of the Socialist League anarchists. It is worth saying that these had in more ebullient moments been pointed to as signs of strength and decentralised self-activity. His proposal to form the 'Associated Anarchists', a group with a "non-compulsory" (!) agreement to be a condition of membership, missed the point — what precisely was this new group to do? In the event they published a few issues of yet another paper — the *Alarm* — and fell apart within a year. They had at least managed to produce a little more than the Anarchist-Communist Alliance, which existed only as the imprint on a manifesto issued in 1895. They too had nothing but 'mere abstractions' to sustain them and no situation to speak to.

Papers began to close. The last number of *Liberty* edited by Tochatti appeared in December 1896. The immediate reason was the ill-health of Tochatti, but it is significant that no one could step in to take his place. It is evident that the paper was difficult to keep going, financially speaking. Excellently produced and devoted to maintaining a dialogue between anarchists, anti-parliamentary socialists and libertarians of more statist inclinations in the I.L.P. and elsewhere, it was a great loss. It was the only anarchist paper that William Morris was prepared to "talk to." Closely in touch with many facets of the socialist movement, it actually managed to have discussions rather than battles in its columns. It is a tribute to its more tranquil spirit that ill-health was all that surrounded its passing.

The *Torch* had temporarily halted its production in June 1896, briefly come back to life in October of that year and then finally collapsed in January 1897. This paper died with considerably more acrimony than *Liberty*. The halt in its production in 1896 was caused by the aftermath of the departure of the Rossetti sisters, Olivia and Helen, from the English anarchist movement. According to the autobiographical novel written by Olivia Rossetti under the pen name of Isobel Meredith (called *A Girl Among the Anarchists*) the reason for their departure was a sudden feeling of pointlessness in their propaganda activity. Other sources seem to indicate that this feeling might have been encouraged by some of the people they had to work with. Particularly, we should point to Tom Cantwell and Ernest Young. Geoffrey Byrne, another member of the Torch group, wrote of them, "With such a pair of despicable, lying, cowardly humbugs I have nothing in common. How could I? I have never lived out of the movement or sponged on Comrades as Cantwell and Young are doing. I was never kept by two girls (whose youthful inexperience prevented them from seeing through the wiles of a lying scab) for nearly two years … and then repaid them by laziness, lying and mischief-making and finally by filth, lice and trouble-making driving them disgusted and heartsick out of the English movement."[8] Principles do not seem to have been Young's and Cantwell's strong point. On several occasions they persuaded some Italian anarchists in the name of the cause to do the donkey work printing their commercial work for nothing. The Italians could not understand English, and it was some time before they discovered that they had been conned.[9] Whatever the reason for the departure of the Rossetti sisters, the real trouble started once they had left. Byrne and F.S. Paul remained in the group, together with Young and Cantwell, to carry on the *Torch*. (Young and Cantwell seemed to have stayed due to some sense of customary right and because their assistance was needed to produce the paper.) Olivia Rossetti was happy enough for Paul and Byrne to continue the paper but, understandably enough, wished to dispose of the financial obligation to rent the office at 127 Ossulston Street. She also offered to sell Paul the printing plant. Paul had not the means to buy it and asked Max Nettlau for financial help.

Now Paul had come under some suspicion as a brash upstart of heterodox opinions. He had rather pushed himself forward as the secretary of the meeting in September 1895 which had been called to discuss the International Socialist Congress scheduled for 1896, which, it was announced, would exclude anarchists. For this presumption he was rather snottily admonished in *Liberty*.[10] Paul had also announced it as his opinion that anarchy would evolve from state socialism and, to the irritation of other comrades, had suggested that participation in elections should not, therefore, be ruled out. Since he also coupled his request for cash with a demand for editorial and managerial autonomy and the right to exclude such undesirables as the Associated Anarchists from the office, his request was rather coolly regarded by Nettlau. Instead the latter approached Olivia Rossetti and bought the plant and took over the office from her. The plant was placed in the hands of a group of trustees largely drawn from the Freedom Group. There were conditions laid down by Olivia Rossetti, however. The plant was to be used in the first place for the *Torch* then for the movement generally and only thereafter for the assorted jobbing printing with which Young supplemented his income. Further, two homeless Italians who were sleeping in the office were to remain at their convenience. The trustees decided to have Cantwell move in the *Freedom* printing plant and to print *Freedom* in Ossulston Street. The result was that despite Nettlau's good intentions and his desire that the printing plant should be at the disposal of the movement as a whole — including F.S. Paul — the office was, to all practical purposes in the hands of Young and Cantwell. The result was that Paul, Byrne and on one occasion Olivia Rossetti were refused entry to the office. The two Italians were summarily evicted from the office by Cantwell at gunpoint. The whole affair left a sour taste in the mouth and did not do the reputation of the Freedom

Group any good at all since it was widely assumed that the whole thing was a forcible takeover. Byrne and Paul got their paper printed elsewhere but, as we have seen, it died a natural death in January 1897.[11]

The Associated Anarchists and their paper *Alarm* collapsed in similarly acrimonious circumstances. Will Banham and Tom Reece 'seceded' from the group, taking with them the type and office necessaries. Carl Quinn wrote to *Freedom* as secretary of the *Alarm* group asking that no further money should be sent in "at any rate for the present." They asked subscribers to write in as "during the course of recent events their addresses have been mislaid" — in all probability Banham and Reece had taken the list with them. They promised to continue the paper.[12] Banham and Reece also wrote to *Freedom* asking for all money to be sent to them since "No other people are authorised to collect monies or transact business on behalf of the *Alarm*." They also promised that the *Alarm* would "reappear at an early date from a new office."[13] The *Alarm* did not reappear from either source. According to Hart[14] some of the twelve or so Associated Anarchists left with Quinn, then burgled the new office that Banham and Reece set up. The latter two then most un-anarchistically called in the police. The result of this minor fracas was a temporary reconciliation which came to a sudden end when Banham and Reece sold the assets, pocketed the proceeds and disappeared.

The extent of the sense of collapse in the movement is indicated by a letter from Marsh (the editor of *Freedom*) to Nettlau in October 1897: "… *Freedom*, financially is in terribly low water and writing round to the groups has produced no effect. I feel it would be disastrous for the paper to cease, even temporarily. *Liberty*, *Torch*, *Alarm* are all dead and if *Freedom* goes our enemies and the reactionary socialists will have it all to themselves."[15] Marsh's depressed mood seemed partly to do with a crisis with the difficult Cantwell who finally left *Freedom* — at least temporarily — the following month. As Marsh remarked: "…you cannot imagine what a time I had. 2½ years with Cantwell is enough to kill anyone …"[16] *Freedom* pamphlets were selling well, but *Freedom* was now totally responsible for the rent of the Ossulston Street premises, and the paper was in some financial difficulties. *Freedom* did survive through the 1890s and the reaction of the Boer War period but only with a considerable amount of help from its friends. It survived because its friends were able to help it — they tended to be the more middle-class (i.e. better off) anarchists; though tribute should be paid to the self-sacrificing efforts of Marsh himself. He had come to the editorship of *Freedom* in 1895 when the paper was suspended for three months when Charlotte Wilson retired. The reason cited for Mrs Wilson's retirement ('domestic affairs') seems to have been real enough: her correspondence indicates that her mother was ill at the time. Yet the rapidity with which any deep connections with the movement were severed also revealed in the same correspondence seems to indicate that it was a welcome relief to give up the responsibility for the paper after her eight-and-a-half-year stint as editor.

Marsh had been a member of the Freedom Group from some time in 1887, following his friend John Turner from the Socialist League. The son of an old Radical, he had met Turner while still a member of the S.D.F. in 1886. He spoke in the discussion meetings from time to time, yet seems to have been a modest and retiring comrade. For this reason he does not seem to have been a 'prominent' member of the Freedom Group. Correspondence indicates that it was not until 1894 that he was invited to meet Kropotkin at his home in Bromley for one of the regular Sunday soirées, though without doubt he had met Kropotkin 'professionally' many times in previous years. This was probably the point at which he was being groomed to take over the editorship. The character of *Freedom* did not change with the change of editor. It seems quite consistent with Marsh's character that the paper should remain largely theoretical in content and comment on events rather than see itself as an agitational instrument *making* events. There is little doubt that Marsh's preferences matched those of Kropotkin whose policy was completely dominant within the Freedom Group. The Nettlau Collection in Amsterdam has many postcards and letters from Kropotkin to Marsh which are friendly in tone yet which are composed of suggestions, exhortations and opinions on the paper. Marsh's letters to Kropotkin are, on the other hand, letters of explanation and occasionally of excuse. They are a clear enough expression of the relationship between the two men.

The group which produced *Freedom* from 1895 under Marsh's editorship had changed somewhat. Its active membership in 1897 was composed of Turner, Wess, Presburg and Nettlau, with Cantwell as printer (at least until October). All these people had at one point been connected with the

Socialist League and the *Commonweal* when it was an anarchist paper. Yet, if Nicoll is to be believed, much of the Commonweal Group had been involved to some extent in the Freedom Group. Certainly Turner and Marsh had long been members. Presburg had written the London reports for *Freedom*. Wess had also contributed to *Freedom*, and Nettlau was a sort of 'man about the movement', anyway. So in reality there was little change in the paper either in form or behind the scenes. Yet the paper now existed in a different environment. It was no longer produced in parallel with other sympathetic publications. The last anarchist paper in Britain to collapse in 1897 was Nicoll's *Anarchist*, which had changed its name to the *Commonweal* in May 1896. At least, after 1897 it only came out sporadically and was no longer influential to any degree. Its almost complete demise was due to a conflict between Nicoll and the Freedom Group. The paper had been in difficulties as evidenced by the necessity to change its format from folio to pamphlet form in mid-1895. And by this time the paper was completely written by Nicoll — presumably in the gaps left to him by the Walsall prisoners' agitation. By 1897 Nicoll had found it impossible to stay in Sheffield since he could not earn a living there by journalism. However, in early 1897 he had published his pamphlet *The Greenwich Mystery*, which has been used as a source for the section on the Bourdin affair in this book. Nicoll had not forgotten his feud with Samuels in the years after Christmas 1893 and his resentment was probably fanned by isolation, poverty and the failure of the Walsall prisoners' campaign. In this pamphlet he made it quite clear that he thought H.B. Samuels had been a police spy and gave strong hints that he considered 'D— ' to have been his willing accomplice. 'D— ', though unidentified, was quite obviously Dr Fauset Macdonald, who had been on good terms with the Freedom Group. Nicoll went much further in his accusations in this pamphlet than his hints in the *Anarchist* in 1894. Nettlau wrote an agitated letter very soon after its publication:

I am sorry that you publish such things as the Greenwich Pamphlet. It does the prisoners no good and brings our cause into ridicule and contempt and it might not be too late to withdraw it from sale altogether. For as to H.B.S. it proves very little. It is all in your way of telling things and a careful reader is soon able to keep both the things, proofs and insinuations, wide asunder. But this is nothing compared to the vile slanders on … D—. This is the worst libel I have seen in print for a long time and it decidedly rivals with Coulon's exploits.[17]

Nicoll's response was anything but conciliatory. In a private note to Nettlau, Nicoll accused Nettlau of cowardice — presumably because in 1894 Nettlau had been prepared to countenance Nicoll's accusations of H.B. Samuels in private letters but not now apparently in public.[18] In print, however, Nicoll went a great deal further. He reprinted the letter from Nettlau in the last issue of the paper published in Sheffield in June 1897 and followed it up with a barrage of mud against Nettlau. It as good as asserted that he had been expelled as a police spy from the Autonomie Club in 1890, accused him of complicity with Coulon and suggested that his private means came from the police. Nicoll also named Macdonald as the 'D— ' in the Greenwich pamphlet. It was extraordinarily stupid of Nicoll, even if his irritation over the movement's refusal to take his accusations of Samuels seriously is understandable. In June 1897 Nicoll also moved from Sheffield to London, intending to continue publication there, and was arrested — though quickly released — for a mocking speech at Canning Town around the subject of the Jubilee of Queen Victoria. Meanwhile there was a flurry of activity over Nicoll's accusations. John Turner went to see Nicoll to ask him to retract but reported him as "quite crazy" and said it was useless to appeal to him.[19] H.B. Samuels, who was now, it appeared, a member of both the I.L.P. and the S.D.F., went (unsuccessfully) to court to try and have Nicoll stopped from continuing to publish the Greenwich pamphlet. He issued a leaflet entitled 'Is D.J. Nicoll Insane?' which used a lot of the material that Coulon had circulated in 1894, and he advertised a meeting in the Athaeneum Hall on 'The History of Greenwich Mystery' to explain his side of it.[20] H.B. Samuels's efforts were greeted with quiet mockery by papers like *Reynold's News*, but Nicoll was under attack from more heavyweight quarters. Kropotkin wrote a protest and sent it to Marsh, but he also wrote a retraction which Nicoll was to sign, and which he sent together with a covering note to Nettlau: "Dear Friend, I read with indignation Nicoll's accusations. I am persuaded that, by different sophisms, he — a man to whom … I never trusted has been brought this campaign. ... Nicoll must be *compelled to sign* a retraction and beaten if he does not."[21] So much for the 'gentle anarchist prince' image.

Kropotkin's influence was great. The protest, cleaned up grammatically, had been circulated by Marsh to various quarters and was thereby in addition to Kropotkin signed by Marsh, Turner, Presburg, Wess, the Hydes and Mrs Dryhurst of the Freedom Group, Charlotte Wilson and, among others, Sam Mainwaring and James Tochatti. It was published in *Freedom's* June/July issue. In addition to protesting about Nicoll's insinuations about Macdonald and Nettlau (H.B. Samuels was significantly not mentioned) and laying the blame on "intellectual and moral faculties" which had been "sadly affected by solitary confinement," it also declared a boycott: "Whatever the cause may be, one can only say that Nicoll's wicked insinuations are the worst of libels. Under the circumstances we feel compelled to dissociate ourselves entirely from Nicoll until he has withdrawn — without reserve and as publicly as he has published — these shameful slurs upon the honour of our two friends. We leave it to comrades elsewhere to act as they think such conduct deserves." Nicoll would neither sign Kropotkin's retraction nor publish one of his own. His clearly developing paranoia could find in this response to his 'revelations' a major confirmation of their truth. The complexity of his response was increased by the fact that his remarks on the Jubilee in this particular issue of the paper also resulted in the police seizing 200 copies. His bitterness towards the Freedom Group, which he rightly saw as the origin of the boycott, was as deep as the effect of the boycott seems to have been. He wrote later:

I had with me my little boy. The struggle would have been hard enough for us under any circumstances, but it was made ten times harder by this 'Protest' and by the lies and calamnies that were diligently circulated by Mr Joseph Perry (Presburg) who appears to be employed for this purpose. Soon we found ourselves without a home, and were compelled to seek the shelter of the common lodging house. One night even this miserable shelter was denied us; it was raining and we paced the streets of Soho, till weary and tired, we rested in doorways till driven onward. I cannot forget this, nor the long days of hunger and misery ... and if I attack these people bitterly, let those men who have children remember the reason why.[22]

The personal consequences for Nicoll of the boycott were severe, and this point probably marks the beginning of his irreversible slide into paranoid breakdown.[23] A movement at a low level of vigour can be rent apart by conflicts which are personal and political and most disastrously by a combination of both. (This is not to say that there is no element of the personal in 'objectively' political disputes or no element of the political in 'objectively' personal disputes in political movements.) In vigorous times energy can be devoted to more pleasurable constructive pursuits, and the amount left over for destructive wrangling is reduced. Further the movement itself if sufficiently elastic to contain such disputes so that their resolution is encouraged. Without the opportunities for constructive action and without conditions which make for resolution, bitter disputes have both more psychic fuel and more shattering effects. Both the unreasonableness of Nicoll and the intransigence of the Freedom Group and its allies illustrate this well.

As we have seen there were a number of such destructive disputes in the movement in 1896 and 1897 resulting in the collapse of anarchist periodicals. By Christmas 1897 *Freedom* stood alone. While it had been the medium of one tendency among many it had been accepted as such. When it became *the* anarchist periodical it became the focus of criticisms, disappointments and hopes which more properly belonged to the movement as a whole. At a conference which took place at that time (having been postponed first from Easter to Whitsun, then from Whitsun to Christmas 1897) a long discussion took place, ostensibly on the need for a popular anarchist weekly paper. This initially centred

> …on the merits and demerits of *Freedom* … many hot assertions and bitter personal remarks made at the first meeting will not be recorded here. The summary of the criticism of Stockton, Percy, Kitz, W.B. Parker, O'Shea, O'Malley, Banham, Quinn and others is that *Freedom* was described as a philosophical, middle-class organ, not intelligible to the working classes, not up to date in late information and in O'Shea's eyes less revolutionary than *Comic Cuts, Alley Sloper* and Sam Weller. It was edited and managed by an inaccessible group of arrogant persons worse than the Pope and his seventy cardinals and written by fossilised old quilldrivers.

The *Freedom* report continues in a hurt tone: "The serious arguments underlying this often grotesque criticism were that there is, and has always been, a necessity for a weekly popular anarchist paper and *Freedom* being monthly ... never pretended to fill this want ... but the great majority of the meeting was hostile to *Freedom* because it was not what it never claimed to be ... the illogical character of this position was pointed out and now the right idea prevailed to publish a weekly paper themselves and to let the bickering about *Freedom* alone."[24] The Freedom Group replied to the accusations made against it saying that they had appealed for help (without success) from their critics who were really the inaccessible ones. The columns of *Freedom* were open for criticism but none had been sent. They were indignant that they should be so abused when they published "the only paper that has managed to struggle through these trying times." They declared themselves ready to wish every success to a weekly paper, should one appear. Yet they did not seem properly able to understand the situation. Attempts had been made to reorganise the movement at the conference but since the emphasis in the movement was so much on propaganda, the sole remaining anarchist paper had assumptions thrust upon it which it was not only designed to disappoint but which it hardly seemed to recognise. To be sure, *Freedom* had its own troubles and was struggling to keep going but it could have been a little more helpful.

It had been agreed at the conference that *Freedom* should be approached and inquiries made as to excess type and the possibility of other help. The reply was to be sent to a 'West London Anarchist Group' which was formed at the conference. The nature of the reply to perhaps rather ambitious suggestions from the meeting can be seen in the letter Kropotkin sent to Marsh:

> Dear Friend, I just received a letter from Gumplowicz, telling me that at the last Conference there was a bitter opposition to *Freedom*, that the comrades wanted to stop it and so on.
>
> I don't know how it came that Gumplowicz consider himself of the Freedom Group; How can he when his ideas are ultra-individualist, bitterly opposed to our Communist lines, and altogether — what has he to do in *Freedom*.

At any rate, *Freedom* being the paper of a small group which lives from voluntary work and contributions of a small group — no one has any right 'to stop' *Freedom*, so long as that group wishes to publish it.

As to a new paper, you know that I am always delighted at the appearance of every new paper and the more would I be delighted to see a weekly published in England.

But Gumplowicz writes they have decided (who has that right, except you and the Freedom Group) that the new paper will be printed in Freedom's office.

Are you agreed with that? Is it really your idea.

I think that the best way to keep kindly relations between the two papers — if a new one appears — is not to print them in the same office.

That is the rule deduced from long practice in France ... it must end in petty quarrels about petty things — to say nothing of the difficulties of printing the two papers — the same week at the end of the month — to keep the composition for pamphlets and so on.

Of course I can give no definite opinion upon this subject (!JMQ) but it seems to me that the printing of the two papers in our small office would only lead to create bad relations.

It is a very serious question and I should earnestly advise the *Freedom* comrades — I mean you, Wess, Nettlau, Presburg — to take no hasty steps.[25]

So much for Nettlau's intention to purchase the *Torch* plant and take over their office for the benefit of the movement as a whole. So much, too, for the proposed weekly paper. The project foundered in frustration and apathy. Nothing further was mentioned until an appeal appeared in the June 1898 issue of *Freedom* for funds to start a weekly paper. The following month they acknowledged £2–£3 which, they said, was "not sufficient."

They also said "...we appealed to you who are interested to communicate with us, and for reasons unknown to us, have so far received no response ..." Nothing further was said and no new weekly paper appeared.

The decline of anarchist morale in 1896 and 1897, represented concretely by the collapse of systematic open-air or written propaganda, could be laid at the door of apathy and the sense of defeat both in the working class in general and the anarchists in particular. In 1898 there were clear signs that a real period of reaction was under way. The ruling-class strategy of judiciously balanced quantities of force and fraud (in Morris's terms) was becoming weighted in the direction of force. In industrial terms this manifested itself in a very determined opposition to trades unions by the employers. They improved their national communications and organisation and with the aid of blacklegs organised by themselves or by the Free Labour Association were able to defeat the engineering workers in a lockout in 1897–1898. Similarly, dock strikes were defeated in 1899–1900. There were also increasing attacks in more 'political' areas. Instead of containing manifestations of 'subversive' or popular activity the authorities were now harassing groups and individuals whose activities were not particularly public or 'disruptive'. A foretaste had been given in July 1897 when a "vile and unfair attack [was] made by the whole press — with few exceptions — against asylum" when Spanish refugees arrived in Liverpool.[26] These people had fled from Spain in the face of the brutal repression of every possible kind of opponent to the government and the Church. Some 400 prisoners had been packed into Montjuich prison, Barcelona, and many had died as a result of appalling tortures. The Freedom Group had conducted a modestly successful campaign on behalf of the refugees.

The reaction began to get under way when two Russians, Burtzev and Wierzbicki, were arrested and charged in London in early 1898 with "having persuaded or endeavoured to persuade divers persons unknown to murder the Tsar of Russia."[27] In a Russian-language magazine for which the two men were responsible, an article had appeared urging revolutionary action in Russia and praising those revolutionaries who had made attempts on the life of the Tsar. This prosecution seems to have been instigated at the request of the Russian government, and it resulted in the imprisonment of Burtzev for eighteen months. In actual fact there was probably more to the prosecution than the article in question. At a later date Burtzev is mentioned as running a one-man counter-espionage operation against the activity of Tsarist spies among Russian émigrés in Paris.[28] This kind of activity, more than any revolutionary sentiments in a magazine, was likely to have aroused the vindictive anger of the Russian government. There was no great outcry against this prosecution, which could be compared to — say — the agitation around the trial of Johann Most. As *Freedom* put it: "The danger at the moment is the indifference of the British people."

Another prosecution that could conceivably have roused 'the people' from their indifference was the prosecution of George Bedborough, secretary of the Legitimation League and editor of its magazine, the *Adult*. He was prosecuted on a number of charges which centred on his having sold copies of Havelock Ellis's book *Sexual Inversion*. The fascinating details of the case involving the activities of a brilliant international confidence trickster, 'de Villiers', and the craven cowardice of Ellis, the bold sexologist, can be found elsewhere.[29] The result was a rather inglorious partial plea of guilty by Bedborough who was pressed on the one hand by the defence committee to become a martyr and on the other by the police, who (quite rightly) pointed out that neither Ellis nor de Villiers were supporting him. Bedborough was effectively bound over and renounced any connection with the Legitimation League or the *Adult*. As a result they both collapsed. And in the face of this withdrawal little passion was aroused by the case. What is most relevant to us is the motivation of the police in prosecuting Bedborough.

The Legitimation League, founded in 1895, had been originally set up to press for equal legal rights for illegitimate children. Its discussions, however, expanded to most matters sexual, and it included in its ranks those who were fighting for sexual liberation as well as cranks and, in the case of de Villiers, a more or less genteel pornographer. It had conducted a successful agitation in its first year to have Miss Edith Lanchester, a sympathiser, released from a lunatic asylum where she had been confined by her family and the family doctor when she had announced her intention of living with a man to whom she was not married. This had brought the League into prominence. The interest of the police had increased when they found that anarchists were regularly attending the meetings of the League and propagandising there. Sweeny, the detective in charge of this investigation, regularly attended meetings of the League and reported that the anarchists were rounding out the Legitimation League's call for an abolition of the marriage laws with a call for the abolition of all laws. Lilian Harman, an American anarchist, co-editor with her father of the magazine *Lucifer*, who had been imprisoned for living with the father of her child when unmarried to him, visited Britain and gave a number of successful lectures. She was also elected honorary President of the League. Thus, when an opportunity arose in the shape of Ellis' book *Sexual Inversion*, for which Bedborough had become an unofficial agent, the police arrested him. In Sweeny's words they were "convinced that we should at one blow kill a growing evil in the shape of a vigorous campaign for free love and anarchism and at the same time, discover the means by which the country was being flooded with books of the 'Psychology' type."[30] The campaign in defence of Bedborough over the summer of 1898 involved Henry Seymour and two previous 'martyrs' in the cause of free speech, Holyoake and Foote. However it did not involve Ellis, who decided he was a scholar not a fighter. Neither did it involve de Villiers, who was concerned, sensibly in view of his previous assorted identities, to avoid contact with the police. Finally with Bedborough's plea of guilty to a number of his charges the case was indefinitely adjourned. From Sweeny's memoirs it is quite clear that the police had every intention of smashing the Legitimation League and closing down the *Adult* and only needed an excuse which would not get them into the choppy waters of accusations of repression of free speech. It is interesting that the political police should so readily jump into questions of morality. We have grown used to psychological-political analyses which relate authority to moral authoritarianism with the result that although self-appointed guardians of sexual morality still plague us they are faced with a pointed counter-attack. In 1898 sexual repression was respectable and attacks on 'free love' propaganda could be conducted with equanimity and self-satisfaction. Yet it is a surprise that it should be so readily assumed that the police should treat it as a political matter.

The prosecutions of Burtzev and Bedborough were specific instances of a more intensive general harassment. This harassment could not be related to a particular wave of anarchist activity comparable to the bombings in Paris in the early 1890s. At that time, however, a measure of international police cooperation had developed and had continued. It was to be given a more definite political form by the international conference, popularly known as the Anti-Anarchist Conference, called by the Italian government in late 1898. The specific basis for the conference was the assassination of the Empress of Austria by the Italian anarchist Lucheni earlier that same year. It was proposed that all participants should ban all anarchist publications, send all anarchists back to their own countries and ban publication of details of anarchist trials and actions. And while in England these proposals never took the form of laws and the public stance of the British government remained 'liberal', in practice the police without hindrance from above seem to have acted in sympathy with the intentions of the conference. In March 1899, *Freedom* was writing "Italian comrades are being systematically coerced and terrorised by Scotland Yard ..." Letters of English and foreign anarchists were being tampered with and the number of people being followed by the police increased. This seems to have been an advance on the situation in mid-1898, which was already pretty tight. According to David Nicoll, the Fitzroy Square area swarmed "with vermin in the shape of spies ... you can't speak to an acquaintance without a gentleman of suspicious appearance walking up to you to listen to the conversation." People were again being followed to work and their employers told of their employee's dangerous political ideas — resulting all too often in the sack. On one occasion, someone who was being followed by Detective Sweeny wilfully misunderstood the situation and deciding that he must be a beggar offered the detective a piece of bread. He was arrested on some trumped-up charge but later acquitted at his trial.[31] Kropotkin, at a Chicago Commemoration meeting in November 1898, spoke of the implications of the Anti-Anarchist Conference: "Take it as a law of history. The so-called scientific people may ignore it but it has had not one single exception in the past. Never has an advanced party been prosecuted, without all more or less advanced parties and even mere reform parties being included in the prosecution and a screw being put on their activities. Only those who become the tools of reaction are spared in such times." He linked the attacks of reactionaries with the passivity of the masses. "Who would have dared to foretell 20 years ago," he said, "...nay ten years only when Morris wrote in *Tables Turned* that the revolution was, not 'coming' but had already begun — who would have dared to foretell the sudden revival of militarism, of ritualism and of Catholicism which we now witness in Europe."[32] In England the wave of popular reaction centred on the war fever surrounding the Boer War (1899–1902). With few exceptions the anarchists were in no position to run a coherent campaign against the war. The S.D.F., poisoned at source by the jingoism of Hyndman and others, was not particularly disposed to oppose the war. Initial opposition came from the Liberals and the I.L.P. The anarchists seemed to be largely sunk in apathy. There were few communications in *Freedom* from old London activists and what few there were consisted of commentary and generalisation rather than reports of activity. Only the groups in Liverpool, Leeds and Glasgow rose at all to the situation. These were the only towns in which outdoor speakers had been active and other propaganda had been steadily carried on for a length of time before the war started. For the rest, the mood seems to be expressed by a report from a visitor to Aberdeen which was, he said, "five or six years ago ... practically, as far as numbers and enthusiasm go, the stronghold of Anarchism in Great Britain ... I called on Harry Duncan, and found him rather despondent about the future of the movement. ... He finding himself unsupported has gone into Trade Union work; where he thinks, if the returns are not so great, they are at least quicker. His ideas have undergone a change, he has perhaps less hope in the future."[33]

Further indications of apathy come from the reception given to three of the Walsall anarchists on their release after serving seven and a half years of their ten-year sentences. A rather sedate tea and social evening was held and Charles, Cailes and Battola were presented with about £20 from a fund collected mainly, it would appear, among Jewish and other foreign anarchists. There were no riotous receptions like those that greeted Nicoll on his release, nor do provincial anarchists seem to have invited them to do speaking tours round the country. Charles went quietly back to Norwich where he married, Cailes remained in the Soho area and Battola seems to have disappeared. Meanwhile the first anti-war demonstration had been broken up in Trafalgar Square by jingo crowds. The only anarchist group to take up the cry in any exceptional way was in Leeds. They organised an anti-war demonstration for 1st October 1899 at which there were nine anarchist speakers. They reported that it was "the most successful and orderly meeting held in this part of the country on that matter." Liberal meetings had been a fiasco "but our meeting with the Anarchist as opposed to the Capitalist and Imperialist spirit put plainly, enthused the workers for there was a concrete exposition of a social state based upon their interests compared with a condition of things based upon their misery and degradation. ... Out of a crowd of 2,000 only 16 voted against the resolution. This meeting has done us a lot of good in the town and since then our meetings have been well attended and enthusiastic."[34]

The matter was not allowed to rest there, however. The Leeds group continued its activities with a series of meetings, working through the local branch of the 'South African Conciliation Committee'. "To wind up these meetings," reported Billy MacQueen, "we had a monster demonstration which, unfortunately for the health of some of the comrades, turned out to be a jingo demonstration. It was a day! All the scum of the pubs of Leeds were turned out — being called up by means of placards inviting them to give us a 'Scarborough Welcome'. And they *did*."[35] In fact Billy MacQueen was nearly lynched and many people were badly beaten about. The following week Matt Sollitt, a veteran Socialist League anarchist, went to the place where the "monster demonstration" had been held and repeated almost word for word Billy MacQueen's speech.[36] It was a brave thing to do, and he remained unmolested. Yet the suppression of anti-war activity intended by the 'Scarborough Welcome' and incited, it was assumed, by Conservative agents seems to have been successful. Leeds anarchists, it was reported, had had to give up outdoor meetings "owing to the lack of speakers."[37] The same team of anarchist speakers existed as before the riot and the reason given rings hollow. It was too dangerous for further outside meetings to be held and it might have been better to admit it. Shortly afterwards, Billy MacQueen, who had largely been responsible for the exceptional activity of the Leeds anarchists, was forced by unemployment to emigrate to America. In Liverpool and Glasgow the regular outdoor meetings were kept up, though, particularly in Liverpool, it was a continual battle against jingoist opposition.

The London anarchists did contribute their mite to the anti-war movement. In early 1900 an anti-war meeting was held with speakers which included Tom Mann and Emma Goldman, the American anarchist, together with Sam Mainwaring and Harry Kelly. There was some jingoist opposition but nothing particularly violent. However, the tide was rising, and although anti-war meetings usually instigated by non-anarchist bodies continued to take place the opposition they encountered increased. After a large meeting at the Queens Hall in mid-1901 where quite a battle took place, the hall was closed to 'controversial' meetings. And it seemed that other halls would be closed, too. *Freedom* commented with some accuracy and considerable gloomy satisfaction:

Here is the situation and we as Anarchists have a right to say a word on the moral of it. Seven years ago [i.e. 1894] when the May Day demonstration held by Anarchists was brutally attacked and broken up by Scotland Yard, with the help of some unofficial roughs, there was no outcry by Liberals, Radicals or Democrats. Later on when Anarchist Clubs were raided, when halls were closed against us, when extraditions went on apace, when Bourtzeff was sentenced, contemptible indeed was the attitude of these parties. Today it is you ... who are the 'Anarchists' in the eyes of the Government. ... *He who will not fight for the liberties of others will surely endanger his own.*[38]

In fact by November 1901 the closure of halls to anti-war meetings seemed to have been systematic — even routine.

The practical work of abolishing free speech has been going on for the last two years. Some newspapers, politically and morally corrupt, especially the *Daily Chronicle*, the *Globe* and the *Pall Mall Gazette* announce the day before the meeting that a 'pro-Boer' meeting will be held. Immediately the police authorities with the paper in hand approach the owner of the hall threatening that disorder will take place and that they — the police — will not be able to protect the hall against the aggressors. The frightened hall proprietor mostly refuses the hall and the meeting is put off.

This hypocritical and (in reality) despotic suppression was done with Miss Hobhouse in her humanitarian crusade against the war atrocities. The same trick was repeated twice with our meetings; twice the halls were refused the last day before the meeting — organised and advertised long before in papers by posters and handbills. Our Government stained with the blood of innocent children, is capable of any violation of popular rights. Are they not attempting to crush our trade unions and the right of combination? ... Did they not impose new burdens on the working classes?[39]

The suppression was not only hypocritical and despotic, it was successful and it needs to be stressed that the anarchist movement emerged from the

Boer War period almost completely destroyed. There was no sense of losing a battle to go on to greater things; the movement felt more or less completely defeated by the reactionary war fever that had gripped the population.

The mood of the movement was despondent and apathetic in the extreme. In one of a number of (unsuccessful) morale-building attempts, Harry Kelly wrote a piece for *Freedom* which took as its starting point the arrest of Most and MacQueen in New York under the 'Criminal Anarchy' Laws. "Small in numbers as we are," he wrote, "it is safe to say that 19 out of every 20 Anarchists in the country would have known absolutely nothing about this … were it not for Barton's note in Reynold's newspaper …." Anarchists, he went on to say, had no means of communication except *Freedom* "and as it is only published monthly, that method is very slow, and alas I don't believe half the comrades read *Freedom*."

There were not more than three active groups in the whole of Great Britain, and they were not in regular contact with one another. Compared to the position seven years before the situation was catastrophic. Though he could well see reasons for this in the war and general apathy he was of the opinion that an organising effort would overcome the difficulties. Whatever the truth of this he shows clearly the effect of the war and its concomitant apathy. He also shows the effect on groups of a stance that left no activity open but general propaganda:

> Groups have stood alone and the half dozen or dozen comrades in each group have discussed and split hairs until there were no more hairs to split and nothing to discuss and then died a natural death. Take Canning Town for example. It is a place where splendid meetings used to be held, plenty of literature sold and any amount of interest and enthusiasm created for our ideas. An active group existed there for years. The comrades were all working men who tired out from a hard day's work were unable to read very much. They derived almost all of their knowledge of anarchism from lectures and open air meetings.

But fewer and fewer comrades visited them, leading to less interchange of ideas "and the group fell a prey to mysticism and spiritualism and the comrades lost all their old time spirit and activity." *Freedom* discussion meetings had been 'suspended indefinitely'. "We got down to an average attendance of six comrades — two of whom were Tolstoyans ... generally we seem to be becoming weaker instead of stronger ... the time is ripe for someone to write a book on 'Modern Society and Moribund Anarchy'."

"Ladies and gentlemen, we are becoming back numbers. ... Shall we organise this movement or shall some historian write opposite our names a few years hence: Interesting — but died through lack of energy."[40]

*Freedom* itself came out sporadically during the war, often missing a month. Over the whole period Marsh, the editor, was sending out private appeals and publishing others in the paper for cash to support the paper.

The public sale of *Freedom* as advertised in the paper itself was restricted to outlets in the north Soho area and Aldgate, both of them areas with a high concentration of foreign exiles (presumably where native jingoism could not affect open sales). It is likely that the circulation of the paper declined to as low as 500 copies per issue during this period. The paper really did seem on the edge of collapse. It was announced in January 1902: "The condition of our finances not permitting us to promise a regular issue of *Freedom*, we shall issue the paper as often as circumstances will allow and hope that all comrades will make an effort to resume and continue the monthly publication."

Attempts were made to reorganise the paper, though in rather a confused way. Kropotkin wrote to Marsh, 15th October 1902: "...It was *my* idea to propose the revival of the *editing* meetings of *Freedom*, once a month ... before the appearance of the number as I think that all these talks about *Freedom* being not well managed from the business point of view are of no avail, so long as we have not tried everything we can to *render the paper more interesting*. It was awfully dull lately and neglected by the contributors, including myself. Let us try and give more life to the contents of the paper first ..." Good intentions alone did not suffice and Kropotkin was writing an agitated letter a month later "...no *Freedom* yet! What is the reason? Want of ms [manuscripts]? Want of money? Or Cantwell's contrariness? What is the reason and what has to be done? The first thing for a paper is to be published on certain dates. Can we obtain that? Write me dear friend, all you think about. What is to be done? Wait? But that will not help. Whatever paper may appear — a paper dealing with the theory of Anarchism … will always be required."[41] *Freedom* did survive; but it was several years before it did anything but limp along.

This eventual revival was the result of circumstances outside *Freedom*, based in the development of a new wave of working-class militancy leading up to the period known as the Syndicalist Revolt. *Freedom* remained the paper it had been from the beginning, largely separate from events, unaware of small-scale developments until it was informed of them by activists, commenting on major conflagrations from a distance. The new militancy infused *Freedom* rather than the other way round. This period brought with it a new wave of activists and encouraged many old anarchists to emerge from 'retirement'. Yet there were organic connections between the movement of the 1890s and the Syndicalist period. Outside the discussions of anarchist theory, outside the publication of anarchist newspapers and a systematic propaganda of anarchist ideas, individuals and groups of militants had had no option but to fight and struggle for existence. This had been their situation when anarchism had first appealed to them. When the formal movement had more or less collapsed the conditions which had inspired their great hopes survived the temporary collapse of those hopes. Their struggles continued. Anarchism survived in holes and corners, in partial, even dispirited battles. Sporadic attempts at revivals were made to subside again. Yet hidden influences were at work which were to make such revivals more successful. It is proper that we should show these false starts and hidden beginnings so that they can take their place as a modest contribution to one of the great periods of working-class self-activity in our history. But first let us look at one response to the collapse of anarchist hopes for a revolution in Britain. These were the anarchist colonies which it was hoped could provide on a small scale the free social relations which the world did not seem prepared to provide on a large one.

## Chapter 12

# COOPERATIVE COLONIES

Cooperative enterprises of a utopian kind in England have suffered the fate of all enterprises designed as rehearsals for a great change that has not yet come. They have been defeated and have collapsed, or they have changed and become absorbed, being no longer dangerous. Yet they represent a continual and continuing attempt to place the relationships of work and living on a basis which differs severely from the norm that has existed since the Industrial Revolution. Their makers have attempted to realise in a concrete way ahead of time the conditions they desire or expect in society as a whole. They have attempted in varying degrees to achieve communism in property, cooperation in production and a rather indefinable quality of freedom with sympathy and mutual care in personal relationships which Morris called "good fellowship" and Orwell "decency." Revolutions have furnished us with examples where such activity has occurred on a general scale — notably in Catalonia and Aragon in the early days of the Spanish Civil War and Revolution in 1936–1939. Yet in such cases the very scale of the operation means the making of revolution. Even in times of an expansive movement in less than revolutionary periods such colonies may have a generally accepted exemplary and experimental role. And while the utopian cooperators in non-revolutionary times may see their role as exemplary to encourage some general development, the spirit of the enterprise cannot but be affected by the loneliness of it all. The desperate need to live in good fellowship is unsupported by the general social situation or a specific social movement. Inevitably, therefore, no matter how much the intention is to provide an example to others, the world at large appears hostile and the enterprise tends to represent not so much an attack on the 'old world' but a withdrawal from it.

These remarks do not, of course, apply to more 'hard-headed' ameliorative measures such as the retail cooperatives which have grown into chains of

supermarkets hardly distinguishable from other such enterprises. It has
to be readily admitted that the beginnings of such cooperatives were not
without idealism, heartache and sacrifice. Yet the commercial viability of
these enterprises seems to have been seen not as a crass necessity for survival
but as an assumed virtue. They had originally been intended in Owen's
time to provide money for communities. From the beginning, therefore,
they were oriented towards profitable trading. However "they were ...
foredoomed to find that the very sensible innovations which permitted the
shops to survive and compete for life, also worked against the fulfilment
of any more adventurous hopes."[1] Retail cooperatives therefore moved
quite rapidly out of the utopian socialist sphere of influence. The utopian
cooperators were concerned to make a new life and only in passing to ease
the conditions of the present one. They were in intention revolutionary
rather than reformist. The history of English utopian cooperators by no
means starts and finishes with the anarchist movement. From the time
of Robert Owen through the times of the Chartists and the International
men and women had attempted to make a world in the here-and-now
compatible with their desires. The movement continues to this day in such
disparate forms as the workers' communes of the Autonomous Assemblies
in Italy and the various imitators of the Woodstock nation. Yet for a
while libertarians, if not anarchists, moved to the centre of the tradition
in England. We have seen that no matter how subjectively revolutionary
these enterprises were, objectively they represented a withdrawal from the
fray in the absence of a general revolutionary movement. In 1893, perhaps
the question was open; by 1896 this type of colony represents a self-
protective shell against a hostile world. Thus we are forced to look at them
both as a separate world of their own and in the context of a demoralised
movement.

Straddling the gap between the cooperative colonies and the retail
cooperators were the cooperative workshops. These were started for every
reason, from the sharing of resources, through attempts to find work for
blacklisted workers, to attempts to live socialism in working hours at least.
This is a confused area and much more work needs to be done on it. However,
the *Labour Annual* for 1898 reported a great growth in productive co-ops.
They were, it said, selling most of their products through distributive co-

ops and were facing bitter opposition from private employers, particularly in Scotland where participants were being blacklisted by employers.[2] This *Labour Annual* also advertised a necessarily incomplete pamphlet, *Cooperative Workshops in Great Britain*, in 1897, which nevertheless ran to sixty pages. Some trades were more susceptible to cooperative working than others. Boot and shoemaking, with its relatively high ratio of skill to capital costs seems to have been in the lead. It was, in fact, the policy of the more militant Leicester branches of the Boot and Shoe Union in the 1890s to press the union as a whole to devote some of its funds to financing cooperative enterprises both productive and retail.[3] But this more ambitious general programme seems to have been based on the experience of existing small-scale workshops — it is worth noting that Battola, one of the Walsall anarchists, was working in a shoemaking cooperative in Soho at the time of his arrest. Cooperative workshops also existed in light engineering, printing, tailoring and other areas.

A growth in the number of cooperative colonies in England paralleled the rise in the number of cooperative workshops. In 1898, four communities were reported as existing in England. By 1899 there were eight; and this seems to have represented a high point, for by 1900 the number had dropped to six.[4] The most interesting of these from the anarchist point of view, and one of the earliest, was the colony at Clousden Hill Farm near Newcastle-on-Tyne. The direct inspiration for this colony was a series of articles by Kropotkin, written for the magazine *Nineteenth Century* which represented the groundwork of a book later published as *Fields, Factories and Workshops*.[5] In these articles Kropotkin developed ideas which seem relatively unremarkable now, yet represented a considerable advance in their time. Kropotkin used the most up-to-date technological information to show the real material possibility of the anarchist-communist ideal of productive units small enough to allow federal organisation which would be both largely self-sufficient and easily self-managed on direct democratic lines. In place of woolly ideas of the 'simple life' Kropotkin assessed the possibilities of such an existence both economically and technologically. It should be stressed that Kropotkin was not calling for the formation of colonies as kinds of pilot plant for the revolution. His works were intended to develop the possibilities open to revolutionaries in the event of general social reconstruction. This was made quite clear by him in a letter sent to the anarchists who set up the Clousden Hill colony when they invited him to become their treasurer.[6] The colonists had seized upon the practical proposal made by Kropotkin that intensive agriculture under glass could find a favourable environment near coal mines where coal could be bought relatively cheaply without massive haulage costs. By early 1895 plans were well advanced, finance was forthcoming from an unnamed 'wealthy London anarchist' and land was being bought. Kropotkin refused the treasurership on the grounds of his general opposition to colonies as a pre-revolutionary tactic and in particular because of their low success rate. He was sympathetic, however, and for several years kept in touch with them and in a minor way lobbied for their support. For a few years the colony seemed to be making progress. A report in *Freedom*, August 1897, on the second anniversary of the colony was optimistic. They believed that they were showing workers both what could be done with little capital and also demonstrating the practicality of the anarchist lifestyle. They had leased eighteen acres of land, one quarter of an acre being under glass in four greenhouses. One, they proudly related, gave a rich crop of cucumbers — twenty a week! They were distributing their produce through retail cooperatives but were careful to preserve their own autonomy. They had no wage system. "Every member works according to his or her ability and enjoys equally all the Colony can grant." Matters of common concern were discussed at weekly meetings, while in all other matters the individual was completely free. The colony at that time was composed of fifteen men, two women and four children. The report finishes by saying that they needed more women. For a later history of the Clousden Hill Colony we have to rely on a rather hostile source, W.C. Hart. He says the colony was undermined by inexperience and internal bickering despite its initial prosperity. Numbers of people began to leave and finally two of the colonists bought out their colleagues. A flower business started by these two proved unsuccessful and came before the Newcastle Bankruptcy Court in April 1902.[7]

Hart seems to imply that this marks the end of Clousden Hill. Another distinctly anarchist colony was founded at Whiteway, near Stroud, Gloucestershire, in 1897. This seems to have been more straightforwardly 'simple life' in conception, without the technological point-making of

Clousden Hill. It was founded by Samuel Bracher, a Gloucester journalist who put a considerable amount of money into the scheme.[8] The membership of the colony expanded from eight to forty quite rapidly. By 1900 the colony was reported to have had 'friction'. It had burned its title deeds and declared that it "recognises no laws or external rule. ... At present the group have no 'prospects' and desire none."[9] An unattractive picture is painted of this period by a hostile witness: "While some worked hard, the majority sponged idly. ... No idea can be given of the indolence and sheer animalism of this Whiteway Anarchia with its lawless licence and its cadging. So disgusted were some of the Colonists that they renounced Anarchy straightway and on an adjoining farm started a cooperative colony based on laws and authority, the chief law being 'He that will not work, neither shall he eat'."[10] Among the people who left were the founder and his family. Other contemporary accounts do not seem to mention a split, though they do mention the movement of a number of people from a mainly Tolstoyan anarchist colony between Croydon and Purley to Whiteway as well as the 'friction' referred to above. It might easily have been this change of personnel which accounts for a different picture given elsewhere of the same colony — though admittedly it could easily be the one "based on laws and authority" referred to above. This author however emphasises the continuity of events rather than otherwise and calls it an anarchist colony.[11] An early raid by a local farmer provoked by the "lack of sense of ownership" of the colonists, which involved him and his labourers stripping the colonists' potato crop was never repeated though he was not resisted. Tramps came and could be as lazy as they wanted. "They were never told to go; but somehow the tramps went and they did not return. Perhaps the life was too lazy for them." (It is worth pointing out that being told to go is not the only way of being told to go.) The colonists operated as far as possible on a system of barter and dispensed with fashion, readily taking to sandals as popularised by Edward Carpenter. Well after the turn of the century it was said that "...so far their harvests have not failed them ... they have had many a surplus over their wants and this has been spent on luxuries which they cannot grow or manufacture such as books and a piano." The colony survives to this day and in the 1930s provided a place of retirement for several anarchists of our period including Tom Keell and Fred Charles.[12]

The Purley/Croydon colony, about which not much information seems to be available,[13] also provided the inspiration for an experiment in Leeds which lies somewhere between a colony and a cooperative workshop with more general social aspirations. In *Freedom* for November 1898, Billy MacQueen reported that: "Some while ago our comrade J.C. Kenworthy came to Leeds and in a number of public meetings tried to bring home to his audience the possibility of living up to the ideal even today. This notion went home in one or two cases, and set folk thinking; with the result that a year ago G. Gibson, who had hitherto been a prosperous cycle manufacturer and electrician, decided to throw his works into the movement."

It was originally set up for victims of the engineering lockout of 1897 but they didn't fall in with it:

> so it was started with a few comrades gathered from various parts ... it was decided to have the thing thorough (and to this) no doubt is due its success ... the essentials were truth, frankness and good fellowship — the expressions of pure healthy life.
>
> They have not formal membership; no rules, no formal admission.
>
> If one thinks their place is there, they go. Only such accounts as are necessary to determine the question of weekly loss or gain are kept. There is no recognition of 'fair' or 'equal' division of wages. Each man or woman in connection takes from the treasury such as they need.
>
> Work if it is worth doing at all, ought to be done well, and, acting up to this, the Brotherhood make the question of profits quite secondary. If there are any they are to be ploughed back.
>
> The idea of a communal home has already been attained and an agricultural colony is possible.
>
> At present the efforts ... are mostly centred in the making of bicycles and various electrical apparatus. One comrade makes the clothing that is needed by the others, whilst another mends their boots and soon hopes to be making them. Comrades wanting anything in the shape of bikes, etc., should make an enquiry. The address is: Brotherhood Workshop, 6 Victoria Rd., Holbeck, Leeds.
>
> The experiment is extremely interesting to us who have approached Anarchy from another road, because now, after one year's running,

the workshop is living proof that folk call live together harmoniously without the aid of law or excessive organisation. In this case it must exercise a great influence for good upon the general movement.

For all the optimism of the report, by 1900 the colony was not doing well, though it had inspired an offshoot in Blackburn: a communal workshop doing electrical work with about ten members.[14] It is probable that the Leeds colony closed down shortly after this.

The actual colonies themselves represented concrete examples of a rather general aspiration in the anarchist movement. We find, for example, the Edmonton, London, anarchist group reporting in early 1898 that they had started a cooperative (presumably retail), the profits from which were to be set aside for a colonising scheme. "This we have conducted for a year in accordance with our principles," they said, "and our increasing prosperity is evidence of the practical nature of such principles."[15] In both Leeds and Manchester at different times the anarchist groups ran cooperative print shops which were basically used only for propaganda.

John Turner himself had been the manager of the Socialist Cooperative Federation whose headquarters had been in Lamb's Conduit Street, Holborn. Fred Charles at a later date was part of an Oxford Builders cooperative, which involved a hundred building workers.[16] The continuing concern for the cooperative movement and for its wider possibilities was based in a theoretical position which was most clearly expressed in Kropotkin's pamphlet *The Development of Trades Unionism*, which first appeared as an article in *Freedom* in March 1898. Here Kropotkin was developing his evolutionary ideas in the more tranquil years of his British exile. Less concerned with questions of immediate revolutionary activity, he was now searching for the historical, social and scientific ground which would nourish the *gradual* growth of a libertarian society. This led him to examine the processes going on around him for hopeful signs. He found them in the trades unions, in cooperatives and in municipal organisation.

He saw that as they stood they were not anarchist organisations, yet if they were to take up a unified federalist and "encroaching control" stance then they would inevitably lead to anarchism. The agitational question of how this change of direction was to be achieved was not discussed.

These ideas were broadly acceptable to the anarchist movement, which saw the cooperatives as an early prefiguration of the society they desired. This area of sympathy is to be found in writings and speeches at all times, though in times of violent class confrontation it tended to sink into the background. In times of reaction and sluggishness, cooperation would emerge as a major concern which could absorb energies which it did not seem profitable to apply in other areas.

*Chapter 13*

# ANARCHISM AND THE ORIGINS OF THE SYNDICALIST REVOLT, 1889–1910

Socialists develop theoretical ideas of the nature of their society, the nature of a more desirable future and the manner of the transition between them. Mass action develops through forms designed for immediate use which can have great implications hardly perceived by the majority of participants. Socialist theory and mass action may not combine on any great scale. When they do both are transformed. The result is an explosion of popular creativity, a 'positive self-consciousness' which makes particular struggles into general ones and abstract discussion into urgent questions of practice. The implications of such situations are revolutionary and circumstances can make them so.

Two such 'pre-revolutionary' situations occur in our period. One is that of 1889–1893, the other is the period of the Syndicalist revolt, 1910–1914, and again after World War One. It is the latter which concerns us here, although some further remarks on the former are necessary. Though the socialist movement as a whole was massively concerned in the organisation of trades unions in 1889–1890 the net result of its concern in the later 1890s was an increase in electoral activity using trades unions as a base. Remarks appeared in various socialist papers (here disregarding the anarchists for the moment) which criticised the new trades unions. Yet the gist of these criticisms was that trades union activity by itself was not sufficient to bring about socialism. See for example a comment in *Justice*: the men "were led to expect too much and now find they cannot accomplish everything with their trade unionism — that it is but a very imperfect weapon with which to fight the capitalist — they are throwing it over altogether as no good, instead of using as a means to something better. This is wrong. Stand by your unions men! And use them to conquer political power for your class."[1] The context makes it clear that 'political power' means power through institutions like parliament. Since the concern of these socialist bodies was to gain political power through existing institutions they had something of a vested interest in belittling the power of trades unions or of 'economic struggles' for social change. It is not surprising, therefore, that they showed little concern with the *structure* of trades unions and their fitness in providing a focus for such change. With the anarchists the situation was rather different. Hostile to electoral activity, they were more concerned with the possibilities for 'non-political' trades union activity. It is true that against the anarchist revolutionary yardstick the trades unions would be rejected in disgust by some sections and that the pro- or anti-trades-union debate tended to dominate. Yet at the same time among the pro-trades unionists there was a real concern to disentangle the nature of trades union struggles and to assess the necessary conditions for trades unions to become revolutionary. The results of this investigation were patchy and inconclusive in the face of events. Yet at various times and in various ways they articulated the pragmatic concerns that were to be systematised by syndicalism.

The anarchists in the late 1880s and early 1890s were hostile to 'officialism' — bureaucracy as we should call it — counterposing spontaneous solidarity. They preached solidarity between skilled and unskilled sections and a concern for the unemployed by those in work. They were interested in extending the tactics used by workers in struggle and saw such extended struggles as rehearsals for revolution. They opposed calls for nationalisation. A few examples will suffice here. The rejection of nationalisation was for the most part from first principles, based in hostility to the state. Yet points could be made which showed an astute assessment of the situation. Of the social democrats' statist obsessions, *Freedom* commented: "So anxious are they to put … economic administration under state control that they are perpetually urging us not to wait for the repair of the ancient political machine, i.e. not to concern ourselves with mere politics but to joyfully confide railways or land or what not to the control of Salisbury and Balfour or Gladstone and Morley or Rosebery and Co., tomorrow if only those chosen of the people can be persuaded to undertake the task."[2] The point remains valid to this day. Have the miners, now enjoying all the benefits that nationalisation can bring, been more noticeably content with their lot? Have the railwaymen? Yet the 'socialist' calls continue for nationalisation as some kind of panacea.

The general tactical outlines for trades union activity were formulated at the Zurich Anarchist Congress in 1893. This took place during and after the chaotic International Socialist Congress of that year from which the anarchists were expelled on the votes of the German social democrat machine. The "practical, business-like and orderly" meetings showed the direction that was already being followed by the anarchists in the French trades union movement. General propaganda for the general strike, seen as a preparatory step for revolution, was to be coupled with practical demands such as the eight-hour day. In each particular situation direct action by the workers themselves rather than the use of legislative bodies was to be stressed. Anarchists should not try and build a party but make a movement. They should enter trade organisations as agitators, not office seekers. Anarchists should be "champions of the weakest and worst off, not flatterers of those who had slightly bettered their position." They should use every opportunity to preach rebellion.[3] Delegates at these meetings included Mowbray and Roland of the West End tailors.

Mowbray, at least, propagandised these principles. In a piece on 'Trades Unionism and the Unemployed' he developed the general principles for English conditions. The trades unions were saying that unemployed men should not offer themselves for less than the union rate and otherwise did nothing for the unemployed, looking down on them with contempt. Meanwhile a largely ineffective policy of organising parades of the unemployed was going on outside the unions. When a drastic drop in union membership took place the unions would bestir themselves, but only to the extent of holding discussions with vestries. This had the effect of demobilising an already less than powerful unemployed agitation. What should be done, Mowbray said, was to immediately campaign round the following policy with both the organised and unorganised workers: Overtime should be stopped immediately; a day of eight hours or less should be enforced to absorb the unemployed; cooperative production should be started; and piecework should be abolished. Otherwise, said Mowbray, it was the unions' fault if there was blacklegging. Political lobbying would do no good, economic power had to be applied to achieve economic ends.[4] In a later article he urged people to join unions as 'trade' members — that is, members who were not involved with Friendly Society benefits and activities: "The sooner the Friendly Society part of Trades Unionism is killed the better," he wrote. If trades unions were to fight capitalism they should stick to economic struggle, and a "closer watch on officials and a general cutting down of useless expenditure would do no harm."[5] In some quarters these points were understood and modest attempts were made to implement them.[6] These have to be understood as suggestions to be taken in conjunction with 'self-help' by the unemployed along the lines of C.C. Davis at Birmingham.

A more spectacular attempt to commit a union to direct action had already been made in Leicester by George Cores, an anarchist on the executive committee of the Leicester branch of the Boot and Shoe Makers Union. Unemployment in the trade was high, and Cores moved a resolution at a meeting of about 250 members which stated that "hundreds … are in such a state of starvation that they will be compelled and entitled to take the means of subsistence by illegal means unless help is speedily forthcoming." Alderman Inskip, a former official of the union, attempted, to oppose it. He was shouted down, much to his astonishment, and the motion was carried by acclamation. Inskip, however, organised a further meeting with about 1,000 members present, and despite appeals by Cores to "resent official dictation" the resolution was defeated. The meeting broke up in such extreme disorder, however, that this result was of dubious value.[7]

We have already seen how direct action was urged upon the miners during their strike in 1893, by the *Commonweal* and by local anarchists. The miners, it was suggested, should burn the coal stocks, sabotage the machinery, pay no rent and loot food shops. Any distaste for a lip-licking relish for the spectacular ought not to hide from us the consistency of these suggestions with both the French syndicalism then developing, and the ideas which later became current in England. In practical terms, however, the response to these calls by the anarchists was limited, though the Hull dock strike echoed them. As time passed, the social and political situation in the late 1890s and early 1900s became less and less conducive to expansive direct action and anarchists in the unions were forced by circumstances to be cautious.

The anarchists in England, however, did provide the means whereby the ideas of the French revolutionary syndicalists could reach a wider audience. The earlier contacts between the revolutionary French and the reformist

English trades unions had been fraught with misunderstanding. At an international congress called by the Parliamentary Committee of the T.U.C. in 1888 in London, Tortellier, "a notorious Anarchist" and a delegate from the Joiners Union in Paris, put an amendment on the question of the eight-hour day. This was to the effect that the workers could expect nothing from legislators and could "only rely on their own strength." A social democrat commented later: "Had M. Tortellier meant the strength of organisations or of Trade Unions he would have said so. But for several years it has been notorious that this Anarchist believes only in the strength of insurrection, aided by the chemical resources of civilisation. This resolution, which really proclaimed as plainly as in common prudence it was possible to proclaim, that revolution — violent physical force revolution — alone could solve the problem ... was cordially endorsed by the English delegates. ... So anxious were the English to avoid Socialism [i.e. Labour representation] that they fell into the arms of the dynamite party."[8]

With the development of the new unionism and in response to physical and legal difficulties the interest of trades union leaderships in Labour representation in Parliament grew. Freakish happenings like the 1888 congress were not relished and social democrats in the trades unions were determined to make sure they were not repeated. At the 1896 International Workers' Congress in London they tried to enforce a strict application of the Zurich resolution expelling anarchists from the proceedings. Will Thorne, the socialist secretary to the congress, wrote to an inquirer: "In reply I may say that all Trades Unions recognise the necessity of political action: that being so the Zurich resolution covers them. But these people who are complaining about not being admitted to the next international congress don't believe in the necessity of political action: That being so the Zurich resolution will shut them out. Best wishes from, yours fraternally, Will Thorne."[9] However, Tom Mann and Keir Hardie, among others, protested strongly at the conference sessions and appeared at an anarchist meeting welcoming the foreign anarchist delegates to repeat their protests.[10] After much heat the congress voted that no one should be excluded. The French trades unions, together with the Dutch, who were also influenced by libertarian and syndicalist ideas, made a significant showing at the congress, much to the distaste of the social democrats.

Something of the new French movement began to filter into anarchist propaganda in England. The 'International Notes' in *Freedom* gave regular snippets of news. Occasional articles appeared which showed a French influence without necessarily making any great effort to adapt the theory to English practice.[11] The propaganda tended to remain general: "In every factory and every field toil the men and women we wish to educate and enlighten. We do not seek their votes; we ask them to think and to act, to unite and to organise, to encourage the spirit of solidarity on all occasions and ... use the weapon they have in their own hands ... the GENERAL STRIKE."[12] Yet, in private discussion, anarchists were talking over the practical problems which were to become so much of a general concern in a later period. Of unions in London it was said in 1901 that they were either too small and ineffective or too big. In the latter case the result was branch apathy and 'uncontrolled officialism'. The activity of social democrats, which involved capturing positions in the unions, then using those positions as a base for a political career, was said to be undermining the ability of the unions to fight economic battles.[13] It was this rather submerged, more pragmatic stream of thought of the anarchist activists that was to be of more immediate influence in the later stormy period. *Freedom* can be criticised for smothering particular cases with overgeneralisation. Nevertheless the French influence was persistent, if small, in its columns through the years of reaction in the Boer War.

After the Boer War the French syndicalist influence was to be augmented from another direction. This had its origins in battles within the S.D.F. during the war which initially had little to do with direct action and anti-officialism, except insofar as it was directed towards the leadership of that body. A group of Scottish rebels had grown increasingly irritated by the group round Hyndman, who effectively controlled both justice and the organisation itself. Their anger was directed at the opportunist and chauvinist backslidings of this controlling group from Marxist principle. Their attacks were given theoretical content by the writings of the American Daniel de Leon and increasingly expressed through the columns of the New York de Leonist newspaper the *Weekly People*. The rebels controlled the Scottish branches of the S.D.F. and from this base started to produce a paper — the *Socialist* — in opposition to *Justice*, from August 1902. Unable to quickly swing the English branches behind them, though there was considerable discontent in the English ranks, they seemed to have resolved on a split at an early date. The crunch came in 1903 at the S.D.F. annual conference, and the Scots — who were expelled — returned to form a separate party, the Socialist Labour Party (S.L.P.), named, on James Connolly's blunt suggestion, after the name of de Leon's American organisation. The English Marxist purist malcontents within the S.D.F. were expelled in 1904 and formed a separate Socialist Party of Great Britain (S.P.G.B.) — the precipitate action of the Scots had completely alienated the majority of the more difficultly placed English. The S.P.G.B. — which some wags were later to suggest stood for the 'Small Party of Good Boys' — never escaped from the status of completely uninfluential sect. It has been suggested by an informed observer[14] that the S.L.P. would have suffered the same fate had it not been for events in America which de Leon's disciples in Scotland slavishly copied.

The American S.L.P. had first had a 'party-centred' attitude to trades unions which had led to the formation of an initially successful S.L.P.-dominated separatist Socialist Trade and Labour Alliance. This was seen as a bulwark against and a refuge from corrupt and opportunist trades unions and their officials ('labour fakirs'). The emphasis shifted, however, and a number of different groups (including anarchists who approached the question from a different direction) began to give industrial organisation the first place and see *industrial* unionism not only as a transcendence of sectional trades unionism but as the basis of a new socialist society. Industrial unionism both organised the workers as a class and provided the form through which the workers would control industry and society. Political power gained through elections represented only a rubber stamping of a position already gained by industrial action. This shift in emphasis was enthusiastically supported by de Leon and so was its practical outcome, the Industrial Workers of the World (I.W.W.), which was formed in 1905. After some confusion the British S.L.P. endorsed this radical shift from orthodox social democratic practice. They assiduously distributed American industrial unionist pamphlets and took steps to set up their own industrial union. In the event a propaganda body, the

Advocates of Industrial Unionism, was founded in Binningham in 1907 to form the core of such industrial union.

But the influence of industrial unionist ideas was considerable among all the socialist groups before this time, though the various uses to which these ideas were to be put were not all to the liking of the sectarian and dogmatic S.L.P. It is not at all easy to trace the way in which ideas are adapted and changed, used or discarded, in a culture that is largely unwritten. For all the documentary evidence available to us — files of newspapers, memoirs, conference reports, etc. — we still cannot properly grasp the shifts in atmosphere and ideas that are often of greater importance than any formalisation in organisational splits and reshuffles. Nevertheless it is clear that on the speaking pitches, in the arguments in tea shops and pubs, industrial unionism became a topic of importance from about 1904 onwards. The evidence would seem to show that there was a quickening of the pulse of socialist thought by mid-1903. *Freedom* was writing: "There is not the slightest doubt that we are on the eve of a new revival of the Socialist movement in this and other countries." It pointed out however that whatever form this new socialism took it would not be social democratic since one of the reasons for its emergence was "precisely the failure of Social Democracy to bring about the great changes which mankind needs."[15] And *Freedom* was right.

This sense of waking up is reflected in the anarchist movement in the reports of groups published in *Freedom*. They do not show a uniformly steady growth. Groups report after having come into being and are full of enthusiasm. A spread of anarchist ideas gets going and then seems to rather fade away — at least as far as reports go. Without the most detailed knowledge of the socialist milieu in a particular town or area of a city at a particular time it is impossible to say to what extent there was a constant anarchist presence. Nor is it possible to accurately gauge the effectiveness of anarchist propaganda when we know it took place. With this in mind it is nevertheless true to say that in London, Leeds, Birmingham, Dundee, Paisley, Glasgow, Edinburgh, Oxford and Hull, a revival of propaganda took place between 1903 and 1905. In London, Sam Mainwaring, the veteran Socialist League anarchist, published two numbers of a paper called *The General Strike* in September 1903 and March 1904. Mainwaring, a member of the London Trades Council for the Amalgamated Society of Engineers, used his experience to give a detailed denunciation of officialism in trades unions. (This was in the context of unofficial action on the Clyde which was crushed because the Engineering Union officials would allow no strike pay.) The paper also gave news of strike movements abroad. As an attempt to apply French syndicalist thinking to English conditions it was a brave start. However, 1904 was a year of quite widespread unemployment, particularly in the engineering trades, and Mainwaring had to leave London for South Wales in search of work. There was no one prepared to carry on the paper and no further issues were published.

The movement in Scotland was less transient in its revival in 1903. Groups were active in Paisley, Dundee and Glasgow, and later in Edinburgh. (The Paisley group formed round a nucleus expelled from Paisley I.L.P. in 1902 for being tainted with anarchist ideas.) The propaganda took the traditional forms of open-air speaking, literature distribution, etc., but as in Mainwaring's case there was a noticeable shift in emphasis towards syndicalism. Paisley and Glasgow cooperated in bringing out a paper, the *Voice of Labour*, in January 1904, which urged direct action trades unionism. Only one issue appeared. With this disappointment the head of steam seemed to drop somewhat. Nevertheless a motion at Paisley Trades Council which called upon that body to "come into line with those Trades Unions which stand on the basis of the General Strike" was carried by a large majority.[16] The Dundee anarchists were working on the project of forming "a labour union on Libertarian lines."[17] The prospects of success for this latter venture are hard to assess. Such a union did not come into existence, yet in 1907 the Dundee anarchists were trying to reform the Jute Workers Union on federalist lines. This project, too, fell through. In Leeds attempts were being made to form an 'International Revolutionary Labour Union' in May and June 1906, its object being "to obtain Labour's *immediate* demands without resorting to political tactics. In other words, what is known as Direct Action and the General Strike are the means chosen for compelling capitalist concessions while overthrow by revolutionary means is kept constantly in view."[18] Regular meetings were being held. Nothing more is heard of this experiment shortly after this point, though it is probable that it was of some importance among immigrant Jewish workers.

These unsuccessful beginnings in papers or separatist trades unions are important because they show the direction in which anarchist ideas were running. They show, too, that there was enough confidence (or over-confidence) in the anarchist movement to allow some militants to go ahead with these projects. Poor organisation as much as lack of response to their propaganda explains their demise. By 1905 there was beginning to be publicity for French syndicalists in the British press generally. Yet some preparatory work had already been done by the anarchists and the movement as a whole was becoming more extensive and confident despite its early setbacks. Industrial unionist and syndicalist ideas were being absorbed and experimented with. They needed time and changing conditions to bear fruit.

Guy Aldred, a curious figure of some importance in our story, was an obsessively regular attender at open-air meetings from 1902 onwards, in "North London, Clerkenwell Green, Hyde Park and other centres of discussion." In him we have a particular example of the way in which these new ideas were developing. In his memoirs,[19] in accounts of his activities which betray a colossal egoism, we can find tantalising glimpses of the incredible variety of causes espoused as a myriad of religious, free-thought and political speakers as well as pure cranks battled for a hearing. This variety both explains the general development of ideas more as a process of seepage than anything else and also demonstrates the difficulty of separating one ideological strand from many. Aldred himself developed from a Christian 'boy preacher' to a free-thought propagandist. By March 1905 (at the age of eighteen) he had become a socialist and had joined the S.D.F. and was speaking from their platform in Clerkenwell Green and elsewhere. But by this time he had already been completely unimpressed by de Leon as a person, though he took some note of his ideas. He had heard him speak on Clerkenwell Green in 1904 — the greatest effect being apparently that he read Bakunin as a result of de Leon's bitter denunciations of anarchism. From the S.D.F. platform Aldred kept up his free-thought propaganda, often mentioned Bakunin in a friendly manner and was being courted by the S.P.G.B. By 1906 he was reading industrial unionist material with quickening interest and, he says, "I studied Anarchism and began to associate with Anarchists." This eclectic sprint through most of the ideological fields open to him, in late 1906, left him an anti-parliamentarian near-anarchist. It is tempting, if wrong, to see in him a model development. As a necessary corrective perhaps it should be said that W.C. Hart's book *Confessions of an Anarchist*, which chronicled the disillusionment of an anarchist militant of the 1890s, was also first published in 1906. If Aldred represented the wave of the future there were also considerable cross-currents.

Nineteen hundred and six was, without doubt, a key year. In January there was a landslide Liberal election victory which brought with it thirty Labour Party M.P.s together with thirteen Liberal-Labour M.P.s representing the miners. Great things were hoped for from the Labour representatives; yet they turned out to be, from the point of view of the socialists, a complete disappointment. They were cautious in the extreme, tail ending the Liberals in most things and did not even allow themselves flamboyant window dressing to please their public. Even the moderate *Reformers Hand Book* for 1907 had harsh things to say of them: "...their half measures have pleased nobody ... On many matters both legislative and administrative they have exhibited an almost incredible political cowardice." For the more militant socialists this represented the failure of the parliamentary tactic rather than any lack of suitability of the candidates. In John Burns they had an example of a man who had risen to cabinet rank directly out of his fame as a leader of the 1889 dock strike who had apparently lost any sympathy for the people he represented. In the conformist and careful behaviour of the Labour members they had an example of the muffling effect that parliament had on socialists. Direct action, industrial unionist and syndicalist propaganda began to appear far more relevant. As Aldred puts it: "My Anti-Parliamentarian and Socialist Revolt against Labourism dates from the elevation of John Burns to Cabinet rank, and the definite emergence of the Labour Party as a factor in British politics."[20]

The worsening economic condition of the working class deepened the relevance of the new ideas. Between 1900 and 1914 prices steadily rose, with an accelerating rise after 1905. Wages lagged behind the rise in prices and a real drop in living standards was taking place. Depression and unemployment was to hold back active discontent temporarily (though many strikes took place in 1908 in attempts to stop wage cuts) but by 1911 the country's economy was booming and unemployment was low. This situation encouraged a rise in trades union membership, steady after 1905 and extremely rapid after 1911. At the same time the trades union leaderships were absorbed in parliamentary manoeuvrings and were nervous of spoiling the election image of the Labour Party and the alliance with the Liberals. Trades union caution was also due to the fact that the leaderships had emerged in the difficult period of the 1890s. The rapidly developing rank-and-file discontent therefore found itself in opposition to parliamentary action as a means of improving their livelihood and found itself frustrated by a cautious and reformist bureaucracy within the unions. Thus the period from the disappointments of 1906 to the explosions of 1910–1914 was a most important one of preparation in an atmosphere of deepening bitterness.

Certain changes had taken place in the nature of the anarchist movement by this time. In the early 1890s the working-class anarchist movement was based on a network of militants who had developed in a libertarian direction within the Socialist League. *Commonweal*, the *Anarchist* and *Liberty* were all edited by ex-Socialist League militants. *Freedom* and the *Torch* also involved people who had been intimately involved with the League. Inevitably, therefore, there was a certain 'party' sense about the movement at that time. (The phrase 'anarchist party' was actually used by some anarchists in this period, though admittedly the word also then had the sense of 'body of opinion'.) The sense of common organisational origins gave a sense of unity and separateness.[21] With the collapse of every paper except *Freedom* and the apparent demise of the British anarchist movement this sense was lost. As we have seen, *Freedom*, now not one of a number of anarchist papers but *the* anarchist paper, came under attack at the 1897 conference as a middle-class paper, out of touch with the working class, and so on. Various muffled pleas, denunciations and individual initiatives connected with the need for a popular anarchist propaganda paper emerged from time to time. Before 1907, however, no successful attempt was made.

The result was that, though *Freedom* was used as a medium for national communication between groups by furnishing addresses and so on, the growth of the anarchist movement after the Boer War was not centred on *Freedom*, nor did it emerge en bloc from any one socialist group as a result of a major split. Its growth was decentralised, originating in the activity of odd local militants, the occasional pamphlet sold through an I.L.P. club bookstall or whatever. The process might be helped by the occasional visit by someone like John Turner, who after 1898 was stumping the country as national organiser for the Amalgamated Shop Assistants Union and delivering speeches to anarchist-sponsored meetings on the side. Contact with the local English-speaking Jewish anarchists could play its part. The various socialist bodies often provided the service for socialists which Marx said capitalism did for the workers: it brought them together and out of their association produced a counter-consciousness. Anarchist groups often emerged from disputes within S.D.F. or I.L.P. branches. So while *Freedom* and Freedom Press pamphlets could provide some theoretical armament, the growth of the anarchist movement was dependent on local organisation. These circumstances firmly placed the anarchists in their immediate socialist milieu and left them open to new currents in all the socialist groupings. They were not just bringing ideas from outside, they were developing them on the spot. This might not be particularly convenient from the historian's point of view, yet it does explain a pervasive anarchist influence without any apparent strong organisation at the centre of it.

For if *Freedom* was the centre it was a hollow one. If the militant anarchists were a part of the wider movement, *Freedom* was apart from it.

It was not a question of the movement controlling the paper — for better or worse the traditional anarchist mode of publishing newspapers has been by an autonomous group more or less sensitive to criticisms from the rest of the movement. There was a group of two involved in publishing *Freedom* with a passive group of contributors who took little part in editorial activity. Aldred wrote later "...the Freedom Group, at this time, as a group never functioned. I never saw its members and they certainly never held regular meetings. Nor did the group seek converts. It operated as a close corporation or not at all. Its policy was decided by Keell who was incapable of really intelligent decision inspired by imagination; and Marsh whose attitude was dilettante."[22] The comments are hostile in spirit but substantially true in fact. (Keell had joined *Freedom* in 1903 as printer, on the illness of Cantwell, who died in December 1906.) Marsh's ability to keep the paper afloat through the difficult years of the Boer War and reaction was no guarantee that he would be able to take advantage of and speak to the new militancy. Anarchists sold *Freedom* because there was nothing else, but the critical attitudes of 1897 persisted: Marsh and Keell devoted their energies to *Freedom* and took no part in the general movement as speakers, etc., and so remained insulated from criticism.

However, one man who had contributed to *Freedom* and in the loosest sense was a member of the Freedom Group was more in touch with the general movement. This was John Turner. He was in close touch with the Jewish anarchists of the East End[23] and had spoken at many of their meetings. He had achieved some notoriety and much publicity after being refused entry to the United States in 1903, and as an anarchist was held in Ellis Island for several months pending an appeal. As I have said, he used his job to enable him to speak to meetings up and down the country and seems to have been an able exponent of anarchist ideas. Since his contributions to *Freedom* were on labour topics and he was himself a trades union official the new mood in the working class was immediately apparent to him. He took steps to publish a paper which would fill the need for popular propaganda and which was to be used as a base round which to organise 'direct actionist and anarchist groups'. This was the *Voice of Labour*, the first number of which was published in January 1907 as a weekly — the first such anarchist paper since the *Commonweal*.

The paper ran until September of the same year. Its policy was outlined in its first issue: "Direct Action ... is what we stand for ... we shall insist at every turn that nothing is gained without activity in organisation, in agitation, in the Strike in all its forms and that only by these means will the workers in the end be able to claim their own." This activity was constantly counterposed to parliamentary passivity in every issue of the paper. Yet though the paper was written in a much more punchy style than *Freedom* and though the coverage of labour disputes in Britain and abroad was full and relevant, there were developing contradictions in the paper. The direct action talked of by John Turner was action instigated and directed by the official structures of the unions. His propaganda was fundamentally directed towards trades unionists and was designed to encourage them to fight directly for gains in wages and conditions rather than allowing Parliament to mediate these demands. Even here he was prepared to compromise. For example, his union, the Shop Assistants, was committed to abolishing the 'living-in' system, where employees not only lost a job if they were sacked but also lost a roof over their heads. This commitment was being followed through with some success by industrial action, but at the same time the Shop Assistants Union-sponsored M.P. was pressing for legislation to make the living-in system non-compulsory. John Turner's comment was only that industrial action might well succeed before the bill was made law.[24] Thus Turner stood for militant official trades unionism, though he was prepared to countenance parliamentary action if it had any prospects of success.

What he did not understand, and in his position probably could not understand, was the rising tide of anti-officialism in the unions. When revolts against the officials of a union took place it was his opinion that it was because the officials were not doing their job and they had to be weaned from whoring after parliamentary gods in order to do so. It does not seem to have occurred to him that the question which was to be increasingly put was: Who should control the unions, the officials or the membership? Militant reformist leadership might reduce tension, but it could not abolish the developing horizontal split in the unions.

Much can be explained by John Turner's experiences.[25] From the time of the Harrow Road 'riots' in 1891 until its amalgamation with another small union in 1898, Turner had been the (unpaid) president of the United Shop Assistants Union. On amalgamation the total membership of the union was approximately 700. Turner became paid national organiser and threw himself into a recruiting drive around the country. The membership grew rapidly as a result of prodigious efforts on his part. But his experiences in the 'United' Union had brought about a change of approach. Branches then had come into being as different workplaces had come into conflict with their employers and then faded away as victory or defeat seemed to make union membership less important or more dangerous. Now Turner, to ensure a stable membership, had introduced unemployment and sickness benefits and as a result had members "of a good type, paying what was, for those days, a fairly high contribution." His policy worked, but he was now primarily organising a union, whereas previously he had been primarily organising conflicts with employers. By 1907 the pressure had relaxed somewhat and Turner was a fairly comfortably off trades union official of some importance. By 1910 the Shop Assistants Union had a membership of 13,000 in the London area, making it the largest union in the district.[26] In 1912 John Turner became president of the union. Although he called himself an anarchist until he died it did not show itself in his union activities. Heartbreaking experience as it might have been, the small union before 1898 had been anarchistic, that after 1898 was no different to the other 'new' unions either in power distribution or policy. There were straws in the wind by 1906. The executive of the union was being seen in some quarters as a bureaucratic interference with local militancy and initiative.[27] And complaints were to grow. By 1909 Turner was being accused from one quarter of playing the "role of one of the most blatant reactionaries with which the Trades Union movement was ever cursed."[28]

Thus though he was, theologically speaking, an anarchist, his social position made him a somewhat anomalous editor of a paper preaching direct action. Things started quite well. Turner recruited Aldred after hearing his progressively anarchistic speeches from the S.D.F. platform on Clerkenwell Green. Aldred, whatever his faults, was blessed with incredible energy, and he was soon speaking at open-air meetings the length and breadth of London. A number of already existing anarchist groups were federated to form the rather grand-sounding Industrial Union of Direct Actionists (I.U.D.A.). There were six groups in London, at Clerkenwell, Lambeth, Plaistow, Walthamstow, Walworth and Whitechapel. Outside London there were groups at Leeds, Liverpool, Dover and, peculiarly enough, Weston-super-Mare. Involved in this venture were old Socialist League anarchists like F. Goulding and Charles Mowbray, as well as new militants like Charles Lahr, A. Ray, F. Large, Beavan (Liverpool), Melinsky (Leeds) and S. Carlyle Potter (Dover).[29] This federation should not be taken seriously. Each of the groups concerned carried on much as before with their open-air propaganda. The elaborate business with which Aldred surrounded the I.U.D.A. did not alter the situation materially. Nevertheless 1907 was a year of increasing activity among anarchists. The *Voice of Labour*, though never out of financial difficulties, had a rising circulation (though no figures were provided) which continued to rise despite an experiment in bringing out ½d [halfpenny] editions which newsagents refused to sell.[30] There were hopes that the paper might soon become self-supporting. Yet the paper suspended publication in September. The reasons given were financial. There was more to it than that.

Aldred was with John Turner — apart from the foreign correspondents — the most regular contributor to the *Voice of Labour*. His memoirs indicate that Turner had rather taken him under his wing. Yet Aldred could not but be aware of Turner's position as a trades union official and the hostility towards such people in industrial unionist material. (The S.L.P., for example, did not allow trades union officials to join.) The break came after Aldred's visit to Liverpool in late August 1907. Liverpool had provided critics of the Freedom Group in previous years. This critical attitude did not seem to have changed and Aldred reports that "the local comrades anxiously discussed with me Kropotkin's relationship to the Freedom Group." Aldred continues, "On my return to London I gradually fell out 'with the Freedom Anarchists. ... Their Anarchy was merely Trade Union activity which they miscalled Direct Action. Their anger knew no bounds when I insisted that Trades Unionism was the basis of Labour Parliamentarianism. ... In 1907 I denounced John Turner as a Labour Fakir. The description was correct and was uttered when challenge drew it forth."[31] The occasion was a shop assistants' strike in Kentish Town when Aldred refused "to write an article in the *Voice of Labour* booming J. Turner's conduct ... when we knew he was acting treacherously towards the parties concerned and sending Anarchism to the devil into the bargain."[32]

The *Voice of Labour* collapsed through internal dissension as much as lack of cash. John Turner was to be a regular speaker at the larger anarchist meetings in the London area and to write pieces in *Freedom*. He also spoke on behalf of Mann's organisation, the Industrial Syndicalist Education League. But the *Voice of Labour* was to be his last real agitational effort in the movement for twenty years. From this point on he increasingly turned to purely trades union matters. Aldred however never ceased to play the role of agitator. In fact in the last issue of the *Voice of Labour* an advertisement appeared for a new fortnightly journal, the *Herald of the Revolt,* to be edited by Aldred and scheduled to appear on the first Saturday in October 1907.

For one reason and another the *Herald of Revolt* did not appear until 1910. Firstly there were difficulties over printing a number of pamphlets. Then Aldred became involved with Rose Witcop (the seventeen-year-old youngest sister of Milly Witcop, the companion of Rudolf Rocker). Though the relationship was sober enough in all conscience it caused domestic ructions on both sides. (These were not soothed by a pamphlet by Aldred published in late 1907 advocating free love.) The result was that Aldred and Rose Witcop set up home in Shepherd's Bush, a suburb on the then far west of London — well away, in fact, from their previous East London haunts. Here Aldred began a local propaganda, and the rather artificially constructed I.U.D.A. fell into its constituent parts. Since the *Herald of Revolt* was apparently intended to fill the gap left by the demise of the *Voice of Labour* and to be the I.U.D.A. journal, the immediate purpose of the paper disappeared. Then in 1909 he became involved in publishing a paper called the *Indian Sociologist,* which resulted in a twelve-month jail sentence. The paper, published from Paris by a group of Indian nationalists, had been printed in England for three issues. It had been suppressed when a prominent Indian civil service officer was assassinated in London by an Indian nationalist. Aldred took it upon himself to print another issue of the paper because it was banned rather than because he agreed with the aims of Indian nationalism. He was speedily arrested and jailed.[33]

Yet despite the absence of a popular anarchist propaganda paper the movement continued to grow. In November 1907 the movement in London was reported as gaining strength. The same month a conference was held in Manchester and the 'International Anarchist Federation of the English Provinces' was formed. This was intended to make speaking tours possible by sharing expenses where possible and to help isolated anarchists to conduct propaganda. The following month a meeting of the Federation numbering forty delegates had representatives from Manchester, from two groups in Liverpool, from Cardiff, Swansea, Newcastle-on-Tyne, Glasgow and Southport. Groups were being formed in Birmingham, Sunderland and, hopefully, in Burnley. And this time the activity was sustained.

In Liverpool during 1908 the anarchists "set themselves the task of building up an industrial organisation, appealing to all who can act in sympathy from a class-conscious and non-parliamentary viewpoint to assist."[34] Discussions were being held with the I.L.P. and S.D.F. members and had met with an initially enthusiastic response. The experiment foundered, whether because of the militant anti-parliamentary attitudes of the anarchists or because of nervousness of losing initiative on the part of the other groups involved. This was a most successful propaganda exercise, however, since the questions of syndicalism, direct action and anti-parliamentarianism had been hotly discussed for several months. The Liverpool Direct Action Group kept on pounding away at their syndicalist propaganda.

In 1908 the anarchists were active in the unemployed agitation in Leeds, where some 15,000 people were out of work. Following on their propaganda a 'Leeds Non-Political Committee on Unemployment' of 350 people was formed. Its aims were to organise the unemployed on the basis of direct action throughout the United Kingdom; to block manipulation by political parties; to assess the extent of unemployment and distress; and to organise unemployed and employed together to demand their full share of production. The unemployed were holding two meetings a day in Victoria Square with thousands present and were addressed by speakers including Kitson, an anarchist described as "the organiser of the unemployed." On 17th September, a crowd of 5,000 gathered at 9pm to demand that the 200 people who had not eaten that day be fed. The mayor was sent for (it appears he thought it politic to come) and a deputation waited on him "stating that if the hungry people did not get food that night in a peaceful manner they would have to get it by force." Seven pounds was hurriedly gathered together and spent on food at midnight.[35] At a demonstration on 24th September, 20,000 people were present and propaganda was started to organise a No Rent campaign to force aid for the unemployed.

However the authorities had their revenge. A joint demonstration of unemployed and suffragettes was attacked by the police when it attempted to hand in resolutions to Asquith, who was visiting. Kitson was rather badly beaten and arrested. His arrest brought Charley Kean from Birmingham who continued the agitational work. When he left, however, the agitation degenerated and fell into the hands of "politicians" who indulged in "mere begging," to quote *Freedom*. In Deptford, London, a vigorous 'direct action' unemployment agitation was likewise under way and led to several clashes with the police and a number of arrests.

By September 1909 the London anarchists had held conferences to discuss a maximum use of their propaganda forces and had established eight regular speaking pitches. These were manned by a group of speakers including Ray, Ponder, Kitz, Pain, Barrett and others. This did not include other people who were speaking more irregularly — or individualistically — in Hyde Park, Regent's Park or Victoria Park and other places. At the same time debates with I.L.P. and S.D.F. branches increased and a common understanding was beginning to develop with sections of the industrial unionists — particularly with the Industrialist League. Similarly, outside London new groups were emerging in Leicester, Bradford and Huddersfield. Propaganda was conducted in Edinburgh, Kilmarnock, Paisley, Darlington and Hull, which indicates that even if there were no groups in some of these places, there were contacts with individuals. In the provinces, too, the emphasis seems to have been on syndicalist, direct-action and industrial unionist ideas.

There had been developments in these ideas. As we have seen, John Turner had tried to adapt French syndicalism to orthodox English trades unionism. There were anomalies in his position, yet it was the one largely taken by Tom Mann in following years and represented one persistent aspect of the upsurge. A persistently grumbling anti-officialism was more audible in industrial unionist quarters. Here too there had been adaptations to English conditions. The S.L.P. had formed the British Advocates of Industrial Unionism in 1907, which was as far as they felt able to go in forming an organisation on the pattern of the I.W.W. When the I.W.W. split in 1908 after political action ceased to be an aim of the organisation a split developed within the B.A.I.U. The 'anti-political' faction in which E.J.B. Allen was prominent — he had been editor of the B.A.I.U. paper, the *Industrial Unionist* — set up a paper in London in June 1908 called the *Industrialist*. Its anti-parliamentarianism at this point was pragmatic and represented a reading of de Leonism in conflict with the de Leonists. Since economic power preceded political power for the bourgeoisie, the argument ran, this must be the case for the working class. Economic power for the working class "consists in their unity and organisation on class lines in the workshops."[36] Until this was achieved there was no point in parliamentary action. The membership of the B.A.I.U. included members of the various parties who believed in parliamentary action, as well as those — like the anarchists — who did not. But they had come together "to help to bring about revolutionary unity in the field of industry which must precede all efficient action of whatever sort by the working class."

As a result of the publication of the *Industrialist*, the group responsible were expelled from the B.A.I.U. by its S.L.P.-dominated executive and another organisation, the Industrialist League, was set up. This started with seven branches — all in London except for one in Tredegar and a number of contacts elsewhere — but by August 1909 it was boasting fourteen branches spread round the country. They were concerned at this point to make it plain that they were not an anarchist body, though anarchists were free to join.[37] Yet there were interlocking activities by both anarchists and the Industrialist League. Jewish tailoring workers in the East End who broke away from the A.S.T. over the question of sympathy strikes and who were heavily influenced by Rocker's group round the *Workers' Friend* were helping the Industrialist League speakers.[38] E.J.B. Allen spoke at the anarchist Chicago commemoration meeting at the Charlotte Street club together with Ponder, an anarchist member of the Industrialist League, Rocker and Malatesta. He also spoke at the Charlotte Street club the following month on 'Anti-Parliamentarianism'.[39] It has to be admitted, however, that E.J.B. Allen's relationship with *Freedom* became somewhat cold after the publication of his pamphlet 'Revolutionary Unionism' in June 1909. In the section entitled 'The Treachery of Officials' he detailed a couple of cases of bureaucratic demobilisation by the executive of the Shop Assistants Union — of which John Turner was a member. And while Turner himself rather humorously pooh-poohed these cases, Keell, who had already fallen out with Aldred over Turner's position, could not be expected to remain friendly. The *Industrialist* had, at first, been printed by Keell. It found new printers.

Yet despite this contretemps the anarchist influence within the Industrialist League continued to grow, though it was resisted by some members. (One member, Ponder, was in fact expelled for trying to commit the Industrialist League as a whole to an anarchist line.) In April 1909 the Newcastle anarchists reported that they were forming a club to enable closer cooperation with Industrialists. Anarchists were being invited to speak to Industrialist League branches. In Bradford when the Industrialist League speakers did not turn up for the May Day meeting in 1910 the anarchists were invited to substitute "as kindred spirits." Joint meetings were held, and so on. In fact in some places the Industrialist League proved to be a stepping stone directly to anarchism. In November 1910 an anarchist group in Plymouth reported for the first time in *Freedom*. A group had been expelled from the Plymouth S.D.F. for preaching direct action rather than parliamentary politics. A minority had joined the S.L.P., while the majority joined the Industrialist League. After they had been introduced to anarchism by J. Walters, however, this latter body formed themselves into an anarchist-communist group. The same thing was to happen with the Hull Branch of the Industrialist League where a large majority of the branch seceded in 1912 to form an anarchist group.

The Industrialist League was the largest of the anarchist-influenced industrial unionist groupings. There were several other small groups, however, which had syndicalist and industrial unionist leanings. One of these, the 'Revolutionary Unionists', with members in Liverpool and Brighton became, in Liverpool at least, an integral part of one anarchist group. Perhaps one further point could be made. The Ruskin College strike of early 1909 by left-wing working-class students against the paternalist and anti-socialist administration led rapidly to the formation of a new body, the Central Labour College. This institution proved a very fertile source of creative thinking in the Syndicalist Revolt. Something has been made of contacts between the Ruskin rebels and the S.L.P. Whatever their influence it could not have much affected the influence from another quarter. Fred Charles, the Walsall anarchist and ex-prisoner, not only had a place on the management committee of the new college as a member of the Oxford Cooperative Society but also acted as a "lecturer and tutor in industrial and political history."[40] These positions he held from 1909 until the college moved to London in mid-1911. He was very probably the means whereby George Davison, an extremely rich 'philosophical anarchist', became a considerable financial supporter of the Labour College from about 1910 until 1914.

Thus when Tom Mann returned from Australia in 1910 to put his enormous personal prestige and organisational ability behind the simmering revolt the ground had been prepared. Economically, working-class conditions were being undermined. The trades union hierarchy remained largely wedded to parliamentarianism and moderation, and as union membership increased became increasingly bureaucratic. Yet Parliament had proved an ineffective tool with which to improve the living conditions of the working class and moderation among the officials had curbed effective direct action. The ideas of syndicalism taken from foreign anarchist practice and British anarchist propaganda, and industrial unionism taken from American sources (also influenced by anarchism), had prepared the way ideologically. The result was an explosion of industrial revolt of unprecedented extent and sustained power.

## Chapter 14
# THE INSURGENT VIRUS

The period 1910 to 1914 and the subsequent period during World War One and its aftermath are among the most interesting in British history for the historian of working-class movements. They are also the most difficult to write about, the very scale of events requiring a great deal of detailed original research organised by the skills of an epic novelist. Such a book, though badly needed, has not yet been written. Certainly the present work is not intended to fill that gap. It is, however, preparative to such a work in that it restores to notice the almost completely ignored anarchist contribution. This is not done in the spirit of what has been called the *Jewish Chronicle* style of history writing: that journal without apparent selection, hierarchy or relevance lists every passing achievement of Jews because they are Jews. It is not the intention here to list every activity of anarchists in the period, without reference to significance or context, because they are anarchists.

The anarchists are important because they represent the only left-wing tendency to precede the period of the Syndicalist Revolt with an ideology that harmonised with it and which grew as a result of those events. Anarchists were increasingly active up to 1914. In a very real way the Syndicalist Revolt in this earlier period was nourishing to, and a testing ground for, anarchism. The successes of the working-class movement were the successes of an anarchist movement anywhere and its failings were (and are) the most worrying ones for anarchists.

Yet would it not have been surprising if there had been no anarchist dimension to the Syndicalist Revolt? The strikes of the period (not to mention related events) were marked by spontaneity and solidarity at a quite extraordinary level which culminated in what amounted to a series of local if not quite national general strikes. The working-class militants at the storm centres were hostile to or ignored the representative political system at local or national level. They impatiently swept aside their union leaders when their demands were not met in negotiations. They showed great readiness for conflict with the forces of law and order, and a perceptive minority paid some attention to their subversion. It would indeed have been remarkable if non-political direct action did not become generalised into self-conscious anarchism to a significant extent.

Men and women can be driven to desperate acts by deprivation, yet deprivation does not necessarily lead to desperate action. It is not surprising that people revolt in varying ways — what is surprising is that they put up with as much as they do. The first barrier that has to be overcome is the debilitating sense of impotence. Most people, faced with a situation they do not like, ask in despair, 'What can you do about it?' — and do nothing no matter what the answer may be. Yet sometimes a spark is struck and a struggle is fought and won. There is an astonishing sense of collective power when people find themselves — both literally and metaphorically — in mass struggle. Others can take up the example offered. Yet though people have had plenty of practice at accepting things as they are, they are for the most part short of practice at changing them. An isolated action, whether it results in success or failure, can surprisingly soon sink back into apathy and acceptance. A sustained period of unrest, however, provides people with the practice they need to change their world and a context in which to place ideologies of change. In such a period the sense of collective power is mutually reinforcing and spills out from particular to general grievances. Industrial upheaval generalises into social upheaval, social upheaval glimpses dual power and revolution.

The period of unrest 1910–1914 was rooted in economic deprivation and the power given by relatively full employment to the working class which enabled them to fight it. If one examines only the bald facts of the industrial revolt itself, the sense of the period is lost. Yet the bald facts are striking enough. The average number of 'man' days lost through strikes in a normal year between 1900 and 1909 was 2½ to 3 million. In 1910, 1912, 1913 and 1914 there were about 10 million man days lost. In 1912 the figure was nearly 41 million.[1] Had the war not intervened in the summer of 1914, the autumn of that year would have witnessed, according to one observer, "one of the greatest industrial revolts the world would ever have seen."[2]

This burst of militancy did not keep a static form throughout. It developed in practice and in theory. The needs of the struggle forced people to find organisational forms for that struggle and these forms became generalised as more functions were packed into them. This will become clearer as events are related. Further, while it is convenient to concentrate on major conflagrations as markers along the way, it should be pointed out that militancy spread in many directions and took many different forms. There cannot have been one area of life which was not affected by the new movement, as contemporary newspapers make plain. The first shots in the battle were fired in the north-east. From November 1909 until July 1910 there was a series of spontaneous strikes culminating in a lockout by the employers among the boilermakers of the shipyards. In January 1910 there started a three-month strike by the traditionally moderate Durham miners against an agreement already signed by their union. The north-eastern railwaymen struck for three days in mid-1910, which was sufficient to gain them victory — despite the fact that they were covered by a five-year agreement in force at that time. Though undoubtedly geographical proximity had something to do with it, each of these strikes, albeit without official sanction, took a traditional 'sectional' character. Sympathy there might be between these sections of workers, yet this sympathy found no mutual action.

The lockout in the cotton industry as a reprisal against militant tactics which took place in the autumn of 1910 was similarly 'sectional' in character, though it was marked by a high degree of solidarity among the locked-out workers. But by this time the signs were obvious, as *Freedom* put it, of the "stupendous struggle which is growing on all sides between capital and labour."[3] The full-throated roar of revolt made itself heard from November 1910 in the Cambrian Combine dispute in the South Wales coalfield. A dispute involving seventy men in a seam in one pit spread like wildfire through the whole Combine, involving 12,000 miners. However, the engine men below and winding men on the surface (in unions separate from the South Wales Miners Federation) stayed at work and the employers as a result attempted to continue to run the mines: "...and the direct outcome of that was the police being sent there, later the military — result, riots, trouble of a considerable character, the fight still on because of the incompleteness of the fight on the men's side, consequent upon sectional unionism" — so said Tom Mann at the time.[4] Miners were fired on at Tonypandy by the troops and many clashes took place. It was not until August 1911 that the men were starved into submission. Yet many lessons had been learned and were to be acted on in 1912 — for the miners had not had their spirit broken.

The solidarity of the men in the Cambrian dispute had spread through one industry — taking on the character of a general strike by virtue of the fact that in the Welsh valleys it was the only industry. In 1911 disputes were to spread from industry to industry in different places in a number of what amounted to local general strikes. From January to April 1911 a national printers' strike for a reduction of hours took place. Relatively peaceful and largely successful, it gave no particular foretaste of the storms of the summer. It was remarkable, however, in that the printers produced a daily strike newspaper — the *Daily Herald* — which first concerned itself exclusively with the strike. On 8th February, however, they announced that they were going to introduce new features so as to make the paper "of interest as a General Labour Daily Newspaper." When the paper ceased publication at the conclusion of the strike at the end of April, they were selling shares to finance this venture. The paper was to reappear in April 1912 and was to play an important part in spreading syndicalist ideas. In June 1911 the seamen's strike gave the signal for a massive burst of activity. Starting in Southampton, much to the fury of the almost feudal shipowners, the strike spread to every major port in Britain. The dockers then came out in support of the seamen and over demands of their own.

In Hull the situation reached fever pitch. First every worker on the waterfront struck. The initiative was taken by the unorganised, i.e. non-unionised, workers who struck almost immediately the seamen did. The union members were instructed to stay at work by their leaders and did as they were told until they were dragged out by the force of events.[5] Then the dispute spread to the mills, at first spontaneously and then by means of mass pickets, which clashed seriously with the police. The strikes spread and cement workers and factory girls came out. More police were drafted in from Leeds, Birmingham and London. Conflicts increased. The chief government industrial conciliator, Askwith, arrived to try and sort out the situation, which was unlike anything he had seen before. The military brought in as a reserve force could not be trusted, while in the town fires were started and there was riotous looting. After negotiations a settlement was reached with the strikers' 'leaders'. But when the terms were announced to a crowd of 15,000, relates Askwith, "an angry roar of 'No!' rang out; and 'Let's fire the docks' from the outskirts where men ran off. … I heard a town councillor remark that he had been in Paris during the Commune and had never seen anything like this … he had not known there were such people in Hull — women with hair streaming and half nude, reeling through the streets, smashing and destroying."[6] By July the situation had calmed somewhat, only to burst out again with renewed force in August.

This time the storm centre was Liverpool. The seamen's strike had spread to the docks. This in turn led to a transport workers' strike. At first local, it involved a total stoppage of the docks, railway porters and the tramway men. "Even the road sweepers declined to work."[7] Troops were moved into the town and two gunboats were moored in the Mersey with guns trained on the working-class quarters. Emboldened by this support, the police made a sudden attack on a massive peaceful strike meeting of 80,000 on 13th August. Though sections of the crowd fought back as best they could, panic had seized it and it was batoned from the Plateau. "Those who tended the wounded were struck; those who were already wounded were struck; and the children were not forgotten in the mad charge," wrote a *Freedom* correspondent. The result was naturally enough an escalation of violence. "Every worker is now talking of revolution and redress."[8] Fires were lit in the street as barricades to stop the movement of police and soldiers. Fierce clashes took place continuously between strikers and police and at least five police horses had to be destroyed as a result of their injuries. Martial law was proclaimed. The troops, however, "increased disorder because they were stoned by the strikers. … They had to retreat under showers of kidney stones with which the mob armed themselves."[9] The troops were being leafleted by the anarchists and others, and meetings of soldiers were addressed by a local anarchist, S.H. Muston, who reported that "There were many instances of disaffection among the troops during the strike" which had been hushed up.[10] During clashes two men were shot dead and others injured by troops.

The transport strike spread to other places. Nationally the railwaymen's leaders were forced to call a strike in order to stay in control. By mid-August

150,000 railwaymen were out. A strike in the London docks had started at the same time as that in Liverpool. Here too it was the non-union workers who initiated the fight. According to one source, "…the men who declared war and afterwards sustained the fight with revolutionary vigour were the non-unionists. The union leaders waited until they saw the strike would succeed before they identified with it. They merely climbed into notoriety on the backs of the suffering strikers."[11] The power in the hands of the strikers was unprecedented. The anarchist leaflet 'Anarchy and the Labour War' issued in August 1911 rightly stressed the novelty of the situation in the "Lord Mayor of Manchester … obtaining passports from the strikers for necessities to pass through the streets. … Who would have suggested that the London provision traffic would have been maintained by permission of the strikers only?" In Dundee the strikers forced blacklegs to leave the town, the troops could not be trusted and the strikers "only allowed household coal and flour through the cordons."[12] Contemporary observers were impressed by the solidarity of different sections of workers, the rapidity with which disputes spread and the violence of the confrontations involved. Violence there certainly was: at the end of the successful strike on the London docks the returning workers poured into the docks to find blacklegs still there. The result was a battle which lasted on and off for two days where the weapons used seem to have been revolvers and stevedores' hooks.[13] Yet the most impressive thing was the level of autonomous self-organisation of the workers. The strikers of 1889–1890 had called in 'outside' organisers. The strikes of 1910–1911 were progressively managed out of the ranks of the strikers themselves, managed, be it said, in opposition not only to the employers but overwhelmingly to their supposed leaders in the unions.

The tensions within the working class were expressed in the literature and the organisations arising from the labour war. The new sense of solidarity between different groups of workers gave rise to urgent demands from the rank and file for the sweeping away of 'sectional' boundaries between these groups. Here industrial unionism became relevant. Yet the experience of the first years of massive confrontation had also led to great distrust of the leaderships of unions large and small. And the sense of being able to organise separately from these leaderships had become a manifest fact. But in what way was organisation on a larger scale designed to transcend sectional barriers to do this without involving the very leaderships they had grown to distrust? The industrial unionist's dream of revolutionary industrial unions organised separately from the reformist unions was a non-starter in Britain: the unions were established well enough and were flexible enough in practice to make this impossible. Yet the dream persisted. Another possibility was to change the leadership of the unions or to bring them more firmly under rank-and-file control: this was constitutionally, at least, a long-term project. The trades union hierarchies, then as now, were well protected against their rank and file. A more immediately practical possibility was to organise at the base in such a way as to maximise solidarity and to minimise official interference. In practice attempts were made with varying emphasis and success on all these levels, and inevitably there were ambiguities which represented both confusion and conflict and the richness of solutions being worked out in practice. A central figure both from the point of rich ambiguity and his involvement in the events of the time was Tom Mann. From the time of the London dock strike of 1889 and before he had revealed himself as an astonishingly able union organiser. Unlike so many of his contemporaries he never seemed to hanker after a quiet niche in trades union office or politics. His political ideas followed from his organising efforts rather than the other way round. As one result his political contacts were wide and heterogeneous. When he was, from 1898 to 1901, the landlord of the Enterprise pub in Long Acre in London's Covent Garden his establishment was used for meetings by the Young Ireland Society, the Central Branch of the S.D.F., the Friends of Russian Freedom (which included Kropotkin) and a club called the Cosmopolitans which included among its guests Malatesta, Louise Michel and Morrison Davidson. This was typical of the man. Probably the only reason the I.L.P. is not in the list is that their tendency towards teetotalism would not allow them to have meetings in a pub!

When he returned to England in 1910 after a spell of organising in Australia he was a convinced industrial unionist, in the sense that he was hostile to sectional unionism and believed that direct action was the means whereby workers won their demands. His convictions had grown out of his Australian experiences. During the Broken Hill dispute in 1909, railwaymen, good union men all, had transported troops 1,500 miles from the eastern seaboard to break the strike of another section of workers. The Arbitration Bills, passed to stop strikes occurring by putting conflicts between capital and labour before an 'impartial' body, had proved to be heavily biased against the workers. Men who advocated or led strikes were put in jail, yet employers could ignore the rulings of arbitration with impunity. It seemed clear to Tom Mann that solidarity had to transcend sectional boundaries and the workers had to rely on their own direct action rather than on the efforts of legislators. The long-term project was the revolutionary overthrow of capitalism.

On his return to England he cooperated with a Walthamstow journalist, Guy Bowman, in bringing out a small periodical, the *Industrial Syndicalist*. This amounted to a series of eleven monthly pamphlets issued from June 1910 to May 1911 which developed these ideas in the context of the situation in Britain. They represented a combination of industrial unionism and continental syndicalism — thus the title. Tom Mann saw the task he had set himself clearly: "It is a big order we are here for: nothing less than an endeavour to revolutionise the trade unions, to make Unionism, from a movement of two millions, mostly of skilled workers whose interests are regarded as different from the labourers who join with them in their industry, into a movement that will take in every worker."[14] Thus he saw his job involving a vast extension and amalgamation of existing trades unions. He knew what the alternatives were:

> I hold they are wrong who suppose that we have not genuine class conscious proletarians in the Unionist movement. I am quite sure that there are many thousands who understand the Class War, and wish to take their rightful share in the fighting; but as yet they can find no satisfactory outlet. Sooner or later these leading turbulent spirits will find a method — and it would be wise on the part of those occupying responsible positions to endeavour to make it easy for such reorganisations as may be necessary, so that those who are determined to fight may not be compelled to find other agencies.
>
> Personally, I would very much prefer to see the existing machinery made equal to the whole than be driven to the conclusion that new agencies must be brought into existence.[15]

He goes on to ask "...what will have to be the essential conditions for the success of such a movement?"

> *That will be avowedly and clearly Revolutionary in aim and method.* Revolutionary in aim, because it will be out for the abolition of the wages system and for securing to the workers the full fruits of their labour, thereby seeking to change the system of Society from Capitalist to Socialist.
>
> Revolutionary in method, because it will refuse to enter into any long agreements with the masters, whether with legal or State backing, or merely voluntarily; and because it will seize every chance of fighting for the general betterment — gaining ground and never losing any.[16]

He rather fudged the issue of control in the trades unions in his analysis. There was no doubt that his huge activity in the years before World War One played its part in helping along the general unrest. There was no doubt that it was his call to direct action, his denunciation of cautious and sectional leadership which made him such a popular speaker, capable of filling the largest halls. This was certainly the reason why some anarchists, notably those in Liverpool, actively sold the *Industrial Syndicalist*. Yet his policy of amalgamation found him working with "those occupying responsible positions" in the sectional unions who were so mistrusted by "the leading turbulent spirits." He worked with Havelock Wilson during the seamen's strike. He worked with Tillett of the dockers for the formation of the National Transport Workers Federation in 1910 and with the leaders of three competing unions on the railways for the formation of the National Union of Railwaymen in 1912. He was responsible, as much as anyone was responsible, for the channelling of the unskilled strikers of these years into the unions.

Criticisms from orthodox industrial unionists which condemned the 'Federation Fake' and Mann's failure to form 'real' industrial unions missed the point. They seemed to be too interested in the label. Libertarians were much closer to the mark. In an excellent piece in *Freedom* in November 1910, John Paton, a Glasgow anarchist, wrote on 'Tom Mann and the Industrial Union Movement'. He first criticised Tom Mann for his ambivalence over Parliament, which he saw as an unwillingness to tread on the toes of trades union leaders over their proclivities towards political careers. More importantly, he went on to say:

> In deciding for the retention of the present organisations, Mann has quite evidently failed to get to grips with the root of the problem he is facing. The curse of Trade Unionism in this country is the centralisation of executive power with its resultant multiplication of officials. The corresponding stagnation and death of local life and spirit is the inevitable consequence. This centralisation would be enormously extended and developed by Mann's scheme. ... We must decentralise and as far as possible destroy executive power. Let the workers themselves bear the burden and responsibility of decisive action.

As we have seen, in 1911 the workers themselves were to seize the "burden and responsibility of decisive action." Yet for the most part the workers did not look beyond the existing organisations and the growth and amalgamation of the unions was accepted and encouraged as a means of destroying sectionalism. *At the same time* they were taking steps to decentralise (if not destroy) executive power. The consequence was that leaders and led were bound together often uncomfortably and occasionally in a state of open war.

At the base this was represented by the growth of bodies of militants at rank-and-file level. In the South Wales coalfield in 1911, there emerged the 'Unofficial Reform Committee'. This was composed of activists from the Cambrian Combine strike and other pits, and included rebel students from the Ruskin strike of 1909. The Unofficial Reform Committee acted as a coordinating body for the militant workers in the coalfield and provided a means of communication unmediated by the officials. As a result of ideas put forward and amended, changed and rearranged by several delegate conferences a remarkable document, *The Miners' Next Step*, was issued in 1912.[17] This proposed a new constitution for the organisation of the miners on three principles: firstly, that the lodges (branches) should have supreme control. Secondly, 'officials or leaders' were to be excluded from the executive, which was to be a purely administrative body composed of men directly elected by the men for that purpose. Thirdly, agents or organisers were to be directly under the control of the executive. Though some changes were made (or forced) in the union these proposals expressed an ideal which was to be frustrated but persistent. The situation was complicated by the election of four militants to the South Wales Miners' Federation executive in 1911 — an executive which their programme was committed to more or less abolish.

In the engineering industry comparable unofficial developments took place in the shape of the amalgamation committee movement. This took its name because of the vast number of unions (there were well over 200) involved in the industry apart from the Amalgamated Society of Engineers and the desire of the militants to draw these bodies together. Here they were obviously influenced by syndicalist propaganda of the Tom Mann variety. A committee of engineers in Manchester had been set up in 1910 to push the principles of direct action, solidarity and amalgamation.[18] This seems to have been the first early example. Such propaganda activity merged with the already existing workshop organisation. By 1909 shop stewards "were being elected, at least in some shops, in most of the major centres, and their number and function continued to grow."[19] The shop stewards had appeared because of the necessity of workshop negotiations — particularly over piecework prices. As such they were the workshop representative of their union. It was inevitable that the need for mutual support would draw the representatives of the different unions together — although craft jealousies would often drive them apart.

From this point it was a logical step to make the stewards a basis of amalgamation. In Sheffield, for example, a shop steward suggested in 1914 "that all the trade unionists in any shop should have shop stewards who should form themselves into a committee to represent the workers in that shop regardless of the trade unions they belonged to and thus make the first step towards uniting the unions."[20] This development was by no means restricted to Sheffield — the same idea occurred in many places at about the same time. Thus the amalgamation committee in the workshop both formed what we should now call a joint shop stewards' committee and provided an inter-union basis of coordination and communication separate from the officials. The opposition to the officials was clearly expressed. A pamphlet issued by the Metal Engineering and Shipbuilding Amalgamation Committee described its functions as twofold. Firstly, it was to encourage amalgamation and to eventually seize control of the industry. Secondly, in the meantime it was "to act as a Vigilance Committee, watching and actively criticising the officials of the various sectional Unions and in every way possible stimulating and giving expression to militant thought throughout the Trade Union movement."[21]

There were more than propaganda attacks on officialdom: in the London Amalgamated Society of Engineers, a delegate meeting ordered the Trustees to stop paying the salaries of officials after 1st January 1913, and appointed a lay 'provisional committee' to take charge. The officials refused to leave the union headquarters and barricaded themselves in. The provisional committee and its supporters, however, with the help of the general secretary of the union were able to get into the building and throw out the occupiers, though it was not done entirely peacefully.[22]

Thus as the wave of strikes continued from 1911 through to the outbreak of war a qualitative shift took place in the spirit of the rank and file which found its formal expressions in these rank-and-file movements. In political terms this shift expressed itself in the development of a different kind of socialist milieu. Yet before we see the way in which the anarchists related to this milieu some remarks are in order as to the way in which anarchists were perceived by the socialist movement at this time. In the early 1890s they had been seen as "fools, madmen and rogues," to quote John Burns.

They had been regarded for the most part as bombers and assassins and their doings were related with fascinated horror. It is hard to place exactly where the change came. Political assassinations and bombings by anarchists continued sporadically in Europe. Yet, in England, by 1909, anarchists had ceased to be bogey men. That year saw massive demonstrations over the arrest and execution of Francisco Ferrer in Barcelona. This had followed on from an attempted rising in Barcelona in the last week of July 1909, known as the 'Bloody Week'. Ferrer was a positivist rather than an anarchist but had become widely identified with the anarchists through his Modern School movement. The Modern Schools were libertarian in their methods and trenchantly secular. Through this Ferrer and the schools he founded had earned the undying hatred of the Roman Catholic hierarchy. After the defeated uprising Ferrer was arrested for complicity in the events — though there was no evidence to show that he had either organised, instigated or taken part in them. He was tried before a military court and shot. (A little-known part in all this was taken by an English C.I.D. detective Charles Arrow, 'on loan' to the Spanish authorities. His role was more or less head of intelligence to the military. His memoirs indicate that he enjoyed the organisation of the repression immensely.)[23]

The socialist movement in England participated readily in the protests organised by anarchists and others. They were uncowed by the connections drawn between Ferrer and the attempted revolution and apparently not at all bothered by his anarchist apologists. Rather the reverse: the execution of Ferrer seems to have started some socialists on the path towards anarchism.[24] This unhorrified acceptance of anarchists and anarchism remained unflustered through the events known as the Tottenham Outrage and the Siege of Sidney Street. The first, in January 1909, was an armed robbery followed by a wild chase through north-east London in which a boy of ten and the two robbers were killed and a number of people were injured. The second followed on from a disturbed robbery at a jeweller's shop in the East End in December 1910. Of the five policemen who went to investigate, three were shot dead and the other two badly wounded. Two of the robbers were traced to 100 Sidney Street in Whitechapel, and after a gunfight that lasted much of 3rd January 1911 and involved Churchill, the Home Secretary and the Scots Guards, the house was mysteriously set on fire and the two gunmen inside killed. In both cases the gun-play was blamed on anarchists, though the men involved were either unpolitical or connected with the Lettish Social Democrat combat groups. One of the Sidney Street gang who managed to escape, named Peter the Painter, and others of them had used the Jewish Anarchist Club in Jubilee Street and this seemed to be enough to link them together in the press. Though both events received wide publicity, as did the alleged involvement of the anarchists, the reaction in the socialist movement was not dissimilar to that of the *Industrial Syndicalist*. Under the heading 'The Battle of Stepney' Bowman or Mann wrote: "Problem: if two men can keep 2,000 men employed and hold them at bay in one street, how many men would be required to defeat two or three million men spread over the area of Great Britain?" They promised a £2 2s reward for the best answer.[25]

Such panic as there was seemed to be restricted to the better-off classes. The police began to take an increased interest in the movement. Following on from a report that Peter the Painter had been seen in Glasgow the police visited the Glasgow group's meetings. As a result they went to the employers of some of the members and managed to have at least one of them — George Barrett — sacked and blacklisted. There seemed to be a general increase of surveillance of anarchists and some concern on the part of the authorities to put into action the 1905 Aliens Act which allowed the deportation of undesirable aliens on the strength of, among other things, a magistrate's recommendation. One attempt to use this legislation, however, met with massive opposition and showed just how little notice the working-class movement had taken of the scare stories.

In May 1912, a criminal libel action was brought against Malatesta by a fellow Italian named Bellelli who supported the Italian government's imperialist ventures in Tripoli. Bellelli had circulated information to the effect that Malatesta's opposition to the action of the Italian government was due to the fact that Malatesta was a Turkish spy. Malatesta had circulated a leaflet among the Italians in London declaring his readiness to appear before a court of honour to clear himself of this charge and making slighting references to Bellelli "who used to call himself an Anarchist ... but many look upon him as an Italian police spy."[26] In the court action that followed much play was made of the fact that Malatesta had supplied a bottle of gas to one of the Sidney Street gang. This had been known to the police, who had satisfied themselves that nothing more than an ordinary business transaction had taken place — Malatesta had a one-man business as an electrical engineer. The result of the character assassination in court, however, was that the judge sentenced Malatesta to three months in prison and recommended that he be deported. On appeal both sentence and deportation were upheld. The short term of imprisonment could not be reckoned to affect Malatesta overmuch — he had been to jail before. But the deportation was serious: on the Continent it could be safely assumed that the least he could expect was life imprisonment.

An anarchist campaign to have the deportation stopped rapidly spread to the socialist movement as a whole. The *Daily Herald* gave the case much publicity and published reams of protests from trades unions and meetings up and down the country. Malatesta had many friends in these quarters, having spoken under the aegis of Mann's Industrial Syndicalist Education League on a number of occasions. In fact one letter in the *Daily Herald* referred to Malatesta as "an international Tom Mann." The campaign culminated in a massive meeting in Trafalgar Square organised by Guy Aldred. It had originally been intended to use mainly anarchist speakers (and some ex-anarchists, surprisingly enough, including W.B. Parker, now a Poor Law guardian, and Agnes Henry). In the event, however, the main speakers were drawn from more respectable quarters, including Wedgwood and Cunninghame Graham, M.P.s, and James MacDonald of the London Trades Council. Also speaking were Mrs Tom Mann and Guy Bowman (Bowman had just been released and Mann was still in jail over a 'Don't Shoot!' leaflet). The campaign was successful. On Monday, 17th June, the deportation order was lifted by the Home Secretary.

The most important thing to emerge from these events was that the anarchists were an accepted part of the socialist movement, which rejected political action as a priority and which espoused direct action. The *Daily Telegraph* was right in its facts if wrong in its conclusions when it wrote in March 1912: "The authorities have now, we understand, received evidence establishing the fact that sections of the Communists, the Syndicalists and the Anarchists share common aims and are working together for one common object, and, in fact, it may be said that the present Labour unrest is almost entirely due to a great conspiracy on the part of those agitators to promote dissatisfaction and resentment amongst the working classes."[27]

The way in which various sections of the movement worked informally together is not particularly clear. Yet we can find certain typical situations and incidents which are clues and illustrations. Let us take Walthamstow in north-east London. Guy Bowman lived in the area and published the *Industrial Syndicalist*, the *Syndicalist Railwayman* and the *Syndicalist* in succession from his home. The secretary of the Walthamstow Trades Council, A.G. Tufton of the Carpenters and Joiners, was an enthusiastic exponent of Tom Mann's version of syndicalism. In 1910–1911 the anarchists of Walthamstow were holding three or more weekly outdoor meetings. All this could have been mutually exclusive, each activity distinct from the other. Yet outside Walthamstow Guy Bowman had been in fairly regular contact with anarchists, speaking with them at meetings, visiting Kropotkin, etc. The local Walthamstow anarchists were great debaters and visited local branches of the S.D.F. and I.L.P. They were present at the first meeting of the Socialist Society in neighbouring Leyton formed out of a branch of the S.D.F. expelled for taking up anti-parliamentary ideas. One of the anarchists active in this area was W.D. Ponder who, as we have seen, had been active in the Industrialist League until his expulsion. He was later to take an active part in the North London Herald League. This is an indication of how little the formal separations of groups meant on a local level. The anarchists of Walthamstow worked with the local 'parliamentary socialists' in a free-speech fight at Epping Forest. After the arrest of Tom Mann, Guy Bowman and the Buck brothers in 1912 for advocating, publishing and printing a 'Don't Shoot!' leaflet for soldiers entitled 'An open letter to British Soldiers', a couple of demonstrations took place involving socialists from north-east London whose speaking base was Victoria Park. The second, an anarchist-initiated demonstration with many other groups involved, marched from Victoria Park round Bethnal Green with placards saying 'Don't Shoot!' and "a large number of the proscribed leaflet ... were distributed."[28]

Anarchists were also involved in purely syndicalist activity as the following letter between two local Socialist League veterans, Joseph Lane and Ambrose Barker shows. (Barker lived in Walthamstow.) Lane wrote "...I believe tonight you have your Syndicalist group meeting. I hope you will have a good rally of numbers. Have you seen this month's Syndicalist, somehow I like their fighting policy and the endeavour to get the Trade Unions to throw over parliament and their leaders and become a rank and file fighting force and while Freedom Groups and pure Anarchists are doing good work as educationalists the Syndicalists will do good work among the Trade Unions in the same direction without frightening them with that terrible word Anarchy."[29] These kinds of loose contact and mutual cooperation were to be found all over the country and are probably of more importance historically than has been recognised. It has been far too readily assumed that the formal separations within the socialist movement into specific groups represents a formal separation at all levels. At grass-roots level this is not the case. From formal cooperation and formal switches of allegiance down to the most casual contacts in places like Henderson's bookshop in Charing Cross Road (known to generations as 'the bomb shop') and Charles Lahr's bookshop in Holborn the socialist movement was more a series of overlapping networks than a collection of parties. This milieu was the one in which the anarchists operated in the years just prior to World War One, and further examples will present themselves as we consider the more formally anarchist activities during this time.

In 1912 there was a possibility that the S.D.F. could absorb and co-opt some of the new energy thrown up by the Syndicalist Revolt. In that year the S.D.F. made the greatest leap forward in its history and, uniting with sections of the I.L.P. who were itching for a more revolutionary policy, formed the British Socialist Party (B.S.P.). This claimed 40,000 members in 370 branches on its formation. Yet even before this time the S.D.F. was suffering from internal dissension over the question of direct action. Tom Mann had resigned his membership (taken up on his return to England) in May 1911, unable any longer to reconcile the purely electoral policy of the S.D.F. with his commitment to extra-political struggle. He was not alone as the 'official' history of the S.D.F./R.S.P. says: "Already, Syndicalist influences were at war with the recognised methods and objectives within the B.S.P."[30] The trouble got worse in the larger organisation: "The insidious preaching of Syndicalism, Direct Action and similar forms of anti-political anarchism, although the advocates were few in number worked a tremendous mischief within the British Socialist Party, as it was bound to do in any organisation that had been thus fastened-upon."[31] The extent of the 'tremendous mischief' can be gauged when we see that within two years the membership of the B.S.P. had dropped by half. "In 1914 the membership of the B.S.P. was no more than that of the S.D.F. six years before."[32]

The I.L.P. was also suffering from a similar malaise. Between 1909 and 1911, forty-six I.L.P. branches collapsed and the sale of pamphlets dropped by half. In 1909 there were 28,650 members in 887 branches; in 1914 there were 20,793 in 672 branches.[33] Some of this drop can be accounted for by the secessions to the B.S.P. but this was unstable as the fall in membership of the latter organisation indicated. The other part can be readily assumed to have been due to discontent with a purely electoral policy. The I.L.P. in any case had a minority of old anarchists as members who had presumably joined when their original faith in the imminent revolution had faded — men like Thomas Barclay in Leicester and Alf Barton in Sheffield. It is not suggested that they were leading the I.L.P., but rather that they represented a tradition which younger members could relate to. A member of the I.L.P. at that time remembered an I.L.P. branch in Glasgow: "...its membership represented an extraordinary diversity of ideas. Atheists, Marxists and anarchists rubbed shoulders with Christian socialists like Hardie himself."[34] It is not suggested that to take part in or advocate direct action or to denigrate electoral activity automatically made anarchists. Anarchism was nevertheless to grow in the increasingly numerous political fringe which had fallen out with the B.S.P. and I.L.P.

At this time *Freedom* was looking more healthy than it had for years. Marsh was on the point of retiring in 1912 and wrote to Keell "...I feel the worst troubles of *Freedom* are over. With a circulation rapidly increasing, with literary help coming in so well it only needs steady work and some monetary help to reach a paying point."[35] The circulation of *Freedom* was at that time about 3,000. The imprisonment of Malatesta and the protest meetings at his ordered deportation had increased interest in his writings published by the Freedom Press, which had been given free advertisements in the *Daily Herald*. Reports of anarchist activity around the country showed a healthy movement. The first national conference of anarchists for years took place in Leeds in February 1912. This was originally called to discuss a programme put forward by a local group, the Beeston Brotherhood, which had achieved a certain local notoriety through its communistic lifestyle and its refusal to accept state registration of personal relationships. Their programme proposed: "The abolition of all law; the disbanding of the Army, Navy and police; the suppression of parliament; the abolition of the coinage system." This was undoubtedly acceptable to most of the delegates, but there would have been little point in having a conference to discuss it since there would be nothing to discuss! In the event the forty-five delegates from England, Ireland, Scotland and Wales at the conference discussed more immediate matters. The first was the question of the organisation of propaganda and groups. It was agreed to form three federations, one in Scotland, one for Lancashire and Yorkshire and one for the south of England. These were to make their own arrangements for exchanging speakers, etc. The conference also discussed a projected weekly paper to be called the *Anarchist*. This we shall discuss a little later on. The conference created a great deal of interest in Leeds and one newspaper reported that "a curious crowd in Boar Lane … kept a keen look out for furtive-looking strangers who might reasonably be supposed to be Anarchists."[36] A meeting held on the night of the conference brought 2,000 people to Victoria Square. The conference seems to have been enthusiastic, and one delegate was reported as saying, "We are going to revive the Anarchist propaganda of a quarter of a century ago."[37]

The mood of the conference represented a new vitality in the anarchist movement. One sign of this was the way in which the old Socialist League anarchists started popping up again. We have seen that Lane and Barker were taking an active interest in the new movement. Others included Kitz, who emerged from a long period of inactivity around 1909 and became increasingly involved. His activities were enough to have him boycotted by the employers in early 1910, and from that point he was forced to eke out a precarious living in street markets. He wrote a set of 'Recollections and Reflections' in *Freedom* from January to July 1912. These are important for the information he gives on the Socialist League and other activities of that time, and the present book draws heavily on them. Yet the most important point is that he felt confident enough of an audience for these memoirs. He described himself as "an old man at one time somewhat despondent of the success of the revolutionary cause."[38] He was no longer despondent. Another old militant to emerge from 'retirement' was James Tochatti, who became an active speaker again. His "book-lined cellar under his shop … in which no daylight ever came" became something of a centre in Hammersmith for "young workmen disillusioned by the timid programmes of other parties" and for his old friends among the exiles.[39] F. Goulding had come back into the movement around 1907 and continued to work with Aldred and his paper the *Herald of Revolt* for some years. Ted Leggatt, now the Carmen's Union organiser, was, in addition to his union activities, for which he was roundly condemned as a labour fakir in the *Herald of Revolt*, active among the Jewish anarchists of the East End. Other people who were active enough again to be noticeable were Carl Quinn and W.B. Parker (who seemed to have a slight hankering after anarchy again).

The fact that a weekly paper was being prepared was also significant, pointing to a new spirit in the movement. It also represented how rapidly the movement could grow in a locality when active organisers and speakers were available. In this case the locality was Glasgow, and the man chiefly responsible for the rapid growth of the anarchist movement there was George Barrett. Born George Ballard in 1888 in Herefordshire (Barrett was his adopted name for propaganda purposes), he first became active in the Bristol Socialist Society. This was an electoral organisation and Barrett seems to have become rapidly opposed to political action, for by February 1908 *Freedom* is reporting him disturbing "the otherwise peaceful routine" of this body by advocating anarchism. He later apparently resigned from the Bristol Socialist Society. By mid-1909 he had moved to London and was taking an active part in the movement. Based in Walthamstow, he spoke at meetings the length and breadth of London. Mat Kavanagh wrote of him at this time: "Barrett's energy was tremendous. He spoke almost every night of the week and would often cycle 20 miles each way to address a meeting, and that after a day's work."[40] By April 1910 Barrett had moved to Glasgow. Here he began a solitary campaign of street-speaking with occasional assistance from John McAra from Edinburgh. It was not long, however, before he began to attract a following. In May 1910 John Paton, already an anarchist and recently expelled from the I.L.P., describes his first meeting with Barrett as follows:

> …one evening I saw an unfamiliar figure mounted on a box at one of the speaking pitches. I made one of the half dozen people listening to him. He was engaged in a familiar denunciation of capitalism and a glance at the pamphlets spread on the street told me he was an anarchist.
>
> I studied him with a new interest. There had been no anarchist propaganda in Glasgow for many years, although at one time there had been an active group. The speaker was a tall, good-looking Englishman, extremely eloquent and able, whose speech betrayed his middle-class origin. The passionate conviction with which he spoke

was extraordinarily impressive; he was undoubtedly an unusual personality; the crowd about him swelled in numbers. As the speech developed, my interest quickened with excitement; he progressed from the usual attack on capitalism to a scathing indictment of politicians and particularly the leaders of the Labour Party: here was, at last, being shouted at the street corner, all the criticisms which had become common in the 'left-wing' of the I.L.P., but which we'd keep discreetly for party discussion. My heart rejoiced. But it was much more than a mere attack on personalities; it was a powerful analysis of the causes that produced them.[41]

After the meeting Paton introduced himself to Barrett and his "solitary henchman, a quiet young railway clerk, Dominic. Before we parted that night we three had constituted ourselves the Glasgow Anarchist Group." They began an energetic campaign of propaganda and started to attract members. At their first business meeting called later in the year they had a membership of twenty. By 1st May 1911 they had fifty members. (One of them was Willie Gallagher, later a founder member of the Communist Party and a Communist M.P. He was still a member of S.D.F. at this point but was to more firmly identify himself with the anarchists later in 1912.) The group took an active part in the events round the seamen's strike of that year and began to expand their activities outside Glasgow to Govan and Paisley; and their numbers increased. By June 1912, with the new paper already started, the Glasgow group were holding meetings at two places in Glasgow, and at Paisley, Clydebank, Maryhill and Parkhead. The weekly paper was being prepared from mid-1911. Barrett first approached the Freedom Group, who felt unable to handle the project. It was then decided to produce it from Glasgow. Over the winter of 1911–1912 Barrett went on tour to drum up financial support and to arrange for distributors in the movement. In Scotland and London his tour met with some success and the movement seemed in good shape. In Liverpool, Manchester and Leeds, however, the response was very disappointing and demonstrated that the anarchist revival was, as yet, only patchy. By the time of the 1912 conference at Leeds some £90 had been pledged, but it is unlikely that the paper could have appeared on 1st May and continued for as long as it did without the support of George Davison.[42] This is not to say that sacrifices were not made, and in fact Barrett seems to have hidden the extent of the struggle to keep the *Anarchist* going from Davison.

> George was working at very high pressure, writing articles and doing all the work of editing and often in addition doing many odd jobs — getting the paper rolled off, folding and packing and even rushing to the post, for one or two members of the group got tired, so for weeks the strain was tremendous. ... Fortunately, a sense of humour pulled us through many a time, even when things went into pawn to pay the 'comps' wages.[43]

The paper came out for thirty-four issues between May 1912 and early 1913. It is the opinion of the present author that the paper produced was not what the movement needed at that time. Its tendency was too much to the philosophical and general. George Barrett was a powerful speaker, as the memoirs of his contemporaries attest, yet his writing and the reports of his speeches show him to have been somewhat prolix and rhetorical. Despite some notable contributions — one from A.J. Cook (later secretary of the Miners' Federation of Great Britain) under a pen name — the paper failed through 'lack of support'. The strains set up by the running of the paper also adversely affected the anarchist group that had so rapidly grown up under Barrett's influence. There had already been a tendency towards oligarchy in the group, as Paton's remarks show: "It had been so obvious to me that the bulk of the new members our propaganda had attracted," he says, "had only the most rudimentary conception of what we were after. They were attracted in part by their hatred of their conditions but more by the glamour of George's personality. Indeed, anarchist-communism in its scientific basis was no easy doctrine for untrained and ill-equipped minds to grasp." Early attempts to run the meetings of the group on a Quaker pattern had proved a failure. The result was, as Paton says, that "George and I, in consultation in advance, determined all the activities of the free commune in efficient bureaucratic style."[44]

This oligarchic tendency began to be complicated by ideological disagreements. Barrett shared something of the attitudes of Turner and other members of the Freedom Group who supported a militant trades unionism which left the hierarchical structure of the unions more or less intact. In August, Guy Aldred was also speaking in the area and was roundly condemning trades union officials and all their works and seems to have found a responsive audience. It was reported in October 1912 that at a recent conference of Scottish anarchists: "We had a fairly hot discussion on the differences that have sprung up among us."[45] The nature of these 'differences' is not spelled out, but reading between the lines it would seem to have been a mixture of the dissatisfactions with the organisation of the group and dissatisfactions over the line taken over trades unions. In the issue of the *Herald of Revolt* (Aldred's paper) for May 1913, after the demise of the *Anarchist*, Angus MacKay wrote an account of the Glasgow movement which shows how the movement there had felt excluded by the group round the weekly paper. The effort required for the paper seems to have disorganised the group. Certainly after the collapse of the *Anarchist* the movement in Glasgow suffered something of a relapse. Barrett caught a chill in May 1913 while speaking which rapidly developed into tuberculosis, and he was thereby largely prevented from taking an active role in the movement. He continued to write for the anarchist press and speak at meetings, but his illess was virulent and deadly and he died in January 1917. Nevertheless, at the national conference in March 1913, Barrett, for all his disappointment at the failure of the *Anarchist* was able to be moderately enthusiastic about the movement as a whole:

> A general view of the country today certainly gives more satisfaction than it did at the time of the earlier gathering, but much still remains to be done before it can be said that the Anarchists have responded to the actual demand for Anarchism which the workers are making in all parts ...
>
> With the possible exception of Scotland — and it cannot remain an exception for long — progress has been made in almost every part. The Newcastle district is doing good work and will soon be doing much better. Leeds, of course, is — Leeds, and the Manchester people are still wondering why no one does anything always forgetting that they are the people who should do it; but apart from these two towns, there seems to be some hope of a revival in Lancashire and Yorkshire.

Birmingham is not doing so well as it might, although the one or two that do anything seem to do all that can be done. South Wales and Bristol are the most active of all perhaps, although there is certainly not the huge possibilities here that there are in the Lancashire, Yorkshire or Scottish districts.

At the conference there were forty delegates from Abertillery, Birmingham, Bristol, Durham, Gateshead, Glasgow, Halifax, Hanley, Harlech, Huddersfield, Hull, Liverpool, Manchester, Newcastle-on-Tyne, South Shields and Swansea. There were apologies for non-attendance from six other towns. By far the most impressive report was from South Wales. The anti-leader agitation in the Swansea valley particularly, but generally throughout the mining valleys, "has taken hold of the most earnest section of the mining industry," reported *Freedom*. Small propaganda groups which called themselves 'Workers' Freedom Groups' were being formed — there were already eight of them in the Swansea valley alone. They had published a declaration of principles and a programme "that may be the envy of every Anarchist." This movement is most interesting. It seems to have grown without prominent personalities like George Barrett and to have been an outgrowth of the movement among the miners which had produced the *Miners' Next Step*. At the time of the 1913 conference these groups were reported as "spreading out more and more." At a meeting later in 1913 with 120 people present, the opening of a communist clubhouse at Ammonford was celebrated. They reported: "The Constitution and programme of the Workers Freedom Groups have been shaped upon the model of future society at which they aim, namely Anarchist-communism. Rooms are provided and set apart for library, study circles and discussion circles. No chairman, secretary, treasurer or any other official can play any part in such an organisation."[46] There is very little documentation on this movement in the 'official' anarchist press and local work is necessary before much more can be said. However, it is worth referring to a short description of the miners' movement in South Wales in the 1920s:

When I was a lad, I would creep surreptitiously past the careless stewards into the miners' conferences which were traditionally held in Cardiff's seedy temperance hall. There I would listen to the bright little alert men as they elevated some local issue on the coalfield to the status of a glorious philosophical dialogue — and all of them were anarchists ... the essential sense of locality, the comparatively small pit where all worked (when work was available), the isolation of the valley village or township — all these were similar to the environmental conditions which created the anarcho-syndicalist movement of Spain.[47]

By May 1913 a Workers' Freedom Group had been established at Chopwell in Durham by Will Lawther and others. (Chopwell had long been a militant miners' lodge and continued to be so — Dave Douglass describes it as one of two villages in Durham which were called 'little Moscow' in the 1920s.)[48] The Chopwell anarchists were spreading the propaganda in neighbouring pit villages. In London too the scale of the propaganda was growing. In 1913 and 1914, before the war, there were groups in East and West London, Forest Hill, Marylebone, Notting Hill, Fulham, Harlesden, Deptford and Greenwich. These groups varied in size, but at East London, West London and Deptford between three and five speaking pitches a week were being maintained by each group. Freelance meetings in the parks and other places continued. In May 1913 a large anti-militarist demonstration was organised by the anarchists on the initiative of W.D. Ponder and a group of French anarchists who met at 9 Manette Street, Charing Cross Road. (It is interesting to note that Manette Street was the new name for Rose Street — the same street that had held the Rose Street club at number 6, in 1879.) Two committees were set up, a central one and an independent one in Hackney, East London, which seems to have involved members of the North London Herald League. Seventy thousand leaflets were distributed and there was much cooperation from branches of the railwaymen, carmen, shop assistants and tailoring unions. Branches of the I.L.P. and B.S.P. also cooperated, and the demonstration attracted thousands of people who marched in five processions from Mile End Waste, Highbury Corner, St Pancras Arches, Paddington Green and the Grove, Hammersmith, to Trafalgar Square. In other areas the movement was advancing. At Hazel Grove, Stockport, a communist club was opened in February 1914 with anarchists from Cheadle, Stockport, Reddish,

Oldham and New Mills. The Oldham anarchists were organised in a Workers Freedom Group, which, like the South Wales groups, was run without officials. In May 1914 a new weekly anarchist paper was started from *Freedom*'s Ossulston Street office, named the *Voice of Labour* and edited by Fred Dunn. This emerged from a monthly paper named the *Torch*, which he issued in January and February of that year. Such a weekly paper had been intended earlier, but Barrett, who had been expected to take the editorship, had been incapacitated for a while by illness. Thus the movement had grown to a significant extent while electoral groups had been suffering a decline. Yet we have concentrated thus far on the 'official' anarchist movement — the movement that sent its reports to *Freedom*, that participated in the conferences publicised in its columns. There were other groups and individuals outside this sphere or only partly involved in it. These were for the most part people who had been involved with the more firmly industrial unionist tendencies that looked askance at *Freedom*'s tendency to overlook the vagaries of union leaders. This separation tended to be another of those formal divides which dissolved at grass-roots level. Yet there is no doubt that the view they presented was distinctive and that the journals they produced are of great interest.

The longest lived was Guy Aldred's *Herald of Revolt*. As we have already seen, Aldred had intended to issue a paper of this name after the collapse of the *Voice of Labour* in 1907, but his removal to Shepherd's Bush and his imprisonment for Indian sedition had interrupted him. During his imprisonment he was contacted by Sir Walter Strickland, a wandering eccentric aristocrat, who was to provide a great deal of financial support for Aldred's paper. On his release Aldred issued the first number of his paper in December 1910 with support from Strickland and George Davison. Davison's support did not last long, however — there was a preposterous argument between him and Rose Witcop over the subject of interior decorating, and Davison went off in a huff. The *Herald of Revolt* was issued monthly from December 1910 until May 1914 when its name was changed to the *Spur*, under which it continued until 1921. It is the opinion of the present author that the *Herald of Revolt* was a more vital and interesting paper than *Freedom*. The intellectual development of *Freedom* tended to be a little blinkered by a set of doctrinaire ideas. For all Aldred's undoubted egotism and high self-regard, he was really interested in the spirit of the anarchist philosophy that lay behind general principles. As he himself was to say: "Catchwords have sacrificed freedom to despotism too often. ... Marx's watchword has replaced Christ's; Morris's hymns have superseded Wesley's. The jargon of our faith has changed but it is every whit as lifeless; a dull, heavy, solemn dogma mouthed in unbelief, and twisted and turned to account by every fakir, who finds in the latest jargon a more acceptable cant than in those that have gone before. ... For such ignorant trust in words, the only remedy is live and vital propaganda, steady consistent working towards the ever-coming dawn."[49]

His paper could occasionally seem a little wayward when eclectic collections of rather arcane material were put together. Yet this represented a wide range of interests. Free-thought, the struggle of Carlyle for a free press in the early part of the nineteenth century, continuing concern with Indian affairs — all this material appeared in his paper. This was the result of Aldred's concern for an ongoing *discussion* of ideas rather than a presentation of an already developed position. Aldred delighted in debate and several contemporaries have noted his ready repartee. (One particularly delightful incident was at a meeting on the necessity for free-thought. He said, "When Constantine adopted the Christian religion it was a political dodge, the same as when they put John Burns in the Cabinet." The local Christian militants were incensed at this blasphemy.) On several occasions he was to print selections of the more libertarian writings of Marx under the heading 'Was Marx an Anarchist?' and compared them with similar passages in Bakunin's writings. He also reprinted some 'Anarchist Portraits' by Malato, originally written in 1894, which took as their subjects the 'grands anars' of the terrorist period whom the more 'philosophical' among the anarchists preferred not to talk about. He also printed some excellent pieces by James Timewell who wrote on the regular abuses by the police of their power. Timewell seems to have been a one-man National Council for Civil Liberties at a time when the word of a policeman, even more so than today, could send someone to jail no matter how good the defence case.

Aldred was primarily a propagandist rather than an organiser, though he does deserve the title of agitator. His interventions in the politics of the time were real enough. The *Herald of Revolt* denounced the Freedom Group for its refusal to recognise the fakirdom of John Turner. More spectacularly he accused Hyndman of having a financial interest in the propagation of his jingo ideas.[50] Aldred demonstrated quite clearly that Hyndman had been involved with the 'Colt Gun and Carriage Co. Ltd.', whose shares rose and fell with war scares. He went on to allege that Hyndman's bellicose patriotism was designed to increase the value of these shares: "Hyndman's jingoistic policy is dictated by his financial interests in human murder." His (clearly libellous) allegations were widely reprinted abroad though not taken up in England. At the time of the prosecution of Bowman and the Buck brothers in 1912 it was only through a number of misunderstandings that he did not print the *Syndicalist* during Bowman's imprisonment — apparently *Freedom* had been asked to print it but had declined. When left-wing newspaper sellers were being harassed by the police for 'obstruction' in Hyde Park in 1911 Aldred organised a big 'sellin'.' In addition to a large turnout of left-wing newspaper-sellers he also arranged for a large 'obstructive' crowd to surround the always unhampered Christian Evidence sellers, which created an embarrassing impasse for the police.

Thus Aldred used his journal as an active base rather than as a pontificatory armchair. His main contacts were with the group round the *Industrialist*, which, if not an anarchist organisation, certainly included many anarchists in its ranks. In March 1912 *Industrialist* was writing to *Freedom*: "I find that many Industrial Unionists are avowed Anarchists and many others are virtually Anarchist without knowing it: the balance is rapidly becoming a negligible quantity, as it is being absorbed by the other sections. I hold therefore that all working class Anarchists should join the I.W.W. ... I have been a member of the Industrial League for a considerable time. The other members with whom I happen to be acquainted are also Anarchist Communists and include some of the most influential members of the League." (The Industrialist League had been granted a charter as the English section of the Chicago section of the I.W.W. in late 1910. The Chicago I.W.W. was distinct from the Detroit section, the former being firmly anti-political and 'direct action' in orientation.) In 1911 Aldred was holding joint meetings with Industrialist League speakers. They contributed articles to his paper and he to theirs. Both papers carried advertisements for the other. When the *Industrialist* suspended publication in June 1912 because of financial difficulties, Aldred offered to come to an arrangement whereby the Industrialist League could use half of the *Herald of Revolt* in return for helping its circulation. This arrangement does not seem to have matured, but for several issues members of the Industrialist League wrote pieces of a semi-'internal' nature. However, the Chicago I.W.W. sent an organiser named Swazey to England in 1913, and by the end of that year there were some six branches of the I.W.W. in the country and a newspaper, the *Industrial Worker*, was being published.

Friendly relations were preserved with the anarchists however: the I.W.W. platform in Hyde Park and other places was used by them. Links were close between Aldred, other anarchists, the Industrial League/I.W.W. and groups like the North London Herald League. Henry Sara, for example, was a member of the Industrialist League, then cooperated with Aldred on the *Herald of Revolt* (and also incidentally became for a while Rose Witcop's lover). Aldred spoke often for the Herald League, which included A.B. Elsbury, Beacham and R.M. Fox, all of whom were members of the I.W.W., and the latter two were contributors to Aldred's paper. Elsbury and Fox were at various times editors of the *Industrial Worker*. Fox was active with Ponder in East London in the anti-militarist agitation. An old anarchist associate of Aldred's, Charles Lahr, had a bookshop in Holborn. Fox recalled that "Most of those who clustered round the shop were either members of the I.W.W. or affected by the Syndicalists, industrial unionist, militant labour ideas."[51] I.W.W. members also had lodgings above the shop. It is a further example of a libertarian socialist milieu which effortlessly ignored formal boundaries.

It is not altogether clear what happened to a number of groups that sprang up round Aldred's paper in 1911. A North London Communist Group was the first formed and in February was reported as manning two pitches a week. By May there were three. (One of the speakers was Messer, possibly the same man as the Messer who was a member of the Clyde Workers' Committee in World War One.) Also in May the Hammersmith Socialist Society was advertised — the result of a direct actionist split from the S.D.F. — and the South London Communist Group came into existence.

By October 1911 there were two more groups at East Ham and Manor Park. Yet by mid-1912 there were only two Communist Groups, one in West London and another in Glasgow. Whether the others became merely moribund or, as is more likely, dissolved variously into other anarchist groups, the I.W.W., the Herald League or other groups, is not clear. The reason for their mushroom growth and disappearance is possibly due to Aldred's increasingly widespread propaganda which allowed him less time to concentrate on London. Certainly after mid-1912 he was more or less commuting between Glasgow and West London — the only places where Communist Groups remained in existence.

One other paper is worth notice from the anarchist point of view. This was Jack Tanner's *Solidarity*, which, of course, is significant from other points of view too. Jack Tanner had been involved in the anarchist movement since 1911 when he had become a coordinator of anarchist meetings in London after a meeting in August. He was a regular speaker, and a member for a while of the Marylebone group in 1912 formed out of the anarchist meetings in Regent's Park. He was secretary to the Malatesta Release Committee until Aldred took over. He seems to have become involved in the amalgamation committee movement and in September 1913 *Solidarity* was published as the organ of the Industrial Democracy League, which was a reconstituted form of the Amalgamation Committees Federation. Tanner's precise relationship to the paper at this point is not clear but articles by him appear in the issues which appeared up to June–July 1914. Later on Tanner is more clearly in an editorial role. His anarchist leanings are clear. He quite firmly denounces "the Wage System and the State." Wartime issues of the paper were to include pieces by Stavenhagen, who had written for the *Herald of Revolt*, and reprints of Kropotkin's *Conquest of Bread*. It also included hilarious 'phrenological' studies of prominent labour politicians by the veteran James Tochatti where particular attention was drawn to "bumps of ambition" or "bumps of avarice." Tanner's later activity can be understood more readily if we remember this early training.

## Chapter 15

# WORLD WAR ONE — AND AFTER

When war was declared on 4th August 1914, it came as a surprise. No matter that warning voices had been raised on the danger of war, no matter the direst predictions of the anti-militarists, the fact that a war had started in Europe was a surprise. From our position in history we look back at that bloody waste of life, appalled and wondering. How could people not only allow themselves to be sucked into that war, how could they voluntarily march off into its jaws? Yet in 1914 the only wars that generations had known had been squalid little wars conducted by regular armies in far-flung corners of the world, carving out empires and markets over the bodies of native populations hardly equipped to resist. The exceptions (at the Crimea and the Franco-Prussian War) were many years in the past and had been much less than total wars. The tightening web of alliances arising out of the rival imperialisms of the metropolitan powers had formed almost imperceptibly to the mass of people concerned in their own domestic battles. The speed with which Europe was suddenly at war even surprised the politicians: "We blundered into war," as Lloyd George was to put it. Even *Freedom*, which could be expected to be gloomy in its predictions, talked of "tens of thousands doomed to die" instead of millions. For the raw power of the allies on both sides, in terms of industrial output (in terms of available waste, one might say), was evenly matched. Any major conflict could be guaranteed, outside considerations of brilliant strategic invention, to be long, drawn-out and bloody.

There had been expansive declarations in the international socialist movement of brotherly love and solidarity. It is easy to condemn the comfortably placed socialist politicians, if one is so disposed, for their panic, indecision and final cowardice in the face of their earlier statements that socialist brotherhood could conquer capitalist bloodshed. Yet those statements had been made without any thought as to the context in which such brotherhood would have to operate. They were not brave or

imaginative men for the most part, as they had consistently demonstrated
before this testing time. The majority of them had proved cowards in
small things. Why then expect them to be brave in large ones? Indeed,
the working class, which had taken so much into its own hands in the
years of the Syndicalist Revolt, had already lost if it waited for the 'leaders'
it had so often ignored. *Freedom* had correctly (if glibly) noted in 1910
that the necessity was to convince the workers that if they were "to use
the General Strike *spontaneously* in case of need [it] would do more to
avert the possibilities of capitalistic wars than any one thing we can think
of."[1] The working class of England (not to mention the other countries
involved) showed no signs of taking any such steps. A determined
minority of socialists opposed the war from the beginning — it was, in
fact, an anarchist, W.D. Ponder, who delivered the first recorded anti-war
speech the day after war was declared under the aegis of the North London
Herald League. Yet for the mass of the working class, the atmosphere was
almost one of carnival. As one writer said, "What terrible attraction a war
can have! The wild excitement, the illusion of wonderful adventure and
the actual break in the deadly monotony of working class life! Thousands
went flocking to the colours in the first days, not because of any 'love of
country', not because of any high feeling of 'patriotism', but because of the
new strange and thrilling life that lay before them."[2]

The war was to have a fragmenting effect on the socialist movement
in several ways. Firstly, there was the battle between patriots and anti-
militarists which not only took place between factions but within them.
Then there was the disruptive effect of the government and attendant
patriots, concerned as they were to crush 'pro-German' sentiment. Further,
there were the effects due to the separation between the struggles which
were to develop over conscription and which took place in industry. Yet
in another sense the strains on the socialist movement and the resulting
fragmentation that the war produced were a further lesson in the nature
of the thing that socialism was committed to overthrow. The struggles that
developed against the war itself and within the situation the war produced
were to reintegrate as war weariness grew. This reintegration was given a
strong impetus by the news of the Russian revolutions of February and
October 1917. For the embattled socialists in prison or in the factory this

news brought a great upsurge of hope — if a revolution could take place in a stronghold of reaction what was not possible in the more developed countries of the world? Yet the October Revolution, the Bolshevik revolution, marked the opening of a new era of left revolutionary politics which is only now drawing to a close. The Bolsheviks presented a new organisational concept for revolutionaries. The relationship of the revolutionary party — the Communist Party — to the mass was forthrightly authoritarian and exclusive. The party was to capture control of the organisations from the workers and lead them along the path decided in its centralised decision-making structure. For each country there could only be one Communist Party and since that party represented the only path to revolution, all other tendencies outside the party were not just wrong but *counter-revolutionary*. It is not the purpose of this book to argue the pros and cons of this position. It is abundantly clear, however, that any major success of such a tendency meant severe damage to an anarchist movement, with its pluralism and decentralism. And while the Communist Party remained small in its early years in England, in the face of its succès d'estime the anarchist movement well-nigh withered away.

But let us start at the beginning. Shortly after the outbreak of war the anarchist movement was thrown into turmoil by the chilling news that Kropotkin and a small group round him supported the war against Germany. While the immediate reaction of the vast majority of the British movement was to reject the war and immediate steps were taken to propagandise against it, this sudden change of heart by Kropotkin could do nothing but confuse and damage the movement. Kropotkin had written a series of articles in *Freedom* between May and August 1913 entitled 'Modern Wars and Capitalism'. In this series he demonstrated clearly that the rival market-seeking by the metropolitan states as the agencies of their respective capitalists tended inevitably to encourage military conflict between those states. Yet on the outbreak of war in August he underwent a rapid change of heart. Keell, by now the editor of *Freedom*, described how he met Kropotkin and Marsh "in a noisy Lyons café in Oxford Street."

They were there first and when I arrived, Peter — the old soldier again — was sketching on paper the military situation in France: the Germans he thought would be in Paris in a week. Then we began to discuss the war as Anarchists and I found out at once that Peter and I differed fundamentally. He spoke of German militarism and its barbarity in Belgium, and the duty of the Allies to throw the enemy back over their own frontiers. Marsh was pro-Peter. My arguments cut no ice with them. I pointed out that a victory for the Allies would be a victory for the Tsar and the end of the revolutionary movement in Russia. ... Peter and I discussed what he should write in the next issue of *Freedom*. He evidently thought he could not write a pro-war article in view of my opposition, so we agreed he should do one on Communal Kitchens as he thought there would soon be a food shortage in the country.[3]

This grotesque article appeared in the September issue of *Freedom*. Indeed the communal kitchens that sprang up to distribute food in France after the war was declared in an upsurge of patriotic egalitarianism could be considered examples of mutual aid. But in the context of the time it was equivalent to admiring the smoke plume from a juggernaut which was roaring down on the world. Kropotkin declared himself publicly in the October issue of *Freedom* in an article entitled 'An Open Letter to Professor Steffen'. Gone was all the understanding of a conflict irrelevant to the mass of those who were to be swallowed by it. He wrote, "I consider that the duty of everyone who cherishes the ideals of human progress ... is to do everything in one's power to crush down the invasion of the Germans into Western Europe." He asserted that "Since 1871 Germany has been a standing menace to European progress ... *the territories of both France and Belgium MUST be freed of the invaders.*" His latent francophilia and germanophobia had become rampant. Keell replied in an article entitled 'Have The Leopards Changed Their Spots?' (This referred to the combatant states rather than Kropotkin's immediate circle.) He said, "The more I study the evidence the more certain I am that the growing commercial as well as military power of Germany was a challenge to Britain and the Allied Powers and the supremacy of one or other is the sole point at issue. And the workers are slaughtering each other to decide it. They will gain nothing by this war. Whatever the result may be, they must lose."

The November issue was largely devoted to a symposium on the war, where the pro-war 'anarchists' and the anti-militarists debated the issue.

It also included a forthright letter from a Scottish anarchist, Robert Selkirk, condemning Kropotkin's article. Cherkesov — one of Kropotkin's old friends — was furious and told Keell, "*Freedom* cannot be an open tribune and *Freedom* must stop." Keell went to see Kropotkin in Brighton and there was a strained and partially bitter confrontation between them; Kropotkin was particularly annoyed at Selkirk's letter, where he was called a recruiting sergeant by implication. Keell replied that "he who wills the ends wills the means." Kropotkin more or less asked for Keell's resignation, which Keell refused to give. Kropotkin reasserted Cherkesov's statement that *Freedom* must not be a 'free tribune' and Keell seems to have agreed — but on the side of not admitting pro-war articles. At tea another guest was a wounded British officer on leave. On the mantelpiece were arrayed the flags of the Allies. Keell was glad to get out. He and Kropotkin never met again. Keell, in consultation with a number of anarchists, decided that from now on *Freedom* would be against the war. Whatever criticisms can be made of Keell he showed great courage in standing up to pressure from Kropotkin who had been revered to an almost sickening extent in the anarchist movement. Secular saints have their dangers when dead; alive they are a constant implied menace. Keell was the braver when we remember that he too was a positive worshipper of Kropotkin.

His difficulties were not over, however. He had more or less declared unilateral independence, and his alleged 'seizure' of *Freedom* was the subject of some lobbying — by Turner and Cherkesov, according to Keell. The result was that George Cores went to the next annual conference in Stockport at Easter 1915 armed with a bitter denunciation of Keell. This denied that the matter was anything to do with a pro- or anti-war position but rather a matter of Keel's undemocratic seizure of the paper. Cores had not enjoyed a good relationship with Keell before this time. Correspondence in Amsterdam shows that when Marsh retired from the editorship of *Freedom* in 1912 he was suggesting that Cores and Keell should run the paper jointly. Yet Keell became sole editor at this time, and it is interesting to note that in another context Keell boasts that he was able to stop Cores and other anarchists using the Ossulston Street office as a social meeting place at around that time. Other letters show that Keell had a close group of friends who constituted the new group that produced *Freedom*. So Cores had some justice on his side. But the overriding question at the conference was the war, and Keell's emphasis on the anti-war reasons for his action unanimously won the approval of the anarchists nationally.[4] It cannot be denied that in ignoring this Cores showed something of a pettiness of spirit. But it must be stressed that Cores was not leading a pro-war faction at the conference and his later activities showed it.

Kropotkin's pro-war sentiments did not only shake the Freedom Group. Aldred's paper, now renamed the *Spur*, devoted much space in the autumn and winter of 1914–1915 to detailed rebuttals of Kropotkin's position, some from Aldred, others from Malatesta and Rocker. Yet, in one sense, the fact that so much time could be spent on discussions of pro- or anti-war positions was an indication that the fight had not yet become desperate; it was a time when there was room still to attempt to persuade rather than to grit the teeth and endure. From August 1914 into 1915 there was voluntary recruiting into the army. The Defence of the Realm Act (D.O.R.A. for short) was not introduced until March 1915. This made it an offence, among other things, to try and 'obstruct' recruiting by words or deeds 'likely to disaffect'. The fact that it was introduced at such a relatively late stage is an indication that voluntary recruitment was working. The opposition to the anti-war agitators by patriots was constant and largely spontaneous before this point. Meetings were attacked with monotonous regularity, sometimes platforms were smashed, sometimes the speakers were violently handled. Meetings were banned by the police and free-speech fights were fought.

Yet it was noticeable that the influence of anti-war propaganda was growing. The circulations of anti-war papers like *Freedom* and the *Spur* grew rapidly. The North London Herald League, in which many anarchists and libertarians were involved, was holding meetings in Finsbury Park and had its share of difficulties. But its opposition to the war struck a sympathetic chord. In response to official appeals to the upper class to release servants for army service one of them asked the crowd, "Have you got a sweating employer or a rack-renting landlord you can spare? Let him join up to fight for humanity, for civilisation, for democracy, for the women and children, for all those causes in which he has always been so enthusiastic." Before D.O.R.A. came into being the North London Herald League had grown from 50 to 500 strong.[5] James Tochatti, speaking against the war in Plymouth, was asked what he would do if the country were invaded. He answered that if the people wished to fight then let them and if the government really trusted the people they would be armed. But no, the government wanted the war to be under their control, for their ends which were not the people's ends. He was cheered. Gallagher was to recall a piece of verse pasted up next to every poster in Glasgow with its picture of Kitchener saying 'Your King and Country Need You'. The verse ran:

Your King and Country Need You
Ye hardy sons of toil
But will your King and Country need you
When they're sharing out the spoil?[6]

It was both in response to the growing influence of anti-war propaganda and the beginnings of difficulties over recruitment that led to the passing of D.O.R.A. From this point on there were increasing numbers of arrests and fines and jailings for statements or literature likely to prejudice recruitment. The homes of private individuals were raided and literature seized all over the country. The offices in London and Manchester were raided in the summer of 1915. There was increasing propaganda in the 'respectable' press for conscription. The activities of jingo crowds became more dangerous, and they were being progressively urged on and — it was suspected — paid by the country's 'leaders of opinion'. Conscription was introduced in January 1916. From this point on the struggle took on a new bitterness. Almost immediately arrests were made for refusal to register for conscription. Meetings against conscription were broken up by jingoist crowds at Finsbury Park and by the police in Harlesden where anarchists were active. Henry Sara, Meacham, Cores, to mention but three names, were arrested several times and given short terms of jail or fined. Arrests were being made for private conversations where people made statements 'prejudicial to recruiting'.

Those arrested first for refusal to register were forcibly put in khaki. Henry Sara was arrested on 13th April 1916, savagely beaten, put in khaki, beaten again for refusing to take orders and finally transferred to Parkhurst gaol. He was luckier than the thirty-four conscientious objectors who were arrested, put into khaki, taken to France and there sentenced to death for refusing to obey orders. The sentences were eventually commuted at the last minute. And the game with the conscientious objectors began. They were at first given sentences in prison of some months, then returned to barracks where they would again refuse to take orders. This time they would receive longer sentences. Then the process was repeated, and they would get a further, longer sentence. Many took the option of the 'Home Office scheme'. This was working at jobs not connected with war production, though officially they had accepted induction into the army by accepting such work; Guy Aldred refused to register, appeared before a court in April 1916 and was sent to prison. (Rose Witcop now took up the editorship of the *Spur*.) In August, Aldred decided to take the Home Office scheme and was sent to a granite quarry at Dyce near Aberdeen. Here he continued his anti-war propaganda and became a member of the camp committee with Bonar Thompson. Aldred and Thompson spoke on anti-war platforms after work and at weekends all over Scotland. Aldred also issued two numbers of an anti-war paper from Dyce entitled the *Granite Echo* in October and November. Yet Aldred was haunted by the fact that he was not resisting the war to the fullest extent and in November voluntarily ceased work at Dyce and returned to London where he was arrested and sent back to prison.

Meanwhile *Freedom* and the *Voice of Labour* had been raided and Keell and Lilian Wolfe had gone to prison. The *Voice of Labour*, a monthly since the outbreak of war, in April 1916 printed an article called 'Defying the Act'. This was "written by 'one of those outlawed in the Scottish hills,' claiming that 'a number of comrades from all parts of Great Britain have banded themselves in the Highlands, the better to resist the working of the Military Service Act'. Lilian [Wolfe] later recalled being in bed with influenza when the group met to discuss the article, 'and me, of all people, dissuading them from cutting out part of it, which a few thought a bit too much'. In May the *Voice of Labour* reported the arrest of most of the outlaws, and there is no evidence that there were more than a few people involved for more than a few weeks. But the idea was dangerous."[7] A leaflet was made out of the article, 10,000 were distributed and some were intercepted by the police. As a result the office at Ossulston Street was raided and Tom Keell and

Lilian Wolfe were arrested and charged with distributing a leaflet which would prejudice recruiting. They were both fined, and refusing to pay the fine they were sent to prison, Keell for three months, Lilian Wolfe for two.

As a result of the raid printers refused to print further issues of the papers. Nevertheless the papers were continued. P.S. Meacham, who had been doing the donkey work round the *Freedom* office for some years, describes how this was done.

I went with F. Sellars and A. Mancer to the Freedom Press for nearly four months (April, May, June, July 1916) daily expecting arrest under the 'Military Service Act'. I spent one week, amidst the friendly chaffing of comrades, clearing the printing machine and getting it in order. Comrade Sellars the compositor could find no printers who would machine *Freedom*. He came downstairs looked at the machine, sighed and said we shall do nothing with that. I thought otherwise.

With emery cloth, oil can and spanner I spent from 8am on Monday morning till 6pm on Saturday — one week — I spent doing nothing but turn the handle in half-hour to one-hour shifts to make the machine run smoothly. After one week it did and we were able to defy the attempts of the authorities so that *Freedom* and the *Voice of Labour* were printed whilst Keell was in prison. F. Sellars, A. Mancer and myself. No one helped us those 14 dreary weeks, daily expecting arrest, to bring out *Freedom*. Sellars laid on the paper, I turned the wheel for one-hour spells which Mancer took off. Mancer gave me ten minutes' rest. In this manner the papers were brought out. On July 27th 1916, we printed 4,000 sheets on one side. Cut in half these would have made 8,000 4-page *Freedom* papers. Of these over 7,000 were ordered but alas A. Mancer had a nervous breakdown on the Friday and could not turn up till on the Saturday am. At 9am we were raided and it was a finish as far as we were concerned. Four months — 18 months — 2 year sentences for refusing to become soldiers (the hired assassins of the propertied class) was the fate both of Comrade Sellars and myself — Mancer's case was tragic. We found he had been taking drugs to bony himself up — alas too much did he take — with the result — a nervous collapse. He put on Khaki but the lamp still flickered. He deserted from time to time — walking to London seeking the help of comrades to hide from the military.[8]

In this raid the press was seized. Had it not been for the friendly services of the I.L.P. press *Freedom* would have been stopped. The *Voice of Labour* ceased production after August as result of the raid and the thinning of the ranks by arrests under the Military Service Act. *Freedom*, though it was raided twice more during the war, managed to continue to appear and trenchantly oppose the war.

The movement in the workshops, factories, etc. during World War One has for the most part been the preserve of Bolshevik influenced historians. Even one of the most recent and detailed accounts, Kendall's The *Revolutionary Movement in Britain*, shares not so much a Marxist as a Leninist perspective. The problems raised by this movement still remain unexamined by libertarians, and the massive research groundwork necessary remains undone. Since the purpose of the present book is to consider the specifically anarchist movement such a massive project has not been undertaken. Nevertheless some remarks are in order. There is no doubt that important sections of the wartime movement formed the nucleus round which the Communist Party was formed. That this represented a clean break with their previous anti-electoral, anti-leadership stance is underlined by Kendall. Yet while the movement in wartime was clearly an extension of the pre-war direct-action movement it is still too much regarded as a staging post between the Syndicalist Revolt and Bolshevism. One of the major difficulties for the libertarian historian is that the militant anti-war stance of the anarchist movement as a whole meant that many anarchists were in prison as conscientious objectors and their struggles and treatment were a major concern of the anarchist press. The decentralised development of anarchism in the pre-war years, particularly in South Wales and Durham but in other places too, meant that its activities were overwhelmingly local in orientation. It did not report to the anarchist press with any regularity. Thus its activities are hidden in a welter of local occurrences. We are generally given only tantalising glimpses of anarchist activity. One of the men arrested in Glasgow in February 1916 at the same time as John Maclean was Jack Smith, an engineering worker anarchist associate of Aldred's. The strike committee in the Clyde February 1915 strike met in an anarchist bookshop run by a man named McGill and his wife. They ran a paper and played an active propaganda role with the distribution of libertarian propaganda. Such examples indicate that further research would give positive results.

Yet this research would of necessity have to be a general study of the industrial working-class movement as a whole. This was as taken by surprise by the outbreak of war as any sections of the left. The union leaders reacted variously. In the mining industry they made strenuous efforts to prevent conditions being undermined. In engineering, things were very different. Here the union leaders, in the name of patriotism, threw up all the conditions hard won over decades of struggle. There was no sign of a comparable throwing over of profits. Yet between the outbreak of war and February 1915 prices rose 23 per cent. Whereas a strike by miners was through the union in March 1915 and won a wage rise commensurate with the cost of living, the Clyde strike of February 1915 was against the union as well as the employers. The result of the undermining of the standard of living of the working class and the pusillanimous attitude of the trades union leaders in the engineering industry led to a massive increase of influence of the shop stewards' movement. This was further underlined by the extremely low level of unemployment caused by the wartime shortage of labour. The engineering industry became the storm centre of rank-and-file opposition, first to the effects of the war and progressively to the war itself. Firstly, they fought to preserve some sort of standard of living in the face of soaring profits and prices. Secondly, they fought against the effects of conscription. This took the form of trying to keep as many men as possible exempt from conscription. The fact that skilled men stood the best chance of escaping did lead to an element of craft elitism. Nevertheless a massive strike in Sheffield which began to spread to other centres in November 1916, when an A.S.E. member had been 'illegally' conscripted, was able to force his return from France.

This led to a counter-attack on the part of the state. A strike in Barrow in March 1917 was defeated before support could be organised by the threat of mass arrests. Trade card exemption was withdrawn by the government in April 1917. A small strike over a local example of dilution in Rochdale set off a wave of strikes which spread over many centres in England — though not to Barrow and Scotland — until by mid-May over 200,000 men were on strike. This was fundamentally against the withdrawal of exemption. The government determined on a strong line and at the point where the London stewards were attempting to contact their Glasgow comrades the 'ring leaders' were arrested. Rather than create martyrs, the government threatened them with life imprisonment, and they signed an agreement to abide by a 'yellow dog' arrangement made by A.S.E. officials with the government. The strike wave rather fizzled out. Yet it was evident that discontent was widespread. The seemingly never-ending demand for cannon fodder for the battlefields, the meaningless slaughter, the privations of the home population had all led to increasing war-weariness. On the other hand, there was the astonishing news from Russia. The most reactionary government in Europe had been overthrown by a revolution!

The impact of this event should not be underestimated. Aneurin Bevan was later to recall "the miners when they heard that the Tsarist tyranny had been overthrown, rushing to meet each other in the streets with tears streaming down their cheeks, shaking hands and saying: 'At last it has happened.'"[9] (When the news reached conscientious objectors in the prisons there was great excitement. Almost immediately strikes were organised in Wormwood Scrubs.) A wave of strikes which took place in May 1917 almost certainly owed something to the news of the Russian Revolution for their origins. A Royal Commission on Industrial Unrest in June and July showed that discontent in the country was at a very high level. In South Wales, for example: "The influence of the 'advanced' men is growing very rapidly and there is grounds for belief that under their leadership attempts of a drastic character will be made by the working classes as a whole to secure direct control by themselves of their particular industries."[10] A convention was called in Leeds in June 1917 to discuss the setting up of workers' and soldiers' councils. Though little came of it, it is worth mentioning because in the speeches of such unlikely Bolsheviks as Ramsay MacDonald we can clearly see the stirring of revolutionary ideals in the previously most moderate of the delegates as a result of the news from Russia.

As the war ground towards a conclusion the threads of war-weariness, revolutionary pacifism, industrial unrest, mutinous rumblings in the army and navy and the promise of the Russian Revolution began to come together. They were never to be fully integrated; the unrest was decentralised though massive; but there was an increasing sense of the connections between these phenomena. In 1918, the last year of the war, over 1,100 disputes were recorded, costing nearly six million man days. (Among the strikers were the London police.) Open mutiny was reported among British troops in France and the last loads of conscripts for France had to be under armed guard to prevent desertions. All the anti-parliamentary, direct-action sects were growing in numbers and influence and others were forming.

In 1919, with the peace, this simmering unrest boiled over. Nearly 35 million man days were lost in disputes in which 21 million workers were involved. Mutinies to accelerate demobilisation were a regular occurrence. The loyalty of troops returning from France was so low that it was considered impossible to rely on them should civil disorder break out. The conscientious objectors in several prisons were completely out of control. After cell wreckings and hunger strikes they were released, at first on parole and then unconditionally. Revolutionary sentiments were widespread. Basil Thompson, the Special Branch man in charge of surveillance of domestic unrest, writes of February 1919 when a large 'Hands Off Russia' meeting took place: "There was a large strike on the Clyde at the moment, and many of the speakers really believed that it was the beginning of the General Strike which was to merge into Revolution. At that moment we were probably nearer to very serious disturbances than we have been at any time since the Bristol Riots of 1831."[11]

That there was no revolution at this time can be put down to several factors. Revolutions are seldom consciously planned, they *happen*. And usually the spark that sets them off is some crass act of oppression or an attempt at it by the authorities. The mood of the people in 1919 was bellicose. Yet while the atmosphere was thick with talk of revolution, the strikes and the mutinies were overwhelmingly for immediate demands that could be settled. As long as no general confrontation was allowed to develop from which neither side could withdraw, the government was safe. The government, furthermore, could rely on the majority of members of trades union and Labour Party hierarchies to accept piecemeal settlements. The authorities played this most difficult situation with consummate skill, delaying, testing out the opposition, withdrawing from negotiations, reopening them, arresting people here, buying them off there. The revolutionaries, on the other hand, though they saw with varying degrees of clarity the revolutionary potential of the activity around them, and saw in Russia an example of what was possible, were nevertheless only able to articulate general aspirations rather than concrete methods. In any case most of them were too busy "making a strike when we should have been making a revolution" as Gallagher was later to remark. One result was that the spirit of revolt ran down the plughole of electioneering. In the autumn of 1919 the municipal elections gave Labour a series of sweeping victories which were to be the foundation for the parliamentary victories of 1923 which confirmed the Labour Party as the new Opposition. By 1924 the first ever Labour government was coming into office. The situation had slipped from near-revolution to Ramsay MacDonald in five years.

It can also be argued that the Russian example, initially so inspiring, was to prove more of a hindrance than a help in the crucial three-year period at the end of the war. Hard news from Russia was rather difficult to come by in the years between 1917 and 1919. The newspapers of the time, particularly those of a more epileptically right-wing tendency, were full of stories describing the random slaughter of foreigners, the plots of the Elders of Zion, the nationalisation of women and so forth. The October (Bolshevik) Revolution was reported initially as anarchist. It is not surprising then that a certain confusion reigned on the left as to the differences between, for example, the soviets (the spontaneously formed people's councils) and the Bolshevik Party, which had captured some of the more important ones and on whose behalf it claimed to speak. Though the left could easily unite to oppose intervention by Britain to obstruct the Revolution, an opposition shared by many soldiers and sailors itching for either insurrection or demobilisation, the nature of the Revolution itself remained something of a mystery. *Freedom* remarked that "Our great difficulty nowadays is the lack of information about the working men and women of Russia. Even in Bolshevik Russia there are 80 million ... besides Lenin and Trotsky, and we want to know how they are using their new-won freedom."[12] It was to take some time to prove just how cruelly untrue were, for example, Jack Tanner's words when he asserted of the Bolsheviks in early 1919: "The common ownership of the land is part of their programme, hence they derive full support from the peasants. ... Industry is also controlled by committees of workmen who receive the products of their labour ... one of the best features of the Bolsheviks is their plan of 'decentralisation' which in essence is a form of 'local autonomy'."[13] This, at a time when the labour force on the Russian railways had been put under what amounted to army discipline, one-man management was being introduced into the factories, peasant insurrections were widespread and the Bolshevik policy of War Communism called for the strictest control from the centre!

The anti-parliamentary, direct-action-oriented left, including the anarchists, were tending to see in the Russian Revolution the consummation of their own hopes in the absence of solid information. Some anarchists, perhaps the more abstractly sectarian of them, were asserting that the Bolsheviks were a government and as such were no better than any other government. Some information on Bolshevik anti-anarchist activities was beginning to emerge in mid-1919 (though the first attacks had been made over a year before). But the bulk of the movement, including most of the activists, took a lot more convincing. And that is not hard to understand; with the class war raging around their ears and with so many lies being told about Russia, they were most unwilling to denounce a revolution that their dreams clung to. In reply to an anti-Bolshevik letter from an Austrian anarchist, Guy Aldred, for example, wrote in his paper:

I understand comrade Grossman is opposed to Bolshevism whereas I am definitely Bolshevik. Grossman contends that the dictatorship of the proletariat is unnecessary. I suggest to him that it is inevitable. ... My comrade fears that, even under a Soviet administration, a fight must take place between intellectual and manual upstarts for power and bureaucratic posts. ... This would be a serious objection, if the dictatorship did not work for its own overthrow and by destroying property society, make directly for the day when the control of persons shall give way to the administration of things.

Aldred even went so far as to say that "those Anarchists who oppose the dictatorship as a transitional measure are getting dangerously close to supporting the cause of the reactionaries. ... If abstract Anarchism is opposed to the social revolution ... it must be repudiated by every soldier of the red flag."[14]

He was to re-emphasise this point in the issue of the following month (October). As if to stress where the attention of many anarchists was being directed he also wrote: "At the present moment the entire revolutionary movement is drawing closer and closer together on a platform of practical revolutionary effort. The Workers' Socialist Federation, the Socialist Labour Party and the Communist League, including a large section of the Anarchist movement, are seeking some organised and disciplined means of expressing their Communist convictions and Bolshevik aims." At the same time he was calling for a "disciplined boycott of the ballot box."[15] But in December an article by Grossman was published in Aldred's paper which spelled out anarchist objections to the Bolshevik regime, noting its suppression of the anarchists, its arbitrary authoritarianism, its government by decree, etc. Significantly, the article went unanswered. By August 1920, Aldred's commitment to Bolshevism began to waver. He began to qualify his use of the phrase 'dictatorship of the proletariat', making it clear that he meant by it only the actions of the proletariat necessary to defend their revolution. Moves towards communist unity were being made by the central cliques of various groups, and this Aldred criticised on the grounds that unity should be made at the grass roots and any other process could only contradict the principles of local autonomy and mandated delegates. He qualified his use of 'discipline', asserting that for him it meant only the right of people in revolutionary groups to expect all their members to work hard and to exclude those who did not: centralism was not implied. Aldred, it would seem, was not a proper Bolshevik at all.

Yet the major question was to become that of electoral activity. This has been described as 'only' a tactical question. Yet the British socialist movement, if it had a tradition at all, had one of being low on general philosophy but intensely concerned with day-to-day tactics. These were a matter of principled commitment. In British socialist politics it was a change of tactics that by implication forced a change in general political commitment rather than the other way round. And of these tactical considerations, electoral activity had marked, by implication, the boundary that separated reformists from revolutionaries. This had been asserted by the Socialist League and confirmed by the career of the S.D.F. It had been reaffirmed by the syndicalist rebels in the face of the Labour Party's career after 1906. For revolutionaries in Britain anti-parliamentarianism was an article of faith. It is with this in mind that we should consider the shock wave that passed through the revolutionary groups when the Third International, founded in 1919, announced that all member-parties should take part in elections and when Lenin underlined this in his *Left-Wing Communism: An Infantile Disorder* and insisted furthermore that any English Communist Party should affiliate with the Labour Party. This was the cause of much resentful debate among British would-be Communist Party members with the Moscow seal of approval. Sylvia Pankhurst crossed swords with Lenin in her *Workers' Dreadnought*. Aldred denounced what he called Lenin's fatal compromise.[16] At the Second Congress of the Third International in Moscow in August 1920, Gallagher pleaded with the delegates not to force upon the Scottish revolutionaries parliamentary "resolutions which they are not in a position to defend, being contradictory to all they have been standing for until now."[17] Tanner told the congress: "Most of the active men [in the shop stewards' movement] have been members of the political socialist parties but have left them because they were not travelling along the right road."[18] Nevertheless, in the face of Bolshevik insistence and prestige, the congress unanimously endorsed the Russian position. Indeed some delegates, like Gallagher for example, seem to have come back completely brainwashed.

For those libertarians who were incapable of swallowing electoral politics the progress of the unity negotiations in 1920 did not encourage participation. The involvement of the B.S.P. was an insult as far as they were concerned, tainted as it was, in their opinion, with opportunism and elections. The hole-and-corner politicking that was going on, with Russian money to ease any change of principles; the strange bed fellows that this began to attract all this left a bad taste in the mouth. Rose Witcop commented in a bitter article, designed in part as an answer to a correspondent who inquired why Aldred was not playing a prominent part in unity negotiations: "The pioneers of Communism in this country who stood for the 'Coming Social Revolution' and understood what they meant while these eleventh hour converts were urging municipal pawnshops, have struggled against parliamentarianism for years." But now "you may be a communist and believe in all the exploded Social Democrat theories; the chief thing, indeed the only thing, is that you must belong to the Communist

Party. Instead of asking why Aldred's name is not included in the list of Communist Party leaders, our comrade should have asked why the names of Arthur Henderson and Mrs Snowdon were omitted."[19] (The latter two were prominent right-wing Labour Party hacks.) By January 1921, Aldred and the groups connected with him were firmly against affiliation to the Third International. Yet the desperate seriousness with which the problem had been considered was significant. It was now clear that the Russian Revolution had become a central concern of the revolutionary left and that now it was impossible to get on with the matters in hand without continuous glances over the shoulder at the Russian example. It marked the beginning of a change in the terms of left-wing politics which in the end could only be destructive of libertarianism. And perhaps not only of libertarianism. The Communist Party formed at the end of 1920 was still, in form, representative of the English left-wing tradition. It was rapidly to be Bolshevised; with strict centralism enforced by 1923. But already the disputes and bad feeling which its formation had given rise to had had their effect. An industrial correspondent of the *Times* was to remark with some satisfaction in 1921: "It is not too much to say that Bolshevism, has become a source of weakness rather than strength in the revolutionary movement. And not in this country only. Everywhere it has been a source of embittered discord and rather a hammer to break up rather than a cement to unite."[20]

The number of groups who remained outside the Communist Party and the level of their activity has been, perhaps, underestimated. (After all, it had been claimed that 20,000 people were represented in unity negotiations, while in 1921 the party only had a membership of between three and five thousand.) But the prestige of the Russian Revolution was not with them and this, taken together with a lack of subsidy and sudden changes in the economic and political situation, was to make their work well nigh impossible. For the post-war boom collapsed suddenly. By the end of 1920 there were three quarters of a million people unemployed; by June 1921, two million. By the end of 1921, wage cuts had been forced on six million workers. There were defensive strikes, bitterly fought. But the mood had changed; people who in 1919 had been shouting for revolution were now looking for work. The unemployed, it is true, rapidly became a problem to the authorities through their turbulence but they had no economic pressure to bring like strikers have. In the atmosphere of gnawing anxiety that any slump induces, no matter how much it is mixed up with anger and bitterness, the authorities felt confident enough to suddenly move against the 'dangerous agitators'. The authorities had been badly frightened in the summer of 1920. The Russian successes in their war against interventionist Poland had brought about the threat of war on the Russians from the British government. In an almost reflex action the whole of the labour movement had responded to the threat of war with the threat of a general strike. It was this threat as much as the subsequent reverses of the Russian fortunes that ensured that war was not declared. The slump gave the government its chance to take its revenge — or to "crack down on subversive elements" if that version is preferred. In 1921 over 100 'communists' were arrested and jailed for variations on the theme of sedition. One of them was Guy Aldred. He and Rose Witcop had run the *Spur* (the successor to the *Herald of Revolt*) as individuals, and the Glasgow Communist Group had decided that a 'party' organ was required. This duly appeared as the *Red Commune* in February 1921. Aldred and three others were arrested and charged with sedition for its declarations in favour of the "destruction of Parliamentary government and the substitution of the Soviet or revolutionary workers' system of administration." Aldred was kept in prison for four months awaiting trial and was eventually sentenced to a year in prison. His companions were jailed for three months. The *Red Commune* and the *Spur* never reappeared.

Where the government repression could not do the job the economic depression was more effective. Revolutionary morale dropped catastrophically. Willie Gallagher was later to say that whereas in 1918 100,000 people had marched on May Day in Glasgow, in 1924 only 100 could be mustered. The effect of this on the revolutionary left outside the Communist Party was predictable. The *Workers' Dreadnought*, for example, which survived the repression and the jailing of Sylvia Pankhurst, quietly folded in 1924 — interestingly enough on a progressively anarchist note.

During the post-war period we have described the 'official' anarchist movement round *Freedom* proceeded along well-worn grooves. *Freedom* remained more or less disconnected from events, but anarchists continued to speak on street corners and take part in the activities around them. The attraction of Russia was strong, particularly when the Revolution was viewed as Soviet rather than Bolshevik. An unwillingness to play into the hands of reactionaries also led them to stifle criticism. Even when overwhelming evidence became available that the Bolsheviks were systematically persecuting all their political opponents it was nevertheless possible for John Turner to go on a T.U.C. delegation to Russia and, despite private doubts, sign the report which represented a glowing advertisement for the Bolshevik regime. Not that the anarchist movement was ineffective; it still found an audience. One activist was to write:

> When we resumed in 1919 and had opposition from paid speakers ... I was surprised to find that our propaganda previous to the war and during same till April '16 had been so effective. The questions put by sympathisers made these meetings ineffective, so much so that we did not refer to the opposition when speaking. Locally our groups meet indoors at different comrades' houses, some weekly, some fortnightly, some monthly. ... I always find the Communist Party attacking the Anarchist Communist ideas in various parts of London. At our meetings it is only 1 in 10 times that the audience can stand on the pavement. Every year, regular as clockwork we get agents provocateurs trying to break up our meetings and trap us 'into making statements liable to lead to arrest'.[21]

Yet the optimism of this account (written in 1928) must be compared with the account Emma Goldman gives. She arrived in England from Russia in 1924 with the intention of rousing protests against the Bolshevik persecution of anarchists — which she had seen at first hand. A small committee of people grouped round *Freedom* attempted, on her initiative, to publicise the situation but with little success. Perhaps she concentrated too much on 'prominent personalities'; perhaps her *Freedom* associates were not closely enough attached to the movement at large; yet she convincingly portrays the anti-Anti-Bolshevik mood of the times. One socialist told her: "It would spell political disaster to my party to declare to its constituents that the Bolsheviks had slain the Revolution." Of the British anarchist movement she says: "The older rebels were disillusioned by the collapse of the Revolution. The younger generation, as far as it was interested in ideas (which was little enough) was carried away by the Bolshevik glamour."[22] Meetings organised by her committee met with little response. "Not even in my pioneer days in the United States," she said, "had I found it so bitter to break new ground as I did in this venture."[23]

The collapse of anarchist self-confidence in the 1920s was as rapid as it had been in the mid-1890s. By 1924 the movement was in deep depression and disarray. By the time of the General Strike of 1926 the movement was so fragmented that anarchists were only able to take part in that struggle on an individual basis. The General Strike represented the last resurgence of the spirit of 1910–1920; as if from slumber people organised themselves and that organisation was still developing when the trades union leaders called off the strike after a little more than a week. Indeed one reason for the calling off of the strike was that the trades union leaders saw their grip on the situation slipping. That their grip had not completely slipped is illustrated by the way the order to return to work was obeyed. But the defeat of the General Strike had catastrophic consequences for anarchism. "The unions were beaten. Syndicalism — 'direct action' — were dead for a generation and more."[24] And the spirit which the popular commitment to direct action as a general principle represented was the essential element which the anarchist movement needed to sustain it. In 1927, it appeared to contemporaries, anarchism was dead. As if to mark its passing *Freedom* ceased publication.

This caused a great flurry in the chicken coop — though the word 'chicken' is perhaps inadvisable, since most of the participants were ageing veterans. Keell, who had edited the paper up to this point, wanted to remove to Whiteway colony, taking the pamphlets of the movement with him and continuing to keep in postal contact with the movement. *Freedom*, he declared, had to be closed down due to lack of support. A group of veterans which included George Cores, Ambrose Barker and John Turner (people who had been anarchists, be it noted, from the time of the Socialist League) demanded the right to take over the paper and were prepared, they said, to pay the debts involved. Keell said that "For many years these people have never come near us to help and have never lifted a finger, let alone their voice in Anarchist propaganda. ... We have a right and we shall exercise that right to decide where Freedom Press literature shall be housed."[25] His enemies replied in turn that Keell had made it impossible for any of them to work with him, that he had made *Freedom* his own family affair. They further alleged that Keell was now due for retirement but could only draw his pension from the Society of Compositors if he no longer worked at his trade. He was being dog in the manger about the whole affair, they said, if he could not run *Freedom* then he was not going to let anybody else do it. All the mutual recriminations of 1914–1915 when Keell had allegedly 'seized' *Freedom* were revived. Nevertheless *Freedom* did close down and Keell retired to Whiteway taking the pamphlets with him. From 1928 to 1932 he issued an occasional *Freedom Bulletin* from Whiteway. The veterans were only able to restart *Freedom* in 1930. It was to continue until 1933, though only against great odds which, for example, caused it to reduce its size in 1932. It is a curiously depressing paper with memories of the old days interspersed with obituaries.

In holes and corners the anarchist movement survived. There were occasional street-corner speakers — my friend George Cummings remembered George Frost speaking on 'Penniless Hill' in Hunslet, Leeds.

Albert Meltzer, who came into the movement in the mid-1930s, was to come across the last remnants of the once powerful Welsh miners' anarchist movement. He mentions Jim Colton — who married Emma Goldman to give her British citizenship — once one of a number of "popular Welsh and English speakers [who] were ostracised, thrown out of their jobs and had to fight grimly to keep their place in the Union — because they opposed the dictatorship in Russia." He describes how he went in 1938 "to speak at a local I.L.P. meeting on Spain in a Welsh valley. 'Take care of those at the back,' whispered the chairman. 'Those are the Wrecking Brigade.' They were a group of Welsh-speaking women who took great pleasure in 'giving hell' to the Labour and C.P. speakers — especially with 'toffee-nosed' English accents. But to their, and my, delight we proved to be fellow-Anarchists. The 'Last of the Mohicans' in the valley were four women, and two elderly miners."[26] Albert Meltzer told me that when he became an anarchist he was the only young person in an old people's movement. It is on this rather depressing note that this history closes.

## Chapter 16

# IN CONCLUSION:
# CONTINUITY AND CHANGE
# IN THE ANARCHIST MOVEMENT

The anarchist movement did not cease circa 1930. Anarchism was to enjoy something of a resurgence in the later 1930s, largely inspired by the activity of the anarchists in Spain during the Civil War and Revolution of 1936–1939. The younger militants of that time, or at least some of them, are still active in the movement, and the events of that time and the years since then are still live issues and matters of polemic. (It would be a brave historian who tried to argue too much with the living, particularly since the tone of voice of history is one which implies that the events it describes are past and done with. My comrades would not relish that.) The anarchists have since shown the same astonishing ability to suddenly come from nowhere when everybody had assumed that they were finished with as they did in the years before World War One, though perhaps on a smaller scale. The movement of the 1930s and 1940s died away. A new movement emerged out of Campaign for Nuclear Disarmament (C.N.D.) and the Committee of 100 and too dispersed. The student movement of the late 1960s again showed strong libertarian proclivities. And that too seems to have largely disappeared. I do not propose to talk about these movements in this book for the same reason that I do not want to talk about the movement of the late 1930s. A bare mention, however, is sufficient to bear out the general thesis that has emerged throughout the book that the anarchist movement grows in times of popular self-activity, feeds it and feeds off it, and declines when that self-activity declines.

The anarchists have preached direct action, spontaneity and self-activity and evidently grow on what they preach. But they have also been consistent utopians. By that I mean that they have placed the possible forms of a non-authoritarian society at the forefront of their propaganda, desperately concerned to demonstrate their practicality. In times of popular self-activity they seem to be able to convince people. This combination of utopian aspiration and immediate tactical creativeness seems to be distinctively anarchist. Up to now, however, we have stressed the positive aspect, the moments of upsurge and self-confidence. What of the periods in between, the periods of depression and even despair? Periods like 1896–1909 or 1921–1936 seem to have been able to wipe out, almost without trace, movements that two years before looked healthy and even indestructible. So much of the movement seems to have depended on the mood of the moment, on action in the receptive here and now, that when the mood changed the movement collapsed like a house of cards. Of course a few die hards keep up a propaganda; of course people drift off into issue politics, and revolutionary energy is applied to reformist ends. But for the most part the wider sense of possibility is lost. This is a conclusion drawn as much from my own experience of the movement in recent years as it is from my work on the movement historically.

Quite often the lack of *organisation* is blamed by anarchists and others for the anarchist failure to survive beyond periods of great excitement. It is quite true that the more hierarchical political groups and parties have a higher survival rate in times of depression, which has been the subject of some anarchist jealousy. (It is worth pointing out, however, that their ability to level off the troughs means that they level off the peaks too: in periods of intense activity they often act as a brake on events.) Yet when this jealousy in its extreme form inspires anarchists, most un-anarchistically, to form some kind of party structure (as has happened) the result has always been failure. For 'organisation' in itself is not an answer: the differences between hierarchical groups on the left with their 'successes' and anarchist groups with their 'failures' is not just a question of hierarchy. Organisations do not exist for the sake of it, they exist to *do* something. The party structures of the authoritarian left are rehearsals for their version of the future, they are governments in preparation. For the authoritarian left, day-to-day activity and the hoped-for future are linked in the actual form of the party. Their strategic aim is the growth in size and influence of the party, an aim quite consistent with their eventual goal of seizing power. For anarchists such a logic of development is the grossest contradiction.

As we have seen, the anarchists in England have paid for the gap between their day-to-day activities and their utopian aspirations. This gap consists basically of a lack of strategy, a lack of sense of how various activities fit together to form a whole, a lack of ability to assess a general situation and initiate a general project which is consistent with the anarchist utopia, and which is not only consistent with anarchist tactics but inspires them. Such general anarchist projects have existed, perhaps the best examples being the anarcho-syndicalist trades unions of Spain and France. Leaving aside questions that have been raised as to bureaucratic developments within them, it is clear that daily bread and butter questions were solved with tactics derived from anarchist politics. Their organisational structures were decentralised, encouraging local initiative, yet coordinated on a national scale.

The anarchist movement in England has shown itself capable of a progression of initiatives taken according to circumstance. Take, for example, the beginnings of the squatters' movement in London. Here a group of anarchists, after a campaign over conditions in a hostel for the homeless, cast around for a solution for these people's housing problem. A campaign was started which first demonstrated against long-term empty housing, progressed to symbolic occupations of empty property and finally moved homeless families into houses. They then fought the local Borough Council to a standstill. This, unfortunately, was as far as advanced thinking seems to have gone, because splits developed as to whether confrontation or cooperation with local councils was the better policy. Nevertheless their campaign was directly responsible for inspiring large numbers of homeless or badly housed people to do likewise to the tune of some 20,000 properties in London alone. For all that, the squatters' movement as a whole is without a strategy for the future and will degenerate unless some serious thought — and action — is taken. Another significant step has been taken in the shape of projects designed to 'serve the struggle' (if Chairman Mao is not too out of place here). Here the development of printing facilities, local newspapers, meeting room facilities, information services, etc. are seen as part of a coherent whole which expedites local struggles without attempting to control them.

Yet this kind of activity has not developed beyond such linked tactics. They are an advance upon sporadic one-off actions, but they do not begin to develop a wider strategy and rely too much on the vulnerable activity of a few people. Meanwhile the mass of the people work at boring, frustrating jobs, producing shoddy and often useless things. They live in inhuman housing in an increasingly alienated environment. The decisions that control their lives are made by an elite without consultation or control, except of the most symbolic kind. And it is only when anarchist strategies develop that move from pin prick defiance and piecemeal defence to confront and change all this that the anarchist movement will make history instead of being dependent on it. The ebb and flow of self-activity will ensure that the anarchists are among those "ye have always with you, both in sickness and in health." But only if the British anarchist movement goes beyond the involvement with the immediate it has been so good at will it escape the fate its history seems to have determined for it.

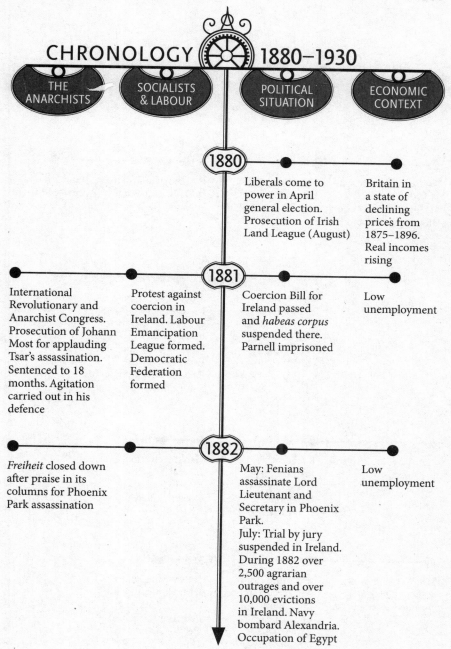

CHRONOLOGY 1880–1930

THE ANARCHISTS

SOCIALISTS & LABOUR

POLITICAL SITUATION

ECONOMIC CONTEXT

**1880**

Liberals come to power in April general election. Prosecution of Irish Land League (August)

Britain in a state of declining prices from 1875–1896. Real incomes rising

**1881**

International Revolutionary and Anarchist Congress. Prosecution of Johann Most for applauding Tsar's assassination. Sentenced to 18 months. Agitation carried out in his defence

Protest against coercion in Ireland. Labour Emancipation League formed. Democratic Federation formed

Coercion Bill for Ireland passed and *habeas corpus* suspended there. Parnell imprisoned

Low unemployment

**1882**

*Freiheit* closed down after praise in its columns for Phoenix Park assassination

May: Fenians assassinate Lord Lieutenant and Secretary in Phoenix Park.
July: Trial by jury suspended in Ireland. During 1882 over 2,500 agrarian outrages and over 10,000 evictions in Ireland. Navy bombard Alexandria. Occupation of Egypt

Low unemployment

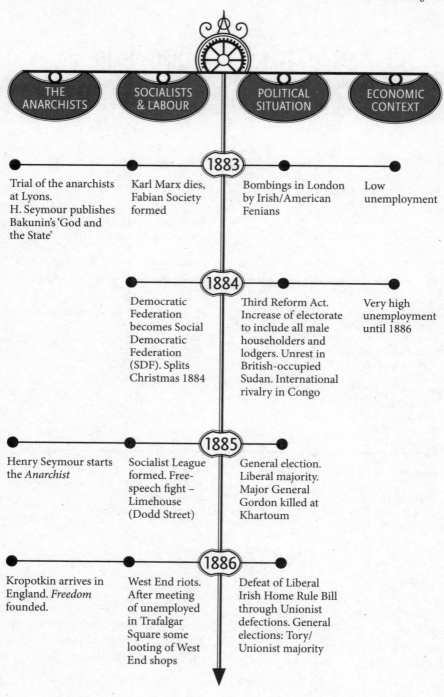

### THE ANARCHISTS | SOCIALISTS & LABOUR | POLITICAL SITUATION | ECONOMIC CONTEXT

**1883**

Trial of the anarchists at Lyons.
H. Seymour publishes Bakunin's 'God and the State'

Karl Marx dies, Fabian Society formed

Bombings in London by Irish/American Fenians

Low unemployment

**1884**

Democratic Federation becomes Social Democratic Federation (SDF). Splits Christmas 1884

Third Reform Act. Increase of electorate to include all male householders and lodgers. Unrest in British-occupied Sudan. International rivalry in Congo

Very high unemployment until 1886

**1885**

Henry Seymour starts the *Anarchist*

Socialist League formed. Free-speech fight – Limehouse (Dodd Street)

General election. Liberal majority. Major General Gordon killed at Khartoum

**1886**

Kropotkin arrives in England. *Freedom* founded.

West End riots. After meeting of unemployed in Trafalgar Square some looting of West End shops

Defeat of Liberal Irish Home Rule Bill through Unionist defections. General elections: Tory/Unionist majority

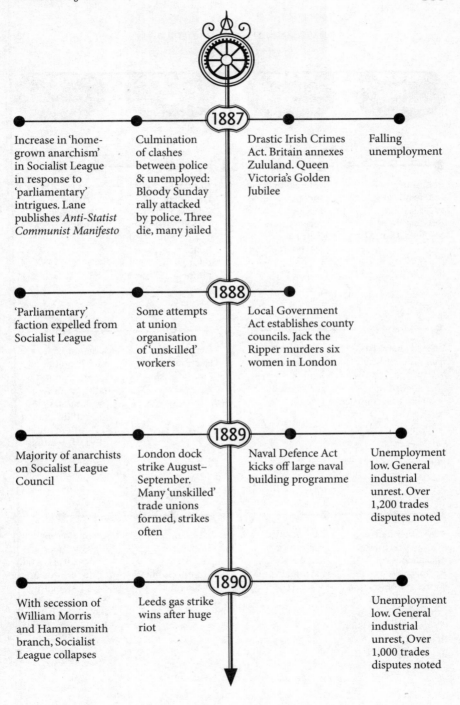

**1887**

Increase in 'home-grown anarchism' in Socialist League in response to 'parliamentary' intrigues. Lane publishes *Anti-Statist Communist Manifesto*

Culmination of clashes between police & unemployed: Bloody Sunday rally attacked by police. Three die, many jailed

Drastic Irish Crimes Act. Britain annexes Zululand. Queen Victoria's Golden Jubilee

Falling unemployment

**1888**

'Parliamentary' faction expelled from Socialist League

Some attempts at union organisation of 'unskilled' workers

Local Government Act establishes county councils. Jack the Ripper murders six women in London

**1889**

Majority of anarchists on Socialist League Council

London dock strike August–September. Many 'unskilled' trade unions formed, strikes often

Naval Defence Act kicks off large naval building programme

Unemployment low. General industrial unrest. Over 1,200 trades disputes noted

**1890**

With secession of William Morris and Hammersmith branch, Socialist League collapses

Leeds gas strike wins after huge riot

Unemployment low. General industrial unrest, Over 1,000 trades disputes noted

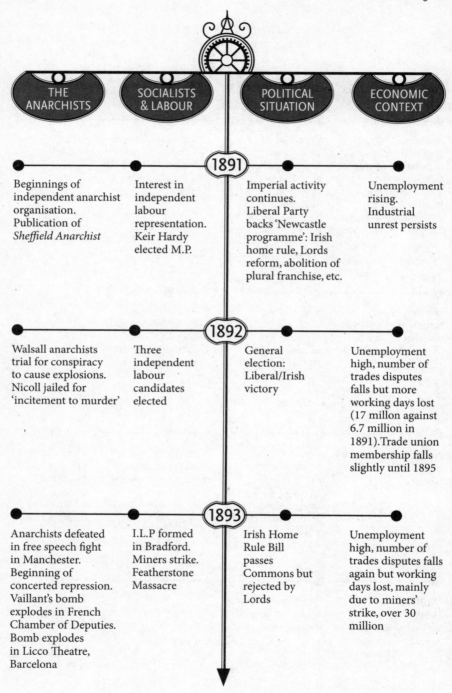

**THE ANARCHISTS** | **SOCIALISTS & LABOUR** | **POLITICAL SITUATION** | **ECONOMIC CONTEXT**

**1891**

| | | | |
|---|---|---|---|
| Beginnings of independent anarchist organisation. Publication of *Sheffield Anarchist* | Interest in independent labour representation. Keir Hardy elected M.P. | Imperial activity continues. Liberal Party backs 'Newcastle programme': Irish home rule, Lords reform, abolition of plural franchise, etc. | Unemployment rising. Industrial unrest persists |

**1892**

| | | | |
|---|---|---|---|
| Walsall anarchists trial for conspiracy to cause explosions. Nicoll jailed for 'incitement to murder' | Three independent labour candidates elected | General election: Liberal/Irish victory | Unemployment high, number of trades disputes falls but more working days lost (17 millon against 6.7 million in 1891). Trade union membership falls slightly until 1895 |

**1893**

| | | | |
|---|---|---|---|
| Anarchists defeated in free speech fight in Manchester. Beginning of concerted repression. Vaillant's bomb explodes in French Chamber of Deputies. Bomb explodes in Licco Theatre, Barcelona | I.L.P formed in Bradford. Miners strike. Featherstone Massacre | Irish Home Rule Bill passes Commons but rejected by Lords | Unemployment high, number of trades disputes falls again but working days lost, mainly due to miners' strike, over 30 million |

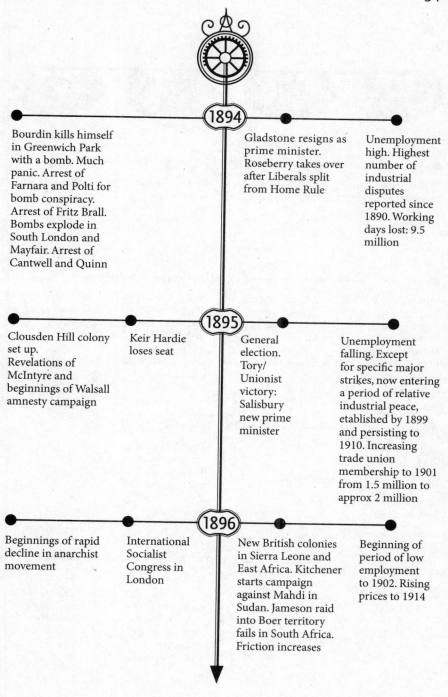

**1894**

Bourdin kills himself in Greenwich Park with a bomb. Much panic. Arrest of Farnara and Polti for bomb conspiracy. Arrest of Fritz Brall. Bombs explode in South London and Mayfair. Arrest of Cantwell and Quinn

Gladstone resigns as prime minister. Roseberry takes over after Liberals split from Home Rule

Unemployment high. Highest number of industrial disputes reported since 1890. Working days lost: 9.5 million

**1895**

Clousden Hill colony set up. Revelations of McIntyre and beginnings of Walsall amnesty campaign

Keir Hardie loses seat

General election. Tory/ Unionist victory: Salisbury new prime minister

Unemployment falling. Except for specific major strikes, now entering a period of relative industrial peace, etablished by 1899 and persisting to 1910. Increasing trade union membership to 1901 from 1.5 million to approx 2 million

**1896**

Beginnings of rapid decline in anarchist movement

International Socialist Congress in London

New British colonies in Sierra Leone and East Africa. Kitchener starts campaign against Mahdi in Sudan. Jameson raid into Boer territory fails in South Africa. Friction increases

Beginning of period of low employment to 1902. Rising prices to 1914

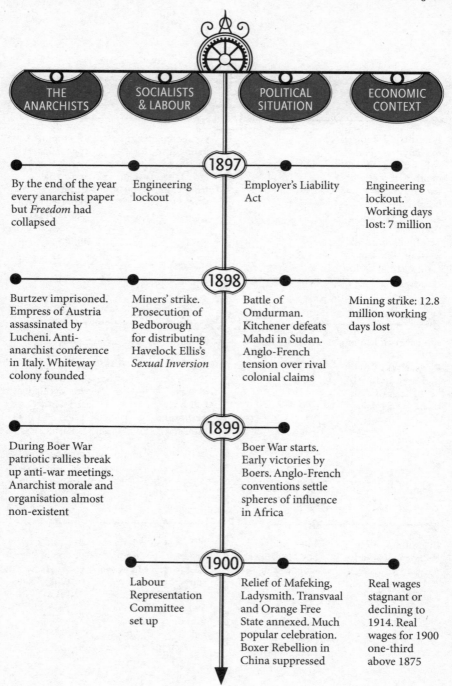

THE ANARCHISTS | SOCIALISTS & LABOUR | POLITICAL SITUATION | ECONOMIC CONTEXT

**1897**

By the end of the year every anarchist paper but *Freedom* had collapsed

Engineering lockout

Employer's Liability Act

Engineering lockout. Working days lost: 7 million

**1898**

Burtzev imprisoned. Empress of Austria assassinated by Lucheni. Anti-anarchist conference in Italy. Whiteway colony founded

Miners' strike. Prosecution of Bedborough for distributing Havelock Ellis's *Sexual Inversion*

Battle of Omdurman. Kitchener defeats Mahdi in Sudan. Anglo-French tension over rival colonial claims

Mining strike: 12.8 million working days lost

**1899**

During Boer War patriotic rallies break up anti-war meetings. Anarchist morale and organisation almost non-existent

Boer War starts. Early victories by Boers. Anglo-French conventions settle spheres of influence in Africa

**1900**

Labour Representation Committee set up

Relief of Mafeking, Ladysmith. Transvaal and Orange Free State annexed. Much popular celebration. Boxer Rebellion in China suppressed

Real wages stagnant or declining to 1914. Real wages for 1900 one-third above 1875

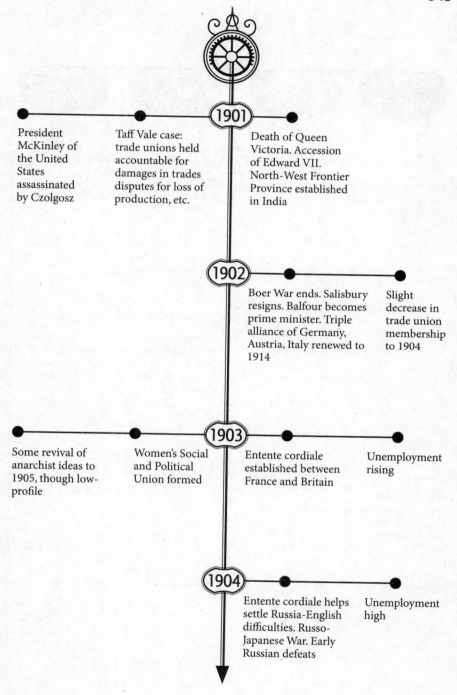

**1901**

President McKinley of the United States assassinated by Czolgosz

Taff Vale case: trade unions held accountable for damages in trades disputes for loss of production, etc.

Death of Queen Victoria. Accession of Edward VII. North-West Frontier Province established in India

**1902**

Boer War ends. Salisbury resigns. Balfour becomes prime minister. Triple alliance of Germany, Austria, Italy renewed to 1914

Slight decrease in trade union membership to 1904

**1903**

Some revival of anarchist ideas to 1905, though low-profile

Women's Social and Political Union formed

Entente cordiale established between France and Britain

Unemployment rising

**1904**

Entente cordiale helps settle Russia-English difficulties. Russo-Japanese War. Early Russian defeats

Unemployment high

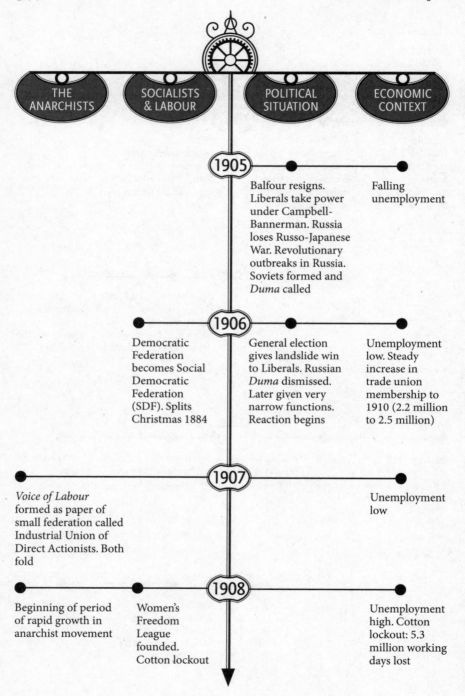

THE ANARCHISTS | SOCIALISTS & LABOUR | POLITICAL SITUATION | ECONOMIC CONTEXT

**1905**

Balfour resigns. Liberals take power under Campbell-Bannerman. Russia loses Russo-Japanese War. Revolutionary outbreaks in Russia. Soviets formed and *Duma* called

Falling unemployment

**1906**

Democratic Federation becomes Social Democratic Federation (SDF). Splits Christmas 1884

General election gives landslide win to Liberals. Russian *Duma* dismissed. Later given very narrow functions. Reaction begins

Unemployment low. Steady increase in trade union membership to 1910 (2.2 million to 2.5 million)

**1907**

*Voice of Labour* formed as paper of small federation called Industrial Union of Direct Actionists. Both fold

Unemployment low

**1908**

Beginning of period of rapid growth in anarchist movement

Women's Freedom League founded. Cotton lockout

Unemployment high. Cotton lockout: 5.3 million working days lost

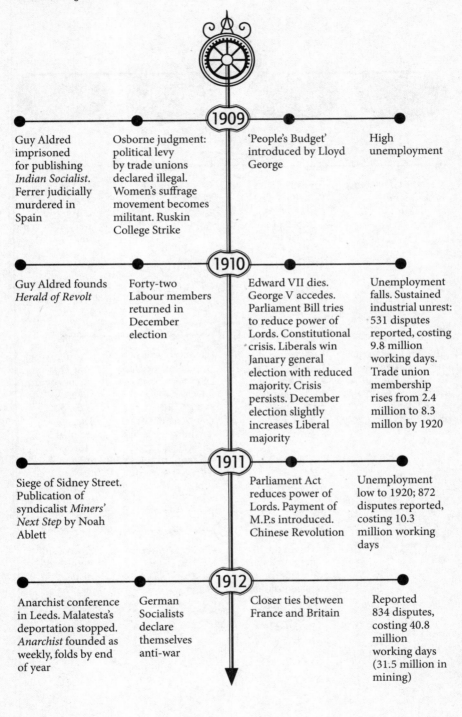

**1909**

Guy Aldred imprisoned for publishing *Indian Socialist*. Ferrer judicially murdered in Spain

Osborne judgment: political levy by trade unions declared illegal. Women's suffrage movement becomes militant. Ruskin College Strike

'People's Budget' introduced by Lloyd George

High unemployment

**1910**

Guy Aldred founds *Herald of Revolt*

Forty-two Labour members returned in December election

Edward VII dies. George V accedes. Parliament Bill tries to reduce power of Lords. Constitutional crisis. Liberals win January general election with reduced majority. Crisis persists. December election slightly increases Liberal majority

Unemployment falls. Sustained industrial unrest: 531 disputes reported, costing 9.8 million working days. Trade union membership rises from 2.4 million to 8.3 millon by 1920

**1911**

Siege of Sidney Street. Publication of syndicalist *Miners' Next Step* by Noah Ablett

Parliament Act reduces power of Lords. Payment of M.P.s introduced. Chinese Revolution

Unemployment low to 1920; 872 disputes reported, costing 10.3 million working days

**1912**

Anarchist conference in Leeds. Malatesta's deportation stopped. *Anarchist* founded as weekly, folds by end of year

German Socialists declare themselves anti-war

Closer ties between France and Britain

Reported 834 disputes, costing 40.8 million working days (31.5 million in mining)

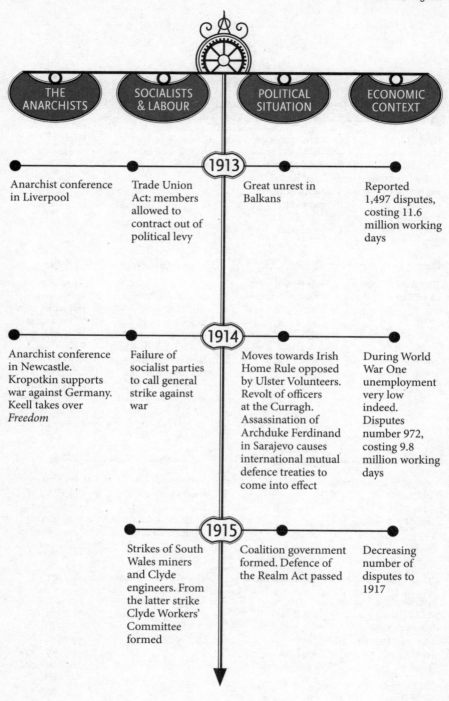

**THE ANARCHISTS** | **SOCIALISTS & LABOUR** | **POLITICAL SITUATION** | **ECONOMIC CONTEXT**

**1913**

Anarchist conference in Liverpool

Trade Union Act: members allowed to contract out of political levy

Great unrest in Balkans

Reported 1,497 disputes, costing 11.6 million working days

**1914**

Anarchist conference in Newcastle. Kropotkin supports war against Germany. Keell takes over *Freedom*

Failure of socialist parties to call general strike against war

Moves towards Irish Home Rule opposed by Ulster Volunteers. Revolt of officers at the Curragh. Assassination of Archduke Ferdinand in Sarajevo causes international mutual defence treaties to come into effect

During World War One unemployment very low indeed. Disputes number 972, costing 9.8 million working days

**1915**

Strikes of South Wales miners and Clyde engineers. From the latter strike Clyde Workers' Committee formed

Coalition government formed. Defence of the Realm Act passed

Decreasing number of disputes to 1917

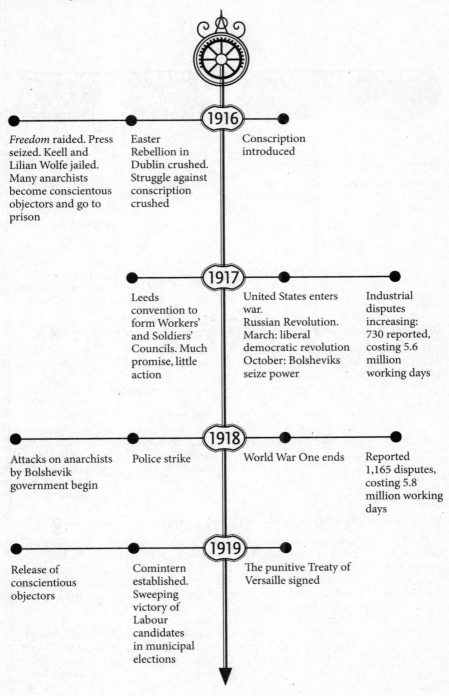

**1916**

*Freedom* raided. Press seized. Keell and Lilian Wolfe jailed. Many anarchists become conscientous objectors and go to prison

Easter Rebellion in Dublin crushed. Struggle against conscription crushed

Conscription introduced

**1917**

Leeds convention to form Workers' and Soldiers' Councils. Much promise, little action

United States enters war.
Russian Revolution.
March: liberal democratic revolution
October: Bolsheviks seize power

Industrial disputes increasing: 730 reported, costing 5.6 million working days

**1918**

Attacks on anarchists by Bolshevik government begin

Police strike

World War One ends

Reported 1,165 disputes, costing 5.8 million working days

**1919**

Release of conscientious objectors

Comintern established. Sweeping victory of Labour candidates in municipal elections

The punitive Treaty of Versaille signed

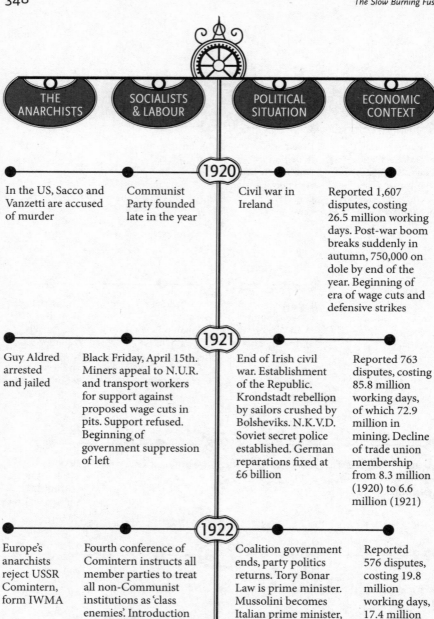

|  | THE ANARCHISTS | SOCIALISTS & LABOUR | POLITICAL SITUATION | ECONOMIC CONTEXT |
|---|---|---|---|---|
| **1920** | In the US, Sacco and Vanzetti are accused of murder | Communist Party founded late in the year | Civil war in Ireland | Reported 1,607 disputes, costing 26.5 million working days. Post-war boom breaks suddenly in autumn, 750,000 on dole by end of the year. Beginning of era of wage cuts and defensive strikes |
| **1921** | Guy Aldred arrested and jailed | Black Friday, April 15th. Miners appeal to N.U.R. and transport workers for support against proposed wage cuts in pits. Support refused. Beginning of government suppression of left | End of Irish civil war. Establishment of the Republic. Krondstadt rebellion by sailors crushed by Bolsheviks. N.K.V.D. Soviet secret police established. German reparations fixed at £6 billion | Reported 763 disputes, costing 85.8 million working days, of which 72.9 million in mining. Decline of trade union membership from 8.3 million (1920) to 6.6 million (1921) |
| **1922** | Europe's anarchists reject USSR Comintern, form IWMA | Fourth conference of Comintern instructs all member parties to treat all non-Communist institutions as 'class enemies'. Introduction of strict 'democratic centralism' to British Communist Party | Coalition government ends, party politics returns. Tory Bonar Law is prime minister. Mussolini becomes Italian prime minister, Stalin Russian Communist Party General Secretary, secret police reorganised as O.G.P.U | Reported 576 disputes, costing 19.8 million working days, 17.4 million were in engineering. Trade Union membership falls to 5.6 million, (static to 1926) |

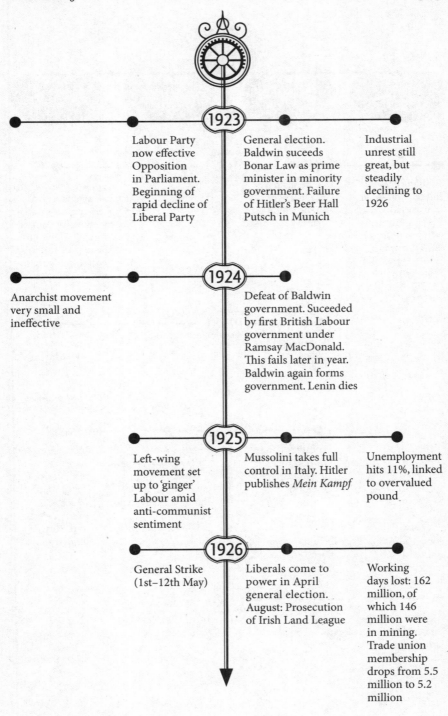

**1923**

Labour Party now effective Opposition in Parliament. Beginning of rapid decline of Liberal Party

General election. Baldwin suceeds Bonar Law as prime minister in minority government. Failure of Hitler's Beer Hall Putsch in Munich

Industrial unrest still great, but steadily declining to 1926

**1924**

Anarchist movement very small and ineffective

Defeat of Baldwin government. Suceeded by first British Labour government under Ramsay MacDonald. This fails later in year. Baldwin again forms government. Lenin dies

**1925**

Left-wing movement set up to 'ginger' Labour amid anti-communist sentiment

Mussolini takes full control in Italy. Hitler publishes *Mein Kampf*

Unemployment hits 11%, linked to overvalued pound

**1926**

General Strike (1st–12th May)

Liberals come to power in April general election. August: Prosecution of Irish Land League

Working days lost: 162 million, of which 146 million were in mining. Trade union membership drops from 5.5 million to 5.2 million

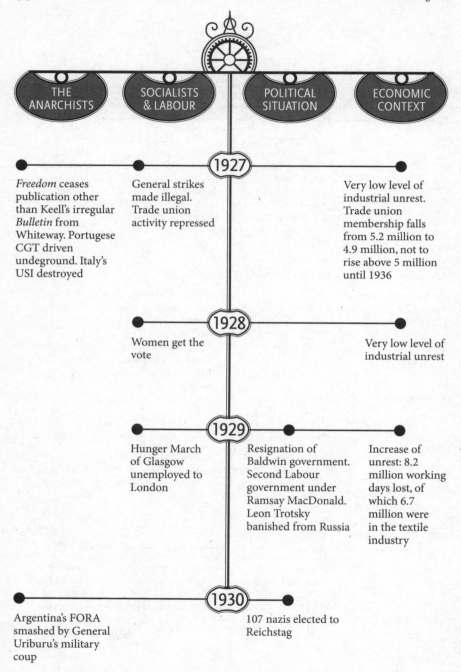

## 1927

**THE ANARCHISTS**

*Freedom* ceases publication other than Keell's irregular *Bulletin* from Whiteway. Portugese CGT driven undeground. Italy's USI destroyed

**SOCIALISTS & LABOUR**

General strikes made illegal. Trade union activity repressed

**ECONOMIC CONTEXT**

Very low level of industrial unrest. Trade union membership falls from 5.2 million to 4.9 million, not to rise above 5 million until 1936

## 1928

**SOCIALISTS & LABOUR**

Women get the vote

**ECONOMIC CONTEXT**

Very low level of industrial unrest

## 1929

**SOCIALISTS & LABOUR**

Hunger March of Glasgow unemployed to London

**POLITICAL SITUATION**

Resignation of Baldwin government. Second Labour government under Ramsay MacDonald. Leon Trotsky banished from Russia

**ECONOMIC CONTEXT**

Increase of unrest: 8.2 million working days lost, of which 6.7 million were in the textile industry

## 1930

**THE ANARCHISTS**

Argentina's FORA smashed by General Uriburu's military coup

**POLITICAL SITUATION**

107 nazis elected to Reichstag

# BIBLIOGRAPHY

To paraphrase Kropotkin, the history of anarchism does not reside in books — at least as far as England is concerned. Nevertheless two books must be singled out for special mention even though the first is hostile to anarchism and the second never seems to have heard of it. These are E.P. Thompson's *William Morris* and Walter Kendall's *The Revolutionary Movement in Britain*. E.P. Thompson's book exhaustively covers the Socialist League period and Morris's relationship with the anarchists and gives a more detailed picture of the early socialist movement than I had space to do. Outside these areas, particularly when he is dealing with anarchists, he should be treated with caution. Walter Kendall's book is only about a part of the revolutionary movement in Britain but gives a fact-packed summary of some of the developments on the left before and during the Syndicalist Revolt and is particularly interesting in his detailed accounts of the formation of the Communist Party of Great Britain. He ignores the anarchist contribution completely. But both books deserve respect because they have gone to the primary sources and in their central concerns have demythologised important parts of the history of the left. The books mentioned below are only some of the books I have looked at during the writing of the present work. A few other titles will be found in the footnotes. The books here listed, however, are those where more than a paragraph or even only a sentence is of interest to would-be historians of anarchism. The bulk of the information for this book has come from a close examination of periodicals and the private papers of anarchists, but the following works do repay examination.

ALDRED, G.A., *Dogmas Discarded*, Glasgow, 1940.

_____. *No Traitor's Gait!*, Glasgow. Issued in approximately monthly parts from 1956.

_____. *Rex v. Aldred*, Glasgow, 1948.

ALLEN, E.J.B., *Revolutionary Unionism*, Huddersfield, 1909.

CALDER-MARSHALL, A., *Lewd, Blasphemous and Obscene*, London, 1972.

CARLSON, A., *German Anarchism*, Metuchen, New Jersey, 1972.

CARPENTER, E., *My Days and Dreams*, London, 1916.

CLYNES, J.R., *Memoirs*, London, 1937.

COATES, K. and TOPHAM, T., *Workers' Control*, London, 1970.

CRAIK, W.W., Central Labour College, London, 1964.

*Documents of the First International*, 4 vols., London/Moscow, 1964.

FISHMAN, W.J., *East End Jewish Radicals*, London, 1975.

FOX, A., *A History of the National Union of Boot and Shoe Operatives*, Oxford, 1958.

FOX, R.M., *Smoky Crusade*, London, 1937.

FREEMANTLE, A., *This Little Band of Prophets*, New York, 1960.

GALLAGHER, W., *Revolt on the Clyde*, London, 1949.

GLASIER, J.B., *William Morris and the Early Days of the Socialist Movement*, London, 1921.

GOLDMAN, E., *Living My Life*, London, 1932.

HART, W.C., *Confessions of an Anarchist*, London, 1906.

HENDERSON, P. (ed.), *Letters of William Morris*, London, 1950.

HULSE, J.W., *Revolutionists in London*, Oxford, 1970.

*John E. Williams and the Early History of the S.D.F.*, London, 1886.

KENDALL, W., The *Revolutionary Movement in Britain*, London, 1969.

KROPOTKIN, P., *Memoirs of a Revolutionist*, London, 1908.

LATOUCHE, P., *Anarchy!*, London, 1908.

LEE, H.W. and ARCHBOLD, E., *Social Democracy in Britain*, London, 1935.

LONGONI, J.C., *Four Patients of Dr Deibler*, London, 1970.

MANN, T., *Tom Mann's Memoirs*, London, 1923.

MARX, K. and ENGELS, F., *Selected Correspondence*, London, 1934.

NETTLAU, M., *Anarchisten and Sozial-Revolutionäre*, Berlin, 1931.

NEVINSON, H.W., *Fire of Life*, London, 1935.

NICOLL, D.J., *The Ghosts of Chelmsford Gaol*, Sheffield, 1897.

_____. *The Greenwich Mystery*, Sheffield, 1897.

_____. *Letters From the Dead*, London, 1898.

_____. *The Walsall Anarchists*, London, 1894.

NOMAD, M., *Dreamers, Dynamiters and Demagogues*, New York, 1964.

PATON, J., *Proletarian Pilgrimage*, London, 1936.

ROCKER, R., *The London Years*, London, 1956.

SHADWELL, A., *The Revolutionary Movement in Britain*, London, 1921.

SHIPLEY, S., *Club Life and Socialism in Mid-Victorian London*, London, 1971.

SWEENY, J., *At Scotland Yard*, London, 1905.

TAYLOR, J., *Self-Help to Glamour: The Working Men's Clubs 1860–1972*, London, 1972.

THOMPSON, B., *Queer People*, London, 1922.

THOMPSON, E.P., *William Morris*, London, 1955.

WOODCOCK, G. and AVACUMOVIC, I., *The Anarchist Prince*, London, 1950.

See also the bibliography in Kendall and Nettlau's *Bibliographie de l'Anarchie*, Brussels, 1897, if a wider range of titles of a more general or more theoretical bent is required.

The periodicals whose files I have consulted are: *Alarm*, *Anarchist*, *Anarchist* (Sheffield), *Black Flag*, *Commonweal*, *Daily Herald*, *Freedom*, *Freiheit*, *Herald of Revolt*, *Industrialist*, *Industrial Syndicalist*, *Islington Gazette*, *Justice*, *Labour Annual*, *Liberty* (Boston), *Liberty* (London), *Reynold's News*, *Sheffield Anarchist*, *Shop Assistant*, *Solidarity*, *Spur*, *Times*, *Torch*, *Voice of Labour*, *War Commentary*, *Weekly Times and Echo*, *Workers' Dreadnought*.

# NOTES

## A PERSONAL INTRODUCTION

1   P. Kropotkin, *Memoirs of a Revolutionist*, London, 1908, pp. 255–6.

## CHAPTER 1: RADICALS, EXILES AND SOCIALIST BEGINNINGS

1   Club and Institute MS appeal, dated January 1873; quoted in John Taylor, *Self Help to Glamour: The Working Men's Clubs, 1860–1972*, History Workshop Pamphlet No 7, London, 1972.

2   John Taylor, op. cit.

3   Quoted in John Taylor, op. cit.

4   The biographical information on Kitz is taken from his 'Recollections and Reflections', in *Freedom*, January–July 1912, and also from Stan Shipley, *Club Life and Socialism in Mid-Victorian London*, History Workshop Pamphlet No. 5, London, 1972.

5   Quotes to this point from *Freedom*, January 1912. For the ex-members of the British Federation of the First International he mentions, see *Documents of the First International*, London/Moscow, 1964. Of particular interest is George Harris, who was viewed with suspicion by Marx because of his contacts with anarchists and others involved with the unorthodox Section 12 of the International in New York.

6   Shipley, op. cit.

7   *Freedom*, February 1912.

8   Andreas Scheu, *Unsturzheime*, quoted in E. P. Thompson, *William Morris*, London, 1955, p. 319.

9   Ibid.

10  Ibid., *Principles of the Social Democratic Party of Germany and of the Social Democrats of America* were published in English in 1877. They were reprinted in the pamphlet published by Sketchley in 1879.

11  A most detailed source on the German anarchist movement is Andrew R. Carlson, *German Anarchism*, Metuchen, New Jersey, 1972.

12  P. Kropotkin, *The Spirit of Revolt*, translated by D.J. Nicoll, Sheffield, 1898.

13  Carlson, op. cit., p. 143.

14  *Freedom*, April 1897.

15  Letter, Marx to F. A. Sorge, 5th November 1880.

16  *Freedom*, March 1912.

17  See the English-language *Freiheit*, 24th April 1881, and *John E. Williams and the Early History of the S.D.F.*, London, 1886.

18  MS autobiography of Ambrose Barker, *Memoirs of a Revolutionist*, kindly lent to me by Stan Shipley.

## CHAPTER 2: THE LABOUR EMANCIPATION LEAGUE

1  Mat Kavanagh in *War Commentary*, 5th May 1945. Lane himself says both that he arrived in London 'around 1867' and that he saw the railings pulled down in the Reform Riots.

2  From verbal reminiscences of Ambrose Barker to E.P. Thompson. See the latter's *William Morris*, p. 325.

3  John Lord was the treasurer of the *Freiheit* Defence Committee. The minutes of the International Conference are given in Nettlau, *Anarchisten und Sozial-Revolutionäre*, Berlin, 1931.

4  Kropotkin, *Memoirs of a Revolutionist*, p. 411.

5  Shipley, op. cit., pp. 34–5.

6  Ambrose Barker, MS, see Chaper 1, note 18.

7  Shipley, op. cit., p. 36, footnote.

8  Joe Lane was involved with the production of the *Radical*.

9  *Justice*, 11th July 1896.

10  *Freedom*, February 1912.

11  H.W. Lee and E. Archbold, *Social Democracy in Britain*, London, 1935, p. 50.

12  Joe Lane, various memoirs, International Institute of Social History, (I.I.S.H.) Amsterdam. Punctuation added.

13  Mat Kavanagh, *War Commentary*, 5th May 1945.

14  Lane memoirs.

15  Lee and Archbold, op. cit., p. 50.

## CHAPTER 3: THE DEMOCRATIC FEDERATION AND THE SOCIALIST LEAGUE

1  Frank Kitz, *Freedom*, April 1912. Following quotes from Kitz from same source.

2  Lane memoirs. Subsequent Lane quotes from same source.

3  Lee and Archbold, op. cit., p. 44.

4  Ibid., p. 42.

5  Marx, letter of 11th April 1881.

6  Marx to Sorge, letter of 15th December 1881, op. cit., p. 397.

7  Lee and Archbold, op. cit., p. 51. The stepping-stone programme remained the only programme of the Federation until the surprises of the 1884 conference.

8  See quote in Thompson, op. cit., p. 344.

9  See Marx to Sorge, letter of 5th November 1880, 'In any event Most has performed the good service of having brought together all the ranters — Andreas Scheu, Hasselman — as a group.'

10  See Thompson, op. cit., and Carlson, op. cit.

11  Quoted in Thompson, op. cit., p. 321.

12  Thompson, op. cit, p. 355.

13  Engels to Sorge, letter of 29th April 1886.

14  William Morris, 'How I Became a Socialist', *Justice*, 16th June 1894.

15  Answer to a question at a meeting, quoted by J.B. Glasier, *William Morris and the Early Days of the Socialist Movement*, London, 1921, pp. 21–2.

16  Two examples are Edward Aveling in London and Thomas Barclay in Leicester.

17  Lee and Archbold, op. cit., p. 58.

18  Ibid., p. 57.

19  Manifesto reproduced in *Bulletin of Society for Study of Labour History*, No. 14, Spring 1967.

20  Quoted in Thompson, op. cit., p. 396.

21  *Letters of William Morris*, Philip Henderson (ed.), London, 1950, pp. 203–4.

22  Lane memoirs. Punctuation added.

23  Lane is here referring to the 'stepping stones'. See note 7.

24  E.P. Thompson argues this case persuasively.

25  The letter was written after the conference and the first meeting of the new council.

26  See Thompson, op. cit., p. 448, for Engels's activities here.

27  Frank Kitz, *Freedom*, April 1912.

28  Quoted in Thompson, op. cit., p. 444.

29  Letter, Lane to Barker.

30  Lane memoirs.

31  Mile End, Stratford and Hoxton branches; material in Socialist League archive, I.I.S.H.

32  MS minutes, S.L. archive.

33  Garrett, *Man in the Street*, London, p. 141. My thanks to Anna Davin for this reference.

34  P. Latouche, *Anarchy!*, London, 1908, p. 78.

35  *Club and Institute Journal*, 17th July 1886.

36  William Morris, *Commonweal*, 31st July 1886.

37  Latouche, op. cit., pp. 46–7.

38  See movement of unemployment figures in Chronology.

## CHAPTER 4: THE *ANARCHIST* AND *FREEDOM* ... AND DAN CHATTERTON

1   See e.g. *Liberty*, 25th August 1883.

2   For more detail see A. Calder-Marshall, *Lewd, Blasphemous and Obscene*, London, 1972, pp. 181–2.

3   *National Reformer*, September 1884, quoted in *Liberty*, 3rd January 1885.

4   Fabian Tract 41, London, 1892.

5   *Anarchist*, August 1885.

6   Mat Kavanagh, biographical sketch of James Harrigan, *War Commentary*, 24th February 1945.

7   *Anarchist*, 15th October 1885.

8   *Anarchist*, 9th December 1885.

9   Quoted in the *Anarchist*, March 1886.

10  See G. Woodcock and I. Avacumovic, *The Anarchist Prince*, London, 1950, p. 203ff.

11  Ibid.

12  From Stepniak's *Underground Russia*, quoted in the *Anarchist*, September 1885.

13  *Anarchist*, 1st January 1886.

14  *Anarchist*, 20th April 1886.

15  See letter, C. M Wilson to Marsh, Marsh papers, I.I.S.H.

16  See C.M Wilson to Sparling, 7th March 1886, S.L. archive, and the *Anarchist*, June 1886.

17  Quoted in the *Anarchist*, June 1886.

18  Letter, C.M. Wilson to Sparling, 29th June 1886, S.L. archive.

19  See Carlson, op. cit.

20  Letter from Reuss to S.L. council, 3rd July 1886, S.L. archive, and letter from H. Charles to the *Anarchist*, October 1886.

21  Woodcock and Avacumovic, *The Anarchist Prince*, London, 1950, p. 205.

22  This is an accurate account taken from Nicolas Walter's biographical sketch in the *Match*, November 1973.

23  H.W. Nevinson, *Fire of Life*, London, 1935, p. 52.

24  J.W. Hulse, *Revolutionists in London*, Oxford 1970, p. 91.

25  See letters of F.C. Slaughter (F. Charles) and C.M. Wilson, S.L. archive.

26  Engels to Sorge, 29th April 1886.

27  Quoted in the *Commune*, November 1926.

28  *Commonweal*, D. Nicoll (ed.), 3rd October 1903.

29  Frank Kitz, *Freedom*, May 1912.

30  Quoted in A. Freemantle, *This Little Band of Prophets*, New York, 1960, p. 158.

31  *Anarchist*, Sheffield, August 1895. From an article written on the death of Dan Chatterton.

32  Mat Kavanagh, biographical sketch of Dan Chatterton, *War Commentary*, 24th February 1945.

## CHAPTER 5: ANARCHISM DEVELOPS IN THE SOCIALIST LEAGUE

1  The draft proposals of the Avelings. See Chapter 3.

2  Morris to Jane Morris, 15th June 1886, *Letters*.

3  D128-131, S.L. archive.

4  Letter written summer 1887, *Letters*.

5  Engels to Sorge, 29th April 1886.

6  Motion by Donald, 20th September 1886, S.L. archive.

7  See letter of Morris to J. B. Glasier, 1st December 1886.

8  Binning to S.L. council, 3rd June 1886. S.L. archive.

9  Circular 'To members of the Socialist League', F173, S.L. archive.

10  MS minutes, S.L. archive.

11  Report of Norwich branch to 1887 conference, S.L. archive.

12  *Freedom*, November 1887.

13  *Commonweal*, 10th March 1888.

14  *Freedom*, November 1887.

15  Lane memoirs.
16  Morris in *Commonweal*, 19th November 1887.
17  Cunninghame Graham, *Commonweal*, 10th November 1888.
18  *Freedom*, January 1888.
19  Internal circular of 1887, F173, S.L. archive.
20  Weekly letters, D95-100, S.L. archive.
21  This is probably the significance of the 'missionary fund' made up of money collected at public meetings, etc., by members of the Bloomsbury branch. According to practice this was to be handed into the office for *Commonweal* expenses, etc., although with council permission — which seems to have been given freely enough — branches could use such money for local propaganda. The Bloomsbury branch, however, didn't hand in their money, refused to account for it and were rude about it when asked. A motion condemning them for this was notified in the internal letter for 4th July 1887. The probable use of the money was for 'working the provincial branch' on behalf of the parliamentarians.
22  'To the members of the Socialist League', F174, S.L. archive.
23  Nor were the anti-parliamentarians above a bit of misrepresentation: the Hackney branch claimed eighteen members in the conference minutes; yet Secretary Cores's membership list reveals only eleven names.
24  Hackney branch circular, 1888, 1533, S.L. archive.
25  Report of Bloomsbury branch, B43, S.L. archive.
26  Mandates of Bloomsbury delegates, B36, S.L. archive.
27  Morris to Glasier, 1888, *Letters*.
28  Ibid.
29  MS notes of a conversation with Fred Charles, I.I.S.H.
30  Morris to Glasier, 15th December 1888, *Letters*.
31  *Freedom*, July 1912.
32  *Freedom*, May 1888.
33  Morris to Glasier, 27th July 1888, *Letters*.
34  Glasier, op. cit.
35  *Commonweal*, 18th May 1889.
36  *Freedom*, October 1889.
37  *Commonweal*, 31st August 1889.
38  *Commonweal*, 7th September 1889.
39  *Freedom*, October 1907.
40  *Freedom*, October 1889.
41  *Commonweal*, 7th September 1889.
42  Debate at the Patriotic Club, Sunday, 25th August 1889. From *Freedom* of September 1889. The word 'expropriation' has a special meaning here. Kropotkin's pamphlet of that name had been published by Seymour in English in 1886. It visualises the progress of the revolution where the people "As soon as they have made a clean sweep of the

Government ... will seek first of all to ensure to themselves decent dwellings and sufficient food and clothes." But in order to ensure no return of previous exploitation, expropriation "must apply to everything that enables any man — be he financier, mill owner or landlord — to appropriate the product of another's toil." Essentially expropriation is the process of communalising property and capital.

43  *Commonweal*, 9th November 1889.
44  Handbill in Nettlau Collection, I.I.S.H.
45  *Commonweal*, 30th August 1890.
46  Latouche, op. cit., p. 60.
47  J.R. Clynes, *Memoirs*, London, 1937, pp. 53–4.
48  *Commonweal*, 16th August 1890.
49  Morris to Glasier, 6th April 1890, *Letters*.
50  *Commonweal*, 12th July 1890.
51  Morris to Nicoll, 19th July 1890, *Letters*.
52  *Freedom*, July 1912.
53  *Commonweal*, 22nd November 1890.
54  *Commonweal*, 15th November 1890.
55  *Commonweal*, 23rd May 1891.
56  *Commonweal*, 29th November 1890.
57  Morris to Glasier, 5th December 1890, *Letters*.
58  *Commonweal*, 5th April 1890.
59  *Commonweal*, April 1891.
60  *Commonweal*, Nicoll (ed.), Christmas 1904.
61  *Belfast Weekly Star*, quoted in *Commonweal*, March 1891.
62  See for example handbill headed 'MURDER' in W.C. Hart, *Confessions of an Anarchist*, London, 1906, p. 42.

## CHAPTER 6: THE WALSALL ANARCHISTS

1  *Reynold's News*, 14th April 1895.
2  *Times*, 16th January 1892.
3  I.e. at the Socialist congresses held in Paris that year.
4  This was, in all pedantry, a mistake. The letter was signed 'Degnai'.
5  *Times*, 22nd January 1892.
6  *Anarchist*, Sheffield, Vol. 2, No. 8, 1895.
7  *Commonweal*, No. II, May 1898.
8  See S.L. archive, K1137, 1138.
9  D.J. Nicoll, *The Walsall Anarchists*, London, 1894.
10  J.C. Longoni, *Four Patients of Dr. Deibler*, London, 1970, p. 16.
11  He arrived in mid-1890.
12  *Commonweal*, 21st May 1892.
13  Letters K1239-1240, S.L. archive. See also Deakin's confession.

14  Ted Leggatt, letter to *Reynold's News*, 21st April 1895. See also article by P. McIntyre, *Reynold's News*, 14th April 1895, and Edward Carpenter, *My Days and Dreams*, London, 1916.

15  *Anarchist* (Sheffield), Vol. 2, No. 20, 1895.

16  D.J. Nicoll, op.cit.

17  In the Brotherton Collection, Brotherton Library, University of Leeds.

18  *Commonweal*, 24th October 1891.

19  *Commonweal*, 5th December 1891.

20  Whom I suspect, on very little evidence, to have been the young Billy McQueen.

21  This would appear to be Cyril Bell.

22  *Shop Assistant*, 30th August 1924.

23  *Times*, 17th October 1891.

24  *Times*, 1st January 1892. See H.S. Salt's introduction to *Selected Poems of J.E. Barlas*, London 1925, for some biographical details. He had been "batoned and floored" on Bloody Sunday and had been a member of both the S.D.F. and the Socialist League.

25  W.M. Thompson was also the editor of *Reynold's News*.

26  *Birmingham Daily Post*, 10th February 1892.

27  A notice warning about his activities had appeared in *Justice* the previous year, on 18th April 1891.

28  *Justice*, 5th November 1892.

29  *L'Internationale*, which was distributed in England by Coulon.

30  *Commonweal*, No. II, 15th May 1898, and Good Friday 1909.

31  See Longoni, op. cit.

32  *Times*, 29th March 1892.

33  *Times*, 4th April 1892.

34  It changed little for the Walsall defendants that this later turned out to be a plot got up by a highly professional agent provocateur. See Central News telegram of 21st April, quoted *Freedom*, May 1892.

35  *Freedom*, May 1892.

36  *Times*, 5th April 1892.

37  The Chief Inspector was Colonel Majendie who gave evidence at this and other anarchist trials for the prosecution.

38  *Justice*, 9th April 1892.

39  Leaflet in Nettlau Collection.

40  A. Coulon, *Anarchy is Too True a Doctrine* ..., British Museum.

41  *Anarchist* (Sheffield), Vol. 2, No. 20, 1895.

42  Edward Carpenter to Alf Mattison, 7th April 1892. Brotherton Collection, Leeds University Library.

43  *Anarchist* (Sheffield), Vol. 2, No. 20, 1895.

44  Nicoll, *Anarchy at the Bar*, London, 1894. The 'dear friend' is Fred Charles.

45  See *St James's Gazette*, 9th April 1892.

46  *Anarchist* (Sheffield), Vol. 2, No. 20, 1895.

47  The headquarters were at 7 Lamb's Conduit Street, W.C.1. "This is the only Society in the United Kingdom," they announced, "founded on TRUE cooperative principles: Self-employment by the workers; Eight Hours Day; TU wages the minimum pay; No Interest to Shareholders; No Dividend Grabbing; Sweaters boycotted." *People's Press*, 24th January 1891.

48  *Anarchist* (Sheffield), Vol. 2, No. 20.

49  Nicoll, *Anarchy at the Bar.*

50  *Anarchist* (Sheffield), Vol. 2, No. 20.

51  *Anarchist* (Sheffield), Vol. 2, No. 21.

52  W.C. Hart, op. cit., p. 45.

53  *Reynold's News*, 7th April 1895.

54  *Anarchist* (Sheffield ), Vol. 2, No. 21, 1895.

55  *Times*, 25th April 1892.

56  *Anarchist*, 20th April 1886.

57  *Commonweal*, 30th April 1892.

58  J. Sweeny, *At Scotland Yard*, London, 1905.

59  *Times*, 2nd May 1892.

60  *Times*, 7th May 1892.

61  Nicoll, *Anarchy at the Bar.*

62  This is quite literally true. Some of the documents had disappeared by the time Nicoll was released.

63  *Times*, 7th May 1892.

64  Published Sheffield, 1897.

65  *Commonweal*, Christmas 1904.

66  See the series of articles in the *Evening News*, London, December 1894, particularly 18th and 19th of that month.

67  See Chronology.

68  *Commonweal*, Christmas 1904.

## CHAPTER 7: H.B. SAMUELS AND THE *COMMONWEAL*

1  See S.L. archive K2628, and *Labour Annual*, 1896.

2  Nicoll, *The Greenwich Mystery*, Sheffield, 1897.

3  *Freedom*, June 1893.

4  *Times*, 28th January 1893. The two men at the back of the court were George Cores and Billy MacQueen. The account in *Freedom*, March 1893, makes it quite clear that they were rather severely beaten up by the police.

5  Nicoll, *The Greenwich Mystery*, and *Commonweal*, 1st May 1893.

6  See account of a meeting addressed by Tochatti in the Italian quarter in *Commonweal*, 25th June 1893.

7  See e.g. W.C. Hart, *Commonweal*, 13th May 1893. Also later reports from Hart in *Freedom* and other examples in the present book.

8   *Islington Gazette*, 3rd July 1893.

9   *Commonweal*, 8th July 1893.

10  Quoted from the press of 21st September in *Commonweal*, 30th September.

11  *Commonweal*, 28th October 1893.

12  See *Commonweal*, 14th October 1893 to 20th January 1894.

13  *Times*, 9th November 1893. *Freedom* later asserted that the bomb had exploded prematurely, killing the person carrying it who was waiting for the opportunity to hurl it at Marshal Campos, who had massacred peasants at Xeres. Pallas had already made one attempt on Campos's life and had been executed.

14  *Morning Leader*, 12th November 1893, quoted in Nicoll, *The Greenwich Mystery*.

15  *Times*, 13th November 1893.

16  *Commonweal*, 25th November 1893.

17  Trafalgar Square had been reopened for meetings by the Liberal government elected in 1892, doubtless as a result of Radical pressure, to the accompaniment of rhetorical flourishes. To close the square must have taken some pressure with these on record.

18  *Freedom*, January/February 1894.

19  *Times*, 18th December 1893.

20  *Commonweal*, 23rd December 1893.

21  *Commonweal*, 31st March 1894.

22  *Times*, 5th January 1894.

23  Sweeny, op. cit., pp. 208–9.

24  *Commonweal*, 30th September 1893.

25  See agenda in *Commonweal*, 25th November 1893.

26  *Commonweal*, Christmas 1904; Nicoll, *The Greenwich Mystery*; Nicoll to Nettlau, letters in Nettlau Collection.

27  *Commonweal*, Christmas 1904.

28  Letter to Nicoll by L.S. Bevington, quoted in Nicoll, *Letters from the Dead*, London, 1898.

29  *Labour Annual*, 1896. His subsequent political career did not live up to this early promise: suspected of dabbling in explosives "he was forbidden to hold office or lecture for a year with the result that the Kilburn branch changed its name and refused to be deprived of his services." See P. Thompson, *Socialists, Liberals and Labour*, London, 1967, pp. 160–62.

## CHAPTER 8: THE GREENWICH PARK EXPLOSION

1   This incident inspired Joseph Conrad's novel *The Secret Agent*, which, however, bears little resemblance to the real events. See Norman Sherry, *Conrad's Western World*, London, 1971, which is both good reading and a more or less accurate unravelling of Conrad's sources.

2   L.S. Bevington to Nicoll, *Letters from the Dead*.

3   *Greenwich Mystery*.

4   See Central News report in the *Times*, 16th February 1894. The Central News was a news agency which, interestingly enough, had employed Reuss, the German police spy, at one time.

5   "Walsh, the big bully of the force, a ruffian noted for his savage attacks on little boys and blind men." *Commonweal*, No. III, July 1898.

6   *Times*, 17th February 1894.

7   'Death to Carnot!' — Carnot was the President of France. He had refused to commute Vaillant's death sentence. The placard is interesting taken together with an account of a London anarchist meeting described in *Figaro*, 7th February 1894, where speakers asserted that bombs killed the innocent as well as the guilty and advocated the use of the knife or gun. It was apparently a general sentiment — an anarchist, Santo Caserio, assassinated Carnot four months later, with a dagger.

8   The house at 30 Fitzroy Street had already been lived in by François, whom the French police had extradited for the Café Very bombing. Fritz Brall had also lived there.

9   "According to a reporter of the Press Association": Nicoll, *The Greenwich Mystery*.

10  Quoted ibid.

11  Ibid. Coulon, however, depended rather heavily on self-advertisement for his reputation as a Scourge of Anarchy and need not be assumed to be telling the truth.

12  *Times*, 20th February 1894.

13  Ibid.

14  *Times*, 24th February 1894.

15  'Dynamitism', in *Commonweal*, 24th June 1893.

## CHAPTER 9: THE COLLAPSE OF THE *COMMONWEAL*

1   *Commonweal*, 13th April 1894.

2   Ibid. Also *Freedom*, April i894.

3   *Freedom*, May 1894.

4   Ibid.

5   See *Liberty*, May 1894; *Commonweal*, 13th April 1894; *Freedom*, May 1894.

6   See the *Times*, 4th and 5th May; also *Commonweal*, 17th November 1907 — at which time Farnara was still in Dartmoor.

7   *Times*, 2nd and 19th June 1894. The words 'dynamite guide' seem to be a bit of poetic licence: the pamphlet's German title is R*evolutionäre Kriegwissenschaft*, or *Revolutionary Warfare*.

8   Hart, op. cit., pp. 20–1.

9   Latouche, op. cit., pp. 133–4.

10  In *Collection of Anarchist Placards* in French, British Museum. Many are given as originating from the 'Imprimerie Anarchiste, Londres'. Date from Glasier, op. cit., p. 126, who says the leaflet was issued by the Autonomie Club.

11  Glasier; op. cit., p. 126.

12  Hart, op. cit., pp. 2 and 13.

13  Max Nomad, *Dreamers, Dynamiters and Demagogues*, New York, 1964.

14  See documents in Nettlau Collection.

15  Nicoll, *Letters from the Dead*.

16  Nicoll, *The Greenwich Mystery*.

17  A reference, one supposes, to creatures like Reuss and McCormack who made a bit extra from journalism to supplement their regular retainers as spies.

18  Nicoll, *The Greenwich Mystery*. 'Isobel Meredith' (Olivia Rossetti) gives a more dynamic fictional account in her novel *A Girl Among the Anarchists*, London, 1903.

19  *Commonweal* meetings were on the Tuesday before the paper came out on a Saturday. Thus, according to Nicoll, Samuels had been first accused two weeks before Tuesday, 5th June, i.e. 22nd May.

20  Nicoll, *Letters from the Dead*.

21  Hart, op. cit., p. 45.

22  Account of events and trial from *Freedom*, August 1894; *Times*, 2nd, 5th, 10th, 17th, 21st June, 1st August.

23  *Commonweal*, 15th May 1898.

24  Nicoll to Nettlau, letters in Nettlau Collection.

25  *Commonweal*, Christmas 1904.

26  Nicoll, *Letters from the Dead*.

27  Ibid.

28  *Commonweal*, 20th June 1897.

29  Nicoll, *Letters from the Dead*.

30  *Anarchist* (Sheffield), 26th August 1894.

31  Quoted in *Commonweal*, 8th August 1907.

32  *Commonweal*, 20th June 1897.

## CHAPTER 10: THE MOVEMENT IN 1894.

1   *Islington Gazette*, 22nd August 1893.

2   A letter from Tom Maguire quoted in E. Carpenter's introduction to Tom Maguire, *A Remembrance*, Manchester, 1895.

3   Blair-Smith in the *Anarchist* (Sheffield), 18th March 1894.

4   *Times*, 8th August 1894.

5   *Weekly Times and Echo*, 3rd December 1893.

6   *Evening News*, 17th December 1894. Article by Zitrik (pseudonymous).

7   H.W. Nevinson, op. cit., p. 53.

8   Latouche, op. cit.

9   Quoted in Max Nomad, *Apostles of Revolution*, New York, 1961, p. 298.

10  Max Beer, *History of British Socialism*, London, 1940; also *S.D.F. Conference Report*, 1895.

11  *Justice*, 7th May 1892.

12  *Commonweal*, 12th June 1898.

## CHAPTER 11: THE MOVEMENT IN DECLINE

1   For the details see *Reynold's News*, 19th May 1895.
2   *Reynold's News*, 14th April 1895.
3   *Anarchist* (Sheffield), Vol. 2, No. 18, 1895.
4   *Anarchist* (Sheffield), Vol. 2, No. 19, 1895.
5   See paragraph or so on current activities at the beginning of Nicoll, *The Ghosts of Chelmsford Gaol*, Sheffield, 1897.
6   See article by Henry Seymour, *Liberty*, October 1895.
7   In a letter to *Liberty*, January 1896.
8   Byrne to Stapleton of the Canning Town Group for general circulation, August 1896. Nettlau Collection.
9   Hart, op. cit., Chapter XIV.
10  *Liberty*, October 1895.
11  See letters from Byrne, Nettlau and O. Rossetti in Nettlau Collection.
12  Quinn to *Freedom*, 10 November 1896. Nettlau Collection.
13  Banham and Reece to *Freedom*, 12th December 1896. Nettlau Collection.
14  Hart, op. cit., p. 86.
15  Marsh to Nettlau, 3rd October 1897. Nettlau Collection.
16  Marsh to Nettlau, 25th November 1897. Nettlau Collection.
17  Nettlau to Nicoll, 29th April 1897. Reprinted in *Commonweal*, 20th June 1897.
18  Nicoll to Nettlau, n.d., I.I.S.H.
19  Marsh to Nettlau, 29th June 1897. Nettlau Collection.
20  See leaflets in I.I.S.H.
21  Nettlau Collection.
22  *Commonweal*, 15th May 1898.
23  Later issues of his *Commonweal*, which continued until 1907 with gaps of up to a year between each issue, are evidence of an unfolding, almost classic, paranoid condition. The truth of socialism becomes the property of a kind of masonry of which Nicoll was one of the few members. William Morris became Solomon's architect Hiram, with whom the secret of the building of the great Temple died. His death had been caused by a conspiracy which at first involved Samuels, MacDonald and Turner, but which was then expanded to reveal a vast homosexual/Jesuit/reactionary conspiracy involving the Catholic Church in general and people such as Charlotte Wilson, Edward Carpenter and Keir Hardie in particular.

Despite some lucid periods, he steadily declined into the condition that Guy Aldred found him in some time after 1907: "The paper stopped and Nicoll sold sheets of paper, bearing ridiculous crayon scrawls. He was unable to work and met comrades with a cracked laugh, a smile that horrified, and a mysterious manner. His talk was always about spies. He gained a precarious living from small sums given to him by comrades who recalled his past services to the movement or had learned of them. He became a kind of tradition and menace combined" (Aldred, *Dogmas Discarded*, II, Glasgow, 1940, p. 68). He died in St Pancras workhouse in 1919.

24  *Freedom*, January 1898.
25  Kropotkin to Marsh, 30th December 1897, Marsh archive, I.I.S.H.
26  *Freedom*, February 1898.
27  Ibid.
28  See M. Nomad, *Dreamers, Dynamiters and Demagogues*, New York, 1964.
29  In Calder-Marshall, op. cit.
30  Sweeny, op. cit., p. 186.
31  *Commonweal*, July 1898.
32  *Freedom*, December 1898.
33  *Freedom*, October 1899.
34  *Freedom*, January/February 1900.
35  *Freedom*, September/October, 1900.
36  See Rudolph Rocker's account in his *The London Years*, London, 1956.
37  *Freedom*, September/October, 1900.
38  *Freedom*, July 1901.
39  *Freedom*, December 1901.
40  MS in Nettlau Collection. Published in *Freedom* in bowdlerised form.
41  Kropotkin to Marsh. Both letters in Marsh archive.

## CHAPTER 12: COOPERATIVE COLONIES

1   Coates, K. and Topham, T., *Workers' Control*, London, 1970, p. xxxii.
2   *Labour Annual*, 1898, p. 88.
3   See Alan Fox, *A History of the National Union of Boot and Shoe Operatives*, Oxford, 1958. Cooperatives were set up on a branch basis, though with but modest success. See pp. 181–5. Some of these productive co-ops were long-lived however: "of the 42 cooperative production societies composing the Cooperative Production Federation in 1950, 16 were footwear societies" (p. 637).
4   *Labour Annual* for each year. Either the editors became bored or the decline was catastrophic because no mention is made of colonies in succeeding issues.
5   First published in London in 1899.
6   Reprinted in *Liberty*, March 1895.
7   Hart, op. cit., p. 79.
8   Hart, op. cit., pp. 79–81, says some £1,200.
9   *Labour Annual*, 1900.
10  Hart, op. cit., p. 81.
11  Latouche, op. cit., pp. 136–8.
12  And some like Lilian Wolfe who bounced back to invigorate the movement for years.
13  The *Labour Annual* for 1900 reported it as being "not yet self-sufficient." Members included Norman St John and J.C. Kenworthy.
14  *Labour Annual*, 1900.
15  *Freedom*, February 1898.

16  See Yann Cloare and Georges Darien, *L'Ennemi du peuple*, Paris, 1972, p. 88.

## CHAPTER 13: ANARCHISM AND THE ORIGINS OF THE SYNDICALIST REVOLT

1   *Justice*, 6th June 1891.
2   *Freedom*, May 1889.
3   *Commonweal*, 30th September 1893.
4   *Commonweal*, 6th January 1894.
5   *Commonweal*, 20th January 1894.
6   See letter from O.G., *Commonweal*, 17th February 1894.
7   *Commonweal*, 25th November 1893; also Alan Fox, op. cit., pp. 185–6.
8   Adolphe Smith, *A Critical Essay on the International Congress*, London, 1889.
9   *Liberty*, January 1896. See also Eleanor Marx Aveling's introduction to a translation of Plekhanov's *Socialism and Anarchism*, published in 1896 for a smearing attack on the anarchists designed to bolster the campaign to keep them out of the congress.
10  *Freedom*, August/September 1896.
11  E.g, 'New Tactics in the Economic Struggle', *Freedom*, February 1898.
12  *Freedom*, August 1900.
13  See 'Methods of Propaganda', *Freedom*, July 1901.
14  Walter Kendall, *The Revolutionary Movement in Britain*, London, 1969, gives more details of these developments.
15  *Freedom*, August 1903.
16  *Freedom*, August 1904.
17  *Freedom*, October 1904.
18  *Freedom*, June 1906.
19  Aldred, *No Traitor's Gait!*, published in approximately monthly parts from 1956 onwards.
20  Aldred, *Dogmas Discarded*, II, p. 39.
21  Though for the militants who survived into the syndicalist period it represented a body of memories and inspiration of extraordinary power. John Turner, Frank Kitz, Sam Mainwaring, Ambrose Barker, in various snippets of autobiography, all pay eloquent testimony to the education they received in the League.
22  Aldred, *No Traitor's Gait!*, Vol. 2, No. 1, p. 303.
23  For the East End Jewish movement see W.J. Fishman, *East End Jewish Radicals*, London, 1975.
24  *Voice of Labour*, Vol. 1, No. 4, 9th February 1907.
25  For the most detailed accounts of his union career see *The Shop Assistant*, 19th October 1912 and 30th August 1924.
26  P. Thompson, op. cit., p. 59.
27  See the section entitled 'The Treachery of Officials' in E.J.B. Allen, *Revolutionary Unionism*, Huddersfield, 1909.
28  *Industrialist*, November 1909.
29  Aldred, *No Traitor's Gait!*, Vol. 2, No. 1.

30  *Voice of Labour*, 29th July 1907.

31  Aldred, *No Traitor's Gait!*, Vol. 2, No. 1.

32  *Herald of Revolt*, June 1912.

33  For details see Rex v. Aldred, by the latter, Glasgow, 1948.

34  *Freedom*, August 1908.

35  *Freedom*, October 1908.

36  *Industrialist*, June 1908.

37  *Industrialist*, July 1909.

38  *Industrialist*, November 1908.

39  *Freedom*, December 1908. E.J.B. Allen was later expelled from the Industrialist League for taking part in the election campaign for Victor Grayson in Colne Valley. (Industrialist League Executive minutes, 9th October 1916.) He then joined Tom Mann's Industrial Syndicalist Education League.

40  See W.W. Craik, Central Labour College, London, 1964, pp. 82, 90, 95–6. Craik claims that S.L.P. attempts to recruit at Ruskin were a failure. He was there at the time. Tom Bell, who claims otherwise, was not.

## CHAPTER 14: THE INSURGENT VIRUS

1   See Chronology.

2   Quoted in Geoff Brown's introduction to reprint of *Industrial Syndicalist*, London, 1974.

3   *Freedom*, October 1910.

4   *Industrial Syndicalist*, January 1911.

5   *Herald of Revolt*, May 1912.

6   G.R. Askwith, *Industrial Problems and Disputes*, London, 1920, p. 150.

7   P. Gibbs, *Pageant of the Years*, London, 1946, p. 180.

8   *Freedom*, September 1911.

9   P. Gibbs, loc. cit.

10  *Freedom*, September 1911.

11  *Herald of Revolt*, September 1911.

12  *Freedom*, January 1912.

13  See J.W. Major, *Quayside Crooks*, London, c. 1930, p. 51.

14  *Industrial Syndicalist*, Vol. I, No. 6.

15  *Industrial Syndicalist*, Vol. I, No. 1.

16  Ibid.

17  Reprinted by Pluto Press, London, 1973.

18  *Industrial Syndicalist*, Vol. I, No. 3.

19  H.A. Clegg, A. Fox and A. F. Thompson, *A History of British Trades Unions*, Vol. I, Oxford, 1964, p. 132.

20  J.T. Murphy, *New Horizons*, London 1941, pp. 44, 45.

21  Quoted in C.H. Stavenhagen, *Industrial Unionism: Labour's Final Weapon*, London, probably 1917. (Second edition advertised February 1918.)

22  See R.M. Fox, *Smokey Crusade*, London, 1937, p. 140.

23  C. Arrow, *Rogues and Others*, London, 1926,Chapter XXII.

24  E.g. John Paton; see below.

25  *Industrial Syndicalist*, Vol. I, No. 6.

26  *Daily Herald*, 20th May 1912 and ff.

27  *Daily Telegraph*, 20th March 1912.

28  *Freedom*, April 1912.

29  Lane to Barker, 17th December 1912, I.I.S.H.

30  Lee and Archbold, op. cit., p. 183.

31  Ibid., p. 185.

32  W. Kendall, The *Revolutionary Movement in Britain*, London, 1969, p. 28.

33  Ibid., p. 37 and footnote.

34  J. Paton, *Proletarian Pilgrimage*, London, 1936, p. 206.

35  Marsh to Keell, 21st March 1912, I.I.S.H.

36  *Daily Despatch*, 24th February 1912.

37  *Daily Despatch*, 26th February 1912.

38  *Freedom*, July 1912.

39  G. Slocombe, *The Tumult and the Shouting*, London, 1936.

40  Quoted in introduction to Barrett's *The First Person*, London, 1963.

41  Paton, op. cit., p. 119ff.

42  Davison had made a lot of money working for Kodak. In addition to supporting the Central Labour College, the *Anarchist* and other things mentioned in the text, he also supported W.F. Hay, a Syndicalist miner from Wales during a speaking tour of the northern coalfields.

43  As note 40.

44  Paton, op. cit., pp. 221 and 232.

45  *Freedom*, October 1912.

46  *Freedom*, April 1913.

47  Leo Abse, *Private Member*, London, 1974.

48  Dave Douglass, *Pit Life in County Durham*, Oxford, 1972, p. 68.

49  *Spur*, June 1914.

50  *Herald of Revolt*, July 1911, reprinted February 1913.

51  R.M. Fox, op. cit., p. 184.

## CHAPTER 15: WORLD WAR ONE — AND AFTER

1  *Freedom*, June 1910.

2  William Gallagher, *Revolt on the Clyde*, London, 1949, p. 18.

3  Keell to Karl Walter, 17th November 1936, reprinted *University Libertarian*, Nos. 7 and 8.

4  See letters of Cores and Keell to Nettlau in I.I.S.H. One gives details of Cores's denunciation of Keell in 1915.

5  R.M. Fox, op. cit.

6   Gallagher, op. cit., p. 30.

7   N.W. in *Freedom*, 25th May 1974.

8   P.S. Meacham to Nettlau, 29th February 1928, I.I.S.H.

9   Quoted in the introduction to *British Labour and the Russian Revolution*, London, n.d.

10  Quoted in Kendall, op. cit., p. 163.

11  B. Thompson, *Queer People*, London, 1922, p. 297.

12  *Freedom*, February 1912.

13  *Solidarity*, January 1919.

14  *Spur*, September 1919.

15  *Spur*, October 1919. The Workers' Socialist Federation was Sylvia Pankhurst's organisation, grouped round the *Workers' Dreadnought*. The Communist League was probably Aldred's organisation.

16  *Spur*, May 1920.

17  Quoted in Kendall, op. cit., p. 229, footnote.

18  Ibid., p. 231.

19  *Spur*, August 1920.

20  A. Shadwell, *Revolutionary Movement in Britain*, London, 1921. Reprinted from the *Times*.

21  Meacham to Nettlau, 1928, I.I.S.H.

22  Emma Goldman, *Living My Life*, London; 1932, Vol. 2, pp. 963 and 968.

23  Ibid., p. 972.

24  Margaret Cole, *Life of G.D.H. Cole*, London, 1971, p. 160.

25  Keen to Nettlau, 25th August 1928, I.I.S.H.

26  *Black Flag*, January/February 1975.

# BIOGRAPHIES

## ALFRED BARTON

Alfred Barton was born on 30th July 1868 at Kempton in Bedfordshire, the son of a foundry labourer Henry Barton and his wife Eliza, née Savill. Self-educated, he became well informed in philosophy and history, especially classical history. He was able to read several languages. Not much is known of his early years in Bedfordshire. His first job was in a public library at the age of 12. He left home around 1890 to go to Manchester. Here he became a member of the Socialist League, and already had strong anarchist tendencies. He worked first as a clerk and then in Rylands Library. He threw himself into the work of the League which began an intensive propaganda campaign. Active alongside him was Herbert Stockton (an odd job man and later an industrial assurance agent according to George Cores), who ran a drapers shop in Levenshulme, and his brother Ernest.

Very active during the free speech fight led by the Manchester anarchists (1893–1894) during which he was arrested. Barton married Eleanor 'Nellie' Stockton (born 1872/1873) sister to Herbert and Ernest in 1894. She was one of many young women who supported the open air meetings. She was a very prominent member of the Women's Cooperative Guild and like her brothers described herself as an anarchist-communist. The Bartons moved to Sheffield in 1897. Here Alf joined the Independent Labour Party and started moving away from his radical positions. He gained a reputation in Sheffield as 'The Monolith Orator'. He had by now abandoned anarchism, joined the Shop Assistants Union and was its delegate to the Trades Council. In 1907 he was elected councillor for Brightside Ward, but lost the seat in 1910. Discontented with the Labour Party, he joined the British Socialist Party in 1911, issuing the pamphlet *The Universal Strike*, which harked back to his anarchist ideas, in the same year. He regained Brightside in 1913 as a B.S.P. candidate and without Trades Council support and held it until 1920. He supported World War One. After a brief period with the Communist Party he rejoined the I.L.P. After two unsuccessful parliamentary contests he rejoined the Trades Council in 1926, becoming an alderman in 1929. He died on 9th December 1933. Nellie eventually emigrated to New Zealand where she died in Papatoetoe on 9th March 1960.

## CYRIL BELL

Cyril Bell, medical student and lecturer, who gives the information in *Commonweal* that he was a "mountain devil" from mid-Wales, was active in Scotland, Sheffield and London. He spoke in Edinburgh in 1891 for the anniversary of the Chicago martyrs. Later he was secretary of Louise Michel's Free School in Fitzrovia, London.

## LOUISA SARAH BEVINGTON

Louisa Sarah Bevington was born into a Quaker family on 18th May 1845, in St John's Hill, Battersea. The occupation of her father was described as a 'gentleman'. She was the oldest of eight children, seven of whom were girls. She started writing verse at an early age.

Not long after she published her second volume of poems in 1882, she went to Germany and in 1883 married a Munich artist Ignatz Felix Guggenberger. The marriage lasted less than eight years, and she returned to London in 1890. She began to frequent anarchist circles, restarting her career under her maiden name. By the mid-1890s, Bevington knew many London anarchists and was recognised as an anarchist poet. She probably became acquainted with anarchism through meeting Charlotte Wilson, who had jointly founded the anarchist paper *Freedom* in 1886.

Rejecting the tactics of the bomb and dynamite being espoused by some anarchists in Britain, she associated with the anarchist paper *Liberty* (subtitled *A Journal of Anarchist Communism*), edited by the tailor James Tochatti from January 1894. She wrote many articles and poems for it, as well as for other anarchist papers, like the *Torch*, edited by the two young nieces, Helen and Olivia, of the artist Dante Gabriel Rossetti. She was involved in efforts to set up an organisation, the anarchist-communist Alliance and wrote an Anarchist Manifesto for it, which was distributed on 1st May 1895 (the Alliance appears not to have survived long). She translated Louise Michel's essay on the Paris Commune into English and was a good friend of the author.

At the age of 50 in 1895, Bevington was still active but was suffering from bad health, namely heart disease that had been afflicting her for years. She managed to write some articles for *Liberty* in that year and her last collection of poems for Liberty Press.

She died on 28th November 1895 in Lechmere, as the result of dropsy and mitral disease of the heart. Her funeral at Finchley cemetery was attended by her old comrade James Tochatti, Kropotkin, and the Rossetti sisters, among others.

## GUSTAVE BROCHER

Gustave Brocher was born in Delle, France in 1850. He was raised by his father in a Fourierist tradition. Despite this he studied theology and became a priest but appears to have rejected this, and then went off to Russia as a private teacher. He went to London in 1875, where he eventually joined the Vpered! group and became a socialist.

In 1879 he became an anarchist under the influence of Paul Brousse and co-edited the newspaper *Le Travail* (Labour) between 1880 and 1881. He became active in the Socialist League and anarchist circles in London. He chaired a committee to organise a London Anarchist Congress in 1881, and he represented the Iowa Icarians at the International Social Revolutionary and Anarchist Congress on 14th to 19th July 1881.

He met Victorine Rouchy there, and they later got married in 1887 and adopted five orphans of the Paris Commune. He contributed articles to Henry Seymour's monthly paper the *Anarchist* (1885–1887). With Frank Kitz he published an English language *Freiheit* in defence of Johann Most, and seven issues of this appeared from April to June 1881.

Hammersmith Socialist Society minutes report that he lectured to the branch twice in 1885 on 'The Phalanstere' and 'The Icarian Communities'. The August 1885 *Commonweal* reports his singing of the old song from the French Revolution, 'La Carmagnole,' at the first annual League conference. Between 1885 and 1897 he published three French translations and readers in London. In 1891 he moved to Lausanne in Switzerland. Later he returned for a while to London. An 1893 issue of *Freedom* lists him as a speaker, and he may well have been the Brocher at Mary Mowbray's funeral in 1893 who spoke as a representative of a 'French Anarchist Section' of the League.

He taught at the academy of Fiume in Italy from 1911 to 1914. He contributed to many anarchist periodicals and publications like the *Encyclopédie Anarchiste* and, as a militant freethinker from the 1880s on, to numerous secularist papers. He was editor of *La Libre Pensée* (Free-thought) from 1918 until his death.

He wrote several books between 1915–1918 in France on Russian topics, and edited selections of a *Dictionaire des Athées* (Dictionary of Atheists). His pamphlet *Absurdités et atrocités de la Bible* (Editions de L'Idée Libre) appeared in 1926.

## NANNIE FLORENCE DRYHURST (MRS DRYHURST)

Hannah Ann Robinson was born in Dublin on 17th June 1856. She was the daughter of Alexander Robinson a dyer and Emily née Egan. Her sisters called her Nannie, and she decided to change her name to Nannie Florence. This was because she had a friend called Florence who died young. After her father's death in the mid-1870s she became a school governess in Ireland and then London where she looked after Nellie Tenison an Irish doctor's daughter. The doctor may have sexually harassed her, as indicated in letters, and she suddenly returned to Ireland.

Doctor Tenison was the family doctor of the Dryhurst family, and this may have been how she met Alfred Robert Dryhurst, usually known as Roy. They became engaged in 1882 and were married in August 1884. There seems to have been some ambivalence from Nannie towards the relationship, which had been conducted for a long time in the form of letters. Nevertheless the marriage took place. A year later a daughter, Norah, was born in London, and three years later another daughter, Sylvia (who as Sylvia Lynd was to become a poet and novelist).

Nannie was passionate about the Irish independence struggle. She gravitated towards the group around Charlotte Wilson and became involved in the anarchist movement from the late 1880s. She had broken with the Fabians and became an anarchist-communist and atheist. She became a regular correspondent for *Freedom* from the beginning. As William Wess wrote in a memoir in *Freedom* of January 1931: "speaking, debating, handing out bills, or going around with the collection plate; nothing was too much or too little for her to do." She often edited the paper whilst Charlotte Wilson was away, as well as "writing up notes and comments on contemporary events, corresponding with comrades all over the country; getting them to send up reports of propaganda; putting ship-shape all their notices and reports" (Wess). She spoke French, German, and Irish Gaelic and was an experienced translator (she was also an accomplished artist and painted Christmas cards to order). This was of great use in her translation of articles for *Freedom*, and she translated Kropotkin's book *The Great French Revolution* into English. At the beginning of the 1890s she replaced Wilson as editor for a short while.

She taught at the International School, the anarchist free school set up at 19 Fitzroy Square in London in the early 1890s by the exemplary French anarchist and Communard Louise Michel, working alongside her and Charlotte Wilson, Agnes Henry and Cyril Bell. In 1897 she was active in giving support to Spanish anarchist refugees fleeing from savage repression. She visited and financially supported the anarchist colony at Clousden Hill, near Newcastle, which existed from 1895 to 1902.

She began a long affair with the journalist Henry (H.W.) Nevinson whom she first met in February 1892. This relationship finally collapsed in 1912. It was through her that Nevinson briefly became involved with the Freedom Group and became a close friend of Kropotkin.

In 1906 she became a member of the Georgian Relief Committee, travelling there on fact-finding visits. She learnt Georgian from the anarchist associate of Kropotkin, Vladimir Cherkesov, and the following year spoke at an international conference at the Hague on the subjection of Georgia by the Tsarist Empire. Her involvement in helping the Georgian cause meant a distancing from editorial work with *Freedom*. She became honorary secretary of the Nationalities and Subject Races Committee and also returned to her support for Irish independence. She wrote occasional articles on Irish history for the *Daily Chronicle* and Irish papers. She was a friend of W.B. Yeats and appeared in his play *The Land of Heart's Desire* in June 1904. She died in 1930.

She was slight and graceful and was described by the rural writer George Sturt in 1889 as "surprisingly young looking" with high cheekbones, dark eyes and her hair in a coiled plait.

## AGNES HENRY

Born in Tipperary, Ireland, in 1850 Agnes Henry was to later inform historian of anarchism Max Nettlau in the questionnaire that he sent to English and foreign anarchists that from her youth she had participated in movements to alleviate suffering.

Most of her life was spent studying kindergarten theory, which she regarded as essentially anarchist. In the 1880s she ran a kindergarten in Trinidad.

In anarchist newspaper *Freedom* of July 1887 there appeared an article by her arguing against the prohibition of women workers from the pit brow (the 1886 Mines Regulation Bill).

She went for a while to Italy and as a result of her experiences there was able to write an article for *Freedom*, 'How Italian Risings are Promoted and Suppressed by the Italian Government', in July 1891. It would appear that she got to know various leading lights in the Italian anarchist movement like Errico Malatesta and the lawyer Saverio Merlino. In 1890 she translated a collection of fairy tales by the German writer Wilhelm Hauff entitled *The Cold Heart*. This book was used in many schools.

She participated in an experiment in communal living at 29 Doughty Street, near Mecklenburgh Square, Bloomsbury at the Fellowship House until it closed in 1892. It had been set up by the Fellowship of the New Life, a group which advocated a more ethical approach to life and "the cultivation of a new character in all." Other members included Edward Carpenter and Havelock Ellis. The Fabian Society emerged from this group.

She then moved to St Augustine's Road, Camden. Here *Freedom* set up office in February 1893 with the printer William Wess, moving there with the type. *Freedom*'s office was in the damp basement, which had a bad effect on Wess's health so the composing was moved. Together with Louise Michel she ran the International School in Fitzrovia at 19 Fitzroy Square.

She wrote *Women under Socialism* in March 1892 and gave a 'Wednesday lecture' at the Hall of Science in London on 'Women's Position under Anarchy'. She opposed state maternity support.

She was to say: "In anarchism I see the only base for women to escape marriage without love and obligatory maternity and the degrading laws and servile customs to which women of all classes have been subjected for so long."

In April 1893 she went on a speaking tour to Scotland to promote anarchism.

When Alfred Foster, an unemployed activist and anarchist, was arrested in Peckham in March 1894 she offered to put up bail but was rejected because she was a woman.

In November 1895 she was due to lecture on anarchism to the Birmingham branch of the Independent Labour Party, but this invitation was withdrawn because the Party feared that "she might advocate violence."

She adopted a young girl Adelaide, with an age variously given as six or eight, whom Nettlau described as "run wild." This was the daughter of the Italian anarchist Antonio Agresti, who was then able to marry Olive Rossetti and move to Italy (both these former anarchists ended up as avid supporters of Mussolini).

Around this time, in January 1895, she moved to Paris and from June of that year until March 1896 lived in Pont Aven in Brittany, trying to earn a living by teaching and by translating. The Decadent poet Ernest Dowson records encountering Henry and the child there.

She returned to England in April 1896. In a letter in *Seed-Time*, magazine of the Fellowship, she said that she would be "exceedingly glad" to meet a small family to share a house with her in North Walsham, "if possible in the Associated Home System" that had been adopted by Fellowship House.

She had to move to find a suitable school for the child, which was Suffield Park Girls School in Cromer, which disapproved of competition.

In 1896 she published *Anarchist Communism in Relation to State Socialism*, put out by James Tochatti's Liberty Press. In September of the same year she brought out *The Probable Evolution of British Socialism Tomorrow*.

The same year she was deeply involved in the activities of the Associated Anarchists founded by Carl Quinn, which made an effort to develop effective organisation within the British anarchist movement. As a result she moved away from the group around *Freedom*. Unfortunately the Associated Anarchists were only able to bring out a few issues of their paper *Alarm* and fell apart within a year.

Also in 1896 she attended the congress of the Second International held in London, acting as a delegate for French syndicalists unable to attend, along with Archie Gorrie, John Bullas, Alf Barton, J. Welsh and John Headley.

In April 1897 a letter from Agnes Henry appeared in the paper of the Independent Labour Party, the *Labour Leader*, in which she stated that it had almost persuaded her to join the I.L.P. In July she explained that she was now anxious to join it, rather feebly justifying her decision as an anarchist-communist to join a political and parliamentarian party.

George Robertson, an Edinburgh anarchist, was to reply that "you can take part in no political contest without renouncing your claim to Anarchism." The Italian anarchist Merlino's move to reformism seems to have influenced her.

She was one of quite a few anarchists in this period to move over to the I.L.P., representing some loss of nerve within the movement (others were Archibald Gorrie and a while later Tom Barclay, both of Leicester, John Headley of Great Yarmouth, Alf Barton, W.B. Parker, Tom Pearson, John Paton, etc.). Other indications of this demoralisation were the collapse of both open-air and printed propaganda, with the movement not recovering until around 1903.

Agnes Henry was listed on the Roll of Honour of Suffragette Prisoners 1905–1914 (compiled by the Suffragette Fellowship around 1950 based on recollections of participants) and appears to have been one of those arrested during the pre-World War One actions.

She felt enough allegiance to her old comrade Malatesta to speak on his behalf at Trafalgar Square, alongside anarchist speakers, when he was threatened with deportation in 1912.

## FRED LARGE

An anarchist from Walthamstow, house painter by trade. He was active in Aldred's Industrial Union of Direct Actionists in 1907. Fred later moved to the Whiteway colony in 1914, when he was 33 years old, and remained there until 1926, during which time his wife left him and moved to Leamington. He emigrated to Canada. (Nellie Shaw, *Whiteway: A Colony on the Cotswolds*)

## BILLY MacQUEEN

William 'Billy' MacQueen was born on 14th January 1875 at 34 Charlotte Street, London W1. Son of Robert MacQueen, a painter, from a family of tailors originally from Scotland, William started in the painting trade before leaving home. He later worked as a commercial traveller and always used his going around the country in the job to do anarchist propaganda. He became an active anarchist in Manchester and Leeds at the end of the 1890s.

He was a good public speaker, especially in Burnley where his speeches on the market square worried the Social Democratic Federation, the Marxist group headed by Henry Hyndman. Anarcho-syndicalist Rudolf Rocker said that he was the best of the English speakers in Leeds and an "able and extremely likeable young man." He arranged meetings for the visiting American anarchist Emma Goldman in Leeds on her tour in 1895. He organised a massive and successful demonstration on 1st October 1899 in Leeds with nine speakers and a crowd of 2,000 in opposition to the Boer War. He was badly beaten and nearly lynched by a jingoist mob after his speech against the Boer War in 1900 at a following demonstration in Leeds.

He was the driving force behind the activity of the Leeds Anarchist Group. For a time he lived in a house with Solomon Ploschansky and Hanna Kiselevsky, both anarchists. He wrote articles for the anarchist paper *Freedom*, and he edited an anarchist monthly in Leeds called the *Free Commune* (1898–1899) with an associate, Henry.

He became friends with Rudolf Grossmann (Pierre Ramus) the Austrian anarchist. Together with the anarchist Alf Barton of Manchester (see libcom.org/

history/manchester-anarchists-fight-free-speech) he brought out the *Anarchist Newsletter* in 1900 with a view to promote means of communication between the comrades (31st August 1900). He brought out an English translation of German Johann Most's *Communist Anarchism* in 1901. He continued to bring out pamphlets in Leeds under The Free Commune imprint, before moving to Hull, a centre for German anarchist refugees.

Unemployment and the persuasion of Most led him to emigrate to the States, and he became editor of the anarchist paper *Liberty* in Paterson and New York (1902–1903). He was imprisoned for five years as a result of agitation during the Paterson strike of 1902 with Luigi Galleani and Rudolf Grossmann when they all addressed a mass meeting.

They were all arrested for inciting a riot under the newly introduced Criminal Anarchy laws along with Johann Most. He jumped bail, but returned to face trial. He was released after three years on condition he leave the US and never return. His health broken, as a result of the appalling prison conditions, due to which he contracted TB, he returned to England and died soon after at the age of 33 in 1908.

## TOUZEAU PARRIS

Thomas Collins Touzeau Parris, usually known throughout his life as Touzeau Parris, was born in Honiton, Devon in 1839. He attended Bristol Grammar School and Bristol Baptist College. He became a Unitarian minister and chaplain for Samuel Courtauld, the mill owner. He helped his father sell books in Bristol. He became a secularist and was an agent for the secularist newspaper *The National Reformer* in Clifton, then a suburb of Bristol.

When in 1877 two leading secularists, Charles Bradlaugh and Annie Besant, were put on trial for publishing a work on birth control, Touzeau Parris and his wife Annie moved up to St John's Wood in London to help with the defence committee.

He became a lecturer for the National Secular Society and was very popular on the speaking circuit.

From 1884 his firm of gelatine manufacturers, based in South Acton, appeared in business directories. In 1885 he was living in Hammersmith, and in September of that year wrote to William Morris offering his help to organize against the prosecution of Morris and other socialists arrested after a police raid on the International Club at 7 St Stephen's Mews. He appears to have joined the Socialist League in that year.

In July 1886 he lectured to the Hammersmith branch of the League on socialism from an anarchist point of view and appears to have developed anarchist-communist positions. Later in the 1880s he became a neighbour of Morris, living at 23 Upper Mall until 1902, and becoming his good friend. Whilst continuing to be an anarchist, he remained, like James Tochatti, with the Hammersmith Socialist Society after the split in the League in November 1890, and despite the rejection of anarchism by the H.S.S. in their manifesto. In February 1891 he was a member of the committee set up to organise a meeting to commemorate the Paris Commune, where Kropotkin and Gustave Brocher spoke. He was a propagandist and speaker for the H.S.S. at the pitch at Bridge End Road and continued to lecture for the H.S.S. even though at a meeting on the 6th May 1892 (from which he was absent) there was questioning of anarchist views being expressed at the H.S.S. outdoor meetings. Fortunately, Philip Webb and Morris put forward a motion which led to the subject being dropped. He gave a graveside speech at the funeral of Mary Mowbray in that year. In 1894 he contributed articles to Tochatti's anarchist-communist paper *Liberty*.

On 13th January 1893 he sponsored a motion on establishing an alliance of all socialist groupings and was one of the five on the committee set up as a result. He was still a member of the H.S.S. in 1896 and was its delegate to the International Socialist Congress held in London in that year. His last recorded activity as an anarchist was his participation in the meeting to commemorate the Chicago martyrs in 1896. In 1907 he fell seriously ill and as a result fell into poverty. His comrades rallied round to support him and Tochatti was to write to George Bernard Shaw to thank him for a cheque that he had written to help out saying that he was "still the old Parris, only very weak." George Meredith was another who contributed to the fund. Parris died the same year at the age of 68 on 28th October at St Columb in Cornwall, the money raised being given to his widow.

## W.B. PARKER

W.B. Parker was a stalwart of the Socialist League and an anarchist within it. He had been a founder of the Social Democratic Federation and appears to have joined the League in 1886. He took a regular part in S.L. propaganda work and was often a speaker and lecturer.

He was living in Dalston in 1885 and in Holborn in 1888. He took part in the benefit to help the Berner Street club run by Jewish anarchists in January 1888.

He again came to the help of the Club when it was attacked by the police on 16th March 1889 and three of its members arrested, speaking at the subsequent defence meeting. In 1888 he was an organiser of the committee set up by the League to celebrate both the Chicago anarchist martyrs and Bloody Sunday 1887 when the police brutally attacked socialists rallying in Trafalgar Square.

He was secretary of the Stoke Newington and Stamford Hill branch of the League and informed the Secretary of the League that he was prepared to take charge of the Kingsland Green speakers' pitch if the League could assure him of a regular supply of lecturers.

In the same year W.B. Parker himself became Secretary of the League and appears to have carried out that role competently.

Alongside Kitz, Mowbray and Nicoll, he addressed large meetings during the dockers' strike of 1889. Again with Nicoll, Mowbray and John Turner he was involved in the 'No rent!' agitation of 1891. He was one of the speakers at the large Hyde Park protest meeting following the arrests of Mowbray and Nicoll in 1892.

In the same year he was secretary of an anarchist group set up in Paddington.

W.B. Parker was one of the fairly considerable number of anarchists who defected to the Independent Labour Party in the 1890s in what can be described as a 'loss of nerve' within the ranks of the anarchist movement. In 1906 he was chairman of Islington Trades Council.

In 1912 he still felt enough loyalty to his former comrades to speak at the large meeting held in Trafalgar Square to protest the threatened deportation of Malatesta.

He was vice-chair of the Islington Trades and Labour Party at the beginning of World War One and indeed he adopted a pro-war stance and he was one of the I.L.P. notables who addressed mass meetings to recruit for the armed forces. He was a Labour Poor Law Guardian for a considerable period of time. He died in the 1930s. Max Nettlau in a letter to Fred Charles in 1930 perhaps rather unkindly describes him as a "very active and plausible comrade, but ... not of an elevated character at all and of no interest to history" but may have had his defection to the I.L.P. in mind.

## HERBERT STOCKTON

Born 1860. Like his brother Ernest, an engineer, and his sister Nellie active in Manchester Anarchists and in the free speech fight of 1893, during which he was arrested twice. Herbert Stockton married and had five children and ran a drapers shop in Levenshulme. He also, according to Cores, joined the Independent Labour Party. Ernest Stockton emigrated to Canada.

## JACK TANNER

Jack Tanner was born on 28th April 1889 in Whitstable. His father had a job as sports manager at Alexandra Palace, so Jack moved as a young boy to London. At the age of fourteen he was apprenticed to an engineering firm in Southwark, but tiring of this he joined the Merchant Navy and travelled around the world. He acquired the nickname of 'Handsome Jack' because of his looks.

On his return he worked as a fitter and turner. He joined the Amalgamated Society of Engineers and became active in it, also joining the Social Democratic Federation. He read Kropotkin and became an anarchist, subsequently involving himself in syndicalist activity (he frequented the shop of the anarchist tailor James Tochatti in Hammersmith and may have first been introduced to anarchism by him). He had a part in the foundation of the National Federation of Women Workers. During the 1910s he was active in the Industrial Syndicalist Education League, subsequently joining the Industrial Democracy League in 1913, and contributing regularly to its paper *Solidarity*, which first appeared as a fortnightly in September of that year, gradually taking more and more of an editorial role. He became a coordinator of anarchist meetings in London after a meeting in August 1911. He spoke regularly at anarchist pitches and was for a while a member of the anarchist group in Marylebone formed in 1912 after a series of anarchist open air meetings in Regents Park.

In 1913 he was secretary of the Ettor-Giovannitti Protest Committee, to defend two Wobblies imprisoned in the USA, speaking alongside anarchist Errico Malatesta. Later in the same year, he was secretary and treasurer of the Malatesta Release Committee after the famous Italian anarchist was arrested by the British police. He was shortly replaced in this role by Guy Aldred. Also in 1913 he chaired the first International Syndicalist Congress in London, attended by delegates from twelve countries. He was involved in the amalgamation committee movement.

Around this time he met Will Lawther, down from Durham (he was to take a similar trajectory to the right as Tanner, though speedier), and they both contributed to the anarchist paper the *Voice of Labour*. He also contributed regular letters from London to *La Vie Ouvrière*, paper of the French syndicalist Confédération Générale du Travail. During World War One he worked as an engineer in the Paris suburbs and was active in the Confédération Générale du Travail. He returned to London in 1917 and worked at the Royal Aircraft factory in Farnborough. The black American writer and activist Claude McKay mentions meeting him at the International Socialist Club in Shoreditch during the war, along with Aldred, George Lansbury, A.J. Cook, Sylvia Pankhurst, etc. The Club was located at 28 East Road, off of City Road.

He wrote a pamphlet, *The Social General Strike*, in 1919. He became active in the Shop Stewards and Workers Committees Movement, and in 1920 attended the Second Congress of the Communist International in Moscow as one of its delegates. He expressed classic syndicalist views at the conference, such as: "A number of those who are active in the shop stewards' movement are not greatly concerned about the formation of the party, because they have been convinced from their experience in other parties that it was a loss of time to share in the work of such parties." He met Lenin there, and on his return joined the Communist Party, although his membership only lasted eight months. In this period he worked in activity for the expansion of the Red International of Labour Unions serving on its London District Committee (the London R.I.L.U., interestingly, produced a short-lived paper called *Solidarity*). After he left the C.P. he had an ambivalent attitude towards it. He was active within the National Minority Movement (a Communist Party front established in 1924 to work within the reformist trade unions) and served on its executive.

He obtained work at the *Evening Standard* and by 1930 was the London District Committee Organiser of the Amalgamated Engineering Union. He became its president in 1939 and served as such until 1953. He remained in an ambiguous relationship with the C.P. He welcomed the World War Two enthusiastically. He saw eye to eye with the C.P. for the need for joint production committees and economic planning in industry in the war years. His increasing right-wing trajectory saw him become president of the Trades Union Congress in 1954. After his retirement in that year he became director of the right-wing Industrial and Research Information Services (I.R.I.S.), which reported on and worked against Communist Party activities in the unions.

He died on 3rd March 1965.

**Nick Heath**

# AFTERWORD

The re-edition of John Quail's classic chronicle of the Victorian anarchist movement, *The Slow Burning Fuse*, is most welcome. It will make readily accessible in hard copy one of the few — and certainly one of the best — texts on British anarchism in the Victorian era. It also provides an excellent opportunity to restate the many merits of this landmark study and assess its contribution to the scholarship of anarchism. It may seem a little facile to argue that Quail's seminal study has not aged. It is nonetheless true, and this is no small feat, given that the book was first published in 1978, and that the research area that it covers has been extensively revisited in the last two decades or so.

One of the highlights of *The Slow Burning Fuse* is the fact that it brings together so many strands that have since generated a great deal of scholarship. Among these are terrorism and the now-familiar concept of propaganda of/by the deed, as well as police surveillance, which occupy the last two chapters, reflecting the deepening influence of these themes in the early 1890s. Quail's remark that "the arrest, trial and sentencing of the Walsall anarchists in 1892 deserve more attention than they have received from the historians of the left in Britain" cannot fail to elicit a smile, since so much research has been produced on this and related issues in the context of the current wave of Islamist terrorism, beginning with 9/11; the work conducted by Richard Bach Jensen, in particular,[1] as well as a lively debate in the journal *Terrorism and Political Violence*, which revisits the era of propaganda by the deed as a point of comparison for Islamist terrorism.[2]

From the perspective of current historiography, an especially interesting aspect is Quail's emphasis on individuals and actions rather than political theory, underpinned by a close attention to the sociological, philosophical, political and organisational dimensions of the movement. As Quail stresses in his 'Personal Introduction', "it is an unfortunate fact that political theory, no matter how worthy or perceptive, is curiously disembodied; it gives no clues to the passions, the heroisms or the squalid conflicts that it inspired. . . . The forms of the movement were shifting and decentralized, making it rather difficult to pin down numbers, events and the particular activists involved and forcing the historian to rely on a myriad snippets of information." This emphasis on individuals and their connections, grounded in a conception of political history as embodied and driven by individuals and the associations they form, is pivotal to the continued relevance and very current feel of the book.

While convergent with other classic studies of grassroots anarchist movements, such as Jean Maitron's comprehensive *Histoire du movement anarchiste français*[3] or Paul Avrich's work on U.S. anarchism,[4] Quail's perspective also has much in common with current investigations into networked activism, charisma, 'history from below' approaches, revisited biography, etc. — all of which have been key themes for historians of anarchism in recent years. These approaches have been increasingly developed since Davide Turcato's influential article on 'Italian anarchism as a Transnational Movement' (2007),[5] with a great wealth of studies examining the role of individuals and their associations in anarchist activism. This has generated a great deal of research into political networks (including some formal network-mapping exercises) and the status of nineteenth-century anarchism as a social movement.

A different take on the same theme is visible in the current interest in biographies of anarchists, for instance Davide Turcato's study on Malatesta,[6] my own work on Jean Grave and Louise Michel,[7] and various authors on Emma Goldman[8] — although it may be argued that these studies of charismatic and highly influential figures are at odds with Quail's ode to 'unsung demi-heroes' and ongoing efforts to explore the role of intermediaries and everyday militants. Similarly, much of the book shows the human dimension of some of the 'big narratives' of socialist history successfully interweaving these various dimensions. The anarchists' engagement with the nascent labour movement in the 1880s, strike organisation and public speeches are considered important events in Quail's history, resulting in a very innovative form of labour history for its time, reconciling levels often regarded as dissociated: practical everyday organisation and activism but also theoretical elaboration, grassroots and 'leaders', everyday activism and major conferences. Quail shows that organisational history rested on constant interactions, especially in militant spaces and practices, and that politics occurred primarily outside party conferences. While networks — one of the central concepts of contemporary anarchist historiography — are not explicitly mentioned, his history is nonetheless informed by a nuanced understanding of networks of places, people, organisations and paper distributors.

The history of British anarchism is embedded in a broader history of British labour and provides a great introduction to the complexities and specificities of labour activism in Britain at a time when socialism was 'a submerged and sometimes only just discernible tradition' derived from Robert Owen. The first chapter starts with the Chartists and the differences between radicalism and socialism, the radical club culture integral to the Socialist Revival and the dilemmas of reform vs. revolution. As such, *The Slow Burning Fuse* sits alongside classics of British radical/ labour history, such as E.P. Thompson's *William Morris: Romantic to Revolutionary* (1977) and Stan Shipley's *Club Life and Socialism in Mid-Victorian London* (1972) in recounting the teeming and complicated early years of the Socialist Revival as seen from the grassroots. Among these books, Quail's is unique is giving centre stage to anarchists, and despite all the work done since on international anarchist movements active in Britain in this period, it continues to stand out due to its rare foregrounding of British activists. It is pleasing to see that even as labour history has become increasingly marginalised in academia, the study of anarchism, especially in a transnational perspective, has opened up great prospects in this area, with significant results: much has been written about the history of syndicalism, with a seminal volume co-edited by Hirsch and Van der Walt[9] and the recent volume *Wobblies of the World: A Global History of IWW.*[10]

This leads us to the broader theme of transnationalism, a dominant trend in recent anarchist historiography. Quail's narrative portrays cosmopolitanism and the role of foreign refugees as essential features of the movement from its very beginning, starting with the 1878 influx of German socialists and Johann Most, as well as examining the role of recognized personalities who were of dual origin, including Kitz. Alongside the focus on British militants — 'native' anarchism, as it is sometimes called — Quail points to the transnational elements of the movement, long before the lexicon of transnationalism became so omnipresent. He conveys quite effortlessly how fluid and nonetheless occasionally fraught the exchanges and connections between these various circles and levels were. Discussing the July 1881 Social Revolutionary and Anarchist Congress in London, he remarks that "the minutes of the proceedings reveal that the English delegates played little part; yet many of the people involved were more or less permanent exiles in London and it was partly through contact between them and the British socialists that a more sophisticated libertarian philosophy was to develop relevant to British conditions."

There are countless leads that have subsequently been explored by historians in a specifically transnational perspective. These include the history of how the early *Freiheit* was smuggled internationally from Britain to Germany by sailors — since then, the theme of paper circulation has gained importance, with a growing focus on anarchist print culture as a medium for propaganda but also anarchist identities and, more broadly, processes of information sharing and exchange. While these processes are now commonly described as networks of dissemination and ideological circulation, they are evidenced and discussed in less scholarly terms in *The Slow Burning Fuse* and are clearly integral to the way Quail understood anarchism as a doctrine of action — the main difference is one of language, as Quail remains (mercifully, some might say) jargon-free.

*The Slow Burning Fuse* has not really aged. This in turn raises interesting questions about the historiography of pre-World War One British anarchism — has the field really barely evolved since 1978? It straddles the gaps between scholarly research and a more militant book, as reflected in the book's relatively short bibliography. The subtitle, 'The Lost History of British Anarchists', invites reflection and may well be the one element in Quail's analysis whose validity has become problematic. It certainly points to a historiographic tradition that for a long time hid the historical importance and the rich but elusive legacies of British anarchism. The book provides a healthy reminder that for some time everything was at play and revolutionary politics might have prevailed; in that sense, it is correct to claim that the revolutionary narrative has been unduly obscured. Just forty years later, is it still correct to claim that this history has been lost?

Not quite. Looking at studies with a British focus, and with pre-emptive apologies for inevitable omissions here, David Goodway, Judy Greenway, Ruth Kinna, Matt Adams and Carissa Honeywell have all done excellent work on twentieth-century anarchism.

The historiographic marginalisation of anarchists has at least been partly revised. There are also countless studies, most of them transnational in nature, where British anarchism features as a secondary focus, for instance Ole Birk Laursen's research into the Indian revolutionary movement in Europe (which prominently features the fascinating figure of Guy Aldred),[11] Pietro Di Paola's work on the Italian anarchist diaspora in London,[12] and, recently, Daniel Laqua's study on German anarchist circles.[13] However, it might be argued that, for all the research it has generated, the transnational turn has also had the unwanted effect of replicating the dominant narrative that British anarchism was insignificant in comparison to the size and relevance of other anarchist movements and perpetuating the erroneous notion that British anarchism was primarily exilic. Quail remains mandatory reading to rectify such interpretations.

There are, of course, a few aspects to which today's reader may object. The main one is the titular reference to 'British anarchists' in a study which is overwhelmingly London-centric, despite close-ups on Walsall and Manchester. Scottish anarchism, for example, is nowhere to be seen, although this may be the result of the chronology adopted — which is also a little unsatisfactory for today's reader. This, however, is a matter for future discussions, which will hopefully continue with the great vigour of recent years. Having been introduced to British anarchism by Quail in the early stages of my PhD, it is wonderful to come full circle and pay homage to this great book. Long may it continue to inspire readers and researchers.

**Constance Bantman, University of Surrey**

## Bibliography

Avrich, Paul. *Anarchist Voices: An Oral History of Anarchism in America.* Oakland: AK Press, 2005 [1995].

Bach Jensen, Richard. *The Battle against Anarchist Terrorism: An International History, 1878–1934.* Cambridge: Cambridge University Press, 2013.

Bantman, Constance. 'Jean Grave and French Anarchism: A Relational Approach (1870s–1914)'. *International Review of Social History* 62 (2017): 451–77.

———. 'Louise Michel's London Years: A Political Reassessment (1890–1905)'. *Women's History Review* 26 (2017): 994–1012.

Binder Leonard. 'Comment on Gelvin's Essay on Al-Qaeda and Anarchism'. *Terrorism and Political Violence* 20, no. 4 (2008): 582–88.

Birk Laursen, Ole. 'Anarchist Anti-Imperialism: Guy Aldred and the Indian Revolutionary Movement, 1909–14'. *Journal of Imperial and Commonwealth History* 46 (2018): 286–303.

Cole, Peter, David Struthers and Kenyon Zimmer. *Wobblies of the World: A Global History of the IWW.* London: Pluto Press, 2017.

Di Paola, Pietro. *The Knights Errant of Anarchy: London and the Italian Anarchist Diaspora (1880–1917).* Liverpool: Liverpool University Press, 2013.

Esenwein, George. 'Comments on James L. Gelvin's "Al-Qaeda and Anarchism: A Historian's Reply to Terrorology"'. *Terrorism and Political Violence* 20, no. 4 (2008): 597–600.

Falk, Candace. *Love, Anarchy and Emma Goldman: A Biography.* New Brunswick, NJ: Rutgers University Press, 1990 [1984].

Ferguson, Kathy. *Emma Goldman: Political Thinking in the Streets.* Lanham, MD: Rowman and Littlefield, 2011.

Hemmings, Clare. *Considering Emma Goldman: Feminist Political Ambivalence and the Imaginative Archive.* Durham, NC: Duke University Press, 2018.

Hirsch, Steven, and Lucien van der Walt, eds. *Anarchism and Syndicalism in the Colonial and Postcolonial World, 1870–1940: The Praxis of National Liberation, Internationalism, and Social Revolution.* Leiden, NL: Brill Academic Publishers, 2010.

Kelsay, James. 'Al-Qaida as a Muslim (Religio-Political) Movement Remarks on James L. Gelvin's "Al-Qaeda and Anarchism: A Historian's Reply to Terrorology"'. *Terrorism and Political Violence* 20, no. 4 (2008): 601–5.

Laqua, Daniel. 'Political Contestation and Internal Strife: Socialist and Anarchist German Newspapers in London, 1878–1910'. In *The Foreign Political Press in Nineteenth-Century London: Politics from a Distance.* Edited by Constance Bantman and Ana Cláudia Suriani da Silva. London: Bloomsbury, 2018.

Maitron, Jean. *Histoire du Mouvement Anarchiste en France (1880–1914).* Paris: Maspero, 1975.

Turcato, Davide. 'Italian Anarchism as a Transnational Movement, 1885–1915'. *International Review of Social History* 52 (2007): 407–44.

_____. *Making Sense of Anarchism: Errico Malatesta's Experiments with Revolution, 1889–1900.* London: Palgrave Macmillan, 2012.

## Notes

1   In particular, see Richard Bach Jensen, *The Battle against Anarchist Terrorism: An International History, 1878–1934* (Cambridge: Cambridge University Press, 2013).

2   James Kelsay, 'Al-Qaida as a Muslim (Religio-Political) Movement Remarks on James L. Gelvin's "Al-Qaeda and Anarchism: A Historian's Reply to Terrorology"', *Terrorism and Political Violence* 20, no. 4 (2008): 601–5; Leonard Binder, 'Comment on Gelvin's Essay on Al-Qaeda and Anarchism', *Terrorism and Political Violence* 20, no. 4 (2008): 582–88; George Esenwein, 'Comments on James L. Gelvin's "Al-Qaeda and Anarchism: A Historian's Reply to Terrorology"', *Terrorism and Political Violence* 20, no. 4 (2008): 597–600.

3   Jean Maitron, *Histoire du Mouvement Anarchiste (1880–1914)* (Paris: Maspero, 1975).

4   Paul Avrich, *Anarchist Voices: An Oral History of Anarchism in America* (Oakland: AK Press, 2005 [1995]).

5   Davide Turcato, 'Italian Anarchism as a Transnational Movement, 1885–1915', *International Review of Social History* 52 (2007): 407–44.

6   Davide Turcato, *Making Sense of Anarchism: Errico Malatesta's Experiments with Revolution, 1889–1900* (London: Palgrave Macmillan, 2012).

7   Constance Bantman, 'Jean Grave and French Anarchism: A Relational Approach (1870s–1914)', *International Review of Social History* 62 (2017): 451–77; Constance Bantman, 'Louise Michel's London Years: A Political Reassessment (1890–1905)', *Women's History Review* 26 (2017): 994–1012.

8   Candace Falk, *Love, Anarchy and Emma Goldman: A Biography* (New Brunswick, NJ: Rutgers University Press, 1990 [1984]); Kathy Ferguson, *Emma Goldman: Political Thinking in the Streets* (Lanham, MD: Rowman and Littlefield, 2011); Clare Hemmings, *Considering Emma Goldman: Feminist Political Ambivalence and the Imaginative Archive* (Durham, NC: Duke University Press, 2018).

9   Steven Hirsch and Lucien van der Walt, eds., *Anarchism and Syndicalism in the Colonial and Postcolonial World, 1870–1940: The Praxis of National Liberation, Internationalism, and Social Revolution* (Leiden, NL: Brill Academic Publishers, 2010).

10  Peter Cole, David Struthers and Kenyon Zimmer, *Wobblies of the World: A Global History of the IWW* (London: Pluto Press, 2017).

11  Ole Birk Laursen, 'Anarchist Anti-Imperialism: Guy Aldred and the Indian Revolutionary Movement, 1909–14', *Journal of Imperial and Commonwealth History* 46 (2018): 286–303.

12  Pietro Di Paola, *The Knights Errant of Anarchy: London and the Italian Anarchist Diaspora (1880–1917)* (Liverpool: Liverpool University Press, 2013).

13  Daniel Laqua, 'Political Contestation and Internal Strife: Socialist and Anarchist German Newspapers in London, 1878–1910', in *The Foreign Political Press in Nineteenth-Century London: Politics from a Distance*, ed. Constance Bantman and Ana Cláudia Suriani da Silva (London: Bloomsbury, 2018).

# INDEX

## EVENTS

Anti-Anarchist Conference 241/2
Anti-Socialist Laws 26/9
Arbitration Bills 288

Bloody Week 292
Boer War 223 231 242 246 262 269/70 342
 343 378

Chicago Martyrs 94 103 111 175
Coercion Bill 36 38

Defence of the Realm Act (D.O.R.A.) 316/7

Explosives Act 142 207 210

Featherstone massacre 172 340

General Strike (1926) 331 349
Greenwich Park Explosion 179 185/6
 189/91 196 209

Hull dock strike 215 260

International Socialist Congress 167 230
 259 341 380
International Syndicalist Congress 382
International Workers Congress 261

Labour Remuneration Conference 67
London dock strike 105/8 111 113 239 267
 287 339

May Day 111 122 129/30 152 159/60 163/4
 176 245 278 329
Military Service Act 318/20
Mines Regulation Bill 375

Paris Commune 25 29 42 373

Reform Act 19/20
Reform Riots 33 342
Revolutionary Conference 112 116
Russian Revolution 34 312 322 325 328 330

Second International 377
Siege of Sidney Street 293/4 345
Social Revolutionary and Anarchist
 Congress 34 373 387
Spanish Civil War 14 249 333
Syndicalist Revolt 248 257 278 281 297 312
 320 351

Third International 327/8
Tottenham Outrage 293

United International Action 112

West End Riots 61 167 338

Zurich Anarchist Congress 259
Zurich resolution 261

## ORGANISATIONS

Advocates of Industrial Unionism 264 276
Amalgamated Engineering Union 383
Amalgamated Shop Assistants Union 269
Amalgamated Society of Engineers (A.S.E.)
 265 291/2 321/2 382
amalgamation committee 291 310 382
Amnesty Committee 226
Anarchist Club 45
Anarchist-Communist Alliance 228
Anti-Broker Brigade 122 153 223
Associated Anarchists 228 230/1 377
Autonomie Club 103 112 125 129 131
 133/4 139 164 182/3 185/6 188/9 197/8
 219 226 234 363

## PEOPLE

## PLACES

## POLICE

## PUBLICATIONS

Charlotte
Wilson

Peter
Kropotkin

Max
Nettlau

Fauset
MacDonald

James
Tochatti

Alfred
Marsh

Rose and Milly
Witkop

Rudolf
Rocker

Guy
Aldred

Tom
Mann

Charles
Mowbray

Agnes
Henry

Tom
Cantwell

Sam
Mainwaring

Tom
Keel

PM Press was founded at the end of 2007 by a small collection of folks with decades of publishing, media, and organizing experience. PM Press co-conspirators have published and distributed hundreds of books, pamphlets, CDs, and DVDs. Members of PM have founded enduring book fairs, spearheaded victorious tenant organizing campaigns, and worked closely with bookstores, academic conferences, and even rock bands to deliver political and challenging ideas to all walks of life. We're old enough to know what we're doing and young enough to know what's at stake.

We create radical and stimulating fiction and non-fiction books, pamphlets, T-shirts, visual and audio materials to educate, entertain, and inspire you. We aim to distribute these through every available channel with every available technology—whether that means you are seeing anarchist classics at our bookfair stalls; reading our latest vegan cookbook at the café; downloading geeky fiction e-books; or digging new music and timely videos from our website.

PM Press is always on the lookout for talented and skilled volunteers, artists, activists, and writers to work with. If you have a great idea for a project or can contribute in some way, please get in touch.

PM Press
PO Box 23912
Oakland CA 94623
510-658-3906
www.pmpress.org

PM Press in Europe
europe@pmpress.org
www.pmpress.org.uk

# FRIENDS OF PM

These are indisputably momentous times—the financial system is melting down globally and the Empire is stumbling. Now more than ever there is a vital need for radical ideas.

In the many years since its founding—and on a mere shoestring—PM Press has risen to the formidable challenge of publishing and distributing knowledge and entertainment for the struggles ahead. With hundreds of releases to date, we have published an impressive and stimulating array of literature, art, music, politics, and culture. Using every available medium, we've succeeded in connecting those hungry for ideas and information to those putting them into practice.

Friends of PM allows you to directly help impact, amplify, and revitalize the discourse and actions of radical writers, filmmakers, and artists. It provides us with a stable foundation from which we can build upon our early successes and provides a much-needed subsidy for the materials that can't necessarily pay their own way. You can help make that happen—and receive every new title automatically delivered to your door once a month—by joining as a Friend of PM Press. And, we'll throw in a free T-shirt when you sign up.

Here are your options:

- $30 a month: Get all books and pamphlets plus 50% discount on all webstore purchases
- $40 a month: Get all PM Press releases (including CDs and DVDs) plus 50% discount on all webstore purchases
- $100 a month: Superstar—Everything plus PM merchandise, free downloads, and 50% discount on all webstore purchases

For those who can't afford $30 or more a month, we have **Sustainer Rates** at $15, $10, and $5. Sustainers get a free PM Press T-shirt and a 50% discount on all purchases from our website.

Your Visa or Mastercard will be billed once a month, until you tell us to stop. Or until our efforts succeed in bringing the revolution around. Or the financial meltdown of Capital makes plastic redundant. Whichever comes first.

# FREEDOM

## ABOUT FREEDOM PRESS

The oldest anarchist publishing house in the English-speaking world, *Freedom Press* was founded in London by a group of volunteers including Charlotte Wilson and Peter Kropotkin in 1886.

The Press has repeatedly been the target of state repression, from crackdowns in the 1890s to raids during World War I and most famously, at the end of World War II. The 1945 free speech case, which saw four editors of its journal War Commentary arrested for causing "disaffection in the armed forces," prompted support from many famous names including Herbert Read, George Orwell, Benjamin Britten, and E.M. Forster. Three were jailed.

Despite this and many other threats, from fascists to organised crime, for over a century Freedom has regularly published works on the philosophy and activities of anarchists, and produced its Freedom Newspaper for the best part of a century. Freedom now maintains an anarchist-focused news site, www.freedomnews.org.uk, and publishes a biannual free journal.

Freedom runs Britain's largest anarchist bookshop at its home of more than 50 years in Whitechapel, in the heart of London. The upper floors of the Freedom building are home to a number of anarchist organisations, and the venue regularly hosts talks, meetings, and events for the wider movement.

### About the Freedom Press Library Series

Freedom Press has partnered with PM Press to republish titles from Freedom's back catalogue, bringing important works back into circulation with new introductions and additional commentary. *The Slow Burning Fuse* is part of this series.

**Freedom Press**
**84b Whitechapel High St**
**London, E1 7QX**

**www.freedompress.org.uk**
**www.freedomnews.org.uk**

### Anarchist Seeds beneath the Snow:
### Left-Libertarian Thought and British Writers from William Morris to Colin Ward
David Goodway
$24.95 • ISBN: 978-1-60486-221-8
6x9 • 448 pages

From Morris to Wilde to Orwell, left-libertarian thought has long been an important but neglected part of British cultural and political history. In *Anarchist Seeds beneath the Snow*, David Goodway seeks to recover and revitalize that indigenous anarchist tradition. This book succeeds as simultaneously a cultural history of left-libertarian thought in Britain and a demonstration of the applicability of that history to current politics. Goodway argues that a recovered anarchist tradition could—and should—be a touchstone for contemporary political radicals. Moving seamlessly from Aldous Huxley and Colin Ward to the war in Iraq, this challenging volume will energize leftist movements throughout the world.

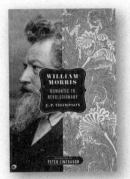

### William Morris: Romantic to Revolutionary
E.P. Thompson • Foreword by Peter Linebaugh
$32.95 • ISBN: 978-1-60486-243-0
5.5x8.5 • 880 pages

William Morris—the great 19th-century craftsman, designer, poet and writer—remains a monumental figure whose influence resonates powerfully today. As an intellectual (and author of the seminal utopian *News from Nowhere*), his concern with artistic and human values led him to cross what he called the "river of fire" and become a committed socialist—committed not to some theoretical formula but to the day by day struggle of working women and men in Britain and to the evolution of his ideas about art, about work, and about how life should be lived.

This book remains unsurpassed as the definitive work on this remarkable figure, by the major British historian of the 20th century.

### The Floodgates of Anarchy
Stuart Christie and Albert Meltzer
$15.95 • ISBN: 978-1-60486-105-1
5.5x8.5 • 144 pages

The floodgates holding back anarchy are constantly under strain. The liberal would ease the pressure by diverting some of the water; the conservative would shore up the dykes, the totalitarian would construct a stronger dam.

But is anarchy a destructive force? The absence of government may alarm the authoritarian, but is a liberated people really its own worst enemy—or is the true enemy of mankind, as the anarchists claim, the means by which he is governed? Without government the world could manage to end exploitation and war. Anarchy should not be confused with weak, divided, or manifold government. As Christie and Meltzer point out, only with the total abolition of government can society develop in freedom.

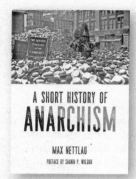

### A Short History of Anarchism

Max Nettlau • Preface by Shawn P. Wilbur
$24.95 • ISBN: 978-1-62963-645-0
5.75x8.25 • 448 pages

Ida Pilat Isca's translation of *A Short History of Anarchism*—a comprehensive, one-volume introduction to the origins of the idea of anarchy and the emergence of the modern anarchist movement—is a particular treasure.

Written to indicate the breadth and diversity of anarchist ideas and practices, in a style that largely allows the historical facts to speak for themselves, it remains remarkably useful and current, despite the years that have passed since its composition in the 1930s. Nettlau's historical account is supplemented by biographical and bibliographical resources—some new to this edition—which aid both readers and researchers interested in navigating the broad river of anarchy.

### New Fields: Early Reflections on Anarchism

Max Nettlau • Edited by Shawn P. Wilbur
$14.95 • ISBN: 978-1-62963-643-6
5x8 • 160 pages

Although essays like "Responsibility and Solidarity in the Labor Struggle" have been widely translated and disseminated, the majority of this work on anarchism's future development remains little known. During his lifetime, only a single collection of these critiques, the Spanish-language *Crítica Libertaria*, saw publication. The present anthology is an attempt to at least begin to remedy that lack, drawing together English-language essays published in *Freedom* and *Mother Earth* with new translations of work originally published in French. *New Fields* captures the reflections, questions, and fears of Nettlau during the early years of the anarchist movement, 1895–1921, allowing modern readers both to experience something of that era and to apply these early critiques and perennial questions to the anarchist practices of our own era.

### Life and Ideas: The Anarchist Writings of Errico Malatesta

Errico Malatesta • Edited by Vernon Richards
Foreword by Carl Levy
$21.95 • ISBN: 978-1-62963-032-8
6x9 • 320 pages

The editor has translated hundreds of articles by Malatesta, taken from the journals he either edited himself or contributed to, from the earliest, *L'En Dehors* of 1892, through to *Pensiero e Volontà*, which was forced to close by Mussolini's fascists, and the bilingual *Il Risveglio/Le Réveil*. These articles have been pruned down to their essentials and collected under subheadings ranging from "Ends and Means" to "Anarchist Propaganda." Through the selections Malatesta's classical anarchism emerges: a revolutionary, nonpacifist, nonreformist vision informed by decades of engagement in struggle and study. In addition there is a short biographical piece and an essay by the editor.